Contents

Dedicated to

My Parents

Dr. Prakash Swaroop Bhatnagar & Mrs. Sarla Bhatnagar

who do their utmost in supporting all my endeavours.

Introducing
News
Media

Introducing News Media

Amjad Ali
(Deputy Librarian)
Aligarh Muslim University, Aligarh

Ess Ess Publications
4837/24, Ansari Road
Darya Ganj
New Delhi-110 002
Phone: 23260807, 41563444
Fax: 41563334
E-mail: info@essessreference.com
url: http://www.essessreference.com

First Published **2006**

ISBN: 81-7000-491-8

Rs.625/-

Published by:
Ess Ess Publications
4831/24, Ansari Road, Darya Ganj, New Delhi-110 002
Tel: 011-23260807, 41563444 Fax: 011-41563334
E-mail: info@essessreference.com
url: www.essessreference.com

Printed in India at:
Printline, New Delhi

CONTENTS

PREFACE

Humanbeings exchanged news long before they could write. They spread it by word of mouth on crossroads and markets. Messengers raced back from battlefields with reports on victories or defeats. Criers walked through villages announcing births, deaths, marriages and divorces. Stories of unlikely occurrences spread like wildfire through preliterate societies. The growth of civilization brought advanced means for generation, collection and distribution of information and also the news.

With the arrival of writing and literacy, news reports gained added reliability in advanced societies like that of Rome and China. Rome had a particularly sophisticated system for circulating written news, centered on the acta, the daily handwritten news sheets, which were posted by the government in the Roman Forum from the year 59 B.C. to at least A.D. 222 and which were filled with news of such subjects as political happenings, trials, scandals, military campaigns and executions. China, too, had early government-produced news sheets, called the tipao, which were first circulated among officials during the Han dynasty.

News media took varied forms. Newspapers, which still dominate the scene in most of the countries, have about 500 years of known existance. In Renaissance Europe handwritten newsletters circulated privately among merchants, passing along information about everything from wars and economic conditions to social customs and human interest. The first printed forerunners of the newspaper appeared in Germany in the late 1400's in the form of news pamphlets or broadsides, often highly sensationalized in content.

The modern newspaper is a European invention. Then came the radio and television followed by the electronic media and of course the Internet in our own time. Internet has revolutionized the process of collection, edititng and

distribution of news. Internet is a better substitute to newspaper, radio and television all taken together since it presents news by stripping sentences and facts from all media sources and their combinations.

The natural home of information is a library and a news library caters to the particular needs of the news media organizations. They hold collections consisting of newspapers, magazines, news broadcasts, cable wire or Internet-based news organizations. Alongwith newspapers, libraries also manage information resources which are stored in files, on tape or microfilm or in computers which are used by news and editorial staff in publishing establishments, such as newspaper and magazine publishers, and in broadcasting establishments.

This book discusses about the emergence of news media, mainly focusing on the newspaper, radio, television and Internet and the accumulation of news media resources in libraries. The management issues and preservation techniques of the news media resources have also been taken up. It is hoped that the book will be useful for the students of Journalism, Mass Communication and Library and Information Science.

Dr. Amjad Ali

Abbreviations and Terms

ABC American Broadcasting Company.

Actives Listeners who call radio stations to make requests and comments or in response to contests and promotions.

Actuality Actual recording of news event or person(s) involved.

Ad lib Improvisation. Unrehearsed and spontaneous comments.

ADI Area of Dominant Influence; Arbitron measurement area.

Adjacencies Commercials strategically placed next to a feature.

Affidavit Statement attesting to the airing of a spot schedule.

AFTRA American Federation of Television and Radio Artists; union made up of broadcast performers: announcers, deejays, newscasters.

Aircheck Tape of live broadcast.

ALA American Library Association. The oldest and largest organization of librarians and libraries in the country, with over 30,000 members.

AM Amplitude Modulation; method of signal transmission using Standard Broadcast band with frequencies between 535 and 1705 kHz.

Amplification Electronically increasing the power of a signal.

Announcement Commercial (spot) or public service message of varying length.

AOR Album-Oriented Rock radio format. Also called Classic Rock.

AP Associated Press; wire and audio news service.

Arbitron Audience measurement service employing a seven-day diary to determine the number of listeners tuned to area radio stations.

ASCAP American Society of Composers, Artists, and Performers; music licensing service.

Ascertainment The formal process of determining a community's needs.

Assignment Desk or News Desk: At broadcast bureaus and stations, the staff responsible for dispatching camera crews and reporters to cover news events.

Attribute To write the name of source of your information when using a quote, of book, or a part of any copyrighted work.

Attribution Statement of the source of information in a news item.

Audio Sound; modulation.

Audition channel Monitoring point separate from program that allows for off-air listening.

Audition tape Telescoped recording showcasing talents of air person; listen off-air.

Automation Equipment system designed to play prepackaged programming.

Availability Vacant air slot for commercial announcement.

Average quarter-hour (AQH) Rating measurement used to estimate the size of a station's audience during any fifteen minute period.

AWRT American Women in Radio and Television.

Back announce Recap of preceding music selections.

Balance sheet A summary of a station's assets and liabilities.

Banner A print media term for a headline for a story of unusual importance, stretching the entire width of the page.

Break The time during the show that commercials are played

Barter Exchange of airtime for programming or goods.

BBC British Broadcasting Corporation

BEA Broadcast Education Association.

Bed Music behind voice in announcement.

Bi-directional pickup pattern Microphone pattern that is sensitive to sound from the front and back but not the sides.

Blasting Excessive volume resulting in distortion.

Blend Merging of complementary sound elements.

BM Beautiful Music radio format. One of the first formats on FM.

BMI Broadcast Music Incorporated; music licensing service.

Book Term used to describe rating survey document; "Bible."

BPME Broadcast Promotion and Management Executives.

Bridge Sound used between program elements.

Broadcast Communicating near and far using radio and television.

BTA Best Time Available, also Run of Schedule (ROS); commercials logged at available times.

Bulk eraser Tool for removing magnetic impression from recording tape.

Call letters Assigned station identification generally beginning with W east of the Mississippi and K west.

Capstan Shaft in recorder that drives tape.

Cardiod pickup pattern Microphone pattern where sound is picked up from front and rejected from the rear.

Cart Plastic cartridge containing a continuous loop of recording tape.

Cash flow Operating profit before taxes, depreciation and interest are subtracted.

Cassette Two reels of tape in a plastic housing.

CD-ROM Compact Disc - Read Only Memory. An almost indestructible disc which is read by a laser and can store the equivalent of 1500 floppy disks or 270,000 pages of information.

CFR Code of Federal Regulations.

Chain broadcasting Forerunner of network broadcasting.

CHR Contemporary Hit Radio format.

Clip A segment of audio or videotape that's included in a story that is broadcast on radio or television or on the Web.

Clock Wheel indicating sequence or order of programming ingredients aired during one hour.

Closed question This type of question doesn't help a interviewee to open up! Closed questions usually prompt a person to answer with simple "yes" or "no".

Cluster Group of announcements; stop set. (see Spot set)

Cold Background (music bed) fade on last line of copy.

Combo Announcer operating own board, engineering show; also refers to co-owned AM/FM operation.

Commercial Paid advertising announcement; spot.

Communications Plan A communications plan is a planning document that answers the following questions: who is the audience, what is the message, what is the desired outcome, and how is the desired outcome going to be achieved? Desired outcomes include awareness of a product, public endorsement for a program, or support during change in the workforce.

Community Relations Reaching out to community stakeholders such as local residents or community groups, in response to a situation or event. The objective is to educate and involve the community in decisions that affect it.

Compact disk (CD) Digital recording using laser beam to decode surface.

Compensation Combination of salary and fringe benefits paid to an employee.

Condenser microphone Microphone with a capacitative electrical element.

Console Audio mixer consisting of inputs, outputs, toggles, meters, sliders and/or pots; board.

Consultant Station advisor or counselor; "format doctor."

Control room Center of broadcast operations from which programming originates; air studio.

Cool out Gradual fade of bed music at conclusion of spot.

Co-op Arrangement between retailer and manufacturer for the purpose of sharing radio advertising expenses.

Copy Material for a newspaper or magazine article.

Copywriter One who writes commercial or promotional copy.

Cost Per Point (CPP) Estimate of how much it costs an advertiser to reach one rating point worth of listeners.

Cost Per Thousand (CPM or Cost Per Mil) Estimate of how much it costs an advertiser to reach 1,000 listeners.

CPB Corporation for Public Broadcasting.

Crisis Communication Responding to crisis situations with communication aimed at minimizing the negative affects of the situation on an organization's image.

Crossfade Fade out of one element while simultaneously introducing another.

Cue burn Distortion at the beginning of a record cut resulting from heavy cueing.

Cue Signal for the start of action; prepare for airing.

Cume Ratings measurement, the number of people who have sampled a radio station.

Cutline Sentences at the bottom of a photo that describe what happened in it, which usually relate to a story. Also called a caption.

Cutline The caption to a picture or other graphic element of a story.

Cutting Editing tape or film.

DAB Digital Audio Broadcasting. There are two competing systems. IBOC favored by the US. Eureka147 favored by Canada and Europe.

DAT Digital audio tape.

Dateline A line at the beginning of a printed news story or news release giving the place and date of the story's origin.

Dead Air A technical error in which no signal is fed for broadcast.

Dayparts Periods or segments of broadcast day: 6-10a.m., 10a.m. - 3p.m., 3- 7p.m.

DDC Dewey Decimal Classification. Classification system used by almost all public libraries.

Dead air Silence where sound usually should be; absence of programming.

Deadline The editor of a newspaper, magazine, or other media outlet sets a deadline. This is the time when they expect an article to be submitted.

Deejay Host of radio music program; announcer; "disk jockey."

Demagnetize remove magnetic impressions.

Demographics Audience statistical data pertaining to age, sex, race, income, and so forth.

Direct Broadcast Satellite (DBS) Powerful communications satellites that beam programming to receiving dishes at earth stations.

Directional Station transmitting signal in a preordained pattern so as to protect other stations on the same or adjacent frequency.

Donut spot A commercial in which copy is inserted between segments of music.

Double billing Illegal station billing practice in which client is charged twice.

Download To take files from another computer or server for use on your own.

Draft A draft of an article before submitting it.

Drivetime Radio's primetime: 6-10 a.m. and 3-7 p.m.

Dub Copy of recording; duplicate (dupe).

Dub: Most commonly, a copy of a film or tape. It can also mean making a completely new soundtrack, as in dubbing English for a foreign film. A dubbed tape is also called a dupe.

EBS Emergency Broadcast System.

Edit To alter composition of recorded material; splice.

Editing The process of reviewing a news story, revising the writing and checking it for mistakes before it is published or broadcast.

Editing/Copy Editing Editing is an important part of the process of producing written materials that are clear and easy to understand. An editor checks for correct grammar and spelling, and appropriate vocabulary and tone. Communicators may edit the writing of others in an organization, or may write and edit materials themselves.

Editor A person who edits material for publication or broadcast.

Editorial A newspaper article written by, or on behalf of, an editor, especially one giving an opinion on a well-known issue.

Encoding videos The process of changing video camera footage into digital footage which can be read and displayed by a computer. (i.e.—RealVideo material)

ENG Electronic news gathering.

Erase Wipe clean magnetic impressions; degauss, bulk, deflux, demagnetize.

ERP Effective radiated power; tape head configuration: erase, record, playback

ET Electrical transcription.

Ethnic Programming for minority group audiences.

Eureka147 Digital Audio Broadcasting System being used by Canada and Europe.

Evaluation An important part of effective communications is setting clear goals for public relations campaigns, and evaluating whether the goals were met after the campaign is over. There are many ways to do this, including surveys, monitoring media coverage and sales figures.

External Communications Communications to external stakeholders to educate, increase awareness and generate acceptance regarding a product or program. Communications strategies may include media relations, special events, investor relations and community relations.

Fact sheet List of pertinent information on a sponsor.

Fade To slowly lower or raise volume level.

FCC Federal Communications Commission; government regulatory body with authority over radio operations.

Feature A longer, more probing article or story (as opposed to an "objective" news item or account). Magazines and newspapers may have a features department or desk.

Feed To send a program or signal. For instance, feeding a program from one station via satellite to other stations.

First Generation The original film or tape. Dubs or dupes are made from it.

Fidelity Trueness of sound dissemination or reproduction.

Fixed position Spot routinely logged at a specified time.

Flight Advertising air schedule.

FM Frequency Modulation; method of signal transmission using 88-108 MHz band.

FMX System used to improve FM reception.

Footage A selection or sections of film already shot.

Format Type of programming a station offers; arrangement of material, formula.

Frequency Number of cycles-per-second of a sine wave.

FTP (File Transfer Protocol) This is a program used to upload files and webpages from a personal computer to a server.

Fulltrack Recording utilizing entire width of tape.

Gain Volume; amplification.

Generation Dub; dupe, tape-recording.

Government Relations Determining how government policy, including laws and regulations, affect an organization; establishing an organization's views on policies; and communicating views about public policy to government representatives.

Grammar The study of classes and functions of words, how words are said, and how words relate in a sentence.

Grease pencil Soft-tip marker used to inscribe recording tape for editing purposes.

Green Room A small room near a broadcast studio in which program guests wait before they are interviewed.

Hot Usually in reference to a microphone meaning it's "on."

Gross impressions Total number of exposures to a schedule of announcements.

Gross Rating Points (GRP) Representation of the total number of exposures to a schedule of announcements, expressed as a percentage of all possible listeners.

Ground wave AM signal traveling the earth's surface; primary signal.

Headphones Speakers worn directly over the ears; headsets, cans.

Heat To cover a particular genre of journalism. (i.e.- Music Journalism or Sports Journalism)

Hertz (Hz) Cycles per second; unit of electromagnetic frequency. (named after Heinrich Hertz).

Hot clock Wheel indicating when particular music selections are to be aired.

Hot Overmodulated. also uptempo AC.

HTML (Hyper Text Markup Language) HTML is the lingua franca for publishing hypertext on the World Wide Web.

HTTP Hypertext transfer protocol. The portion of a WWW address that signifies that a document was created in HTML.

Hype Exaggerated presentation; high-intensity, punched.

Hyperlinks The text on a Web site which can be "clicked on" with a mouse which in turn will take you to another Web page or a different area of the same Web page. Hyperlinks are created or "coded" in HTML. They are also used to load multimedia files such as AVI movies and AU sound files.

Hypertext A system of writing and displaying text that enables the text to be linked in.

IBOC In-Band On-Channel. System that allows digital

broadcasting over current AM and FM frequencies. Major companies promoting IBOC included Lucent and USADR USA Digital Radio, Inc. These companies have merged and are now know as Ibiquity. IBOC is now refered to as HD-Radio.

ID Station identification required by law to be broadcast as close to the top of the hour as possible; station break.

IFLA International Federation of Library Associations and Institutions. The leading international body representing the interests of library and information services and their users.

In the Can A show or portion of it that is complete and ready to broadcast. The tape or film literally is in a can.

Lapel or Lavaliere Mike Smallish microphone attached to a lapel or blouse.

Info-bahn The information super highway (info, as in information and bahn, as in German for highway).

Input Terminal receiving incoming current.

Institutional Message promoting general image.

Internal Communications Any communications method aimed at informing, educating and motivating employees within an organization. Communications vehicles may include newsletters, an intranet, employee events, surveys, staff meetings and information sessions, and a forum for two-way communication with senior management.

Investor Relations Specializing in communicating with an organization's investors.

IPS Inches per second; tape speed: 1 7/8, 3 3/4, 7 1/2, 15, 30 IPS.

ISDN Integrated Services Digital Network. High-speed digital telecommunications lines that can transmit both voice and data.

ISO International Organization for Standardization. A network of national standards institutes from 147 countries

working in partnership with international organizations, governments, industry, business and consumer representatives.

ISSN International Standard Serial Number. A unique eight-digit number, in two groups of four, assigned to a periodical by the International Serials Data System.

Issues Management Identifying and monitoring issues that could affect an organization and preparing appropriate spokespeople to speak on behalf of issues to influence the outcome.

ITU International Telecommunications Union; world broadcasting regulatory agency.

Jack Plug for patching sound sources; patch-cord, socket, input.

Jingle Music commercial or promo; signature, aural-logo.

Jock see Deejay.

Journalism The business or practice of writing and producing news media.

Journalist A person who writes, edits, or reports for a newspaper, magazine or news broadcast.

Key (keying) Turning a sound source on or off from the console.

Kilohertz One thousand cycles per second; AM frequency measurement, kilocycles.

LAN Local Area Network. A network of computers within an institution.

Lead or Lede (pronounced leed) The opening sentence or paragraph of a news story.

Leader or Leader Blank The blank film or tape used at the "head" or start of a program. Can be used to thread a projector or tape machine so the show can go on the air as soon as the machine starts running.

Leader tape Plastic, metallic, or paper tape used in conjunction with magnetic tape for marking and spacing purposes.

Leading **questions** These questions try to lead an interviewee in a certain direction.

Lede (or lead) The first and most important sentence of the story. It sets up what the story is going to be about.

Level Amount of volume units; audio measurements.

Licensee Individual or company holding license issued by the FCC for broadcast purposes.

Line Connection used for transmission of audio; phone-line.

Line-of-sight Path of FM signal; FM propagation.

Liner cards Written on-air promos used to ensure adherence to station image; prepared ad-libs.

Live copy Material read over air; not prerecorded.

Live tag Postscript to taped message.

Loaded words Words that leave people with a distinct and often negative impression.

Local channels Class IV AM stations found at high end of band: 1200-1600kHz.

Make-good Replacement spot for one missed.

MARC MAchine Readable Cataloging. MARC records contain data in standardized format and allow conversion to automated cataloging and circulation systems.

Market Area served by a broadcast facility.

Marketing The process of planning and executing the conception, pricing, promotion and distribution of ideas, goods; and services to create exchanges that satisfy individual and organizational objectives.

Master control see Control room.

Master Original recording from which dubs are made.

MBS Mutual Broadcasting System; radio network.

Media (or Press) Kit Information distributed to reporters which can include a news release, background information, and photos to assist the media in preparing a news article or broadcast.

Media Relations As a function of a public relations practitioner, media relations involves establishing and maintaining

relationships with reporters who cover stories relevant to an organization and the business it performs.

Media Training Training people to speak effectively to the news media for print, radio and television broadcast.

Megahertz (MHz) Million cycles per second; FM frequency measurement, megacycles.

Messages Something an organization wants to communicate to an audience about itself.

Mixdown Integration of sound elements to create desired effect; production

Monitor Studio speaker; supervise on-air sound; aircheck.

Mono Single or fulltrack sound; monaural, monophonic.

MOR Middle-of-the-Road radio format.

Morning Drive Radio's most listened-to daypart: 6:00-10:00 a.m.

MSA Metro Survey Area; geographic area in radio survey.

Multiplexing Impressing two or more signals on one carrier as in FM stereo.

Multitracking Recording sound-on-sound; overdubbing, stacking tracks.

Music sweep Several selections played back-to-back without interruption; music segue.

NAB National Association of Broadcasters.

Narrowcasting Directed programming; targeting specific audience demographic.

NBC National Broadcasting Company.

Network feed Programs sent to affiliate stations.

Network Broadcast combine providing programming to affiliates: CBS, ABC, Mutual, etc.

News (or Media or Press) Release A short report, usually up to two pages, describing an event, an announcement, a discovery or the results of a study, that the organization believes the public should know about.

News block Extended news broadcast.

News Conference An event announcing a newsworthy decision, report or activity to the news media in a forum where reporters are invited to receive information directly from the organization's spokespeople and ask questions.

News Peg The aspect of a story that makes it newsworthy, important, or interesting. The news peg is often timeliness, wide impact, or effect on community.

NPR National Public Radio

O and O's Network or group owned and operated stations.

Off the record This is what people say when they want the information they tell you to be unmentioned. This means that they don't want their names or quotes to be said to anyone or printed in your story.

Off-mike Speech outside normal range of microphone.

Omnidirectional pickup pattern Microphone pickup pattern that picks up sound equally well from all directions.

On the record The opposite of "off the record". This means that you are allowed to use the person's name and quotes for your story.

Online journalism Stories that are written specifically for the Web instead of newspaper, radio, television or magazine. It can include the use of text, photos, graphics, hypertext, audio and video to tell stories.

Open-ended questions These questions encourage the person to talk and share their thoughts and feelings on a subject. It allows them to tell their own story without much prompting from the reporter.

Open-Mike A microphone in use.

Out-cue Last words in a line of carted copy.

Output Transmission of audio or power from one location to another; transfer terminal.

Overdubbing see Multitracking.

Overmodulate Exceed standard or prescribed audio levels; pinning VU-needle.

Pack journalism This refers to large groups of reporters from different newspapers or broadcasting stations who are all after the same big story.

Package A complete story with natural sound and voice over

Packaged Canned programming; syndicated, prerecorded, taped.

Passives Listeners who do not call stations in response to contests or promotions or to make requests or comments; the silent majority.

Patch panel Jack board for connecting audio sources: remotes, studios, equipment; patch bay.

Patch Circuit connector; cord, cable.

Payola Undercover illegal payment to a disc jockey or radio station programmer for playing or plugging a record.

Persons using radio (PUR) Measurement of the number of persons listening to stations in a market.

Photographs "Grip and Grin" These are photos of people receiving awards or diplomas, cutting ribbons or passing out cheques.

Pinch roller Rubber wheel that presses recording tape against the capstan.

Playback Reproduction of recorded sound.

Playlist Roster of music for airing.

Plug Promo; connector.

Pool A camera crew and reporter(s) assigned to cover a story or event on behalf of all media and to share materials with them. Often used when tight space and security are considerations or when it is unlikely that any "news" will be made.

Rating The size of the TV audience as measured by the number of TV-equipped households watching. The total U.S. figure is about 92 million TV households, so each rating point

equals about 920,000 homes watching. A family with more than one set is counted as one unit. Contrast with Share.

Popping Breakup of audio due to gusting or blowing into mike; blasting.

Positioner Brief statement used on-air to define a station's position in a market.

Pot Potentiometer; volume control knob, gain control, fader, attentuator, rheostat.

PRI Public Radio International.

Production The use of studio equipment to combine sounds into a finished product. See Mixdown.

PSA Public Service Announcement; noncommercial message.

Psychographics Research term dealing with listener personality, such as attitude, behavior, values, opinions, and beliefs.

Public Relations/Communications The terms "public relations" and "communications" are often used interchangeably. Public relations explains an organization's actions and policies in a focused, consistent and credible manner, to both employees and publics outside of the organization.

Publics or Audience Any group of people interested in an issue, or a segment of society you seek to interest. Audiences could be employees, customers, shareholders, interest groups, governments or other "publics" outside an organization.

Publish To produce or release a written work for the public to see or hear.

Punch Emphasis; stress.

Quadraphonic four speaker/channel sound reproduction; surround sound.

Qualitative Methods Survey research used to explore consumer reaction to ideas, issues and new products in a forum that allows for in-depth feedback through interviews or focus groups.

Quantitative Methods Survey research, usually conducted by phone or written questionnaire, to determine or measure the proportion of a specified audience who hold a particular viewpoint or behave in a particular way, and the intensity with which the opinion is held or the behaviour is performed.

RAB Radio Advertising Bureau.

Rack Prepare or set up for play or record: "rack-it-up"; equipment container.

RADAR Nationwide measurement service by Statistical Research, Inc.

Rate card Statement of advertising fees and terms.

Rating Measurement of the total available audience.

RCA Radio Corporation of America; NBC parent company.

Reach Measurement of how many different members of an audience will be exposed to a message.

Real Video The format of video files displayed on most Internet sites, such as SNN.

Recut Retake; re-record, remix.

Reel-to-reel Recording machine with feed and take-up reels.

Remote Broadcast originating away from station control room.

Reverb Close echo; redundancy of sound.

Rewind Speeded return of recording tape from take up reel.

Ride gain Monitor level; watch VU needle.

Rip 'n' read Airing copy unaltered from newswire.

rpm Revolutions per minute: 33 1/3, 45, and 78 rpm.

RTNDA Radio and Television News Directors Association.

Running Time How long it takes a show to go from start to finish. Often abbreviated TRT (total running time).

Run-of-station (ROS) Bulk commercial buying plan where station's traffic department will fit the commercials into available time locations. See BTA

Satellite Tour A feed from one point of origination to various

downlink sites. An example is when an author is plugging a new book and is connected in series with several different interviewers in their newsrooms.

Satellite Orbiting device for relaying audio from one earth station to another; DBS, Comsat, Satcom.

SBE Society of Broadcast Engineers.

SCA Subsidiary Communication Authority; subcarrier FM.

Scrum The gathering of reporters around a person who is important to a particular story.

Search ngine A program used by an Internet browser to look for specific words and sort them for information.

Secondary service area AM skywave listening area.

Segue Uninterrupted flow of recorded material; continuous.

Server A computer in a network shared by multiple users. The term may refer to both the hardware and software or just the software that performs the service.

SESAC Society of European Stage Authors and Composers; music licensing service.

SFX Abbreviation for sound effects.

Share The percentage of televisions actually in use that are tuned to a specific program.

Sidebar A short accompanying piece for a larger story, often with a human interest angle. Usually blocked off from the main text.

Share Percentage of station's listenership compared to competition; piece of audience pie.

Signal Sound transmission; RF.

Signature Theme; aural logo, jingle, ID.

Simulcast Simultaneous broadcast over two or more frequencies.

Sitting Mike A microphone on a table.

Sky wave Radio wave that bounces off the ionosphere.

SLA Special Libraries Association. A national association of

librarians who work in special libraries. There are two chapters in Connecticut: Fairfield County and Connecticut Valley. Sponsors meetings, workshops, and an annual conference.

SOT Sound on Tape – Both Nat and Voice come from tape

SOTVO Soundbyte is followed by video

Sound bite Audio portion of interview. See Actuality.

Sound byte any piece of audio handled as an element separate from any video

Spot News: News of immediate interest.

Sound hour Term referring to the programming strategy with an hour of broadcasting.

Source Aperson, written article, book, song, video or film from which to get information

Spec tape Specially tailored commercial used as a sales tool to help sell and account.

Spectrum Range of frequencies available to broadcasters.

Splice To join ends of recording tape with adhesive; edit.

Splicing bar Grooved platform for cutting and joining recording tape; edit bar.

Sponsor Advertiser; client, account, underwriter.

Sponsorship An organization donates money or other resources for an event or program in return for public recognition of its contribution. This often includes placing the corporate logo on signs, advertisements and printed material associated with the event.

Spot set Group or cluster of announcements; stop set.

Spots Commercials; paid announcements.

Stage Manager The individual on the set of a studio who cues the participants and otherwise provides liaison with the control room.

Stakeholders An audience or public who become involved in the activities of a public or private business because they

have an interest or a stake, in the activities of that business.

Stand Up A commentary or report by a TV correspondent seen on camera, usually at the scene of the action. Used to open, close, or bridge the elements of a report.

Station identification Station call letters immediately followed by city of license. for example: WVUD Newark

Station rep company acting in behalf of local stations to national agencies.

Station Broadcast facility given specific frequency by FCC.

Stereo Multichannel sound; two program channels.

Stinger Music or sound effect finale preceded by last line of copy; button, punctuation.

Straight copy Announcement employing unaffected, nongimicky approach; institutional.

Stringer Field or on-scene reporter; freelance reporter.

Subliminal Advertising or programming not consciously perceived; below normal range of awareness, background.

Super: An image superimposed over another image. Often the subject of an interview will be "supered" with identifying information. Also called "titles" or "lower thirds" because of the positioning of words.

Survey Research Gathering opinions, perceptions, behaviours and attitudes regarding issues, ideas, products and concepts through qualitative and quantitative methods.

Sweep link Transitional jingle between sound elements.

Syndication Programs sent to a network of users.

Syndicator Producer of purchasable program material.

Syntax The way that words are put together to make sentences.

Tag Time Last statement of a show, spot, or commercial.

Tag Postscript to taped message.

Talent The paid staff who are seen or heard on the air, often the interviewer.

Talent Radio performer; announcer, deejay, newscaster.

Talk Conversation and interview radio format.

TAP Total Audience Plan.

Tape speed Movement measured in inches per second. See IPS.

TCP/IP Transmission Control Protocol/Internet Protocol. Allows different types of computers to communicate with each other; uses packet-switching to move data among computer networks.

Tease A short clip that "Teases" an upcoming package before the break

Telescoping Compressing of sound to fit a desired length; technique used in audition tapes and concert promos, editing.

TELNET A "terminal emulation" protocol or application program that allows users to log in to another computer on the Internet.

TFN Till Further Notice; without specific kill date.

Time spent listening (TSL) Measurement of average amount of time spent by average listener tuned to a station.

Toll broadcasting Precursor to commercial radio.

Total Survey Area (TSA) Geographic area in radio survey.

Trade-out Exchange of station airtime for goods or services.

Traffic Station department responsible for scheduling sponsor announcements.

Transmit To broadcast; propagate signal, air.

Turnover Measurement of how often listenership changes from time period to time period.

Turntable Ancient device used to play records :-)

Underwriter Program sponsor; noncommercial financial sponsor.

Underwriting Method by which noncommercial stations seek financial support from commercial sponsors.

Unidirectional mike Microphone designed to pick up sound in one direction; cardiod, studio mike.

Upload To transfer files from your computer to another computer or server.

URL Uniform Resource Locator. The address of a WWW site. CLC's URL is http://www.ctlibrarians.org.

VNR: A video new release. The television equivalent of a news release.

VOA Voice of America. U.S. International broadcast service.

Voice-over Talk over sound.

Voice-track Recording of announcer message for use in mixdown.

Volume control Pot; fader.

Volume Quality of sound; audio level.

VOTOPS Video Only – Anchor Speaks over the video. There is usually natural sound on the video

VU Meter Gauge measuring units of sound.

WARC World Administrative Radio Conference; international meeting charged with assigning spectrum space.

Web cast Aa video or audio broadcast that's transmitted over the World Wide Web.

Wheel Program tool indicating sequence or order of programming ingredients aired during one hour.

Windscreen Microphone filter used to prevent popping and distortion.

Wire A source of information for Journalists. The wire itself is an up-to-the-minute source of information for other reporters.

Wire service News gathering organization; for example:AP.

Wireless telegraphy Early radio used to transmit Morse code.

Wow Distortion of sound created by inappropriate speed; miscue.

XM One of two national satellite radio services. (See also Sirius)

1
Fiber to Cyber Media

Paper has been used as the basic material for written communication and the dissemination of information. It dominated the scene of learning for the last many centuries. Paper coupled with the moveable types invented in the 15th century accelerated the rate of growth of the recorded knowledge. It was a cheaper and easily available medium and even mass production was not difficult. From this invention onwards, the quantum of publication was so high that whatever number of books the whole of Europe could have brought out till the 15th century was produced within a year of this invention. Paper became an indispensable reality in every civilized society ever since.

The word paper is derived from the name of the fibrous plant papyrus, which grows abundantly along the Nile River in Egypt. In ancient times, the fibrous layers within the stem of this plant were removed, placed side by side, and crossed at right angles with another set of layers similarly arranged. The sheet so formed was dampened and pressed. Upon drying, the glue like sap of the plant, acting as an adhesive, cemented the layers together. Complete defibering, an indispensable element in modern papermaking, did not occur in the preparation of papyrus sheets. Papyrus was the most widely used writing material in ancient times, and many papyrus records still survive. The known history of papermaking can be traced to about AD 105, when Ts'ai Lun, an official attached to the Imperial court of China, created a sheet of paper using mulberry and other bast fibers along with fishnets, old rags, and hemp waste. In its slow travel westward, the art of papermaking reached Samarkand, in Central Asia, in 751;

and in 793 the first paper was made in Baghdad during the time of Harun ar-Rashid, with the golden age of Islamic culture that brought papermaking to the frontiers of Europe.

The Arabs acquired the art of papermaking as one of the spoils of war. The Central Asian city of Samarkand was fighting the Chinese and captured a number of prisoners, two of whom were papermakers who were released in exchange for teaching the Arabs how to make paper. The Arabs wasted no time in improving papermaking techniques - they were probably the first to make paper from linen - and they spread the techniques throughout the Middle East and into Spain. By the 14th century a number of paper mills existed in Europe, particularly in Spain, Italy, France, and Germany.

The invention of printing in the 1450s brought a vastly increased demand for paper. Through the 18th century the papermaking process remained essentially unchanged, with linen and cotton rags furnishing the basic raw materials. Paper mills were increasingly plagued by shortages; in the 18th century they even advertised and solicited publicly for rags. It was evident that a process for utilizing a more abundant material was needed. At the time when Gutenberg produced his first Bible around 1456, Europe was still predominantly using parchment and vellum for printing, rather than paper.

Parchment is the skin of a sheep or goat prepared for writing; vellum is a fine parchment made from the skins of calves, lambs or kids. Gutenberg printed several copies of his Bible on parchment; to print just one, he had to use the skins of 300 sheep. Now with that kind of resource demand, obviously there were not enough goats and sheep and calves in Europe to allow the mass production of books. So there came the printing press - and no way to realize its potential, until entrepreneurs saved the day by improving and expanding the technology of making paper from linen rags. At first, paper was called "cloth parchment."

With the easy availability of Paper, book production increased and newspapers started appearing in the late 1600s and early 1700s. Newspapers, and the increased communication they offered, began to affect the conduct of government and commerce. Newspapers played an important role in spreading political information in the pre-Revolutionary and Revolutionary period, not to mention during the formative period of nation's institutional and industrial history. Still the booksellers in the Middle Ages seldom had many ready-made books in shops. They were copied down by hand which took a lot of time and resources that everybody was not able to afford. It was done by simply borrow the first few pages of the book and take them home for copying. These pages were usually returned before borrowing the next few pages. There's a story, perhaps apocryphal, about Gutenberg's financial partner - when he offered 20 identical copies of the Bible to a bookseller in Paris, he was quickly forced to flee for his life. People were certain that the only explanation for this bizarre occurrence was that he was in league with the Devil.

The printing press was used to disseminate news in Europe shortly after Johann Gutenberg invented the letter press, employing movable type, in the 1450s. One of the first printed works that might qualify as news was an Italian account of a tournament printed in about 1470. A letter written by Christopher Columbus, reporting on his discoveries, was set in type and circulating in Barcelona before Columbus arrived there in April of 1493. In the sixteenth and seventeenth centuries, thousands of printed newsbooks, short pamphlets reporting on a news event, and news ballads, accounts of news events written in verse and usually printed on one side of a single sheet of paper, circulated in Europe and, to a lesser extent, in the new European colonies in America. The first news report printed in the Americas described an earthquake in Guatemala and was printed in Mexico in 1541.

By the turn of the 19th century, the Industrial

Revolution had taken hold and, when Queen Victoria came to the throne in 1837, the printing industry had been transformed. As had been the case in the second half of the 18th century, the country was gripped by social, political and industrial unrest. Numerous Combination Acts were passed by Parliament up to 1824, designed to prevent workers from combining to organise industrial action, and to prevent their employers from joining together to fix prices.

THE POWER PRESS

The printing press allowed lower cost of printing information on paper. Their subsequent availability, stimulated the foundation of new schools and universities. Because books were now more numerous, educational opportunities that were once restricted to the nobility and upper classes were now becoming somewhat more available to other classes in society, with dramatic increases in levels of education and literacy.

Improvements transformed the world of art. Previously, artists had to practice their techniques and develop their drawing abilities on canvasses that they painted over and over again, so most paintings were actually lost - hidden under layers and layers of new paint. When paper became available as a cheap type of "canvas," artists could go wild practicing their sketching, and now these sketches could be saved. For the first time, drawing became an important art form in itself. The breakthrough in papermaking technology fueled a huge expansion in business that eventually led to the development of the modern corporation, which was unable to function without tremendous supplies of paper. The paper industry in the 1850s crated changes so far-reaching that it was one of the transformation factors in the developing the nations. Not the least revolutionary change was the astounding drop in newsprint prices that advances in papermaking technology allowed.

In Europe and the United States of America, throughout the eighteenth century, there was an intense search for a new fiber source of paper. Contests were held, universities offered prizes, and inventors and laboratories worked feverishly to come up with a new source for paper. Inventors would often print a book on their newly-invented paper that described how the paper was made. And it ended up with books printed on paper made from asbestos, straw, swamp grass, marsh mallow, and esparto dune grass from certain beaches in Spain. The first patent for a paper using deinked waste paper as pat of its fiber source was issued in 1800 in London. It was not until the 1840s that the initial development of the papermaking machine in England and experiments in groundwood pulping in Germany and Nova Scotia enabled the commercial production of paper.

Several major pulping processes were gradually developed that relieved the paper industry of dependency upon cotton and linen rags and made modern large-scale production possible. These developments followed two distinct pathways. In one, fibers and fibre fragments were separated from the wood structure by mechanical means; and in the other, the wood was exposed to chemical solutions that dissolved and removed lignin and other wood components, leaving cellulose fiber behind.

Prior to the invention of the paper machine, paper was made one sheet at a time by dipping a frame or mold with a screened bottom into a vat of stock. Lifting the mold allowed the water to drain, leaving the sheet on the screen. The sheet was then pressed and dried. The size of a single sheet was limited to the size of frame and mold that a man could lift from a vat of stock. Since cellulose fiber is a major constituent of the stems of plants, a vast number of plants represent potential sources of paper; many of these have been pulped experimentally. A rather substantial number of plant sources have been used commercially, at least on a small scale and at various times and places. Indeed, the use of cereal straws for paper predates the use of wood

pulp and is widely practiced today throughout the world, although on a relatively small scale of production. Because many parts of the world are deficient in forests, the development of the paper industry in these areas appears to depend to a considerable degree upon the use of annual plants and agricultural fibers.

There is abundance of bamboo in Southeast Asia, where increased production of paper is greatly needed, Much interest has been displayed in bamboo pulp development. The growing cycle of bamboo is favorable, for the culms can be harvested without destroying the root system. Under ideal conditions of soil fertility and moisture, an established stand of bamboo probably would produce more fiber per hectare (or acre) per year than any other plant. Wild bamboo, however, is difficult to harvest and transport economically; so far, the interest in it has not been translated into any large-scale production. Pulp mills make use of bamboo in India, Thailand, and the Philippines. Considerable quantities of bamboo pulp are said to be made in China.

The development in papermaking brought out new ways of communication of ideas. In the ancient time, the media of communication had durability but lacked portability. This was achieved with the invention of paper. Later, the celluloid medium contributed in reduction of size of documents and made mass transfer of information possible through microfilms, microfiches and ultra fiches. This new medium also presented a different kind of material for understanding of reality and that was in the form of motion pictures. But the route to theses developments goes to the printing technology.

The current information revolution is actually the fourth information revolution in human history. The first one was the invention of writing 5,000 to 6,000 years ago in Mesopotamia; then—independently but several thousand years later—in China; and some 1,500 years later still, by the Maya in Central America. The second

information revolution was brought on by the invention of the written book, first in China, perhaps as early as 1300 B.C., and then, independently 800 years later, in Greece, when Peisistratos, the tyrant of Athens, had Homer's epics—only recited until then—copied into books. The third information revolution was set off by Gutenberg's invention of the printing press and of movable type between 1450 and 1455, and by the contemporaneous invention of engraving. We have almost no documents on the first two of these revolutions, though we know that the impact of the written book was enormous in Greece and Rome as well as in China. In fact, China's entire civilization and system of government still rest on it. But on the third information revolution, printing and engraving, we have abundant material.

At the time Gutenberg invented the press, there was a substantial information industry in Europe. It was probably Europe's biggest employer. It consisted largely of thousands of monasteries, many of which housed hundreds of highly skilled monks. Each monk labored from dawn to dusk, six days a week, copying books by hand. An industrious, well-trained monk could do 4 pages a day, or 25 pages during a six-day week, for an annual output of 1,200 to 1,300 handwritten pages. Fifty years later, by 1500, the monks had become unemployed. These monks (some estimates go well above 10,000 for all of Europe) had been replaced by a very small number of lay craftsmen, the newly minted class of "printers," totaling perhaps 1,000, but spread over all of Europe produce a printed book required coordinated teamwork by up to 20 such craftsmen, beginning with one highly skilled cutter of type, to a much larger number, maybe 10 or more, of much less skilled bookbinders. Such a team produced each year about 25 titles, with an average of 200 pages per title, or 5,000 pages ready to be printed. By 1505, print runs of 500 copies were becoming increasingly common. This meant that a printing team could produce annually 25 million printed pages,

bound into 125,000 books ready to be sold—or 2.5 million pages per team member as against the 1,200 or 1,300 the individual monk had produced only 50 years earlier.

As a result of Gutenberg's invention prices of books felt dramatically. Before it books were such a luxury that only the wealthy and educated could afford them. But when Martin Luther's German Bible came out in 1522 (a book of well over 1,000 pages), its price was so low that even the poorest peasant family could buy one. .The cost and price reductions of the third information revolution were at least as great as those of the present, the fourth information revolution. And so were the speed and the extent of its spread. Cotton was by far the most desirable of all textile fibers. It is easily washable and can be worked up into an infinite variety of different cloths. It was a time- and labor-expensive process. For it took 12 to 14 man-days to produce a pound of cotton yarn by hand, as against 1 to 2 man-days for wool, 2 to 5 for linen, and 6 for silk.

The printing revolution also changed institutions, including the educational system. In the decades that followed, university after university was founded throughout Europe, but unlike the earlier ones, they were not designed for the clergy or for the study of theology. They were built around disciplines such as law, medicine, mathematics, natural philosophy (science).

.Printing publicized every single advance the Portuguese seafarers made along the west coast of Africa in their search for a sea route to the India. Printing provided Columbus with the first (though totally wrong) maps of the fabled lands beyond the western horizon, such as Marco Polo's China and the legendary Japan. Printing made it possible to record the results of every single voyage immediately and create new, more reliable maps. Noneconomic changes cannot be quantified. But surely the impact on society, education, culture—let alone on religion—of the printing revolution was easily as great and

surely as fast, if not faster, as the impact of the present information revolution.

The most important lesson of the earlier information revolution may, however, be found in the fates and fortunes of its technologists. The printing revolution immediately created a new and unprecedented class of information technologists, just as the most recent information revolution has created any number of information businesses, MIS and IT specialists, software designers, and chief information officers. The IT people of the printing revolution were the early printers. Nonexistent and not even imaginable in 1455, they flourished throughout Europe 25 years later and had become great stars. Unlike earlier craftsmen, they were great gentlemen. These virtuosi of the printing press were known and revered all over Europe, just as the names of the leading computer and software firms are recognized and admired worldwide today. Printers were courted by kings, princes, the pope, and rich merchant cities and were showered with money and honors.

By 1580 or so, the printers, with their focus on technology, had become ordinary craftsmen, respectable tradesmen but definitely not of the upper class. Their place was soon taken by what we now call publishers (though the term was not coined until much later), people and firms whose focus was no longer on the "T" in IT but on the "I." This shift got under way the moment the new technology began to have an impact on the meaning of information, and with it, on the meaning and function of the 15th century's key institutions such as the church and the universities. It thus began at the same juncture at which we now find ourselves in the present information revolution as we undergo the shift in business information and, with it, the redefinition of the function and purpose of business.

Changes were also made to the printer's end product and from 1740 most books were sold in paper covered boards. The principle behind this was that it would allow

the buyer to arranging binding to his own taste. A side effect of the move was undoubtedly that it brought the basic price of a book within the financial means of a wider reading public. During the latter years of the century, another new practice was introduced whereby books were sold in subscription copies. These were advertised before publication (allowing the printer to assess demand) and the names of subscribers were often included in the printed copy.

Censorship remained prevalent throughout the 1700s and writing about the government was forbidden, especially in newspapers. The campaign to allow reports on government business was led by John Wilkes, a Member of Parliament, and in 1762 he founded the North Briton. But the establishment was determined to resist the actions of this activist and he was expelled from Parliament and imprisoned for a short time. He became a cult figure both in England and America, whose independence he supported. Two other important political changes were the passing of the first Copyright Act by Parliament in 1709 and the introduction of Stamp Duty on newspapers in 1712. The Copyright Act recognised the rights of authors and illustrators and provided protection for a period of two years after their deaths. The introduction of Stamp Duty was less favourable. It amounted initially to a halfpenny or one penny on the price of a newspaper, depending upon the size. In subsequent years, this amount was to be increased and the duty was not abolished until as late as 1855.

Working conditions made little progress generally and printing on wooden presses remained laborious. The process of inking and manually operating the press had not changed substantially since Gutenberg's invention hundreds of years earlier. A competent printer could expect to produce perhaps 100 printed sheets in an hour. One hundred copies of a 300 page book might therefore take a number of weeks just to print the loose pages p; even

working a 16 hour day, which was not uncommon at that time. But in the latter years of this period, the Industrial Revolution stamped its mark on printing.

As the iron industry grew and mechanisation began to take shape, the life of the wooden press drew to a close. In 1772, William Haas of Basel built a new press where all parts which were the subject of stress were made from iron, including both the bed and the platen. His work was superseded in 1798 when Earl Stanhope built a press made entirely from iron.

At around the same time Friedrich Koenig of Suhl was working on a power press but his first attempt, called the Suhler press, was eventually aborted as was a second. But by 1812 he had built a steam operated twin cylinder machine and within two years this was adopted by The Times newspaper in London. At that time the paper was published by John Walter II, having taken over from his near bankrupt father in 1803 but by 1837 distribution of The Times was approaching the 30,000 mark. This had been made possible by the invention of Koenig's power press. The output of the new machine was 1,100 sheets an hour, more than four times higher than that of the manually operated press previously used by the newspaper.

The invention of lithography and the power press combined to make printing an altogether more affordable medium. Book production, business and personal stationery benefited from the revolution in the sense that these ceased to be almost exclusively enjoyed by large companies and the landed gentry. Printing developed an altogether wider marketplace. But the progress and changes in the industry were not limited solely to the press.

In 1804 Henry and Sealy Fourdrinier bought the patents for a papermaking machine invented five years earlier in France. Bryan Donkin, the Fourdriniers' engineer, made significant changes to the earlier design and the adapted machine formed the basis for modern

papermaking. By 1838, over 100 of the Fourdrinier machines were in operation throughout the UK. By 1837 the industry was almost unrecognizable from its form 90 years earlier. The Industrial Revolution was all but over, Victoria came to the throne, and a period of consolidation was to follow.

The first 50 years of the 20th century were dogged by international unrest and two world wars, the like of which had never been seen before. For the industry, it represented a period of consolidation and moderate progress, with several signs of what was to come in the modern age. The nascent 19th century technological advances started to deliver on their promises. For example, web printing using removable letterpress shells became the norm and the use of etching baths allowed the rapid development of photography.

The use of steam to drive printing presses did not really catch on in spite of the competition going on between advocates of the two modes of electricity, AC or DC. The introduction of transformers based on selenium meant that press manufacturers were not bound to one method at the expense of the other.

With great numbers of young men serving in France and economic priorities often laying elsewhere meant that the quality of print during the First World War and for a time afterwards was extremely variable. A hunger for illustrations of the war resulted however in methods of image capture and reproduction being developed at a phenomenal rate.

Great numbers of weekly periodicals were produced and even today these magazines are immensely popular and can be seen. It speaks volumes for the methods of reproduction that these periodicals catch the mood of the time without appearing overly dated. The demand for copper engravers, woodblock carvers and the like held strong till well after the Second World War.

DESKTOP PUBLISHING

A recent advance in the publication industry is the desktop publishing which began in 1985 with the introduction of Aldus Pagemaker software and the Apple LaserWriter printer for the Apple Macintosh computer. A particularly important feature of desktop publishing systems is that they enable to see on the display screen exactly how the document will appear when printed. Systems that support this feature are called WYSIWYGs (what you see is what you get). The ability to create WYSIWYG page layouts on screen and then print pages at high resolution was revolutionary for a personal computer system. The term "desktop publishing" is attributed to Aldus Corporation founder Paul Brainerd, who sought a marketing catch phrase to describe the small size and relative affordability of this suite of products in contrast to the expensive commercial phototypesetting equipment of the day.

Desktop publishing combines a personal computer, page layout software and a printer to create publications on a small economic scale. Users create page layouts with text, graphics, photos and other visual elements using desktop publishing software such as QuarkXPress, Adobe InDesign, RagTime, the free Scribus, Microsoft Publisher, Adobe Photoshop and CorelDraw. For small jobs a few copies of a publication might be printed on a local printer. For larger jobs a computer file can be sent to a vendor for high-volume printing.

Using a personal computer or workstation to produce high-quality printed documents. A desktop publishing system allows to use different typefaces, specify various margins and justifications, and embed illustrations and graphs directly into the text. The most powerful desktop publishing systems enable you to create illustrations, while less powerful systems let you insert illustrations created by other programs.

As word-processing programs become more and more powerful, the line separating such programs from desktop publishing systems is becoming blurred. In general, though, desktop publishing applications give more control over typographical characteristics, such as kerning, and provide more support for full-color output.

Until recently, hardware costs made desktop publishing systems impractical for most uses. But as the prices of personal computers and printers have fallen, desktop publishing systems have become increasingly popular for producing newsletters, brochures, books, and other documents that formerly required a typesetter.

Early desktop publishing was a primitive affair. Users of the PageMaker-LaserWriter-Macintosh system endured frequent software crashes, the Mac's tiny 512 x 342 1-bit black and white screen, the inability to control letter spacing, kerning and other typographic features, and discrepancies between the screen display and printed output. Behind-the-scenes technologies developed by Adobe Systems set the foundation for professional desktop publishing applications. The LaserWriter and LaserWriter Plus printers included extremely high quality, scalable Adobe fonts built into their ROM memory. The LaserWriter's additional PostScript capability allowed publication designers to proof files on a local printer then print the same file at service bureaus using optical resolution 1200+ ppi PostScript-printers like the Linotronic. Later, the Macintosh II was released which was much more suitable for desktop publishing because of its larger and color screen.

In 1986, the GEM-based Ventura Publisher was introduced for MS-DOS computers. While PageMaker's pasteboard metaphor closely simulated the process of creating layouts manually, Ventura Publisher automated the layout process through its use of tags/style sheets and automatically generated indices and other body matter. This made it suitable for manuals and other long-format

documents. During these early years, desktop publishing acquired a bad reputation from untrained users who created chaotically organized ransom note effect layouts—criticisms that would be levied again against early web publishers a decade later.

The improved typographic controls and image handling of PC and Mac-based publishing systems increasingly attracted the attention of professional publishers. The turning point was the introduction of Quark XPress 3.0 in the 1990s and an ever increasing number of digital typefaces. Xpress became dominate in the publishing world until the early twenty first century. Most recently Adobe InDesign has grown in popularity for its powerful typographic controls and integration with other Adobe publishing products which dominate the design, photography, publishing, printing, and digital media industries.

At present virtually all publishing is "desktop publishing." The superior flexibility and speed of desktop publishing systems has greatly reduced the lead time for magazine publication and accommodates elaborate designs and layouts.

Desktop publishing helped to condition a generation of personal computer users to be on the lookout for "the next big thing." In the late 80s, developers hopefully applied the "desktop" prefix to potential new markets like "desktop presentations," "desktop forms" and "desktop video." All of these markets proved to be important (see PowerPoint, Adobe Acrobat, and miniDV for example), especially desktop video editing. Many cinema length movies are now edited on Apple Final Cut Pro using a few thousand dollars worth of equipment which would have cost tens of thousands just a decade earlier..

THE AUDIOVISUALS

The audiovisual media developed during the last one

hundred years primarily starting from the technique of photography. It was believed and is still in place that a picture is worth a thousand words as it may communicate a huge mass of ideas, which may mean differently to different people. Photography emerged as an effective medium which coupled with the technology of sound proved to be the greatest and the most significant form for presentation of ideas.

The present day photography is the result of the early observations by alchemists and chemists based on the action of light on the photosensitive materials. The technique developed towards the end of the 18th century when the demand for the pictures grew. A major advancement in photography took place with substitution of glass for paper as a carrier for the light sensitive material. In 1851, once the manufacture of photographic materials was established as a commercial industry, the photographic techniques followed steady growth. In 1912 Kodak Company introduced flat film in place of glass plates for making negatives. The technique was advantageous for manufacturers. A few years later, the development in new sensitizing dyes made it possible for preparing panchromatic materials of improved quality.

RADIO

Radio emerged as one of the most potent media of mass communication since it made possible the transmission and reception of signals by means of electronic wave and without the use of connecting wires. Within a century of its invention radio has grown enormously going out of Marconi's workshop to a permanent fixture in almost all the homes the world over.

Radio waves are a form of electromagnetic radiation, created whenever a charged object (e.g. an electron) accelerates with a frequency that lies in the radio frequency (RF) portion of the electromagnetic spectrum. In radio, this acceleration is caused by an alternating current in an

antenna. Radio frequencies occupy the range from a few tens of hertz to a few hundred gigahertz.

Other types of electromagnetic radiation, with frequencies above the RF range are infrared, visible light, ultraviolet, X-rays and gamma rays. Since the energy of an individual photon of radio frequency is too low to remove an electron from an atom, radio waves are classified as non-ionizing radiation.

Electromagnetic radiation travels (propagates) by means of oscillating electromagnetic fields that pass through the air and the vacuum of space equally well, and does not require a medium of transport (such as the aether). When radio waves pass an electrical conductor, the oscillating electric or magnetic field (depending on the shape of the conductor) induces an alternating current and voltage in the conductor. This can be transformed into audio or other signals that carry information. Although the word 'radio' is used to describe this phenomenon, the transmissions which we know as television, radio, radar, and cell phone are all classed as radio frequency emissions.

Early radios ran the entire power of the transmitter through a carbon microphone. While some early radios used some type of amplification through electric current or battery, through the mid 1920s the most common type of receiver was the crystal set. In the 1920s, amplifying vacuum tubes revolutionized both radio receivers and transmitters.

The theoretical basis of the propagation of electromagnetic waves was first described in 1873 by James Clerk Maxwell in his paper to the Royal Society A dynamical theory of the electromagnetic field, which followed his work between 1861 and 1865. In 1878 David E. Hughes was the first to transmit and receive radio waves when he noticed that his induction balance caused noise in the receiver of his homemade telephone. He demonstrated his discovery to the Royal Society in 1880

but was told it was merely induction. It was Heinrich Rudolf Hertz who, between 1886 and 1888, first validated Maxwell's theory through experiment, demonstrating that radio radiation had all the properties of waves (now called Hertzian waves), and discovering that the electromagnetic equations could be reformulated into a partial differential equation called the wave equation.

In 1893 in St. Louis, Missouri, Tesla made the first public demonstration of radio communication. Addressing the Franklin Institute in Philadelphia and the National Electric Light Association, he described and demonstrated in detail the principles of radio communication. The apparatus that he used contained all the elements that were incorporated into radio systems before the development of the vacuum tube. He initially used magnetic receivers, unlike the coherers used by Marconi and other early experimenters. Tesla was the first to apply the mechanism of electrical conduction to wireless practices.

On 19 August 1894, British physicist Sir Oliver Lodge demonstrated the reception of Morse code signalling using radio waves using a detecting device called a coherer, a tube filled with iron filings which had been invented by Temistocle Calzecchi-Onesti at Fermo in Italy in 1884. Edouard Branly of France and Popov of Russia later produced improved versions of the coherer. Popov, who was the first to develop a practical communication system based on the coherer, is usually considered by his own countrymen to have been the inventor of radio. The Indian physicist, Jagdish Chandra Bose, demonstrated publicly the use of radio waves in November of 1894 in Calcutta, but he was not interested in patenting his work.

In 1896 Marconi was awarded what is sometimes recognised as the world's first patent for radio with British Patent 12039, Improvements in transmitting electrical impulses and signals and in apparatus there-for. In 1897 he established the world's first radio station on the Isle of Wight, England. The same year in the U.S., some key

developments in radio's early history were created and patented by Tesla. The U.S. Patent Office reversed its decision in 1904, awarding Marconi a patent for the invention of radio, possibly influenced by Marconi's financial backers in the States, who included Thomas Edison and Andrew Carnegie. Some believe this was made for financial reasons, allowing the U.S. government to avoid having to pay the royalties that were being claimed by Tesla for use of his patents.

In 1909, Marconi, with Karl Ferdinand Braun, was also awarded the Nobel Prize in Physics for "contributions to the development of wireless telegraphy". However, Tesla's patent (number 645576) was reinstated in 1943 by the U.S. Supreme Court, shortly after his death. This decision was based on the fact that prior art existed before the establishment of Marconi's patent. Some believe the decision was also made for financial reasons, to allow the U.S. government to avoid having to pay damages that were being claimed by the Marconi Company for use of its patents during World War I.

Marconi opened the world's first "wireless" factory in Hall Street, Chelmsford, England in 1898, employing around 50 people. Around 1900, Tesla opened the Wardenclyffe Tower facility and advertised services. By 1903, the tower structure neared completion. Various theories exist on how Tesla intended to achieve the goals of this wireless system (reportedly, a 200 kW system). Tesla claimed that Wardenclyffe, as part of a World System of transmitters, would have allowed secure multichannel transceiving of information, universal navigation, time synchronization, and a global location system.

The next great invention was the vacuum tube detector, invented by a team of Westinghouse engineers. On Christmas Eve, 1906, Reginald Fessenden (using his heterodyne principle) transmitted the first radio audio broadcast in history from Brant Rock, Massachusetts. Ships at sea heard a broadcast that included Fessenden

playing O Holy Night on the violin and reading a passage from the Bible. The world's first radio news program was broadcast August 31, 1920 by station 8MK in Detroit, Michigan. The world's first regular wireless broadcasts for entertainment commenced in 1922 from the Marconi Research Centre at Writtle near Chelmsford, England.

DEVELOPMENTS IN THE 20TH CENTURY

In 1960, Sony introduced their first transistorized radio, small enough to fit in a vest pocket, and able to be powered by a small battery. It was durable, because there were no tubes to burn out. Over the next twenty years, transistors displaced tubes almost completely except for very high power, or very high frequency, uses. In 1963 color television was commercially transmitted, and the first (radio) communication satellite, TELSTAR, was launched. In the late 1960s, the U.S. long-distance telephone network began to convert to a digital network, employing digital radios for many of its links.

In the 1970s, LORAN became the premier radio navigation system. Soon, the U.S. Navy experimented with satellite navigation, culminating in the invention and launch of the GPS constellation in 1987. In the early 1990s, amateur radio experimenters began to use personal computers with audio cards to process radio signals. In 1994, the U.S. Army and DARPA launched an aggressive, successful project to construct a software radio that could become a different radio on the fly by changing software.

Many of radio's early uses were maritime, for sending telegraphic messages using Morse code between ships and land. One of the earliest users included the Japanese Navy scouting the Russian fleet during the Battle of Tsushima in 1905. One of the most memorable uses of marine telegraphy was during the sinking of the RMS Titanic in 1912, including communications between operators on the sinking ship and nearby vessels, and communications to shore stations listing the survivors.

Radio was used to pass on orders and communications between armies and navies on both sides in World War I; Germany used radio communications for diplomatic messages once its submarine cables were cut by the British. The United States passed on President Woodrow Wilson's Fourteen Points to Germany via radio during the war.

Broadcasting began to become feasible in the 1920s, with the widespread introduction of radio receivers, particularly in Europe and the United States. Besides broadcasting, point-to-point broadcasting, including telephone messages and relays of radio programs, became widespread in the 1920s and 1930s. Another use of radio in the pre-war years was the development of detecting and locating aircraft and ships by the use of radar (RAdio Detecting And Ranging).

Today, radio takes many forms, including wireless networks, mobile communications of all types, as well as radio broadcasting. Before the advent of television, commercial radio broadcasts included not only news and music, but dramas, comedies, variety shows, and many other forms of entertainment. Radio was unique among dramatic presentation that it used only sound. AM broadcast radio sends music and voice in the Medium Frequency (MF—0.300 MHz to 3 MHz) radio spectrum. AM radio uses amplitude modulation, in which louder sounds at the microphone causes wider fluctuations in the transmitter power while the transmitter frequency remains unchanged. Transmissions are affected by static because lightning and other sources of radio add their radio waves to the ones from the transmitter.

Radio teletypes usually operate on short-wave (HF) and are much loved by the military because they create written information without a skilled operator. They send a bit as one of two tones. Groups of five or seven bits become a character printed by a teletype. From about 1925 to 1975, radio teletype was how most commercial messages were

sent to less developed countries. These are still used by the military and weather services.

Many forms of presentations emerged and met extinction within a short life span of radio spreading over the last fifty years. By 1975, the once-popular nostalgia format was fading, drama radio had been dead for more than a decade, and the disco format was "being studied based on the records played in the growing number of discotheques throughout. Since its development in 1895, the radio has long since been revolutionizing the world. It has become so common that it is very improbable that one could ever pass a day without coming into contact with radio in some shape or fashion. In the beginning, radios were the only form of entertainment other than family outings and live shows such as those seen on Broadway. However, it seems like radio has outlived its passion for the programs and evening news and now concentrates almost completely on music.

The radio not only revolutionized the world but also created a new form of entertainment and education that will more than likely carry on for many centuries to come. Perhaps this invention will soon be able to travel through space, collect tremendous amounts of data from the universe, and spell out for us the reality of new frontiers waiting to be explored. Truly the radio will live on forever.

PHOTOGRAPHY

Photography coupled with sound heralded a new era in field of communication of ideas. It followed the invention and application of a variety of technologies for recording and presentation of information. It began with the art of sight and sound which later transformed into tape slide shows. But with further improvements in synchronization of sound with the moving images, the present day cinematography took its birth.

The development in photography and cinematography brought significant changes in

communication of ideas. Now more sense organs were involved in the perception process. The human nature is so that the maximum of ones total knowledge is perceived through the senses of sight and sound and the new media of communication available as a result of these advancements exploited this potential of man to its fall, facilitating learning at a higher speed and with a greater ease. The trend was on for about thirty years in India from the mid of the last century. The celluloid medium was primarily adopted for entertainment but soon it became equally popular in the academic circles. Film became the medium of instruction within fifty years of its existence.

Cinematographic film consists of a transparent flexible support or base on which is laid a photosensitive adhesive emulsion. They are now available in different widths ranging from 8 mm to 70 mm. The more the width the higher is the cost of the film. They are used for varied purposes depending upon the cost and the quality of the film. The super 8 mm is used very rarely as the infrastructure for production on this format is not generally available. But this is certainly the cheapest cinematographic medium available so far. The 16 mm film is used by most of the institutions for education and development. This has advantage over 8 mm because of comparatively higher resolution being suitable to be magnified on slightly larger screen.

Both the 8 mm and' 16 mm films are used depending upon the size of the audience as well as the cost of the production involved. The 35 mm and 70 mm films are normally used for entertainment and commercial purposes. 'They are suitable for larger gatherings like the audience of feature films in cinema halls. The advertisement agencies produce ads on these formats. The advantage of their having larger width is that the picture contain: very high resolution and does not blow up while magnified on larger screens. Sound for cinematographic films can be

recorded magnetically or optically depending upon the circumstances.

Video is basically a picture and sound recording medium. It is also cheaper in comparison to the cinematographic film. The great advantage of this medium is its instant playback facility. Video productions are generally available on video tapes and video cassettes. Their width vary from super 8 mm to 2". VHS is the most suited format for home viewing and a small gathering. 'The formats of video are changing very fast. In India, within a decade the production studios have witnessed reel to reel videotapes, 1" BCN, 3/4" U Matic in low and high band and currently the Betacam in 1/2". There is also a possibility of shifting the medium to digital in the coming times since this format has certain advantages over the existing ones.

The audiovisual medium was used basically for entertainment purposes but its potential was soon recognized in the academic circles. Film became the medium of instruction. Motion pictures are now available on cinematographic film as well as on video. Their basic and common characteristic is the movement of picture on the screen. The movement is achieved by running a film or video through a projector or player at a speed of 24 frames per second. The stills are recorded in a situation where all of them are comparatively similar and differ only at the point where movement has to be visualized. Motion pictures include silent and sound films as well. Nowadays, nearly all of them are being recorded in color. Motion pictures are being accepted increasingly by the academic circles as a learning aid as well as the medium for preservation of information.

Looking at the newer electronic media of audiovisuals, we find the difference quite visible. The audiovisual programs are being produced mainly on cassettes now which arc becoming cheaper despite the fact

that the human factor is involved in their production and that the human labor is becoming costlier everywhere in the world. Computers, modems, discs, antennas, TV sets, VCRs/VCPs, nearly all the equipment and accessories used in the information storage and retrieval and based on the electronic devices are becoming cheaper. The main reason is the availability of improved technology based on Very Large Scale Integration (VLSI) and the mass production of electronic goods. The cost of audiovisual programs too has gone down about 10 times with the adoption of video in place of celluloid. On celluloid, the shooting of sequences involved much pain and the result was known only after developing the prints whereas video offers instant playback facility. Thus, the wastage of efforts or resources is minimum in the electronic media.

THE DIGITAL MEDIA

The digital media is concerned with creating, sharing, and using information in digital form. Digital information is data that are structured and manipulated, stored and networked, subsidized and sold. Information takes many forms. One way to think about these forms is to distinguish between symbolic information and coded information.

The world defined by strings of 1's and 0's has existed for a long time. The idea of the digital computer originated over 300 years ago in the fertile mind of a German mathematician, Gottfried Wilhelm von Leibnitz. In 1679, Leibnitz imagined a device in which binary numbers were represented by spherical pellets, circulating within a kind of pinball machine controlled by a rudimentary form of punched cards. He described a comprehensive numerical system in which all calculation can be expressed in combinations of 1 and 0—the identical approach that all digital technologies use today.

At present, the digital system uses numbers to represent a concrete object or an abstract idea. Digitization is the process of transforming the object or idea into a

numerical code. The baseline of digital technology is a coding system with only two numbers—1 and 0—hence the term binary. Each numerical place in the system is a bit. In the digital world bits are things; they take up space; they take time to move from one place to another. A collection of bits can be described and counted, much like anything.

A bit-mapped image is a digital picture made up of row after row of bits in a grid. In a digital image, a bit is commonly referred to as a pixel, short for "picture element." As objects, digital images are described in terms of three characteristics: resolution, dynamic range, and pixel size.

The information revolution is still well under way. But it is not happening where information scientists, information executives, and the information industry in general are looking for it. It is not a revolution in technology, machinery, techniques, software, or speed. It is a revolution in concept.

So far, for 50 years, the information revolution has centered on data; their collection, storage, transmission, analysis, and presentation. The next information revolution will surely engulf all major institutions of modern society. But it has started, and has gone farthest, in business enterprise, where it has already had profound impacts. It is forcing us to redefine what business enterprise actually is and should be. This largely underlies the new definition of the function of business enterprise as the "creation of value and wealth," which in turn has triggered the present debate about the "governance of the corporation," that is, for whom the business enterprise creates value and wealth. Yet, despite its importance and impact, the next information revolution has so far been largely ignored by the information establishment.

The improved technology for storage and dissemination of information has made available a wide range of products that accommodate a fairly larger body of

information. Reduction in size of documents by photographic process was one of the first measures in reducing the space required for housing information. All these discoveries were based on optics and chemical processes. The documents required utmost care in handling and preservation and in the normal circumstances it was almost impossible to preserve them beyond a few decades.

Computer is regarded as the greatest invention of all the times. It facilitates the storage, processing and distribution of information much easier with its vast memory speed and accuracy. The advancements in calculator, which was invented to carry out mathematical calculations led to the invention of computer.

A more visible change took place when calculators acquired the capability of processing textual data proceeded by the capacity to process information available in varied formats. Further improvements in computer design during the 1960s enabled the integration of text and graphics, a move that encouraged the development of computer based training programs. Such use was however limited, as programming was costly, slow and cumbersome, and the computing relied on a mainframe, or central computer to do all the work. The release of the first microcomputers during the late 1970s saw computing become more portable and affordable. Ease of use took a quantum leap with the introduction of the Apple Macintosh computer in 1984. Operation of the computer and its programs became more intuitive, largely as a result of research in the area of human-computer interaction.

The adoption of computers in the area of vocational training also increased, with some industries recognizing that the technology offered benefits that were largely cantered on efficiency gains. This was particularly the case in industries such as finance and insurance, manufacturing, health care, and the armed forces where training was a critical but costly component of operation.

These types of organizations, with large staff numbers requiring training to an industry standard, or with staff located across national and international borders, found cost savings could be achieved by using technology to distribute training programs to the workplace, rather than bring staff to a central training centre. Computer programs could deliver training at a time and place convenient to all parties, provide flexibility in terms of progression and pace, generate and score tests, record all interaction between the learner and the system and produce detailed reports of this interaction. These attributes were welcomed in organizations where staff development programs were valued as a means of motivating staff and maintaining the standard of service. These programs are commonly based on competency standards that clearly define objectives, and set standards of performance that may be observed and measured against defined criteria.

The notion of providing training when it was needed to where it was needed was extended through the development of performance support systems. These systems allowed an employee to use a computer as both a tool and a tutor - the tutor would provide step by step assistance in the performance of specific computer related tasks, in much the same way as help "wizards" incorporated within many Microsoft products try to anticipate users needs in designing a new spreadsheet or database. Computer based training has also been a logical choice where there was substantial risk in allowing a novice to train in an operational environment. It is safer and more cost effective to allow the operator of a steel rolling mill to practice the procedure using a computer simulation, or a pilot to manage an engine failure without leaving the ground.

The electronic media has the capability to store, manipulate and transfer information in the form of text as well as audiovisuals. It is also possible to combine both of them. Multimedia is and hypermedia can be cited as

examples. The electronic media is useful in learning both in a classroom situation or individually. It includes information networks and CD ROMs. The information is recorded electronically, hence greater speed, accuracy and memory is available to the users. It is presumed that within the coming decade, the electronic media will supersede all the available media for storage, management and dissemination of information. This will particularly affect the educational institutions as it is more effective and economic both in terms of money and time spent in learning. It will also affect the nature of classroom instruction. A new learning culture is in the offing, which can be seen in the open system of education where attendance in class is not a prerequisite to earn a degree.

The advances in electronics and telecommunications brought newer technology capable of accommodating very large quantities of information in a very little space. Magnetic tapes, CD-ROMs, multimedia and hypermedia are a few examples. CD ROMs have an edge on print as well as online resources. On the one hand they save a lot of physical space required for their print counterpart while on the other hand they allow to work on huge resources independent of online connectivity that is far expensive. The cost of Internet connectivity also suggests that CD ROM technology is more suited to education and research. Document in an ever-increasing number are being directly published on CD ROMs without involving prints. Now experts believe that the shift from page to screen once a fantasy is approaching reality now. Students in many university use textbook that exist online. Similarly there are CD ROMs, which hold valuable academic information and are the only sources of information in certain areas of study like medicine and technology.

In the electronic media, search time has been reduced miraculously. Bulky reference tools like the Chemical Abstracts, Dissertation Index, Index to Higher Theses, encyclopedias and dictionaries, etc. can be searched within

a fraction of a second by just pushing the keys of a computer. Further, the search is very easy as most of the databases are user friendly. Any of the related words can be taken as 'Search Term' and fed into the system for retrieval of information. This is followed by appearance of a detailed list of documents available on the same topic from which one can select the most relevant and pinpointed information and even download it in the memory of the computer or on auxiliary memory for future use. There are some restrictions. Words, which can create hindrance, are debarred from the retrieval process. They are called stop words. This is achieved by maintaining a separate file for them.

Another advantage of electronic media is the updating of the reference tools. Unlike the printed medium, which requires repeating the whole mechanical process for improvement or updating, the information is updated instantly in the electronic media. This is achieved with the push of a button. In fact, the agencies dealing in the electronic sources of information enter into an agreement with the consumers. The same discs can be sent to the agencies and returned updated. Now, with the Electronic Mail facility, updating can be carried out instantly on line. This practically involves no time and saves expenditure as well. In the print as well as the celluloid, mass copying leads to deterioration of prints by way of generation loss. But in the electronic media, the same text can be generated again and again without any loss or deterioration in the quality of the original or its copy.

In a tropical country like India the fluctuation in temperature and humidity leads to deterioration in the quality of print as well as celluloid by way of chemical reactions. This process of degeneration goes on with the passage of time. It is very difficult to maintain quality of print beyond a century and of celluloid beyond a decade. The solution lies to some extent in erection of specialized dehumidified chambers and providing air conditioners but

this too is not practicable for many other reasons such as frequent breakdowns in supply of electricity and the huge expenditure involved.

Now information is available anywhere, anytime and the books will never go out of print like the past tragedies. The change that this is going to bring about in society is as fundamental as the change brought out by the printing press.

Like the printed book, the electronic book or "eBook" will be a special device that is easy to read; has a vertical layout and allows users to flip from page to page. It will be just as comfortable to read as a printed book, yet it will offer more opportunities. The readers will be able to store a whole library of books on a single device of the size of a paperback book. They will be able to search for specific information or look up words while they read. They will also be able to download any book they want from the Internet and any time they want. The electronic book can do a lot of things that a printed book cannot do, and will never be able to do. It's going to change every area of life one can think about where reading goes on.

At present it does not look advantageous to read books available electronically as it is easier in case of a book available on paper but once the technology is popularized and people get them easily available the electronic books will also be advantageous and easy to read. When reading electronically becomes easier, people will want to do it, and the advantages will become obvious.

One advantage is that consumers and businesses will be able to greatly reduce the amount of storage space they reserve for books since they will be able to store hundreds of books on a device the size of a paperback novel. Another is that they will no longer have to weigh themselves down with books while traveling.

Another benefit is that eBooks will offer people with disabilities the same access to books as the rest of the

population. For example, people who are blind will be able to download any book and play software that reads the books aloud. Moreover, people with visual impairments won't be limited to the few books currently available in large print. It means that every book is available in large print sizes automatically because it just comes with the system.

Yet another benefit is that eBooks will reduce the world's consumption of paper. A lot of paper is used in the world's businesses in a year? There's a huge infrastructure in place to deal with that — to grow trees, cut them down, transport them, pulp them, print on them, store that print, transport the printed material and send the unsold books back to the pulp plant to get pulped again and turned into other books. Think of what happens if we eliminate that infrastructure. There's obviously going to be a certain amount of trauma associated with that change. But it's inevitable, and in a world with a finite amount of resources.

Ultimately, books will become cheaper because the infrastructure required to produce them electronically will be far less labor-intensive. Picture what this does to education in third world countries. Countries like China, India and Africa where people are unable to afford books or don't have access to the books they need. As the cost of the hardware drops, these countries will come in the position to set up a local public library anywhere, with instant access to as much content as the Library of Congress, for a fraction of what a library costs today. It will have the same level of access for any village school.

DIGITAL COMMUNICATION

In the early times, it was smoke that communicated meanings to the responders at the other end. Then it took the form. Now information is transferred to other places in a number of ways. The telecommunication has brought a revolution in the ways of sending messages at distant

places virtually without involving any considerable amount of time.

Wire remained the main career of messages for the last two centuries and improvement in wire-based technology increased efficiency of transmitting messages across the geographical boundaries of the nations. Different materials were used to manufacture them ranging from copper, aluminum, steel etc. Recently fiber optics has taken a lead over all the existing wire-based communication devices.

Fiber optics communicates data in digital form and is a very reliable channel for communication of huge quantity of data. A single glass fiber is thinner than the size of a human hair and it can transmit all the characters in dozens of books of the same size across the country in a single second. Such a quantity of information will normally take about 21 hours to send over a copper telephone line. Fiber Optic technology is a cutting edge method of transmitting information over great distances (150 km without using a repeater) using pulses of light.

Fiber optic technology sends data without electricity through a conductor. Instead of electrical signals, modulated light is used to quickly transmit data over great distances through an insulated glass Fiber-type material.

Fiber optics is currently the best long distance communications method because it provides much faster data transfer speeds when compared to traditional interconnection media such as copper wire. The signal cannot be disrupted by outside sources like electricity, rain, humidity, or other things that tend to damage conventional copper wire signals. Fiber Optic Cables are ideal for volatile environments because there is no fear of damage should they break like there is with traditional copper wiring.

Optical Fiber is lightweight compared to copper cabling because it is a thin glass strand and has huge bandwidth because information travels along the Fiber at

the speed of light. Thousands of fibers can be fit in the same amount of space as required for one cable. The developments in fiber optics suggest that the future cost of broadband transmission capability will be within the reach of small organizations and individuals.

Significant developments were made in wireless communication during the twentieth century and many forms. But the most significant mode of communication that revolutionized the process of information exchange in the satellite.

Satellite Communication has turned the entire world into a global village. Satellites relay or transmit information such as TV, phone, weather, military intelligence, and data. Communications satellites provide a worldwide link. In 1960, Echo 1 was launched becoming the first communications satellite. The primitive Echo 1 was an inflatable metallic sphere with instruments that bounced radio signals back to earth. Two years later, Telstar 1 became the first active communications satellite. These satellites orbit the earth at a relatively low altitude. This made them difficult to track and not very suitable for communication. Active satellites receive, amplify, and retransmit signals to different locations. Telstar 1 was responsible for the relay of the first live television broadcast across the Atlantic Ocean.

Weather forecasting has undergone a revolution because of the availability of pictures from geostationary meteorological satellites—pictures we see every day on television. All of these are important aspects of the space age, but satellite communications has probably had more effect than any of the rest on the average person. Satellite communications is also the only truly commercial space technology.

In 1965, when EARLY BIRD was launched, the satellite provided almost 10 times the capacity of the submarine telephone cables for almost 1/10th the price.

Satellites are still competitive with cable for point-to-point communications, but the future advantage may lie with fiber-optic cable. Satellites still maintain two advantages over cable; they are more reliable and they can be used point-to-multi-point (broadcasting). Cellular telephone systems have risen as challenges to all other types of telephony. It is possible to place a cellular system in a developing country at a very reasonable price. Long-distance calls require some other technology, but this can be either satellites or fiber-optic cable. Cellular telephony has brought us a new technological system, the personal communications system (PCS). In the fully developed PCS, the individual would carry his telephone with him. This telephone could be used for voice or data and would be usable anywhere. Several companies have committed themselves to providing a version of this system using satellites in low earth orbits (LEO).

The inherent "broadcast" nature of satellite communications has made direct-broadcast a recurrent theme yet one never brought to fruition. Each year many communications satellites are launched making the process of communication of information more easy and effective day by day. The confluence of satellite and multimedia resulted in making the communication technology available at an unimaginably lower cost to the betterment of the common man although it originated in labs for scientific researchers. Now, Internet services are primarily based on these technologies.

Multimedia represents the convergence between computers, digital video, digital audio and sound synthesis. It has initially culminated the re-evaluation of the ways in which we communicate information combining still and moving images, sound, text and audio. Day to day applications of multimedia can be visualized considering information activities around us. Multimedia is being increasingly adopted for education and training, reference, business,. entertainment etc.

MULTIMEDIA

Multimedia is widely acknowledged as an environment with great potentiality for education. It is able to assist both the people and teachers in new ways since for teacher it provides a means of putting across information and ideal and for students it can represent a one-to-one teaching environment which moves at the required pace. Distribution of multimedia lessons, lectures and courseware on CD ROM or CD-1 discs adds another dimension to multimedia in education providing a vehicle of information to the students to take home. Its potential is enormous for the rural communities and isolated geographical regions where schools are inaccessible. The Open University teaching will certainly depend more upon the means and methods presented by advances in multimedia in the time to come.

The electronic media allows portability as well as durability. Information recorded digitally can last for centuries virtually with no effect of humidity, dust or temperature. The quality of recording is not affected because the information i , not recorded on the surface but within the medium itself. The electronic media seems to be ideal for preservation of manuscripts and other valuable records. There are two ways of recording from paper on to the digital media-one is the transfer of text page wise and the other is that the contents of rare manuscripts may be entered word by word. Thus, not only the life of the documents increases but also they can be retrieved rapidly and made available to the researchers.

THE INTERNET

Internet has emerged as the most powerful medium for storage and retrieval of information. It works round the clock and connects every nook and corner of the globe. With an unprecedented growth in the quantum of knowledge worldwide and the easy accessibility, Internet has become an unavoidable necessity for every institution

of higher learning and research. Internet is continuously growing internationally. Within a short span of ten years, its services have been spread among all the nations of the world. In 1991 it was within reach of 73 countries but within four years of its existence Internet reached 148 countries. The number of Internet users is also increasing tremendously as they are almost doubled after every two years. In the meanwhile Internet widened its scope. Now it is used for storage, manipulation and dissemination of textual data as well as the multimedia.

Internet became more popular by its feature of the World Wide Web in 1991, Tim Berners-Lee, a young scientist working in European Particle Physics Laboratory (CERN) produced Internet's first browser. According to him, "the dream behind the Web is of a common information space in which we communicate by sharing information. "By its application, someone could scan every document or photo or video on the net. It gave an opportunity to share the resources by individuals and organizations on the basis of mutual understanding.

Internet services are easily available and affordable as the cost of connectivity and computer hardware, software has come down considerably during the last few years. Moreover, there has been standardization in the ever-changing configuration of systems. The software has been made more user friendly for computer as well as netsurfing. Now, the services are also being offered through cablel and mobile phones.

2

The Story of Newspaper

Newspaper is a publication which appears regularly and frequently, and carries news about a wide variety of current events. The term is commonly used to refer to daily or weekly publications that bring news of general interest to large portions of the public in a specific geographic area. However, some organizations such as trade unions, religious groups, corporations or clubs may have their own newspapers.

Production of a newspaper like many other media of mass communication is a team work. The news is gathered and then written up by reporters. Photographers shoot pictures to accompany the stories and graphic artists contribute charts and diagrams. Editors assign reporters to stories, check over those stories, write headlines for them, determine where they will be placed in the newspaper and work on the paper's "layout", the arrangement of stories, photographs and art on each page. An editor-in-chief or an executive editor usually supervises the paper's news staff. The newspaper's publisher has overall control of its business and news operations.

General circulation newspapers play a role in commerce through the advertisements they carry; they provide readers with information of practical value, such as television schedules, weather maps and listings of stock prices; and these newspapers provide a source of entertainment through their stories and through such features as comic strips and crossword puzzles. However, one of the most important functions of the general-circulation newspaper a crucial function in a democracy is

to provide citizens with information on government and politics.

Newspapers have about 500 years of known existance. In Renaissance Europe handwritten newsletters circulated privately among merchants, passing along information about everything from wars and economic conditions to social customs and "human interest" features. The first printed forerunners of the newspaper appeared in Germany in the late 1400's in the form of news pamphlets or broadsides, often highly sensationalized in content.

The modern newspaper is a European invention. It owes little or nothing to the Roman acta (No copies of which survived), or to the early experiments in news dissemination developments in China. (Modern newspapers were introduced to China in the nineteenth century primarily by missionaries and other foreigners.)

The oldest direct ancestors of the modern newspaper appear to have been the handwritten news sheets that circulated widely in Venice in the sixteenth century. Venice, like most of the cities that played a major role in the early history of the newspaper, was a center for trade and therefore for information. These Venetian news sheets, known as avisi or gazette, were filled with information on wars and politics in Italy and Europe. They were distributed weekly as early as 1566 and were seen as far away as London. The style of journalism they employed for short sets of news items, forwarded from a particular city, written under the name of that city and the date on which they were sent — was the style that would be used in most early printed newspapers.

The oldest surviving European printed newspapers were both published weekly in German in 1609. The printed newspaper spread rapidly through Europe. Printed weeklies appeared in Basel by 1610, in Frankfort and Vienna by 1615, in Hamburg by 1616, in Berlin by 1617 and in Amsterdam by 1618. An English official at the time

complained that his country was being "reproved in foreign parts" because it lacked a publication to report "the occurents every week." The first newspaper printed in England appeared in 1621. France produced a newspaper of its own in 1631. But printers in Amsterdam, a center of trade and of political and religious tolerance in the early seventeenth century, were exporting weeklies in French and in English as early as 1620. Italy's first printed weekly appeared by 1639 at the latest, Spain's by 1641.

The oldest surviving newspaper written in English appears to have been published in Amsterdam in 1620 by Pieter van de Keere, a Dutch map and print engraver who had lived in London for a few years. This first English newspaper begins not with a title — in those early years papers often did not have consistent names .

The publishers of the early weeklies had to struggle to find fresh news items with which to fill their papers every week. Many, particularly in England, failed to meet this demanding schedule, and their newspapers appeared late. They had to struggle to fulfill what one early publisher called the reader's "expectation of weekely Newes." These struggles sped up the process of printing news. Editors could no longer print items at their leisure; there was always that weekly to fill. The pace of events would soon adapt itself to this weekly schedule, as it would later adapt itself to the schedule of daily newspapers and, in recent decades, of hourly broadcast news reports.

The oldest surviving newspaper actually printed in England appeared On September 24, 1621, under the characteristically long title: "Corante, or weekely newes from Italy, Germany, Hungary, Poland, Bohemia, France and the Low Countreys." Its publisher gave only his initials, N.B., and unfortunately for the history of English journalism, there were two active printers in London with those initials — Nathaniel Butter and Nicholas Bourne. Cases have been made for both of them as England's first newspaper journalist. In Paris, Theophraste Renaudot

began publishing his Gazette de France in 1631. It was the second newspaper printed in France, but it was a particularly thoughtful, though cautious, publication and would survive in essentially the same form until the French Revolution in 1789.

The early newspapers were generally printed in one of two formats in the style of the Dutch papers in which the reports were packed densely only two or perhaps four pages; or the style of the early German weeklies, which were pamphlets in which the news was spread over eight to twenty-four pages. The various English publishers, including Butter and Bourne, who sometimes competed but often worked together on series of early English newspapers, first used the Dutch style, but switched to the German style by 1622.

News items in these early newspapers were still printed pretty much as they came into the print shop. News of a battle in the Thirty Years War, which was then raging on the Continent, might appear under the name of Vienna, Frankfort or Prague or any other of the handful of cities in which it might have found its way into a letter or a newspaper that in turn found its way to that print shop. A newspaper might report under one date that a city was under siege and then under another date that it had fallen. It was a system of journalism that was easy on printers but not on readers. One of the first attempts to change this system, to actually edit stories into more readable narratives, was made in London. This early editor's name was probably Thomas Gainsford, and he appears to have begun work on a series of early English newspapers in 1622.

In the English-speaking world, the earliest predecessors of the newspaper were corantos, small news pamphlets produced only when some event worthy of notice occurred. The first successively published title was The Weekly Newes of 1622. It was followed in the 1640's and 1650's by a plethora of different titles in the similar newsbook format. The first true newspaper in English was

the London Gazette of 1666. For a generation it was the only officially sanctioned newspaper, though many periodical titles were in print by the century's end.

There were forty-three newspapers in print. The press played a vital role in the affairs of the new nation; many more newspapers were started, representing all shades of political opinion. The no holds barred style of early journalism, much of it libelous by modern standards, reflected the rough and tumble political life of the republic as rival factions jostled for power. The ratification of the Bill of Rights in 1791 at last guaranteed of freedom of the press, and America's newspapers began to take on a central role in national affairs. Growth continued in every state. By 1814 there were 346 newspapers. In the Jacksonian populist 1830's, advances in printing and papermaking technology led to an explosion of newspaper growth, the emergence of the "Penny Press"; it was now possible to produce a newspaper that could be sold for just a cent a copy. Previously, newspapers were the province of the wealthy, literate minority. The price of a year's subscription, usually over a full week's pay for a laborer, had to be paid in full and "invariably in advance." This sudden availability of cheap, interesting reading material was a significant stimulus to the achievement of the nearly universal literacy now taken for granted in America.

The industrial revolution, as it transformed all aspects of life and society, dramatically affected newspapers. Both the numbers of papers and their paid circulations continued to rise. The 1850 census catalogued 2,526 titles. In the 1850's powerful, giant presses appeared, able to print ten thousand complete papers per hour. At this time the first "pictorial" weekly newspapers emerged; they featured for the first time extensive illustrations of events in the news, as woodcut engravings made from correspondents' sketches or taken from that new invention, the photograph. During the Civil War the unprecedented demand for timely, accurate news reporting transformed

American journalism into a dynamic, hardhitting force in the national life. Reporters, called "specials," became the darlings of the public and the idols of youngsters everywhere. Many accounts of battles turned in by these intrepid adventurers stand today as the definitive histories of their subjects.

Newspaper growth continued unabated in the postwar years. An astounding 11,314 different papers were recorded in the 1880 census. By the 1890's the first circulation figures of a million copies per issue were recorded. By the 1910's, all the essential features of the recognizably modern newspaper had emerged. In our time, radio and television have gradually supplanted newspapers as the nation's primary information sources, so it may be difficult initially to appreciate the role that newspapers have played in our history.

Early newspaper featured items from all over Europe and occasionally America or Asia. But with very few exceptions they never reported any news about the country in which they were printed. Print shops were tightly regulated; in most countries they required government licenses to print; and they could be quickly shut down if they printed anything that offended the authorities. Europe's rulers allowed them to print newspapers as long as these papers did not presume to discuss any local or national issues or events.

The first major change in this arrangement came in the years before the outbreak of the English Civil War. As Parliament, under the leadership of Oliver Cromwell, struggled with King Charles I, national news suddenly assumed a new importance, and newspapers, liberated by the breakdown in the king's authority, began to feel free enough to discuss it. The first English newspaper to attempt to report on national news was a sedate little weekly entitled, The Heads of Severall Proceedings. In This Present Parliament, which appeared in November 1641.

This paper soon had a number of competitors.

The ideal of freedom of the press was articulated with great eloquence in England 1644 by John Milton in his Areopagitica, which, however, was concerned primarily with books and took little notice of these scruffy, little weekly newspapers. Nevertheless, these newspapers, among the first in the world to escape government control, were conducting an important experiment in what a free press might do.

Along with their political coverage, newspapers in England in the 1640s, according to the historian Joseph Frank, were among the first in the world to use headlines, to print advertisements, to illustrate stories with woodcuts to collect news and to have newsboys, or more commonly newsgirls, sell papers in the streets. They were also among the first newspapers to compete with newsbooks and news ballads in coverage of sensational events like bloody crimes. By 1649, these newspapers had an opportunity to report on a particularly newsworthy national story: "This day the King was beheaded. over against the Banquetting house by White-Hall..."

When, after the beheading of Charles I, Cromwell was able to consolidate his power, he cracked down on the press, allowing only a few authorized newspapers to be printed. But the English press burst free again during the Glorious Revolution in 1688. The Licensing Act lapsed in 1695, and a belief in the importance of a press that had the right to criticize government eventually took root in England and was transplanted to its American colonies.

As newspapers became more reliable and began appearing more frequently, they began to play a major role in commerce, through their advertisements and by printing price listings and market reports. A German newspaper, published by Lucas Schulte, had begun appearing two times a week in 1625. The world's oldest surviving printed daily newspaper, Einkommende Zeitung, appeared in

Leipzig in 1650. The first successful English daily was the Daily Courant, which first appeared in London in 1702. In the early eighteenth century, according to journalism historian Stanley Morison, the newspaper gained "a hold on London's commercial classes which it never lost." At that time, too, great essayists like Joseph Addison, Richard Steele, Daniel Defoe and Jonathan Swift began publishing newspapers filled with their social and political commentaries in London — though these papers were more similar in content to modern-day opinion magazines.

DEVELOPMENT IN AMERICA

In America the first newspaper appeared in Boston in 1690, entitled Publick Occurrences. Published without authority, it was immediately suppressed, its publisher arrested, and all copies were destroyed. Indeed, it remained forgotten until 1845 when the only known surviving example was discovered in the British Library. The first successful newspaper was the Boston News-Letter, begun by postmaster John Campbell in 1704. Although it was heavily subsidized by the colonial government the experiment was a near-failure, with very limited circulation. Two more papers made their appearance in the 1720's, in Philadelphia and New York, and the Fourth Estate slowly became established on the new continent. By the eve of the Revolutionary War, some two dozen papers were issued at all the colonies, although Massachusetts, New York, and Pennsylvania would remain the centers of American printing for many years. Articles in colonial papers, brilliantly conceived by revolutionary propagandists, were a major force that influenced public opinion in America from reconciliation with England to full political independence.

Britain's American colonies, because of their sparse populations and strict governments, entered the world of the newspaper relatively late. Public Occurrences, Both FORREIGN and DOMESTICK was printed in Boston on

September 25, 1690. The Boston News-Letter, America's second printed newspaper, grew out of a handwritten newsletter that had been distributed by the town's postmaster, John Campbell. It was a much tamer affair than Harris's paper — filled primarily with reports on English and European politics taken from London papers. The Boston News-Letter, which first appeared in print in 1704, survived for 72 years. Campbell lost the position of postmaster in 1719, but he refused to give up the newspaper. So, his replacement as postmaster, William Brooker, began printing his own newspaper, the Boston Gazette, on December 21, 1719. A day later, the third successful American newspaper, the American Weekly Mercury, appeared in Philadelphia.

These papers were careful, for the most part, not to offend colonial authorities. The first paper to attempt to give voice to political debate was Boston's third successful newspaper, the New England Courant, which was first printed in 1721 by James Franklin. The Courant was the most literary and readable of the early colonial newspapers, and in its first issue it began a political crusade. The issue was smallpox inoculations, which were first being used in Boston that year used to fight an epidemic. Cotton Mather, one of the most powerful men in Boston, supported inoculation. James Franklin did not. So the first American newspaper crusade was a crusade against smallpox inoculation. The next year, the Courant took on the colonial government, which it accused of failing to do enough to protect the area from pirates. This crusade landed James Franklin in jail.

New York City's first newspaper was the New York Gazette, founded by William Bradford in 1725, but it was the city's second newspaper, John Peter Zenger's New York Weekly Journal, which began printing in 1733, that was to have a major effect on the history of journalism. The New York Gazette was a typical colonial newspaper: It stayed out of trouble by supporting the policies of the

colony's governor. But New York's governor at the time, William Cosby, was a particularly controversial figure, who had alienated many of the most respected individuals in the colony. They wanted a newspaper that would express their point of view, and Zenger, a young German-born printer, agreed to start one. Zenger's Weekly Journal immediately began taking on the colony's administration. Governor Cosby had Zenger arrested on November 17, 1734, charged with seditious libel.

The major limitation on press freedom in England in the eighteenth and the first half of the nineteenth century was the stamp tax, which had the effect of raising the price of newspapers to the point where the poorer classes could not afford to buy them. The Stamp Act passed by the British Parliament passed in 1765 would have placed a similar tax on American newspapers. Americans were not represented in this Parliament, and American newspapers rebelled against the new tax. They printed letters and essays protesting the.

Similar protests reverberated through the colonial newspapers when the British Parliament approved the Townshend Acts in 1767, which imposed taxes on American imports of glass, lead, paint, tea and, significantly, paper. "Nonimportation agreements," policed in large part through the press, led the colonies to another victory. In 1770 all the duties except that on tea were removed.

During these successive waves of protest against the British in America, newspapers appeared with woodcuts of divided snakes, to represent the weakness of the colonies if they remained divided, with woodcuts of coffins to represent the victims of the Boston Massacre; they published list of those "Enemies to their Country" who continued to import boycotted British goods; they serialized radical essays by John Dickinson and, in 1776, Thomas Paine.

Not all the colonial newspapers were on the side of

the anti-British Sons of Liberty. James Rivington's New York Gazetteer, one of the best edited, most attractive papers in the colonies, gave voice to the Tory, or pro-British, as well as the "Patriot" side in the ongoing conflict, in what he called his "Ever Open and Uninfluenced Press." Despite their professed allegiance to the principle of a free press, the Sons of Liberty were infuriated by Rivington's paper, and he responded by taking more openly Tory positions. A group of members of the Sons of Liberty wrecked Rivington's printing plant, and, after the Revolutionary War began, he was arrested and forced to sign a statement of loyalty to the Continental Congress.

Still, for the most part American newspapers in the years leading up to the American Revolution represented something the world had never before seen: a press committed to challenging, even overthrowing, governmental authorities. This remains an unusual and difficult position for newspapers to take. Unlike pamphlets or broadsides, newspapers must appear regularly. Their publishers cannot hide from authorities, and, as proprietors of an ongoing business, they usually have a stake in the stability of the community and therefore in preserving the power of authorities. This tends to make newspapers conservative forces, more likely to try to unify the members of a community than to try to incite them to anti-authoritarian violence.

In the unsettled years after the Revolution, American newspapers remained filled with arguments and anger — now directed not against the British but against their political opponents. Each of the two parties that formed, the Federalists and the Republicans, had their newspapers and these papers had little sympathy for representatives of the other side. For example, this is how The Aurora, a Republican paper published in Philadelphia by Benjamin Franklin Bache, greeted George Washington's retirement as president in 1796: "The man who is the source of all the misfortune of our country is this day reduced to a level

with his fellow-citizens, and is no longer possessed of power to multiply evils upon the United States."

Although it had originally been left out of the Constitution in 1887, freedom of the press was guaranteed in the Bill of Rights, in the First Amendment to the Constitution. Nevertheless, Federalist Party leaders, increasingly uncomfortable with the criticism they were taking from Republican editors and made nervous by the threat of war with France, soon attempted to silence their critics.

In 1798, Congress passed the Sedition Act — probably the most significant threat to press freedom in the history of the United States. The Sedition Act made "any false, scandalous and malicious writing...against the the Government of the United States," the Congress or the president, "with intent to...bring them...into contempt or disrepute" punishable by a fine or imprisonment. Among others, the leading Republican editor in New York, New England and Philadelphia (Bache) were all indicting for violating the Sedition Act or the common-law prohibition against seditious libel, which had been the charge against Zenger. There were at least fifteen convictions.

Thomas Jefferson was elected president in 1800, partly because of resentment over the Sedition Act, and the Act was allowed to lapse. Nevertheless, the experiment with a free press has continued, with the press in the United States eventually demonstrating not only a compatibility with the maintenance of "orderly government," but a talent for it.

There were about 200 newspapers in the United States when Jefferson assumed the presidency in 1801. A printing press was pulled across the mountains to print the first newspaper west of the Alleghenies, the Pittsburgh Gazette in 1786. The first daily newspaper in America was the Pennsylvania Evening Post, published by Benjamin Towne, in 1783. It lasted only 17 months, but by 1801 there

were abou‹ 20 daily newspapers in the country, including six in Philadelphia, five in New York and three in Baltimore. With daily publication, American newspapers were in a better position to cater to the need of merchants for up-to-date information on prices, markets and ship movements. By 1820, more than half of the newspapers in the largest cities had the words "advertiser," "commercial" or "mercantile" in their names. These "mercantile papers" were often published on large, or "blanket," sheets, and they were expensive — about six cents a copy, more than most of the artisans or mechanics in the cities could afford.

In 1833, a paper printed on four letter-size pages and filled with human-interest stories and short police reports appeared on the streets of New York. Its publisher was a young printer named Benjamin Day, and he sold his paper, the Sun, for one penny. The American newspaper with the highest circulation at that time was New York's Courier and Enquirer, a mercantile paper which sold 4,500 copies a day in a city of 218,000. In 1830, perhaps the most respected newspaper in the world at the time, the Times of London, which was founded in 1785 by John Walter, was selling 10,000 copies of day in a city with a population of two million. However, within two years, Day was selling 15,000 copies a day of his inexpensive, little Sun.

The first cylinder press, invented by a German, Frederick Koenig and improved by Napier in England, was first used in the United States in 1825. An improved version of this press, using two cylinders, was developed by Richard Hoe in New York in 1832. Steam engines had first been used to drive presses at the Times in London in 1814. By 1835 Day was using a steam press to print his rapidly growing New York Sun. These new presses made it possible to push circulations much higher. The old Gutenberg-type printing press could print perhaps 125 newspapers an hour; by 1851 the Sun's presses were printing 18,000 copies an hour.

James Gordon Bennett, one of the most creative forces

in the history of journalism, began his own penny paper, the Herald in 1835. Within in two years it was selling 20,000 copies a day, despite a price increase to two cents. A number of penny newspapers had failed in Boston, a couple even before Day started his Sun. That city's first successful penny paper was the Daily Times in 1836. Philadelphia had the Daily Transcript, begun in 1835, and the Public Ledger, in 1836; Baltimore's Sun was first published in 1837 — all selling for a penny.

The "cheap" newspaper arrived in France in 1836 with Emile de Girandin's La Presse. Newspapers were also selling for a penny or two in England in the first half of the nineteenth century; however, there was one major difference between these papers and their American counterparts: The English penny papers had to evade the stamp tax, which by 1815 was up to fourpence on each copy sold, so they were illegal. More than 560 different unstamped newspapers were printed in England between 1830 and 1836. One, Henry Hetherington's Twopenny Dispatch, was reported to have a circulation of 27,000 in 1836.

The English penny papers, because they lived outside the law, tended to be extremely radical in their politics. "Politics is the noble art of dividing society into two classes - Slaves and Robbers, wrote another of Hetherington's papers, the Poor Man's Guardian in 1834. The British stamp tax was abolished in 1855.

Most of the American penny papers were less interested in politics; nevertheless, they did have the effect of bringing many working class people and immigrants in the cities into the political process by providing them with a source of news they could afford. The Sun's motto was the egalitarian statement: "It Shines for All"; and the rise of the penny press has been connected with the spread of Jacksonian democracy in the United States.

The major effect these penny papers had on the

politics of the newspaper, however, may have been the change their mass circulations brought to the economic status of publishers. Bennett, who had started his Herald for $500, became a rich man. The Sun was sold for $250,000 in 1849. Newspapers were becoming big businesses, and the owners of big businesses tend to have more conservative politics.

REPORTING THE NEWS

In the early years of the newspaper, editors obtained most of their news simply by waiting for the post to bring out-of-town newspapers or letters, waiting for someone to stop by with an interesting tidbit they might have heard from a traveler at a tavern. The waits were particularly long in eighteenth- and early-nineteenth-century America, where it often took a couple of months for news from Europe to find its way across the Atlantic and a couple of weeks for it to penetrate through the swamps and forests of the undeveloped continent on which they had settled. The Battle of New Orleans, for example, was fought on January 8, 1815, two weeks after a peace treaty ending the War of 1812 had been signed in Belgium. With these waits came a constant sense of uncertainty: Rumors tended to fill the vacuum; early reports often proved wrong.

.News gathering efforts were more advanced in London. The first major breakthrough came when, in the late eighteenth century, newspapers gained the right to send observers to sit in the gallery in Parliament. No note-taking was permitted in those years. Initially, William "Memory" Woodfall, editor of the Morning Chronicle, was the most successful in writing accounts of the debates, but soon James Perry, one of England's most enterprising journalists, outdid Woodfall by sending teams of reporters to cover the debates in relays. Reporters in the gallery were finally permitted to take notes in 1783, making a knowledge of shorthand the crucial qualification for the job. In another pathbreaking reporting effort, James Perry sent himself

to Paris to observe the French revolution firsthand. In 1807, The Times of London dispatched Henry Crabb Robinson to cover some of the battles of the Napoleonic wars.

In the United States in the early decades of the nineteenth century, reporters, with James Gordon Bennett leading the way, had to fight to win the right to report on trials without being held in contempt of court. News from police court became a staple of the early penny papers. Then, in 1836, Bennett was able to temporarily triple the circulation of his Herald by actually leaving his shop, walking over to the house where a young prostitute had been murdered and investigating the murder himself. As the circulations of these penny papers grew, editors were able to hire additional reporters. The Herald sent one reporter to cover the Mexican War in the 1840s; it sent 63 reporters to cover the Civil War in the 1860s.

However, the most dramatic improvement in the speed, breadth and reliability of news coverage came with Samuel Morse's invention of the telegraph. Newspapers became the major customers of the telegraph companies, and the cost of telegraph transmissions led to the formation of wire services like the Associated Press, which was founded as a cooperative venture by New York newspapers in 1848. That year, Bennett's Herald boasted that it printed "ten columns of highly important news received by electric telegraph" in a single issue. The telegraph for the first time enabled newspapers to fill their pages with news that happened yesterday in cities hundreds, then thousands of miles away. With the successful completion of a transatlantic cable in 1866, American newspapers could suddenly print news from Europe with similar promptness.

Newspaper reporting may have come of age in coverage of the American Civil War. Reporters overcame terrible conditions, sometimes heavy-handed government attempts to censor their reports and, when they crossed enemy lines, the threat of imprisonment as spys, to produce thorough and detailed accounts of issues and battles.

Among the best Civil War reporters were Albert D. Richardson of the New York Tribune, Henry Villard of the New York Herald and two southern correspondents, Felix Gregory de Fontaine of the Charlotte Courier and Peter W. Alexander of the Savannah Republican. This was a period of tremendous growth in newspapers in the United States. There were 3,000 newspapers in 1860, 4,500 in 1870 and 7,000 in 1880.

Newspapers in the eighteenth and the first half of the nineteenth century generally reflected the point of view of one person their publisher.The abolitionist crusader William Lloyd Garrison started The Liberator in 1831 with the expressed purpose, of course, of changing people's minds. John B. Russwurm and Reverend Samuel Cornish brought out the first newspaper published by blacks in the United States, Freedom's Journal, in 1827 with a similar purpose. "We wish to plead our own cause," they wrote. "Too long have other spoken for us." The great black writer Frederick Douglas started The North Star in 1847 "to Attack Slavery in all its forms and aspects."

The mass circulation transformed newspapers into valuable businesses with large staffs,. they started to be seen less as vehicles for one person's opinions and more as providers of information. The rise of the wire services, which distributed stories to many different papers, of many different political persuasions, also tended to reduce the emphasis on personal opinion in news stories, as did the new respect with which facts were treated in the late nineteenth century, thanks to the rise of science and the development of realism in literature.

This new veneration for facts was also connected to the spread, after the Civil War, of the "inverted pyramid" writing style, in which facts were detached from the narrative structures in which they formally were imbedded and arrayed in order of importance: with the most important facts who, what, when, where and sometimes why — placed at the top of the story, in the story's "lead."

Journalism was beginning to be thought of as a profession with its own professional standards. The first School of Journalism was founded at the University of Missouri in 1904. The American Society of Newspaper Editors drafted the "Canons of Journalism" in 1923, which included this dictum: "News reports should be free from opinion or bias of any kind."

Of course, it is not possible for any human utterance to be completely bias free. True objectivity is an unrealizable goal; there are too many possible sides to issues, too many different ways of viewing events, for them all to be treated fairly in a news story. The new emphasis on facts above opinion did not stop muckrakers, like Lincoln Steffens, Ida Tarbell and Jacob Riis from using newspapers, magazines and books to crusade against the injustices they saw in society in the late nineteenth and early twentieth century; nor did it prevent publishers like William Allen White, who purchased the Emporia Gazette in 1895, from using their newspapers to make a personal mark on American politics. Nevertheless, in the second half of the nineteenth century and the first half of the twentieth century, newspapers gradually began trying to keep their opinions restricted to their editorial and opinion pages and out of their news stories.

Some news stories have focused on crime, violence, emotion and sex for as long as news has been exchanged. Such stories can be found in the Roman Acta, in early newsbooks and news ballads and in the first American newspaper, Publick Occurrences. However, there have been periods in the history of American journalism, particularly periods when new audiences were being pursued and the competition for circulation was particularly intense, when sensationalism seemed to play an unusually large role in news coverage and cries of outrage over a decline in seriousness and good taste could be heard.

The era of the penny press, beginning in the 1830s and 1840s, was one such period. Crime news and human

interest stories seemed to occupy larger portions of newspaper columns in those years. James Gordon Bennett, with his eagerness to investigate the details of bloody murders and pass on rumors of sex scandals, even became the object of a "moral war," led by other newspapers, in 1840. Nevertheless, Bennett's Herald became the best selling newspaper in the United States.

The number of newspapers in the United States began to decline dramatically in the first half of the twentieth century . There were once 20 daily newspapers in New York city, by 1940 there were eight, and in that year 25 cities in the United States with a population of more than 100,000 found themselves with only one daily newspapers. Moreover, increasing numbers of the newspapers that survived were owned not by local citizens but by large national newspaper chains.

Reducing the number of newspapers published in a city had obvious advantages for those that survived, so in the early decades of the century increasing numbers of publishers began to merge with or buy out the competition. In Chicago in 1914, the Inter Oceanmerged with the Record-Herald and called itself the Herald. Then, in 1918, that paper merged with the Examiner, leaving Chicago with only two morning papers. In New York in 1916, Munsey consolidated the Press with the venerable Sun, which had been edited by Charles A. Dana from 1868 to 1897.

In 1920, Munsey bought and threw into his mix the Bennetts' old Herald and the associated Evening Telegram. In 1924, Munsey sold the Herald to the owners of Greeley's old Tribune, creating the Herald Tribune. Then Munsey, known as "the great executioner of newspapers," bought the Globe and the Mail. Perhaps the most mourned newspaper to expire in New York during this period was the World, which Pulitzer's heirs sold to Scripps-Howard 1931. The morning World disappeared; the Evening World was merged with a paper Scripps-Howard had picked up

from Munsey's collection, the Evening Telegram, creating the World-Telegram.

The first large newspaper chain in the United States was assembled by E. W. Scripps. By 1914, the Scripps-McRae League, which began with the Cleveland Press and the Cincinnati Post, was publishing 23 newspapers. Numerous new papers were founded, bought, merged, sold or abandoned. By 1929, Scripps-Howard, the new name of the chain, owned 25 newspapers. William Randolph Hearst, after his start in San Francisco and his move into New York, began assembling a similar chain. Hearst owned six newspapers by 1904, but rapidly began adding more at the rate of a newspaper a year from 1917 to 1921. In 1922, he added seven additional newspapers to his chain. By the end of that year, in addition to twenty daily and eleven Sunday newspapers, Hearst owned two wire services, six magazines and a newsreel company — an early array of media and therefore political power, which many at the time considered unhealthy. Such media conglomerates would grow even larger, however, as the century progressed.

Even when there were large numbers of daily newspapers circulating in major cities, many groups felt these papers were not representing their points of view and interests. One solution, especially for immigrant groups who were still more comfortable in another language, was to publish newspapers of their own. Probably the first foreign-language newspaper in America was a German newspaper Ben Franklin helped start in Germantown, near Philadelphia. A French newspaper, the Courrier Francais, was published daily in Philadelphia from 1794 to 1798. Early Spanish language newspapers appeared in New Orleans in 1808 and Texas in 1813. The first native-American newspaper, the Cherokee Phoenix, was printed in Georgia in 1828. The Jewish Daily Forward, printed in Yiddish, first appeared in New York in 1897 but was printing local editions in eleven other cities by 1923.

With the waves of immigration to American cities in the first decades of the twentieth century, came an increased market for foreign-language papers. According to statistics presented by media historians Edwin and Michael Emery, the United States had 160 foreign-language dailies in 1914, and a total of 1323 foreign-language newspapers in 1917.

As the number of newspapers declined and the survivors increasingly fell into the hands of large corporations, the limitations of news coverage in the mainstream press also inspired a growth in press criticism, beginning, in the late 1940s, with the New Yorker magazine writer and former newspaper journalist A. J. Liebling. "Freedom of the press is for those who own one," was perhaps Liebling's most famous statement about the press in his time. He argued in 1961 that the United States, which then had competing daily newspapers in only 61 cities, was advancing toward "a monovocal, monopolistic, monocular press." "With the decline in the 'number and variety' of voices," Liebling wrote, "there is a decline in the number and variety of reporting eyes, which is at least as malign." The Columbia Journalism Review, a forum for such criticism, was first published in 1961.

COMPETITION FROM TELEVISION

Newspapers have had many great successes in this century. They have reported, often with distinction, on wars and politics, and they have covered, occasionally somewhat tardily, the century's dramatic social and technological changes. Investigations like those mounted by Bob Woodward and Carl Bernstein for the Washington Post, on White House involvement in the cover up of the Watergate break in, have played a crucial role in exposing and presumably deterring violations of the public trust.

The Washington Post and the Los Angeles Times have now established themselves as major national news organs, whose political coverage and analyses play an important role in the political process; the Philadelphia

Inquirer Miami Herald and Boston Globe have produced significant, nationally recognized, coverage and investigations; and the New York Times, which for most of the century has been the most respected and influential newspaper in the United States, and the Wall Street Journal, the business daily, are both now printed and distributed. nationally. The New York Times had a circulation of 1.2 million daily and 1.8 million Sunday in 1993; the Wall Street Journal had a daily circulation of about 1.9 million in 1993.

Nevertheless, the newspaper business has been suffering, particularly in recent decades. The trouble started with competition from radio, which began offering another source of news and entertainment in the 1920s. Despite efforts to deny radio stations use of information form the Associated Press, radio made significant gains as a news medium, particularly with its reports on the bombing of Pearl Harbor and the Battle of Britain during World War II. But the true end to the period of perhaps two centuries in which the newspaper was the dominant news source in America and much of the world came with the arrival of television after World War II.

With the average home now keeping a television set on for more than seven hours a day, the amount of time available for reading a newspaper has declined dramatically. In 1940, there was one newspaper circulated in the United States for every two adults, by 1990 one newspaper circulated for every three adults. According to surveys, the share of the adult population that "read a newspaper yesterday" has declined from 85 percent in 1946 to 73 percent in 1965 to 55 percent in 1985. According to one survey, only 8.9 percent of Americans said they kept up with news of the Persian Gulf War primarily though newspapers. Evening newspapers, which were once brought home to provide evening entertainment in homes, have felt the competition from television particularly strongly; they

have disappeared in many large cities.

Newspapers have been struggling, sometimes awkwardly, to fight back. USA Today, a national newspaper introduced by Gannett in 1982, has imitated the short breezy stories featured on television newscasts. It was also one of the first newspapers to make heavy use of color in pictures, maps and graphics. Most major newspapers in the United now use color. USA Today was being printed in 32 locations in the United States and two outside the country in 1993 and had a circulation of more than two million, more than that of any metropolitan daily newspaper.

Newspapers, realizing that their readers will have already heard reports on breaking news stories on television, have also begun emphasizing feature stories and analysis pieces. Fewer stories now employ the inverted pyramid format. In addition, many newspapers have been exploring new technologies and experimenting with the possibility of distributing their stories into the homes of their readers through computers hooked up to telephone or cable television lines. However, hundreds of newspapers have also responded to their troubles, which were made worse by a slump in advertising revenues in the late 1980s and early 1990s, by selling out to large corporations, by merging or pooling resources in joint-operating agreements with former competitors, or by closing down.

The United States had 267 fewer newspapers in 1990 than it had in 1940. By 1992, only 37 cities in the United States had separately owned, competing daily newspapers. In the nineteenth century the United States was said to have more newspapers circulating to more people than any country on earth. A UNESCO survey in the 1980s found the United States nineteenth in the world in per capita newspaper circulation.

Most newspaper companies also own other media outlets: The Washington Post Company, for example, owns

Newsweek magazine, and the Chicago Tribune Company owns a number of broadcast stations. Their newspapers, then, are under the control not of independent publishers but of corporate executives, with other business concerns. Some press critics wonder whether eccentrics like Benjamin Harris, Benjamin Franklin, James Gordon Bennett, Horace Greeley or Joseph Pulitzer could find a place today in such media conglomerates.

Most newspapers also now rely for most of their international and national news coverage on large news services like the Associated Press, Reuters, the New York Times News Service and the Washington Post-Los Angeles Times New Service. United Press International, once the main competitor to the Associated Press, fell upon hard times in the 1980s and early 1990s and underwent many cutbacks in its news gathering staff.

Radio and television stations, cable networks, magazines and new computer information services certainly contribute to the range of information now available to citizens. Most major newspapers have also added opinion pages, which air views that differ from those of the newspaper and its publisher. Still, many press critics fear that the decline in the number of competing newspapers, the increasing corporate ownership of those newspapers that have survived and the standardization of their news coverage have, limited the different voices and the different perspectives on the world available to the people.

MAGAZINES

Magazines often are harbingers of change. When large social, economic or technological shifts begin to reshape the culture, magazines frequently are the first media to move, and the structure of the industry is one reason. Unlike newspapers, most magazines are not so tied to a specific geographic area, but are instead centered on interests or niches. Writers are looking for trends.

Publishers can more quickly than in other media add and subtract titles aimed at specific audience segments or interests. Advertisers, in turn, can take their dollars to hot titles of the moment aimed at particular demographics.

One can, if careful, look at what is happening in the magazine industry and get a reasonably good idea of what the culture at large is interested in and where it may be heading. Magazines 40 years ago, for instance, signaled early signs of the social fragmentation so commonly understood today with the decline of general interest magazines like Look and the rise of specialty magazines like Psychology Today.

First, the news agenda has gotten softer and more oriented to lifestyle rather than traditional hard news. Second, the audience for news in magazines is fragmenting. The large, well-known general interest news weeklies continue on their mission of reaching a mass audience with fair to moderate success. But a small group of news magazines with a very different approach to the coverage, such as The Atlantic, is seeing gains. These magazines have eschewed the conventional wisdom about the need for more pictures and lighter stories. Instead they rely on fewer photos and deal with serious topics. Aimed at a more educated audience, they seem less concerned with getting as many readers as possible and are more focused on getting the right readers. They come out just once a month and charge more per subscription, yet their circulation is growing. Their ad revenues are not near the mass-market competitors, but they are growing.

Beyond these overarching shifts, other magazine trends emerge in the data:

* The overall number of magazines is growing, but much of that is occurring in niche service magazines such as child care, travel or bicycling.
* The largest and most powerful magazine owners are

largely not involved in the service niche. Instead, they are heavily invested in pop culture and entertainment magazines, which have also seen large growth in the last decade.

* There is less interest at the corporate level in traditional news. With a few relatively minor exceptions, publishers are not launching new titles. Among the magazines that exist the audience is flat even as the population grows.
* Perhaps as a result, coverage in the general interest news weeklies (Time, Newsweek and U.S. News & World Report) is edging into lighter areas such as pop culture, health and service. To survive, they are becoming less specialized experts in anything and more a lighter version on every topic.
* The vast majority of the high-profile opinion-making magazines are owned by one of three big media companies.

Overall, the magazine industry is healthy, but its landscape is very different than it was even 10 years ago, let alone 20.

NEWSPAPERS IN INDIA

In India the significance of the fourth estate as the inevitable pillar of democracy and the freedom it enjoys, have contributed to the consistent growth of the print media. It is the print media which is easily accessible and has a more lasting effect on the people than any momentary or oft-repeated events in the visual media. This media has now moulded itself to suit the requirements of the recent Internet revolution and is growing with its readership always on the rise.

The news media has flourished since independence and exercises a large degree of independence compared with many other developing countries. British colonialism

allowed for the development of a tradition of freedom of the press, and many of India's great English-language newspapers and some of its Indian-language press were begun during the nineteenth century. As India became independent, ownership of India's leading English-language newspapers was transferred from British to Indian business groups, and the fact that most English-language newspapers have the backing of large business houses has contributed to their independence from the government.

The press has experienced impressive growth since independence. In 1950 there were 214 daily newspapers, with forty-four in English and the rest in Indian languages. By 1990 the number of daily newspapers had grown to 2,856, with 209 in English and 2,647 in indigenous languages. The expansion of literacy and the spread of consumerism during the 1980s fueled the rapid growth of news weeklies and other periodicals. By 1993 India had 35,595 newspapers—of which 3,805 were dailies—and other periodicals. Although the majority of publications are in indigenous languages, the English-language press, which has widespread appeal to the expanding middle class, has a wide multicity circulation throughout India.

There are four major publishing groups in India, each of which controls national and regional English-language and vernacular publications. They are the Times of India Group, the Indian Express Group, the Hindustan Times Group, and the Anandabazar Patrika Group. The Times of India is India's largest English-language daily, with a circulation of 656,000 published in six cities. The Indian Express , with a daily circulation of 519,000, is published in seventeen cities. There also are seven other daily newspapers with circulations of between 134,000 and 477,000, all in English and all competitive with one another. Indian-language newspapers also enjoy large circulations but usually on a statewide or citywide basis. For example, the Malayalam-language daily Malayala

Manorama circulates 673,000 copies in Kerala; the Hindi-language Dainik Jagran circulates widely in Uttar Pradesh and New Delhi, with 580,000 copies per day; Punjab Kesari, also published in Hindi and available throughout Punjab and New Delhi, has a daily circulation of 562,000; and the Anandabazar Patrika , published in Calcutta in Bengali, has a daily circulation of 435,000. There are also numerous smaller publications throughout the nation. The combined circulation of India's newspapers and periodicals is in the order of 60 million, published daily in more than ninety languages.

India has more than forty domestic news agencies. The Express News Service, the Press Trust of India, and the United News of India are among the major news agencies. They are headquartered in Delhi, Bombay, and New Delhi, respectively, and employ foreign correspondents.

Although freedom of the press in India is the legal norm—it is constitutionally guaranteed—the scope of this freedom has often been contested by the government. Rigid press censorship was imposed during the Emergency starting in 1975 but quickly retracted in 1977. The government has continued, however, to exercise more indirect controls. Government advertising accounts for as much as 50 percent of all advertisements in Indian newspapers, providing a monetary incentive to limit harsh criticism of the administration. Until 1992, when government regulation of access to newsprint was liberalized, controls on the distribution of newsprint could also be used to reward favored publications and threaten those that fell into disfavor. In 1988, at a time when the Indian press was publishing investigative reports about corruption and abuse of power in government, Parliament passed a tough defamation bill that mandated prison sentences for offending journalists. Vociferous protests from journalists and opposition party leaders ultimately forced the government to withdraw the bill. Since the late

1980s, the independence of India's press has been bolstered by the liberalization of government economic policy and the increase of private-sector advertising provided by the growth of India's private sector and the spread of consumerism.

The publishers under Section 19D of the Press and Registration of Books Act, 1867, submit Annual Statements to the Registrar of Newspapers for India. These Annual Statements are the principal source of data for compilation of this Report. However, all publishers do not submit their Annual Statements to this office and the RNI has not been able to verify each bit of information, given in the Annual Statements and therefore, this report cannot claim to be an authentic data bank. It can be described as indicative of the general trend.

Among daily newspapers, the first place went to those in Hindi, totaling 2507 in 2001. Urdu dailies numbering 534 came second and those in English (407) came third. Languages, having more than 100 daily publications in 2001, were Marathi (395), Tamil (366), Kannada (364), Malayalam (225), Telugu (180), Gujarati (159), Punjabi (107) and Bengali (103). In circulation also, the Hindi daily Press maintained its dominance with 2,33,82,867 copies, or 40.42 per cent of total circulation of dailies. English dailies claimed the second position, with a circulation of 87,01,803 copies.

Uttar Pradesh continued to have the largest number of daily newspapers (841), followed by Maharashtra (573), Karnataka (479), Madhya Pradesh (443), Rajasthan (431), Bihar (372), Tamil Nadu (384), Andhra Pradesh (352), Delhi (312), Kerala (226), Gujarat (179), West Bengal (167), Punjab (133), Haryana (122) and Orissa (109). Dailies from Uttar Pradesh with a total circulation of 77,88,600 copies were at the top, followed by Maharashtra 74,52,904, Delhi 56,22,907 and Gujarat 40,50,253.

The Press in Delhi and Maharashtra had the

distinction of publishing newspapers in 17 out of 19 principal languages. Delhi and Orissa came next, with newspapers in 16 languages. Newspapers in 15 principal languages were published from Tamil Nadu, 14 from Andhra Pradesh & West Bengal, 12 from Karnataka and 10 from Kerala. Another interesting feature of the Press in India in 2001 is that as many as 6794 newspapers were published from Uttar Pradesh in a single language (Hindi) followed by Madhya Pradesh (3342 in Hindi), Rajasthan (3016 in Hindi), Maharashtra (2867 in Marathi and 1411 in English), Delhi (2810 in Hindi and 2529 in English), and West Bengal (2508 in Bengali). The States publishing more than 1000 newspapers in a single language were Tamil Nadu (1994 in Tamil), Gujarat (1955 in Gujarati), Karnataka (1764 in Kannada), Kerala (1410 in Malayalam), Bihar (1220 in Hindi) and Andhra Pradesh (1199 in Telugu).

The Hindu, an English daily, published from Chennai and printed at Chennai, Coimbatore, Hyderabad, Bangalore, Madurai, Vishakhapatnam, Delhi, Thiruvananthapuram and Kochi was the largest circulated single edition daily with claimed circulation of 9,37,222 followed by Hindustan Times, English Daily, published from Delhi and printed at New Delhi, Chandigarh, Bhopal, Jaipur, Raipur, Kolkota, Ranchi, Muzaffarpur, Bhagalpur, Varanasi and Patna with a circulation of 9,09,278. Anand Bazar Patrika, Bengali Daily, published from Kolkata came third with a circulation of 8,76,727, whereas The Times of India, English Daily, published from Delhi was fourth with a circualtion of 8,43,874 copies.

The Times of India with nine editions and a total circulation of 21,52,046 copies came first among multi-editon dailies. Malayala Manorama with nine edition claiming a circulation of 12,72,823 copies was at second. Dainik Jagaran with eleven edition and a total circulation of 12,72,715 copies occupied the third position.

Newspapers, owned by Individuals had the largest share in circulation (45.68 per cent), followed by those owned by Joint Stock Companies (43.51 per cent). In 2001, there were 171 common ownership units, which brought out 817 newspapers. Newspapers, belonging to these units, had a circulation of 4,68,99,570 copies, or 40.69 per cent of the total circulation of the Indian Press.

Out of total 45,974 periodicals, 27,027 dealt with news and current affairs while 4,368 were literary and cultural magazines. Apart from these categories, there were periodicals, dealing with various subjects, such as religion and philosophy, commerce and industry, medicine and health, labour, engineering and technology, art, science, children, film, sports etc.

Apart from general newspapers and specialized journals, there were 3590 publications, which were not strictly 'newspapers', although they had a definite periodicity. These publications have, therefore, not been included in the general study of the Press. Chapter X is devoted exclusively to the analysis of these publications, comprising market reports and bulletins, publicity journals, fiction, school and college magazines etc.

THE FUTURE OF NEWSPAPERS

The future of newspapers is cloudy, with overall readership slowly declining in most developed countries due to increasing competition from television and the Internet. The 57th annual World Newspaper Congress, held in Istanbul in June 2004, reported circulation increases in only 35 of 208 countries studied. Most of the increase came in developing countries, notably China.

A report at the gathering indicated that China tops total newspaper circulation, with more than 85 million copies of papers sold every day, followed by India with 72 million—China and India are the two most populous countries in the world followed by Japan with 70 million and the United States with 55 million. The report said

circulation declined by an average of 2.2 percent across 13 of the 15 countries that made up the European Union before May 1. The biggest declines were in Ireland, down 7.8 percent; Britain, down 4.7 percent; and Portugal, where numbers fell by 4.0 percent. One growth area is the distribution of free newspapers, which are not reflected in the above circulation data. Led by the Metro chain of newspapers, they grew 16 percent in 2003.

Another growth area is high-quality tabloids, particularly in the UK, where several of the major broadsheets are experimenting with the format. Newspapers also face increased competition from the Internet for classified ads, especially for jobs, real estate, and cars, which have long been a key source of revenue.

3

Major News Agencies

News agencies are organizations established to supply news reports to organizations in the news trade: newspapers, magazines, and radio and television broadcasters. They are also known as wire services or news services. They can be either corporations that sell news, cooperatives composed of newspapers that share their articles with each other, commercial newswire services which charge organizations to distribute their news. Governments may also control "news agencies," particularly in authoritarian states, like China and Russia. A recent rise in internet-based alternative news agencies, as a component of the larger alternative media have emphasized a "non-corporate view," as being largely independent of the pressures of business media.

News agencies generally prepare articles that can be used by other news organizations with little or no modification, and then sell them to other news organizations. They provide these articles in bulk electronically through wire services (originally they used telegraphy; today they frequently use the Internet). Corporations, individuals, analysts and intelligence agencies may also subscribe. News agencies are distinct from news syndicates that distribute comic strips and other editorial material, such as columns and features, and also from public relations organizations that distribute press releases. Sometimes news agencies have separate arms for such work, but many such organizations are completely separate.

EVOLUTION OF NEWS AGENCIES

As early as the 1820s a news agency, the Association of Morning Newspapers, was formed in New York City to gather incoming reports from Europe. Other local news agencies sprang up, and by 1856 the General News Association comprising many important New York City papers was organized. Out of this agency emerged in the 1870s the New York Associated Press, a cooperative news agency for New York papers that sold copy to daily papers throughout the country; the United Press began in 1882. Ten years later these organizations were merged, but the same year a rival agency, the Associated Press of Illinois, was founded.

In Europe three international agencies had arisen; Agence Havas of Paris (1835); the Reuter Telegram Company of London (1851), known simply as Reuters; and the Continental Telegraphen Compagnie of Berlin (1849), known as the Wolff Agency. These began as financial-data services for bankers but extended their coverage to world news. By 1866 national agencies were arising in many European countries; they covered and sold news locally, relying on the major services for coverage and sales abroad.

After the Associated Press of Illinois signed exchange contracts with the worldwide networks, the United Press went under (1897). In 1900 the Associated Press of Illinois, desiring to restrict its membership, reincorporated in New York state and was thereafter known as the Associated Press (AP); in 1915 the United States forbade the agency to restrict its members' use of other services. A Supreme Court decision in 1945 ended the exclusion of members' competitors. In 1906 William Randolph Hearst founded the International News Service (INS), available to papers of other publishers as well as his own. The United Press Association, usually called United Press (UP) although there was no connection with the earlier organization, became an affiliate of the Scripps-Howard newspapers and sold reports to others.

The AP, UP, and INS grew steadily, and by the 1930s their foreign operations freed them of dependence on the European agencies, which tended to reflect national viewpoints in political news. In 1958 INS was merged with UP, forming United Press International (UPI). After a string of owners in the 1980s, UPI's assets were acquired in 1992 by Middle East Broadcasting Limited. After World War II many agencies, including Reuters, AP, and Agence France-Presse (the renamed Agence Havas) became cooperatives owned by their member publishers. Notable cooperatives allied with Reuters include the Canadian Press, the Australian Associated Press, and the Press Trust of India.

Government ownership of news agencies stems from the early 1900s. In 1904 the St. Petersburg (later Petrograd) Telegraph Agency was founded by the Russian government. In 1918, Soviet Russia founded Rosta by merging the telegraph agency with the government press bureau, and in 1925 Rosta became TASS. Today, as ITAR-TASS it is the official news service of Russia and also provides coverage of the other former Soviet republics. In 1915, Germany established a service called Transocean to broadcast war propaganda. The New China News Agency (Xinhua), founded in 1931 as the Red China News Agency, maintains official news and financial service wires, publishes dozens of newspapers and magazines, has its own advertising and public relations firms, and runs a school of journalism. Since 1990 independent news agencies have appeared in Eastern Europe, including Interfax in Russia and A. M. Pres in Romania.

From 1915 until the 1940s, news agencies in the United States transmitted most copy over telephone wires to teletypewriters in newspaper offices. The late 1940s, however, brought the introduction of Teletypesetter machines, which allowed the stories from the agencies, in the form of perforated paper tape, to be fed into typesetting, or linotype, machines, without the use of human operators.

In using Teletypesetters to save labor, publishers ceded to the agencies some of their editing prerogative, thereby standardizing usage and writing style in newspaper stories.

Newspapers moved from linotype to photocomposition in the late 1960s to 1970s. The data is transmitted by telephone or satellite service, and newspapers reconstruct the information in their own format. Most news agencies also offer their clients photographs, news analyses, and special features; for radio and television stations they transmit news-broadcast scripts. Since the advent of computer technology, many news services have become available on line and some of them are listed below:

MAJOR NEWS AGENCIES

Prominent international news agencies include:

* All Headline News
* Agence France-Presse (the oldest, founded in 1835)
* ANSA (Italy)
* Associated Press (founded in 1848)
* British Broadcasting Corporation
* Bloomberg L.P.
* Reuters
* The Press Association (UK)
* Canadian Press
* Canadian University Press (founded in 1938)
* City News Bureau of Chicago
* Cox Enterprises
* EFE
* EIN News
* Kyodo
* ITIM - Israel
* ITAR-TASS, Russia

* China News Service,China
* United Press International (founded in 1907)
* ANP (The Netherlands)
* Pacific News Service
* DPA (Germany)
* OANA
* Xinhua News Agency, People's Republic of China
* Yonhap, Korea
* Australian Associated Press
* Press Trust of India

Some of the international as well as Indian news agencies are being discussed here in detail:

THE ASSOCIATED PRESS

Associated Press is the the world's largest news organization. It is a cooperative owned by its contributing newspapers and broadcast stations in the United States, who both contribute stories to it and use material written by its staffers. Many newspapers and broadcasters outside the United States are AP subscribers - that is, they pay a fee to use AP material but are not members of the cooperative.

The Associated Press is the backbone of the world's information system serving thousands of daily newspaper, radio, television and online customers with coverage in all media and news in all formats. It is the largest and oldest news organization in the world, serving as a source of news, photos, graphics, audio and video for more than one billion people a day. Its mission is to be the essential global news network, providing distinctive news services of the highest quality, reliability and objectivity with reports that are accurate, balanced and informed. AP operates as a not-for-profit cooperative with 3,700 employees working in more than 240 worldwide bureaus.

AP supplies a steady stream of news around the clock

to its domestic members, international subscribers and commercial customers. It has the industry's most sophisticated digital photo network, a 24-hour continuously updated online news service, a state-of-the-art television news service and one of the largest radio networks in the United States. It also has a commercial digital photo archive, a photo library housing more than 10 million images and provides advertising management services.

AP was formed in May 1846 by representatives of five competitive New York City newspapers, who wanted to pool resources to collect news from Europe. The driving force in its formation was Moses Yale Beach publisher of the New York Sun when he invited the other New York publishers to join the Sun in a cooperative venture in covering the U.S. - Mexican war. The five New York papers joined in the agreement were the Sun, the Journal of Commerce, the Courier and Enquirer, and the Herald and the Express. Until then, newspapers competed by sending reporters out in rowboats to meet the ships as they arrived in the harbor. In 1849 it opened the first bureau outside the U.S., in Halifax, Nova Scotia, to meet ships from Europe before they docked in New York. A brief chronological account of its development is mentioned below:

* **1861:** Facing censorship in covering the American Civil War, reporters first filed under the anonymous byline "from the Associated Press agent."
* **1876:** Mark Kellogg, a stringer, becomes the first AP correspondent to die in the line of duty, at the Battle of the Little Bighorn. His final dispatch: "I go with Custer and will be at the death."
* **1893:** Melville E. Stone becomes the general manager of the reorganized A.P., a post he retains until 1921. Under his leadership, the A.P. becomes one of the world's most prominent news agencies.
* **1899:** AP uses Guglielmo Marconi's wireless telegraph to cover the America's Cup yacht race off

Sandy Hook, New Jersey, the first news test of the new telegraph.

* **1914:** AP introduces the Teletype, which transmitted directly to printers over telegraph wires. Eventually a worldwide network of 60-word-per-minute Teletypes is built up.
* **1935:** AP starts WirePhoto, the world's first wire service for photographs.
* **1941:** AP expands from print into radio.
* **1994:** AP launches APTV, a global video newsgathering agency.

As of 2005, AP's news is used by 1,700 newspapers, in addition to 5,000 television and radio outlets. Its photo library consists of over 10 million images. The AP has 242 bureaus and serves 121 countries, with a diverse international staff drawing from all over the world.

The collapse of United Press International as a major competitor, AP's traditional rival, has left it as the only nationally oriented news service based in the United States. The other rival English-language news services, such as Reuters and the English language service of Agence France Presse, are based outside the United States. It is notable that the AP Stylebook has become the de facto standard for newswriting in the country.

The AP has a straightforward, "just-the-facts" writing style, often using the inverted pyramid style of writing so that stories can be edited to fit a newspaper news-hole without losing the essence of the story. The explosion of media and news outlets with the arrival of the Internet has made such concise writing less necessary, and raised the need for more feature-style writing.

It has also posed a threat to AP's financial structure. On April 18, 2005, at its annual meeting, AP announced that as of 2006 it would, for the first time, begin charging separate fees for posting articles and pictures online. News

outlets that buy AP's news, sports, business and entertainment coverage have previously been allowed to place the material online at no extra cost. The cooperative later backed down from the plan and, in a bid to reach more readers, launched asap, a service aimed at 18–34-year-olds. The Associated Press made available for download the unclassified portions of the dossiers of 59 Guantanamo Bay detainees, which they acquired through Freedom of Information Act requests.

The Associated Press employs some of the best and most experienced journalists in the world. Each is dedicated to the same standards — fairness, balance and accuracy. With a robust network of more than 3,700 employees around the world, AP provides breaking news coverage and compelling enterprise pieces that can't be found anywhere else.

AP's news report reflects the full breadth of international, national, state, sports, business and entertainment news and AP's specialized coverage is widely used at length on newspaper section fronts across the United States and around the world.

FEATURED SERVICES FOR NEWSPAPERS

AP provides everything newspapers and Web sites need to be first with results on election night. AP will offer updated results of all national and state elections, plus online content, year-round pre-election coverage, Web hosting and analytic tools for reporters.

Associated Press Television News is the world's largest video news agency, and the international video news arm of The Associated Press.

With over 80 bureaus worldwide, linked by a network of global satellites, APTN provides the world's most reliable, prompt, and accurate breaking video news, sports, and entertainment content to over 500 broadcast newsrooms, portals, Web, broadband and mobile customers worldwide.

The Associated Press puts power, control and flexibility in the hands of broadcast journalists with ENPS, the world's leading news production system. Introduced in 1997, ENPS is now used by nearly 500 newsrooms in 42 countries.

ENPS combines intuitive functionality, integration features, unparalleled language support and continuing product evolution to help production of news programming become more efficient. Developed by and for journalists, ENPS fits the changing needs of all types of demanding news gathering environments.

AP Digital is a division of The Associated Press that provides news and information to Web sites, wireless operators, corporate and government desktops, information distributors and other commercial and new media applications.

With multimedia production resources and the ability to deliver information on a variety of technology platforms, AP Digital offers immediate access to breaking international, national and local news and topical features and creates interactive products using AP text, photos, graphics, audio and video and selected information from content partners. AP's dynamic product portfolio also includes targeted industry-specific news packages and custom content categories that meet the information needs of specific audiences. Services are offered in English, Spanish, French, Dutch and German.

AP VIDEO SERVICES

News videos produced by Associated Press Television News (APTN) are available through an online feed or hosted platform for Web sites and interactive services. Clips cover U.S. and international news, politics, entertainment, business and human-interest stories, plus daily one-minute world news and financial markets summaries.

AP FINANCIAL NEWS

An enhanced business news service offering detailed US company and world market news, quarterly earnings announcements, coverage of executive changes, regulatory actions, mergers and acquisitions and new product developments for major companies in a full range of industries. AP Financial News goes beyond the top stories of the day to offer reliable, readable breaking coverage of top companies and financial markets around the world.

The Associated Press has received 29 photo Pulitzers, the most of any news organization. AP delivers more than 1,000 photos a day from journalists recording news as it happens around the world. AP photos are an important part of modern-day world history — for more than a century, AP photographers have captured the greatest moments in history, news, sports and entertainment.

AP's digital photo archive includes more than two million historical and recent pictures, and the AP photo library holds an estimated 10 million negatives and prints dating back a century. AP images are also available for use by magazines, book publishers, Web sites and individuals.

AP IMAGES

AP Images is the world's largest bank of historical and recent photos. AP Images provides instant access to AP's iconic images and adds new images every minute of every day from every corner of the world, making it an essential source of photos and graphics for professional image buyers and commercial customers.

AP IMAGES SERVICES

Staffed by experienced photo sales professionals, AP/ Wide World Photos licenses AP images and provides image-related services including assignment photography, custom photo research and image rights and clearances.

The Associated Press is everywhere. Breaking news

transcends borders and so does AP's coverage. The Associated Press has bureaus in more than 120 countries — offering coverage with breadth, depth and context to all major media outside of North America. AP tailors its news and photo reports to reflect the specific regional interests of Latin America, the Caribbean, Europe, the Middle East, Asia and Africa and offers news in four foreign languages — French, Spanish, German and Dutch. Agencies translate AP copy into scores of other languages, from Arabic to Chinese.

Photo and news exchange agreements with national agencies build on the scope of AP's global coverage and deepen AP's penetration of foreign markets. In Germany, Switzerland and France, AP offers a strong domestic component to its news and photo services, much like AP's state reports in the United States.

To keep pace with customer and member needs, The Associated Press offers enhanced services for ad management and delivery. For advertisers and agencies, working with AP makes it easier to buy advertising across multiple newspapers. For newspapers, working with AP enables the advertising and sales departments to focus efforts on sales, as opposed to paperwork.

In keeping with its reputation for fairness and impartiality, the AP maintains a neutral position in the ad management business. AP doesn't represent the buyer, and it doesn't represent one newspaper over another — it simplifies the advertising process by eliminating extra steps and repetitive work.

REUTERS

Reuters is a well known news service that provides reports from around the world to newspapers and broadcasters. However, news reporting accounts for less than 10% of the company's income. Its main focus is on supplying the financial markets with information and trading products. These include market data, such as share

prices and currency rates, research and analytics, as well as trading systems that allow dealers to buy and sell such things as currencies and shares on a computer screen instead of by telephone or on a trading floor like that of the New York Stock Exchange. Competitors include Bloomberg L.P. and Dow Jones Newswires.

The company was founded by Paul Julius Reuter, a German-Jewish immigrant to London who as early as 1851 began transmitting stock-market quotes between Paris and London via the new Calais-Dover telegraph cable. Reuter's agency built a reputation in Europe for being the first to report scoops from abroad, like the news of Abraham Lincoln's assassination. Today, almost every major news outlet in the world subscribes to Reuters. It operates in 200 cities in 94 countries, supplying text in 19 languages.

Reuters was floated as a public company in 1984 on the London Stock Exchange and on NASDAQ in the US. However, there were concerns that the company's tradition for objective reporting might be jeopardised if control of the company later fell into the hands of a single shareholder. To counter this possibility, the constitution of the company at the time of flotation included a rule that no individual was allowed to hold more than 15% of the company. If this limit is exceeded the directors can order the shareholder to reduce the holding to less than 15%. This rule was applied in the late 1980s when Rupert Murdoch's News Corporation, which already held around 15% of Reuters, bought an Australian news company which also had a holding in Reuters. The acquisition meant that Murdoch then held more than 15% and he was obliged to reduce the holding to less than 15% in line with the rules.

At the same time, as a further measure to protect the independence of Reuters news reporting, The Reuters Founders Share Company was set up. This is a company whose sole task is to protect the integrity of the company's news output. It holds one "Founders Share" which can

outvote all other shares in the event that an attempt is made to alter any of the rules relating to the Reuters Trust Principles. These principles set out the company's aim to preserve its independence, integrity and freedom from bias in its news reporting.

Reuters began to grow rapidly in the 1980s, widening the range of its business products and expanding its global reporting network for media, financial and economic services. Recent key product launches include Equities 2000 (1987), Dealing 2000-2 (1992), Business Briefing (1994), Reuters Television for the financial markets (1994), 3000 Series (1996) and the Reuters 3000 Xtra service (1999).

In the mid-1990s the company had a brief foray into the radio sector with London Radio's two stations, London News 97.3 FM and London News Talk 1152 AM, which replaced LBC in 1994. A Reuters Radio News service was also set up to compete with Independent Radio News. In 1995, Reuters established its "Greenhouse Fund" to take minority investments in a range of start-up technology companies, initially in the United States.

Reuters dates from a text news service founded by Julius Reuter. In the second half of last century it expanded to encompass television news and has become increasingly prominent as a provider of real-time and archival financial information services, in competition with Dow Jones and Bloomberg. During the late 1990s it acquired majority or minority stakes in a range of information technology research consultancies such as Yankee Group and specialist market information services such as Datamonitor.

As of 2000 the group employed around 2,150 journalists, photographers and camera operators in 190 bureaus, serving 151 countries, with additional personnel in units such as Yankee. Overall staffing was 18,082 people in 204 cities in 100 countries, with group revenues of

US$5.4 billion. In 2005 it has expanded its image operations with the multimillion pound takeover of the London-based Action Images sports photography agency. That deal provided an archive of seven million sports images stretching over 50 years, with over 1.5m accessible online.

UNITED PESS INTERNATIONAL

United Press International (UPI) has been a leading provider of critical information to media outlets, businesses, governments and researchers worldwide since 1970. UPI is a global operation headquartered in Washington, DC with offices in Beirut, Hong Kong, London, Santiago, Seoul and Tokyo.

UPI licenses content directly to print outlets, online media and institutions of all types. In addition, UPI's distribution partners provide content to thousands of businesses, policy groups and academic institutions worldwide. Its audience consists of millions of decision-makers who depend on UPI's insightful and analytical stories to make better business or policy decisions.

As it approaches the 100th anniversary, the company strives to continue to be a leading and trusted source for news, analysis and insight for readers around the world. UPI is a global operation headquartered in Washington, DC with offices in Beirut, Hong Kong, London, Santiago, Seoul and Tokyo.

UPI was founded in 1907 by E.W. Scripps as the United Press (UP). It became known as UPI when the UP merged with the International News Service in 1958, which was founded in 1909 by William Randolph Hearst. Now, it is owned by News World Communications, a global multi-media company.

Journalists contribute content from all over the world including the United States, South America, Europe, the Middle East, Africa and Asia. Its stories and photos cover a variety of topics including international and U.S. news,

politics, sports, entertainment, health, science and technology.

UPI strives to provide coverage that is fair, balanced and accurate. In addition to its English report, UPI provides news coverage coming out of the Middle East in Arabic and a Spanish-language news report from our correspondents throughout Latin America. UPI's news report is read by millions of global readers each day through our clients and though our distribution partners. Since clients can choose stories that are most appropriate to their business, the readership of each story can differ.

News World Communications, a global media company, acquired United Press International in May 2000. News World's flagship newspaper, The Washington Times, was founded in 1982 and has gained a reputation for hard-hitting investigative reporting and thorough coverage of politics and policy. In addition, News World publishes newspapers and magazines in more than 20 countries and in four languages.

Other News World properties include:

* Washington Times
* The Washington Times National Weekly
* The World & I
* Insight Magazine
* Middle East Times
* Tiempos del Mundo
* Ultimas Noticias
* The World Peace Herald
* Segye Ilbo
* Segye Times USA
* Sekai Nippo
* Chongyohak Shinmun
* Washington Golf Monthly
* Philadelphia Golf Monthly

AGENCE FRANCE-PRESSE

Agence France-Presse is the oldest news agency in the world. It is also the largest French agency and the third largest news agency in the world, behind the Associated Press and Reuters. The agency is based in Paris, with regional centres in Washington, Hong Kong, Nicosia and Montevideo and bureaux in 110 countries. It sends out news in French, English, Arabic, Spanish, German, Portuguese and Russian. It was founded in 1835 by Charles-Louis Havas as Agence Havas.

AFP is a nonprofit autonomous public corporation chartered under a specific 1957 law, operating commercially and independently of the French government. It is administered by a CEO and a board comprising 15 member. AFP also has a superior council charged with ensuring that the agency operates according to its statutes, which mandate absolute independence and neutrality.

The primary client of AFP is the French government, which purchases subscriptions for its various services. In practice, those subscriptions are somewhat a subsidy to AFP. AFP statutes prohibit direct government subsidies.

Established in 1990, AFX News is a wholly-owned AFP subsidiary. Headquartered in London, it also operates a network of bureaus across Europe and works with associate companies in North America

XINHUA NEWS AGENCY

The Xinhua News Agency is the official press agency of the government of the People's Republic of China (PRC) and the biggest center for collecting information and press conferences in the PRC. It is one of the two news agencies in the PRC, the other being the China News Service, and is among the premier world news agencies. It is an institution of the State Council of China. Critics of Xinhua therefore consider it to be an instrument of state-sponsored propaganda.

In many ways, Xinhua is the fuel propelling China's print media. Perhaps unique in the world because of its role, size, and reach, Xinhua reports directly to the Chinese Communist Party's Propaganda Department; employs more than 10,000 people — as compared to about 1,300 for Reuters; has 107 bureaus worldwide both collecting information on other countries and dispensing information about China; and maintains 31 bureaus in China — one for each province plus a military bureau. As most of the newspapers in China cannot afford to station correspondents abroad, or even in every Chinese province, they rely on Xinhua feeds to fill their pages. People's Daily, for example, uses Xinhua material for approximately 25 percent of its stories. Xinhua is a publisher as well as a news agency and it owns more than 20 newspapers and a dozen magazines, and it prints in Chinese, English, and four other languages.

Like other government entities, Xinhua is feeling the pinch of reduced state financial subsidies. Beijing has been cutting funding to the news agency by an average of seven percent per year over the past three years, and state funds currently cover only about 40 percent of Xinhua's costs. As a result, the agency is raising revenues through involvement in public relations, construction, and information service businesses.

In the past, Xinhua was able to attract the top young journalists emerging from the universities or otherwise newly entering the field, but it can no longer do so as easily because of the appeal and resources of other newspapers and periodicals and the greater glamour of television and radio jobs. For example, midlevel reporters for the Xinmin Evening News in Shanghai often are given an apartment, whereas at Xinhua and People's Daily this benefit is reserved for the most senior journalists.

The Xinhua press agency was started in November 1931 as the Red China News Agency and changed to its current name in 1937. It began broadcasting to foreign

countries in English from 1944. The Xinhua headquarters is located in Beijing. The.Xinhua News Agency established its first overseas affiliate in 1948. Now it distributes its news in Asia, Middle East, Latin America, Africa where run the superior offices; in Hong Kong, Macau and many foreign countries and districts. There are more than one hundred Xinhua affiliates.

Today, Xinhua News Agency delivers its news across the world in seven languages including Chinese, English, French, Russian, Spanish, Arabic, etc., as well as news pictures and other kinds of news. It has made contracts to exchange news and news pictures with more than eighty foreign news agency or political news department.

Unlike the People's Daily, which is an organization of the Communist Party of China rather than of the PRC government, Xinhua rarely offers editorials, but rather passes through speeches by government officials. Its position set as a platform of receiving and distributing the information all over the world and thus it covers the world news, live news and exclusive reports.

Like many other media organizations, Xinhua struggled to find the "right line" to use in covering the Tiananmen Square protests of 1989. Although more cautious than People's Daily in its treatment of sensitive topics during that period — such as how to commemorate reformist Communist Party leader Hu Yaobang's April 1989 death, the then ongoing demonstrations in Beijing and elsewhere, and basic questions of press freedom and individual rights — Xinhua gave some favorable coverage to demonstrators and intellectuals who were questioning top party leaders. Even so, many Xinhua reporters were angry with top editors for not going far enough and for suppressing stories about the Tiananmen Square crackdown. For several days after the violence on 4 June, almost no-one at Xinhua did any work, and journalists demonstrated inside the Agency's Beijing compound.

In 2001, Hong Kong-listed media company Sing Tao News Corporation Limited invested in joint ventures with Xinhua News Agency to set up a market information Web site and offer audio and visual services planning and consulting.

PRESS TRUST INDIA

India's largest news agency, Press Trust of India is a non-profit sharing cooperative owned by the country's newspapers. PTI subscribers include 450 newspapers in India and scores abroad. All major TV/Radio channels in india and several abroad, including BBC in London, receive the PTI Service. With a staff of over 1,300 including 400 journalists, PTI has over 80 bureaus across the country and foreign correspondents in major cities of the world including Bangkok, Beijing, Dhaka, Jerusalem, Johannesburg, Islamabad, Kathmandu, Kuala Lumpur, London, Moscow, New York, Washington and

The story of PTI is virtually the story of independent India. The run-up to Independence had also thrown up ideas of running free India's own national news agency as an objective disseminator of information about a resurgent nation, freed of the foreign yoke. "The evolution of the concept of a national news agency was the direct consequence of the spirit of independence that swept the country since the days of the Quit India Movement. "The desire to shake off the imperial domination in the field of news supply was at the heart of this evolving thought," said Ramnath Goenka, the fearless press baron and freedom fighter.

After two years of consultations and planning among senior journalists, newspaper proprietors and national leaders like Pandit Nehru and Sardar Patel, free India's first national news agency, the Press Trust of India, was incorporated in Madras on August 27, 1947. This was within a fortnight of what Jawaharlal Nehru described as India's "Tryst With Destiny" at the historic central hall of

Parliament on the night of August 14-15.

Though PTI began its operations in 1949, its origin goes back to the early years of the 20th Century when its forerunner - the Associated Press of India (API) - was launched by an enterprising Indian, Keshab Chandra Roy. The first Indian to function as a Political Correspondent at the British imperial capital, Roy was a high-school dropout who made a success of a journalistic career and rose to be a nominated member of the Central Legislative Assembly as a distinguished journalist. Working for more than one newspaper at a time, including The Tribune of Lahore, the Indian Daily Mail of Bombay and the Amrita Bazar Patrika of Calcutta, Roy found it easy to have a news pooling arrangement with European journalists to carry on with his work. It was from this experience that the idea of a news agency grew in Roy's mind. Soon he collaborated with three of his professional colleagues - Usha Nath Sen, Durga Das and A.S. Iyengar - to float and run API.

Though the exact time of its birth is somewhat hazy, according to the book 'Reuter's Century: 1851-1951' by Graham Storey, it was started in 1910. K C Roy finally gave up in 1919 his brave effort to run an Indian-owned domestic news agency and Reuters became the sole supplier of foreign and domestic news to the government and to the newspapers of India.The London-based Eastern News Agency, owned by Reuters, merely used the name Associated Press of India. API was to be registered as a private limited company, wholly owned by Reuters, much later in September 1945.

February 1,1949, PTI has reported India's history as it happened, blow by blow, in the best traditions of news agency journalism, with speed, accuracy and objectivity. The first general elections of free India in 1952, the first Asian Games a year earlier, the war with China in 1962, Pandit Nehru's death in 1964, the great split of the Indian National Congress in 1969, the 1971 war with Pakistan

culminating in the birth of Bangladesh, India's first nuclear test in 1974, the emergency in 1975, terrorist violence in Punjab in the 1980s, assassination of Indira Gandhi in 1984 as well as the stirring events of the 1990s, were all reported in detail by PTI journalists, most of them in anonymity.

In the last 50 years, PTI has come a long way, growing in size and stature as the oldest and largest among news agencies of the countries that became free after World War II.

It has arrangements with the Associated Press (AP) and Agencies France Presse (AFP) for distribution of their news in India, and with the the Associated Press for its Photo Service and International commercial information. PTI exchanges news with nearly 100 news agencies of the world as part of bilateral and multilateral arrangements, including Non-Aligned News Agencies Pool and the Organisation of Asia-Pacific News Agencies.

ENGLISH NEWS SERVICE

Available in two forms. The 'core' service covers major developments in diverse fields in a compact form. A more comprehensive segmented service allows papers to pick additional inputs from segments of their choice. National/ Regional, Economic/Commercial, International, and Sports. Core service puts out about 40,000 words and the full segmented service upto 100,000 words per day.

BHASHA Bhasha is the Hindi language news service of PTI. With its own network in the Hindi-speaking states and drawing on PTI files, Bhasha puts out about 40,000 words per day.

STOCK SCAN A screen-based service providing stock market information from major stock exchanges of the country.

NEWS SCAN Displays news in capsule from on video monitors. Major developments in the country and abroad are covered.

DATA INDIA A reference weekly providing a digest on the happenings in India, in a user-friendly alphabetical listing.

ECONOMIC SERVICE A fortnightly journal providing analytical reports on the state of the Indian economy and trends in the corporate world.

PTI MAG A weekly package of eleven special stories on topics ranging from arts to business to science. Available through the wire service as well as through mail.

SCIENCE SERVICE Reports on the developments in the fields of science and technology with particular reference to India in a fortnightly journal.

PTI GRAPHICS A weekly mailer package of 14 graphics, covers all major developments. On special occasions like the budget, graphics are distributed by satellite.

PTI FEATURE A package of four weekly features on topical national, international and general events. PTI-TV Provides spot coverage and makes corporate documentaries on assignment basis.

PHOTO Available in two packages to suit the needs of small and big newspapers. PTI Photo provides pictures on the national, foreign and sports scenes via satellite, dial-up and hand delivery. The full colour service of the Associated Press Of America (AP) is also made available through PTI.

ASIA PULSE An on-line data bank on economic developments and business opportunities in asian countries. Formed by PTI and four other Asian media organisations, Asia Pulse International is registered as a company in Singapore.

UNITED NEWS OF INDIA (UNI)

UNI was launched in March, 1961, and has grown into one of the largest news agencies in Asia. During these years, UNI has acquired an enviable reputation for fast

and accurate coverage of all major news events in India and abroad in all areas including politics, •economics, business, sports, entertainment, stock markets and so on. Its service also provides subscribers with a rich choice in features, interviews and human interest stories. Today, UNI serves more than 1000 subscribers in more than 100 locations in India and abroad. They include newspapers, radio and television networks, web sites, government offices and private and public sector corporations.

UNI's communication network stretches over 90,000 Km in India and the Gulf states. UNI hase bureax in all the major cities and towns of India, including all the state capitals. It has more than 325 staff journalists around the country and more than 250 stringers, covering news events from remote corners. UNI also have Correspondents in major world cities such as Washington, London, Dubai, Colombo, Kathmandu, Islamabad, Dhaka, Singapore, Sydney and Vancouver, bringing to our subscribers stories of interest to Indian readers..

UNI has collaboration agreements with several foreign news agencies, including Reuters and DPA , whose stories it distribute to media organisations in India. It lso have news exchange agreements with Xinhua of China, UNB of Bangladesh, Gulf News Agency of Bahrain, WAM of the United Arab Emirates, KUNA of Kuwait News Agency, ONA of Oman and QNA of Qatar.

UNI is currently a major modernisation programme as part of which most of our major bureax are already linked through a computerised network. We are continuously expanding and extending this network. We are also in the process of implementing a project to deliver news, pictures and graphics to our subscribers through the Internet, using NewsML, the international standard for news transmission.

UNI's wire service is available in three languages — English, Hindi and Urdu. We launched UNIVARTA in

Hindi in 1982 and pioneered a wire service in Urdu in 1992. In 1981, it became the first Indian news agency to serve subscribers abroad and earn foreign exchange for the country by selling its wire service directly to newspapers in the gulf States and in Singapore through satellite channels.

UNI has always adopted an innovative approach. It was the first news agency in the country to launch a Financial Service, a Stock Exchange service and a National Photoservice. UNI also has other services like UNIDARSHAN (Television News Clips and Features), UNISCAN (News Display on Television sets for Hotels, top Government officials and corporate clients), UNIDirect (for top executives in the government, corporate and other sectors) and UNI GRAPHICS (Computer-designed Graphics in ready-to-use form).

4
Radio, TV and Internet

Radio, TV and Internet are the modern means of mass communication. They have changed the way of our perception of reality breaking the long established tradition of understanding through the word of mouth or the written communication. These media broadcast information in a dominant way in the present day society.

Broadcasting started formally in the 1920s, with the widespread introduction of radio receivers, particularly in Europe and the United States. Besides broadcasting, point-to-point broadcasting, including telephone messages and relays of radio programs, became widespread in the 1920s and 1930s. Another use of radio in the pre-war years was the development of detecting and locating aircraft and ships by the use of radar. Today, radio takes many forms, including wireless networks, mobile communications of all types, as well as radio broadcasting.

In an effort to boost radio sales in peacetime, the Westinghouse Electric Corporation (now CBS Corporation) of Pittsburgh, Pennsylvania, established the first commercially owned radio station to offer a schedule of programming to the general public. The station received its license in October 1920 and began service from a studio inside a canvas tent built on the roof of a Westinghouse factory. Frank Conrad, a radio hobbyist and veteran engineer with experience in civilian and military radio research, ran the project. He aired various forms of entertainment, including recorded music generated by a phonograph placed before a microphone. There was no user fees to listeners and carried no paid advertisements;

instead, the station was financed by Westinghouse to encourage people to buy home radio receivers.

Another important early broadcaster was the American Telephone & Telegraph Company (AT&T Corp.). Barred from manufacturing radios by the terms of its telephone antitrust exemptions, AT&T explored the possibilities of what the company called toll broadcasting (charging fees in return for airing commercial advertisements on its stations). The first known instance of an advertiser paying for a broadcast commercial took place in 1922, when AT&T accepted a fee from the Queensboro Corporation to air a 12-minute pitch for the sale of cooperative apartments on WEAF, the company's New York City station. Fearing legal action by radio companies that might threaten its telephone franchises, however, AT&T sold its stations to RCA. In return for leaving the broadcasting business, AT&T was granted the exclusive right to provide the connections that would link local stations around the country to the NBC network.

The sale of radios more than justified the expense of operating broadcasting services for RCA, GE, Westinghouse, and other radio set manufacturers. According to estimates by the National Association of Broadcasters, in 1922 there were 60,000 households in the United States with radios; by 1929 the number had topped 10 million. But increases in sales of radio receivers could not continue forever. Broadcasters needed a new incentive to produce and transmit programs once the home radio market matured. The sale of advertising time loomed as a promising growth area.

In Britain, and in the many countries that followed its lead, broadcasting was developing in a different way. Radio owners paid yearly license fees to the government, which were turned over directly to an independent state enterprise, the British Broadcasting Corporation (BBC). The BBC in turn produced news and entertainment programming for its network of stations. The editorial and

artistic integrity of the BBC was to be insured by its funding mechanism, which was designed to isolate it from immediate political pressures.

In the United States, on the other hand, it was widely accepted that broadcasting was a commercial enterprise that should pay its own way without government aid or interference. However, there was some opposition to the development of broadcasting as a primarily commercial medium. Herbert Hoover, who as secretary of commerce was in charge of broadcast regulation, expressed his disapproval of commercialism at the 1922 Radio Conference in Washington, D.C. By the late 1920s, nonetheless, the direction of broadcasting as an industry, art, and technology in the United States had shifted decisively to mass distribution of popular culture funded by commercial advertising.

Noncommercial broadcasting would play only a minor role in the rise of broadcasting Universities saw radio as a natural tool for broadcasting educational programming to rural areas, and schools such as the University of Iowa, Ohio State University, and the University of Wisconsin established stations supported with funds set aside by state legislatures. There would not be a coast-to-coast noncommercial radio network in the United States until the formation of National Public Radio (NPR) in 1970.

By 1934 almost 600 radio stations were broadcasting to more than 20 million homes in the United States. The radio had emerged as a familiar household item, usually built into a substantial piece of wooden furniture placed in the family living room. It became the primary source for news and entertainment for much of the nation. Despite the Great Depression that affected the economy during the 1930s, American commercial radio broadcasting had grown to a $100-million industry by the middle of that decade.

RADIO IN WORLD WAR II

Radio broadcasting reached its height in global

influence and worldwide prestige during World War II (1939-1945), when it carried war news directly from the battlefront into the homes of millions of listeners. This conflict became, in many ways, a "radio war." American commentator Edward R. Murrow created a sensation with his eyewitness descriptions of street scenes in London during German bombing raids, delivering these accounts from the rooftop of the city's news bureau. American president had often used radio to bypass the press and directly address the American people with his so-called fireside chats during the Great Depression, and he continued to do so throughout the war. The radio speeches of German leader Adolf Hitler helped set the conditions for war and genocide in Europe, and the radio appeal from Japanese emperor Hirohito to his nation for unconditional surrender helped end World War II following the atomic bombings of Hiroshima and Nagasaki.

The National Broadcasting Company began regular broadcasting in 1922, with telephone links between New York and other Eastern cities. NBC became the dominant radio network, splitting into Red and Blue networks. The Columbia Broadcasting System began in 1927 under the guidance of William S. Paley. Several independent stations formed the Mutual Broadcasting System to exchange syndicated programming, including The Lone Ranger and Amos 'n' Andy.

A Federal Communnications Commission decision in 1939 required NBC to divest itself of its Blue Network. This Blue Network network became the American Broadcasting Company (ABC). Around 1946, ABC, NBC, and CBS began regular television broadcasts. Another TV network, the DuMont Television Network, was founded earlier, but was disbanded in 1956.

The first experimental broadcasts, from Marconi's factory in Chelmsford, began in 1920. Two years later, a consortium of radio manufacturers formed the British Broadcasting Company (BBC). This broadcast continued

till its licence expired at the end of 1926. The company then became the British Broadcasting Corporation, a non-commercial organisation. Its governors are appointed by the government but they did not answer to it.

Lord Reith took a formative role in developing the BBC, especially in radio. Working as its first manager and Director-General, he promoted the philosophy of public service broadcasting, firmly grounded in the moral benefits of education and of uplifting entertainment, eschewing commercial influence and maintaining a maximum of independence from political control.

Before the Nazi assumption of power in 1933, German radio broadcasting was supervised by the Post Office. A listening fee of 2 Reichsmarks per receiver paid most subsidies. Immediately following Hitler's assumption of power, Joseph Goebbels became head of the Ministry for Propaganda and Public Englightenment. Non-Nazis were removed from broadcasting and editorial positions. Jews were fired from all positions.

The Reichsrundfunk programming began to decline in popularity as the theme of Kampfzeit was continually played. Germany was easily served by a number of European mediumwave stations, including the BBC and domestic stations in France, the Low Countries, Denmark and Sweden, and Poland. It became illegal for Germans to listen to foreign broadcasts. (Foreign correspondents and key officials were exempt from this rule).

During the war, German stations broadcast not only war propaganda and entertainment for German forces dispersed through Europe and the Atlantic, but provided air raid alerts.Germany experimented with television broadcasting before the Second World War, using a 180-line raster system beginning before 1935. German propaganda claimed the system was superior to the British mechanical scanning system, but this was subject to debate by persons who saw the broadcasts.

Sri Lanka has the oldest radio station in South Asia The station was known as Radio Ceylon. It developed into one of the finest broadcasting institutions in the world. It is now known as the Sri Lanka Broadcasting Corporation. Sri Lanka created broadcasting history in South Asia when broadcasting was started in Ceylon by the Telegraph Department in 1923 on an experimental footing, just three years after the inauguration of broadcasting in Europe.

Gramophone music was broadcast from a tiny room in the Central Telegraph Office with the aid of a small transmitter built by the Telegraph Department engineers from the radio equipment of a captured German submarine. This broadcasting experiment was a huge success and barely three years later, on December 16, 1925, a regular broadcasting service came to be instituted.

Edward Harper launched the first experimental broadcast as well as founding the Ceylon Wireless Club together with British and Ceylonese radio enthusiasts. Edward Harper has been dubbed ' the Father of Broadcasting in Ceylon.'

THE 1950S AND 1960S

Television began to replace radio as the chief source of revenue for broadcasting networks. Although many radio programs continued through this decade, including Gunsmoke and The Guiding Light, by 1960 networks had ceased producing entertainment programs. As radio stopped producing formal fifteen-minute to hourly programs, a new format developed. "Top 40" was based on a continuous rotation of short pop songs presented by a "disc jockey." Famous disc jockeys in the era included Alan Freed, Dick Clark, Don Imus and Wolfman Jack. Top 40 playlists were theoretically based on record sales; however, record companies began to bribe disc jockeys to play selected artists, in what was called payola.

In the 1950s, American television networks introduced broadcasts in color. The Federal

Communications Commission approved the world's first monochrome-compatible color television standard in Dec., 1953. The first network colorcast followed on Jan. 1, 1954, with NBC transmitting the annual Tournament of Roses Parade in Pasadena, Calif. to over 20 stations across the country. An educational television network, PBS was founded.

Shortwave broadcasting played an important part of fighting the cold war with Voice of America and the BBC World Service augmented with Radio Free Europe and Radio Liberty transmitting through the "Iron Curtain", and Radio Moscow and others broadcasting back, as well as jamming (transmitting to cause intentional interference)the western voices.

Radio Luxembourg remained popular during the 1950s but saw its audience decline as commercial television and pirate radio, combined with a switch to a less clear frequency, began to erode its influence. BBC television resumed on June 7, 1946, and commercial television began on September 22, 1955. Both used the pre-war 405-line standard. BBC2 came on the air on April 20, 1964, using the 625-line standard, and began PAL colour transmissions on July 1, 1967, the first in Europe. The two older networks transmitted in 625-line colour from 1969.

During the 1960s there was still no UK-based commercial radio. A number of 'pirate' radio ships, located in international waters just outside the jurisdiction of English law, came on the air between 1964 and 1967. The most famous of these was Radio Caroline, which was the only station to continue broadcasting after the offshore pirates were effectively outlawed on August 14, 1967 by the Marine Broadcasting Offences Act. It was finally forced off air due to a dispute over tendering payments, but returned in 1972 and continued on and off until 1989. The station still broadcasts, nowadays using satellite carriers and internet.

When the Federal Republic of Germany was organized in 1949, its Enabling Act established strong state government powers. Broadcasting was organized on a state, rather than a national, basis. Nine regional radio networks were established.

The Allied forces in Europe developed their own radio networks, including the U.S. American Forces Network (AFN). Inside Berlin, Radio in the American Sector (RIAS) became a key source of news in the German Democratic Republic. Germany began developing a network of VHF FM broadcast stations in 1955 because of the excessive crowding of the mediumwave and shortwave broadcast bands.

Radio Ceylon ruled the airwaves in the 1950s and 1960s in the Indian sub-continent. The station developed into the most popular radio network in South Asia. Millions of listeners in India for example tuned into Radio Ceylon. Announcers like Livy Wijemanne, Vernon Corea, Pearl Ondaatje, Tim Horshington, Greg Roskowski, Jimmy Bharucha, Mil Sansoni, Eardley Peiris, Shirley Perera, Bob Harvie, Christopher Greet, Prosper Fernando, Ameen Sayani (of Binaca Geet Mala fame),Karunaratne Abeysekera, S.P.Mylvaganam (the first Tamil Announcer on the Commercial Service) were hugely popular across South Asia.

The Hindi Service also helped build Radio Ceylon's reputation as the market leader in the Indian sub-continent. Gopal Sharma, Sunil Dutt Ameen Sayani, Hamid Sayani, were among the Indian announcers of the station.

The Commercial Service of Radio Ceylon was hugely successful under the leadership of Clifford Dodd, the Australian administrator and broadcasting expert who was sent to Ceylon under the Colombo Plan. Dodd hand picked some of the most talented radio presenters in South Asia. They went on to enjoy star status in the Indian sub-continent. This was Radio Ceylon's golden era.

THE 1970S, 1980S, AND 1990S

The introduction of FM changed the listening habits of younger Americans. Many stations such as WNEW-FM in New York City began to play whole sides of record albums, as opposed to the "Top 40" model of two decades earlier. In the 1980s, the Federal Communications Commission, under Reagan Administration and Congressional pressure, changed the rules limiting the number of radio and television stations a business entity could own in one metropolitan area. This deregulation led to several groups, such as Infinity Broadcasting and Clear Channel to buy many stations in major cities. The cost of these stations' purchases led to a conservative approach to broadcasting, including limited playlists and avoiding controversial subjects to not offend listeners, and increased commercials to increase revenue.

Land-based commercial radio finally came on air in 1973 with London's LBC and Capital Radio. Channel 4 television started in November, 1982. Britain's UHF system was originally designed to carry only four networks. Pirate radio enjoyed another brief resurgence with a literal re-launch of Radio Caroline in 1983, and the arrival of American-owned Laser 558 in 1985. Both stations were harassed by the British authorities; Laser closed in 1987 and Caroline in 1989, since when it has pursued legal methods of broadcasting, such as temporary FM licences and satellite.

Two rival satellite television systems came on the air at the end of the 1980s: Sky Television and British Satellite Broadcasting. Huge losses forced a rapid merger, although in many respects it was a takeover of BSB (Britain's official, Government-sanctioned satellite company) by Sky. Radio Luxembourg launched a 24-hour English channel on satellite, but closed its AM service in 1989 and its satellite service in 1991. Channel 5 went on air onn March 30, 1997, using "spare" frequencies between the existing channels.

The Government of Sri Lanka opened up the market in the late 1970s and 1980s allowing private companies to set up radio and television stations. Sri Lanka's public services broadcasters are the Sri Lanka Broadcasting Corporation (SLBC), Independent Television Net Work (ITN) and the affiliated radio station called Lak-handa. They had stiff competition on their hands with the private sector.

Broadcasting in Sri Lanka went through a transformation resulting in private broadcasting institutions being set up on the. The 1990s saw a new generation of radio stations being established in Sri Lanka among them the 'Hiru' radio station. In the 2000s public service broadcasters like the Sri Lanka Broadcasting Corporation set up their own FM arm.

Sri Lanka celebrated 80 years of broadcasting in December 2005. In January 2007 the Sri Lanka Broadcasting Corporation will celebrate 40 years as a public corporation.

In 1987, stations in the European Broadcasting Union began offering Radio Data System (RDS), which provides written text information about programs that were being broadcast, as well as traffic alerts, accurate time, and other teletext services.

THE 2000S

The 2000s saw the introduction of digital radio and direct broadcasting by satellite (DBS) in the USA. Digital radio services, except in the United States, were allocated a new frequency band in the range of 1,400 MHz. In the United States, this band was deemed to be vital to national defence, so an alternate band in the range of 2,300 MHz was introduced for satellite broadcasting. Two American companies, XM and Sirius, introduced DBS systems, which are funded by direct subscription, as in cable television. The XM and Sirius systems provide approximately 100 channels each, in exchange for monthly payments.

In addition, a consortium of companies received FCC approval for In-Band On-Channel digital broadcasts in the United States, which use the existing mediumwave and FM bands to provide CD-quality sound. However, early IBOC tests showed interference problems with adjacent channels, which has slowed adoption of the system.

In Canada, the Canadian Radio-television and Telecommunications Commission plans to move all Canadian broadcasting to the digital band and close all mediumwave and FM stations. European and Australian stations have begun digital broadcasting (DAB). Digital radios began to be sold in the United Kingdom in 1998.

Regular Shortwave broadcasts using a digital broadcasting scheme for short and medium wave broadcasts have begun. This system makes the normally scratchy international broadcasts clear and nearly FM quality, and much lower transmitter power. This is much better to listen to and has more languages.

In Sri Lanka in 2005 when Sri Lanka celebrated 80 years in Broadcasting, the former Director-General of the Sri Lanka Broadcasting Corporation, Eric Fernando called for the station to take full advantage of the digital age - this included looking at the archives of Radio Ceylon.

THE INDIAN SCENARIO

All India Radio is one of the largest radio networks in the world and a division of Prasar Bharati (Broadcasting Corporation of India), an autonomous corporation of the Ministry of Information and Broadcasting, Government of India. It is the sister service of Prasar Bharati's Doordarshan, the national television broadcaster. The headquarters is at Akashwani Bhavan, on the Parliament Street next to the Indian parliament. Akashwani Bhavan houses the drama section, the FM section and the National service. The Doordarshan Kendra (Delhi) is also located on the 6th floor of Akashwani Bhavan.

Broadcasting house is an old building next to Akashwani Bhavan. The New Service Division of All India Radio under the Director General (New functions) from this building. Built during the British rule, it is a very popular location and easily recognised building in New Delhi.

Radio broadcasting began in India in 1927, with two privately-owned transmitters at Mumbai and Calcutta. These were nationalised in 1930 and operated under the name Indian Broadcasting Service until 1936, when it was renamed All India Radio.

AIR covers 99.37% of India's populace, the largest democracy in the world with over one billion inhabitants. AIR maintains approximately 200 broadcasting centres around the country and transmits in 24 different languages. In spite of recent penetration by other media such as Cable TV, AIR remains the most common means of gaining access to information and entertainment, as the radio receivers are relatively cheap and affordable.

When India became independent, the AIR network had only six Stations located at Delhi, Bombay, Calcutta, Madras, Lucknow and Tiruchirapalli with a total complement of 18 transmitters - six on the medium wave and the remaining on short wave. Radio listening on medium wave was confined to urban limits of these cities. As against a mere 2,75,000 receiving sets at the time of Independence, now there are about 111 million estimated radio sets in about 105 million household in the country.

AIR today has a network of 214 broadcasting centres with 143 medium frequency(MW), 54 high frequency (SW) and 139 FM transmitters. The coverage is 91.37% of the area , serving 99.13% of the people in the largest democracy of the world. AIR covers 24 Languages and 146 dialects in home services. In Externel services, it covers 27 languages; 17 national and 10 foreign languages.

OBJECTIVE OF ALL INDIA RADIO

Objective of All India Radio are to provide information, education and wholesome entertainment, keeping in view the motto, "Bahujan Hitaya; Bahujan Sukhaya" i.e. the benefit and happiness of large sections of the people, and strive to :

* Uphold the unity of the country and the democrative values enshrined in the Constitution;
* Present a fair and balanced flow of information of national, regional, local and international interest, including contrasting views, without advocating any opinion or ideology of its own.
* Promote the interests and concerns of the entire nation, being mindful of the need for harmony and understanding within the country and ensuring that the programmes reflect the varied elements which make up the composite culture of India.
* Produce and transit varied programmes designed to awaken, inform, enlighten, educate, entertain and enrich all sections of the people, with due regard to the fact that the national broadcast audience consists of a whole series of public.
* Produce and transmit programmes relating to developmental activities in all their facets including, extension work in Agriculture, Education, Health and Family Welfare , Science and Technology.
* Serve the rural, illiterate and underprivileged population, keeping in mind the special needs and interests of the young, social and cultural minorities, the tribal population, and of those residing in border regions, backward or remote areas.
* Promote social justice and combat exploitation, inequality, and such evils as untouchability and parochial loyalties.
* Promote national integration.

NEWS AND CURRENT AFFAIRS

The history of news broadcasting in India is far older than that of All India Radio.The first news bulletin was aired on 23 July 1927, from the privately owned radio station at Mumbai. It was only in August, 1937, that the news unit of AIR came into being, when the first news bulletin was broadcast from Delhi. By 1939 - 40, AIR was broadcasting 27 bulletins and the unit was known as Central News Organisation which was later called News Services Division (NSD). In 1943, an External Broadcast Unit was established under the Director of News. NSD is one of the premier broadcasting organisations in the world reaching more than 97% of the country's population.

Two high - tech studios of international standards, exclusively for news broadcasts were set up by NSD, AIR. From these studios, the phone - in voice - casts from AIR correspondents and experts are directly fed into the bulletins.

AIR news bulletins and news - based programmes lay great emphasis on the schemes announced for the welfare of the scheduled castes / scheduled tribes, minorities and the rural poor. AIR has launched a large number of programmes at national, regional and local levels to explain to the people the various benefits of the social welfare schemes and the means of availing themselves of the benefits of the schemes. Many stations have arranged programmes to educate the young entrepeneurs on the setting up of small scale industries, especially with the aid of the Prime Minister's Rozgar Yojana.

The External Services Division (ESD) of AIR, broadcasts programmes for about 70 hours daily in 24 languages (16 foreign including English and 8 Indian languages). The broadcasts adhere to a definite pattern, and generally consist of news bulletin, commentary on current events, and a review of the Indian press. Newsreels,

talks and discussions on socio - economic, political, historical, and cultural subjects, classical, folk and popular music of the different regions of the country form a major part of the total programme output. These broadcasts project the Indian viewpoint on world affairs, and acquaint listeners living abroad with the current changes and developments in the country's scenario, alongwith providing comprehensive information on India, as a whole. The major services are General Overseas Service, Urdu Service and Hindi Service. ESD transmitters directed to SAARC countries continue to carry 2100 hours bulletin in English, originally intended for Home Services.

NEWS-ON-PHONE SERVICE

All India Radio, after launching the news-on-phone service on 25th February 1998 from New Delhi, is running the service from Chennai, Mumbai, Hyderabad and Patna also. The service is accessible through STD, ISD and local telephone calls. The service is going to be started from 10 more cities — Ahmedabad, Banglore, Guwahati, Imphal, Jaipur, Kolkata, Lucknow, Raipur, Simla and Thiruvanthapuram shortly.

English and Hindi hourly news bulletins can be heard **live** on http://www.newsonair.com. The news in MP3 format can be directly played from the site. In the file name the hourly time of news is mentioned. Text of the English and Hindi bulletins can be read from http://www.newsonair.com/BulletinsInd.html.

AIR ON THE INTERNET

On 2 May 1996, All India Radio got connected on the information superhighway, by mounting an experimental on - line information service on the Internet. AIR daily news update, commentary on topics from current affairs and the significant highlights from the country's newspapers are fed regularly once a day in text mode. The system and home page design for this pilot service has been executed by the Research Department of AIR. The address

for the site is : http:/air.kode.net. This AIR service on the Net has received global appreciation and in the first ten days itself, over 7.5 lakh hits were reported. Most of the users are non - resident Indians and diplomats / officials all over the world. The experience and insightful feedback gathered from this experimental programme will be useful for setting up a regular information service of AIR on the Net.

TELEVISION

Television was started in the United States of America in 1920 on experimental basis. These experiments used a mechanical scanning method with the help of a disc that did not scan a picture rapidly. Picture tube, which was invented in 1923 brought some advantage in the method. By 1930 NBC had set up its TV station in New York. Simultaneously BBC started offering regular TV programmes.

The breakout of second World War reduced the speed of improvement in TV technology but by 1940s and early 1950s television had become a feature of life in the most developed countries.. In 1948, there were as many as 48 TV stations in the United States covering 23 cities through receiving sets which number about half a million. Within the next one decade the number jumped to 533 stations covering 55 million receivers. The other advanced countries mainly Canada, Germany and Japan did not leg behind in the new venture.

Radio's success spurred technology companies to make substantial investments in the research and development of a new form of audiovisual broadcasting called television, or TV. Unlike radio, television broadcasting did not go through a period of experimentation by amateurs. It was obvious to commercial broadcasters that enormous profits were to be made from such an invention as an advertising tool, and the dominant companies in communications technology raced to perfect it.

The invention of television was a lengthy, collaborative process. An early milestone was the successful transmission of an image in 1884 by German inventor Paul Nipkow. His mechanical system, known as the rotating or Nipkow disk, was further developed by Charles Francis Jenkins, who made a telecast of a short film to U.S. government officials in Washington, D.C., in 1925, and by Scottish scientist John Logie Baird, who broadcast a televised image in 1926 to an audience at the Royal Academy of Science in London. In 1928 Herbert Ives, an engineer working for AT&T, offered what was perhaps the most spectacular demonstration of mechanical television to that point, transmitting color images of a bouquet of roses and an American flag to two audiences simultaneously in New York City and Washington, D.C. However, the proven capability of the electronic tube system that had been developed for radio turned financial and scientific attention toward that technology and away from research on the rotating disk.

The earliest U.S. patent for an all-electronic television system was granted in 1927 to a young Philo T. Farnsworth, who transmitted a picture of a U.S. dollar sign using his so-called image dissector tube in the laboratories of the Philadelphia Storage Battery Company (Philco). Meanwhile, the three radio technology powerhouses—General Electric, Westinghouse, and RCA—were cooperating closely with each other. General Electric and Westinghouse owned substantial shares of RCA stock, and the companies shared a collection of radio patents valuable to the development of television. In 1930 they consolidated their television research efforts at an RCA facility in New Jersey under the direction of Russian immigrant scientist Vladimir Zworykin. Historians usually credit Farnsworth, Zworykin, or both with the invention of television.

News, weather, and sports reports are important to many television stations because these reports attract a large audience and account for a large proportion of

revenue. Many radio stations depend on up-to-the-minute news for a major share of their programming. Program production staff, such as producers and announcers, also work on the production of news programs.

Reporters gather information from various sources, analyze and prepare news stories, and present information on the air. Correspondents report on news occurring in U.S. and foreign cities in which they are stationed. Newswriters write and edit news stories from information collected by reporters. Newswriters may advance to positions as reporters or correspondents.

Broadcast news analysts, also known as news anchors, analyze, interpret, and broadcast news received from various sources. News anchors present news stories and introduce videotaped news or live transmissions from on-the-scene reporters. Newscasters at large stations may specialize in a particular field. Weathercasters, also called weather reporters, report current and forecasted weather conditions. They gather information from national satellite weather services, wire services, and local and regional weather bureaus. Some weathercasters are trained atmospheric scientists and can develop their own weather forecasts. Sportscasters, who are responsible for reporting sporting events, usually select, write, and deliver the sports news for each newscast.

NETWORK TV

Network television news was once the most trusted source of information. It also had a monopoly over pictures and television reporting from across the country and around the world. Network news in 2004 is an industry trying to find its place in the changed world of 21st-century journalism. It is also an industry on the brink of generational change, with the retirement of its most visible symbols, the current nightly network anchors, beginning with the stepping down of NBC's Tom Brokaw at NBC later this year.

A detailed look at the content of network news reveals that the evening newscasts are still network television's front page, and by traditional standards still home to its most serious journalism. Nearly 30 million people still watch the nightly news, and the programs remain profitable. But the trend line is ominous. Evening news ratings have dropped 59 per cent since their peak three decades ago. And the audience is aging - nearly 60 years old on average, while the average age of Americans is 35. The economics of evening newscasts is headed in a troubling direction.

The picture for network morning news is quite different. Its audience is stable and even grew in 2003. Morning news shows, which have half the audience of nightly news programs, also enjoy twice the revenue as their evening counterparts, according to available data. Yet the content in the morning is softer. People who get their news from morning programs know a very different world - one that is less global and more oriented around entertainment, celebrity and true crime - than those who get their news from newspapers or evening news.

What the networks believe they can afford to offer the public also has changed. Available numbers suggest that the news divisions have fewer correspondents and off-air journalists to produce the news than they once did, and fewer bureaus or listening posts here and abroad. Foreign bureaus have been cut by more than half. At the same time, the newsgathering technology has become more sophisticated, the editing capabilities and satellite reach more vast and instantaneous.

The net effect is the news at all three organizations tends to be focused on the major stories that have to be covered, leavened with features or sidebars routinely chosen for their appeal to targeted demographic groups. Privately, network veterans say the unexpected is less common. So is the original. There is more homogenization. Large portions of the domestic news agenda, such as the

environment, science, prisons and the poor, content analyses suggest, are often absent. Other topics of special interest to targeted demographic groups, such as healthcare, retirement and financial markets, are emphasized.

The journalists at the networks still address a mass audience that surpasses any other medium. They still possess an institutional memory for news delivery that rivals journalists elsewhere. However, the decline of the television networks as a medium means that these advantages of scale and history are dwindling year after year, although they have not yet been dissipated.

Most likely the future will be determined by the degree to which the news divisions' owners have the imagination and the will to create new business models that employ both traditional and emerging technologies, target both old and new audiences, expand to more channels of transmission and generate new revenue streams.

CABLE TV

The convenience of 24-hour cable TV news, offering the latest breaking headlines at any time of the day or night, represents an enormous structural advantage for cable over network television. Cable has become the television news medium of choice. The network most cited as the No. 1 source for news remains CNN, preferred over the broadcast networks and even its cable rivals.

Cable television's audiences are not as large or as constant as its boosters depict. The growth of its core audience reached a peak. Increasingly, anchors or even control room managers - but not correspondents -are the primary figures in cable..

One of the most deeply held notions that journalists are taught, that they are telling stories, does not strictly apply to cable news. Instead, viewers often see newsgathering in the raw: live interviewing illustrated by

unedited videotape, extemporaneous reporting with little time to write or consult sources. The traditional staple of television news, the produced, written, edited and taped package, has been sidelined. What was once the raw ingredient of journalism is now the product. Hour after hour, across all parts of the day, cable television news features constant repetition, a narrow news agenda, an obsession with headlines, scanty sourcing and little autonomy for correspondents in the field.

Many ideas about cable's audience may also defy conventional wisdom. Contrary to press reports, the cable audience appears to have flattened since 2002. It is not growing. The medium kept none of the viewers it gained during the 2003 war in Iraq, and now that Fox and MSNBC are carried on most systems, continued growth may be harder to come by. As of early 2004, roughly 2.2 million viewers typically watched the three cable news networks every day in prime time, about the same number as in early 2002.

One question is what will happen down the road when television and the Internet begin to merge with the expansion of broadband technology. At that point, cable, broadcast and the Web will more closely begin to compete for the same audience. The convenience of getting television news on demand will become less of an advantage for cable alone. Will differences in content play a bigger role in determining audience preference? Even now, when cable networks and broadcast news go head-to-head - during the first day or two of a breaking news event, or even during the morning news hour - the traditional networks remain the preferred medium.

The technology is not yet there. Television news is still something viewers watch mainly in a passive way. Yet when the technology changes and the media converge, the advantage may depend more on which media and which outlet have the strongest news gathering and storytelling abilities.

LOCAL TV

Viewership of local news has begun to decline, much as it did years earlier in network news. Since 1997, the share of available viewers commanded by local early evening newscasts around the country has dropped 18 percent. The share commanded by late news, which is broadcast after prime time is over, has dropped 16 percent.

The decline in viewership, in turn, is furthering straining the flow of revenue. To pick up the slack, newsrooms are being asked to do more with less, expanding the number of hours of news they produce, often with the same or even lower budgets. According to one survey, the average workload demanded of reporters increased from 1.5 stories a day in 1998 to 1.8 in 2002, an increase of 20 percent.

Commercial and academic surveys suggest at least a portion of the viewers who have stopped watching local television news have done so because they find it repetitive, formulaic, sensationalized or insipid. Brand loyalty is weakening and more viewers, research suggests, are likely to sample stations and churn through them. Other surveys have found that 30 percent of the public is generally convinced that what they see on local television news is improperly influenced by powerful outsiders like advertisers and the political elite.

While technology advances are opening up new possibilities for producing the news, the cost of these advances is also a burden. Stations have to convert to digital technology and build Web sites, and much of that investment is coming at the expense of expanding newsrooms.

These are all the challenges, but there are also numerous reasons for local news professionals to be confident. The decline in viewership is not as steep as in network news. The audience for local television news is still relatively large. Local news remains an enormously

profitable business, still able to draw big audiences and still able to amass huge advertising revenues.

It is still a healthier business than most and is considered, at least for now, much better off than network news. This is one of the major motives behind big networks' current push for deregulation. They want the ability to own more local stations. Advertisers still rely on local television and the authority that the public ascribes to it to sell their products. Local advertisers still often demand that their commercials air during news programs and political campaigns still work to ensure that their ads appear during or around newscasts.

These changes do not seem to have had much effect on how people perceive local television news. The public trusts the local news, although it is ambivalent about certain practices, and relies on it for information. In a 2002 survey, 65% rated local TV news a 3 or a 4 on a four-point scale of believability, about the same as network news and cable, and ahead of newspapers.[6] Local television stations also engage in a number of community service activities that enhance their profile and their reputation, and provide commercial time free of charge for charitable organizations. On-air reporters often participate in various volunteer initiatives and serve as de facto "ambassadors" for their stations. News, weather and sports anchors remain, in many ways, the public faces of their community.

The question for the future of local television news is which way it turns. The biggest threat it faces now is the paradox of an undernourished product that is in oversupply. The market is saturated with news shows. In trying to differentiate one product from another, stations have tended to emphasize branding over content.

The issue is whether the industry, before it reaches the dangerous level of audience decline that has befallen network news, decides to invest in its product to reach out to new audiences, or decides it is a mature industry that should focus on efficiency and profit instead.

Local television became prevalent in the late 1940s and early 50s. Originally, there were only a few stations in large cities that offered a few local shows mixed in with network programming provided by broadcasting companies based in New York. Over time, the relationship was formalized into a system of O&O and affiliate stations. O&O stations are those owned and operated by networks, while affiliate stations are owned by non-network companies but have a contractual agreement to air the programming of a network.

THE INDIAN SCENARIO

In fact, television in India was started as an educational project of UNESCO. Its distinct advantage is the vastness of the geographical area it covers by the telecast. The main disadvantage was the enormous expenditure which has now been reduced considerable with the introduction of the new communication technology. It is a tool for visualization of the events and a visual demonstration of rare and complex materials improve presentation of aspects of physical sciences, medicine, geography and the elements of drama and history.

According to the Ministry of Information and Broadcasting, the following are the objectives of public television in India;

(a) To ac as a catalyst for social change

(b) To promote national integration

(c) To stimulate a scientific temper among the people

(d) To disseminate the message of family planning as a means of population control

(e) To stimulate greater agriculture production by providing essential information and knowledge,

(f) To promote and help preservation of environmental and ecological balance

(g) To highlight the need of social welfare measures

including welfare of women, children and the less privileged

(h) To promote interest in games and sports

(i) To stimulate appreciation of our artistic and cultural heritage.

In the advanced countries, educational television has been developed well. Many institutions offering education with the audiovisual modes have come into existence. The British Open University make wide use of TV-time to beam its various faculty programs. The United States' public television programmes for schools serve teachers and students in the classroom and at home besides National University Consortium consisting of several colleges.

Television promotes the goal of social equality in education catering to the masses of rural background and those living in slums of urban areas. Television increases the effectiveness of instruction and cuts down dropout rates. Television programmes are well planned and better presented than the usual classroom instruction. The students learn from television with their own efforts. They need minimum help from the teacher in case television is pressed into service.

Rapid and continuing change in curricula and instructional methods are made possible through educational television. Courses can be constantly modified not only to update them but to incorporate the constantly changing needs of the society and the expansion of knowledge. This is not possible with some of the advanced electronic media like the videodisk.

The regular daily transmission started in 1965 as a part of All India Radio. The television service was extended to a second city – Mumbai (then Bombay) only in 1972. Till 1975, only seven cities were covered by Doordarshan and it remained the only television channel in India. Television services were separated from radio in 1976. Each office of All India Radio and Doordarshan were placed

under the management of two different Director Generals in New Delhi. Finally Doordarshan as a National Broadcaster came into existence.

National programme was introduced in 1982. In the same year colour TVs were introduced in Indian markets with the Live telecast of the Independence day on 15th August, 1982, followed by the Asian Games being held in Delhi. The eighties were era of Doordarshan with soaps like Hum Log (1984), Buniyaad and mythological dramas like Ramayana (1987-88) and Mahabharat (1988-89) glued millions to Doordarshan. Other popular programmes included Hindi film songs based Chitrahaar and Rangoli and crime thrillers like Karamchand (starring Pankaj Kapoor) and Byomkesh Bakshi.

Now more than 90 percent of Indian population can receive Doordarshan (DD1) programmes through a network of nearly 1400 terrestrial transmitters. About 46 Doordarshan Studios are producing TV software. Presently, Doordarshan operates 19 channels – two All India channels, 11 Regional Languages Satellite Channels (RLSC), four State Networks (SN), an International channel, a Sports Channel and two channels (DD-RS & DD-LS) for live broadcast of parliamentary proceedings.

On DD-1 National programmes, Regional programmes and Local Programmes are carried on time-sharing basis. DD-News channel, launched on 3rd November, 2003, which replaced the DD-Metro Entertainment channel, provides 24-Hour news service. The Regional Languages Satellite channels have two components The Regional service for the particular state relayed by all terrestrial transmitters in the state and additional programmes in the Regional Language in prime time and non-prime time available only through cable operators. Sports Channel is exclusively devoted to the broadcasting of sporting events of national and international importance.

The advent of cable channels and private players has eroded popularity of Doordarshan in recent years. Doordarshan has also been criticised by some, as state media and hence not completly free. The news is often accused of having the ruling party's biased point of view. The coverage of sports and other events often put it at the bottom of the pile. The content is often drab and presentation is monotonous at best. Moreover despite getting huge advertising revenues backed by government funding, the Prasar Bharati posts massive losses each year.

In India, television has come to the forefront only in the past 21 years and more so in the past 13. There were initially two ignition points: the first in the eighties when colour TV was introduced by state-owned broadcaster Doordarshan (DD) timed with the 1982 Asian Games which India hosted. It then proceeded to install transmitters nationwide rapidly for terrestrial broadcasting. In this period no private enterprise was allowed to set up TV stations or to transmit TV signals.

The second spark came in the early nineties with the broadcast of satellite TV by foreign programmers like CNN followed by Star TV and a little later by domestic channels such as Zee TV and Sun TV into Indian homes. Prior to this, Indian viewers had to make do with DD's chosen fare which was dull, non-commercial in nature, directed towardsonly education and socio-economic development. Entertainment programmes were few and far between. And when the solitary few soaps like Hum Log (1984), and mythological dramas: Ramayan (1987-88) and Mahabharat (1988-89) were televised, millions of viewers stayed glued to their sets

When, urban Indians learnt that it was possible to watch the Gulf War on television, they rushed out and bought dishes for their homes. Others turned entrepreneurs and started offering the signal to their neighbours by flinging cable over treetops and verandahs. From the large metros satellite TV delivered via cable

moved into smaller towns, spurring the purchase of TV sets and even the upgradation from black & white to colour TVs.

DD responded to this satellite TV invasion by launching an entertainment and commercially driven channel and introduced entertainment programming on its terrestrial network. This again fuelled the purchase of sets in the hinterlands where cable TV was not available. The initial success of the channels had a snowball effect: more foreign programmers and Indian entrepreneurs flagged off their own versions. From two channels prior to 1991, Indian viewers were exposed to more than 50 channels by 1996. Software producers emerged to cater to the programming boom almost overnight. Some talent came from the film industry, some from advertising and some from journalism.

More and more people set up networks until there was a time in 1995-96 when an estimated 60,000 cable operators were existing in the country. Some of them had subscriber bases as low as 50 to as high as in the thousands. Most of the networks could relay just 6 to 14 channels as higher channel relaying capacity required heavy investments, which cable operators were loathe to make. American and European cable networks evinced interest, as well as large Indian business groups, who set up sophisticated headends capable of delivering more than 30 channels. These multi-system operators (MSOs) started buying up local networks or franchising cable TV feeds to the smaller operators for a fee. This phenomenon led to resistance from smaller cable operators who joined forces and started functioning as MSOs. The net outcome was that the number of cable operators in the country has fallen to 30,000.

The rash of players who rushed to set up satellite channels discovered that advertising revenue was not large enough to support them. This led to a shakeout. At least half a dozen either folded up or aborted the high-flying

plans they had drawn up, and started operating in a restricted manner. Some of them converted their channels into basic subscription services charging cable operators a carriage fee.

The government started taxing cable operators in a bid to generate revenue. The rates varied in the 26 states that go to form India and ranged from 35 per cent upwards. The authorities moved in to regulate the business and a Cable TV Act was passed in 1995. The apex court in the country, the Supreme Court, passed a judgement that the air waves are not the property of the Indian government and any Indian citizen wanting to use them should be allowed to do so. The government reacted by making efforts to get some regulation in place by setting up committees to suggest what the broadcasting law of India should be, as the sector was still being governed by laws which were passed in 19th century India. A broadcasting bill was drawn up in 1997 and introduced in parliament. But it was not passed into an Act. State-owned telecaster Doordarshan and radiocaster All India Radio were brought under a holding company called the Prasar Bharati under an act that had been gathering dust for seven years, the Prasar Bharati Act, 1990. The Act served to give autonomy to the broadcasters as their management was left to a supervisory board consisting of retired professionals and bureaucrats.

A committee headed by a senior Congress (I) politician Sharad Pawar and consisting of other politicians and industrialist was set up to review the contents of the Broadcasting Bill. It held discussions with industry, politicians, and consumers and a report was even drawn up. But the United Front government fell and since then the report and the Bill have been consigned to the dustbin. But before that it issued a ban on the sale of Ku-band dishes and on digital direct-to-home Ku-band broadcasting, which the Rupert Murdoch-owned News Television was threatening to start in India. ISkyB, the Murdoch DTH

venture, has since been wallowing in quicksand and in recent times has even shed a lot of employees. But News Corp has been running a C-band DTH venture in the country which has around 20,000 subscribers.

Doordarshan as a public broadcaster has been successfully discharging its special responsibility to give balanced and unbiased news without sensationalizing as well as by carrying different shades of opinion. Considering the perceived need for a dedicated news channel on Doordarshan's platform and building on its twin advantage, viz., viewers loyalty to DD's in-house news bulletins and the greater revenue potential on account of DD-Metro's terrestrial reach, the Prasar Bharati Board approved the proposal to start a 24-hours news channel in place of DD-Metro. This was subsequently approved by the Union Cabinet in its meeting held on 3 October 2003. Consequent to these decisions, DD-News channel was launched on 3 November 2003 by converting DD-Metro into a 24-hours news channel. Its terrestrial reach is 21.6% by area and 44.9% by population of the country.

DOORDARSHAN NEWS

Doordarshan News quickly gained popularity among the viewers, exceeding its commercial revenue target of Rs. 2 crores, for 2003-04, and the channel earned Rs. 10 crores. The popularity of the channel amongst advertisers continues unabated and the revenue figures for the current year (04-05) have already crossed Rs. 10 crores. The foremost benefit that has accrued to Doordarshan as a result of the launch of the DD News channel is the reactivation of a large volume of quality in-house production. This was achieved through a higher utilization of the in-house infrastructure than hitherto achieved.

In addition to the round the clock telecast of Hindi/ English News on DD- News channel, news bulletins in Hindi/ English are also telecast twice a day on the National Network of DD-1. Regional News Bulletins in different

regional languages are also being telecast in the Regional transmissions of DD-1 from 22 Doordarshan Kendras. Regional News Bulletins are also being telecast in various regional language satellite services channels of Doordarshan.

THE INTERNET

A mere fifteen years ago, hardly any one knew that the Internet existed. Since then, its growth has been astonishing in various aspects. Now, it is hard to decide what to include in estimating its size and measure the growth of the Internet as it is a loose collection of networks. However, because no single entity is in control, nobody knows everything about the Internet. Measuring it is especially hard because some parts choose to limit access to themselves to various degrees.

In the given circumstances however, we have various methods of surveying and estimating the size of the Internet. There are widely differing estimates for the growth rate of the Internet. Over the years, the growth rate of the Internet has not been stable with more rapid growth surfacing in some years compared to others, but a decline has never taken place. A surprising statistic is that a large majority of the Internet growth is due to men. Approximately 70% of the users of the internet are men and 30% women world wide. This is partially due to the dominance of men in the workforce, and the fact that half of Internet users are professional and technically related.

Traffic and the capacity of the public Internet grew at rates of about 100% per year in the early 1990's. A brief period of explosive growth was experienced in 1995 and 1996 with traffic growing at a rate of 1,000% per year, but starting in 1997, traffic slowed back down to the 100% per year rate. If the number of people using the Internet were to keep doubling every year, then by mid year 2005, 100 percent (6,005,829,368) of the world's population would be using the Internet. The number of unique indexable Web

pages has grown from 1 billion in January 2000 to more than 2 billion in June 2000. The number of people who use the Internet on a regular basis has dramatically increased from fewer than 90,000 in 1993 to more than 304 million in 2000. Overall, the online access market showed a sluggish growth of barely one percent, growing from about 68.6 million users at the start of 2001 to 69.3 million by the close of the year according to TR's Online Census report. When compared to a 52 percent growth rate for 2000, the growth was very stale.

Recent studies show that home Internet users account for almost one eighth of the world's population and there is still significant growth potential for Internet access. Analyst estimate that 24 million people used the Internet for the first time in the fourth quarter of 2001, which is an increase from the 15 million who went online in the third quarter. The fastest Internet growing countries are: 1)India, 2)Indonesia, 3)Mexico, 4)Portugal, 5)Slovakia, 6)Romania, 7)Ukraine, 8)Brazil, 9)Estonia, and 10)Soviet. The fastest growing Internet countries are mainly the countries that are just getting the Internet established and realizing its benefits. Countries like the United States where the Internet is already widespread has a smaller growth potential. If traffic on the Internet continues to double each year, data should exceed voice on U.S. long distance networks around the end of 2002.

Once broadband technologies such as cable modems, various DSL technologies, or wireless data links are deployed, residential customers will be able to substantially increase their traffic per house-hold. In the very near future, though, rapid growth is most likely to come from institutions such as corporations, which have the broadband communication infrastructure to increase increased traffic. Costs of providing local access at high speeds from corporate WANs are dropping rapidly with the deployment of HDSL (although that is not reflected in prices yet), and fiber will be increasingly feasible for higher

speeds. Even without novel applications, such as packet telephony and videoconferencing, ordinary Intranet and Extranet applications could lead to continued growth at historic rates. We could also see spurts of growth even faster than 100% per year if some of the novel applications start growing. The public Internet could also grow at high rates if more of the growth in internal private line networks shifts to it.

Apart from the complex physical connections that make up its infrastructure, the Internet is held together by bi- or multi-lateral commercial contracts (for example peering agreements) and by technical specifications or protocols that describe how to exchange data over the network. Indeed, the Internet is essentially defined by its interconnections and routing policies. In an often-cited, if perhaps gratuitously mathematical definition, Seth Breidbart once described the Internet as "the largest equivalence class in the reflexive, transitive, symmetric closure of the relationship 'can be reached by an IP packet from".

Unlike older communications systems, the Internet protocol suite was deliberately designed to be independent of the underlying physical medium. Any communications network, wired or wireless, that can carry two-way digital data can carry Internet traffic. Thus, Internet packets flow through wired networks like copper wire, coaxial cable, and fiber optic; and through wireless networks like Wi-Fi. Together, all these networks, sharing the same high-level protocols, form the Internet.

Some of the popular services on the Internet that make use of these protocols are e-mail, Usenet newsgroups, file sharing, Instant Messenger, the World Wide Web, Gopher, session access, WAIS, finger, IRC, MUDs, and MUSHs. Of these, e-mail and the World Wide Web are clearly the most used, and many other services are built upon them, such as mailing lists and blogs. The Internet

makes it possible to provide real-time services such as Internet radio and webcasts that can be accessed from anywhere in the world.

Some other popular services of the Internet were not created this way, but were originally based on proprietary systems. These include IRC, ICQ, AIM, and Gnutella. There have been many analyses of the Internet and its structure. For example, it has been determined that the Internet IP routing structure and hypertext links of the World Wide Web are examples of scale-free networks. These in turn are built around relatively smaller networks. See also the list of academic computer network organizations. In network schematic diagrams, the Internet is often represented by a cloud symbol, into and out of which network communications can pass.

Although the economics are still evolving, the Internet has now become a major source of news in America. In September 2003, over half of the people in the United States - 150 million - went online, a record for Web use.[1] And half to two-thirds of those who go online use it at least some of the time to get news.

Whether the new medium is replacing the old, however, at this point is less clear. Although some people report getting news online at the expense of getting it from magazines and newspapers, the majority of online news consumers say they spend as much time with print as they did before. Television news, research shows, may be more affected.[2]

The Internet is the medium having the most success attracting young people to news, something that the older media were having trouble with before the Internet even existed.

Economically, producers of Web news are still trying to translate the rising number of people who get news online into the kind of profits to which traditional news media companies are accustomed. Journalism has

traditionally been a slow-growth industry (CNN, for instance, took ten years to turn a profit). The Internet seems no different. Some of the biggest news Web sites are not yet breaking even. And the revenues that media companies do get from their Web activities, while rising, account for only a small fraction of their overall revenue. Gannett makes more revenue from its newspaper division in a week than its online division makes in an entire year.

Still, online advertising revenues are growing at a much quicker pace than those in the traditional media. The Web has also continued to gain prominence with consumers, as evidenced by the $12.2 billion spent online between Thanksgiving and Christmas in 2003, an increase of 42 percent over 2002.

The Web has produced a new breed of online competitors vying for local advertising dollars, especially classified. Their chief rival, the newspaper industry, has kept these new competitors at bay for now, but the battle is far from over.

In the meantime, a handful of giant media companies have come to dominate Web news, at least for the moment. Time Warner, the largest of them, controls two of the top four news sites. Nearly 69 percent of the most popular news Web sites are owned by one of the 20 biggest media companies. There are also a myriad of local Internet news sites, whose goals are not to compete for the nationwide audience but rather to appeal to the local community. Their popularity is harder to track.

The Web is the only part of the mainstream news business that generally is seeing audiences grow, especially among the young. People like the convenience of the Web, its availability at work, its speed for delivering breaking news, and increasingly they are coming to trust the accuracy of the information they receive there. The problem is an economic one. How will Web journalism begin to pay its own way? If people increasingly substitute the Web for

their old media before a robust economic model for the Web evolves, the economic effect could be devastating for journalism. Companies might begin to cut back significantly on their newsgathering abilities, as audiences abandon profitable old platforms in favor of less profitable new ones. The net in this case might weaken, not strengthen, the economic vitality of news organizations and the quality of American journalism.

INTERNET IN INDIA

Internet is growing fast in India. There were 50,600,000 Internet users in India (representing 4.5% of the population) in December 2005, Internet World Stats. (Internet World Stats, December 2005). 50.6 million Internet users were estimated in India at the end of 2005, according to eTForecasts. This represented 4.7% of the total number of internet users worldwide. The number was up from 36.97 million in 2004. (eTForecasts, January 2006).

The Indian Internet population is currently over 25 million and is expected to grow to 100 million by 2007, according to the Internet & Online Association of India (IOAI. Even with millions of Web users in its cities, the Internet penetration rate for India remains well below 5%. Despite India's tech outsourcing power, the country's Internet penetration rate is low, and the greatest growth in usage is in increased time online by established users with 80% of Web users in India have been online for more than 3 years, while user growth was only 8% in the past year.

JuxtConsult, a research firm based in New Delhi, surveyed urban Internet users in April 2005, talking to 30,000 Indian Web users about their lifestyle and their Web use. There are about 17.5 million urban dwellers in India who use the Internet consistently, with an additional 5.2 million who use it occasionally.

Though they may still be relatively few in number, these users are dedicated to the Net. Most access the Web

frequently, with less than 20% surfing the Web less than once a day. Almost 40% use the Net over 5 times a day, and an additional 23% use it 2 to 5 times a day. Usage is heavy as well, with about one-third of urban Indian Web users online more than 3 hours every day, and about one-third of those users on throughout the day.

The combined 22.7 million users make up only 9% of all urban Indians. Since Internet usage is negligible in the countryside, the penetration rate for the entire country comes out to just 2%. This is in line with eMarketer's estimates of 21.3 million Internet users in India for 2004, representing 2% of the population. India falls behind many other major nations when it comes to Internet penetration (though eMarketer expects growth of greater than 20% through 2008).

Over 50% of Web users in Indian metropolitan areas are between the ages of 19 and 30, with an additional 22% between 31 and 40. According to Ipsos-Insight's "The Face of the Web 2003 Study", there were an estimated 3 million Internet users in URBAN India in 2003, representing approximately 19% of the adult population. The findings are based on interviews in thirteen key global markets with more than 7,100 adults, including 3,250 active Internet users.

THE USENET

The Usenet is widely known as Internet News, Net News or just News. It has its origins in the Unix programming community in the United States around 1980. The Usenet, which stands for Unix Users Network, was originally set up as a convenient on-line forum for the discussion of Unix-related issues between a small number of institutions and individuals. It proved to be quite popular and the newsreader software, which was available for free, quickly spread from institution to institution as more people got interested in participating in the discussions.

Very soon discussions of noncomputer topics sprang

up as people discovered a convenient and inexpensive way to have conversations with people of similar interests all over the world. There was an explosion in the number and character of newsgroups, and there are now well over 15,000 worldwide, although not all sites will carry all newsgroups.

Some sites will not carry a particular newsgroup for reasons of policy, politics or moral stance. Others will not carry certain newsgroups which are commercial enterprises and therefore charge the service provider a fee for use. Still other newsgroups are entirely local to a site, and may be used for class discussions, administrative forums or just internal noticeboards.

At first news postings were disseminated on a dial-up basis; one institution with newsreader software would call another institution with newsreader software and they would exchange all non-duplicate news postings on their systems. This process would be repeated again and again, until the messages had been spread to all the institutions which supported a particular newsgroup.

Assuring distribution of messages to all relevant sites often took several days, and responses to posting took a similar time to get back to the original poster. Eventually the system migrated to the Internet and response time became a matter of minutes or hours rather than days.

Now the Usenet which was once dominated by technical discussion, as were so many early computing arenas, is host to millions of nontechnical users. In many cases newsgroups have a core of regular posters who have formed an on-line community and will defend it vigorously if they see it as threatened by outsiders, be they legislators or disrespectful posters. The Usenet is full of people who are discussing mutual interests, hobbies, careers, swapping recipes - you name it, there's probably a newsgroup on the Usenet somewhere. And the beauty is, if there isn't, you can lobby to create one.

Apart from Newsnet, there are many other means provising the news through the Internet. The most widely known among them are the Yahoo and Goole services providing the updated news to the audiences all over the world. Nowadays about all newspapers are simultaneously published through the Internet and they provide easier facility for consultation. Moreover, the live coverage of happennings is also available worldwide through the Internet.

Google News is an automated news aggregator provided by Google Inc. The Google News website was introduced as a beta release in April 2002. The service came out of beta on 23 January 2006. There are different versions of the aggregator for more than 20 languages, with more added all the time.

To quell any charges of reporting bias, the service is fully automated with no human editors. However, the sources included are determined by human review, and their selection has come up for criticism. In March 2005 attention was called to Google's inclusion of the white supremacist National Vanguard magazine, and the resulting controversy forced Google to remove that site from the service. In another case, Google was criticized for not including sources which are censored in China. In the official Google Blog on 9/27/2004, the Google Team wrote: "For users inside the People's Republic of China, we have chosen not to include sources that are inaccessible from within that country."

The service covers the news articles that appeared within the past 30 days on news websites in the language concerned, from various countries; for the English language it covers about 4,500 sites, for other languages less. It provides around the first 200 characters and links to the full article. Some of these websites require a subscription; in that case this is noted in the Google News summary of their articles.

In March 2005, Agence France Presse (AFP) sued Google for $17.5 million, alleging that Google News infringed on its copyright because "Google includes AFP's photos, stories and news headlines on Google News without permission from Agence France Presse."[1] [2] It was also alleged that Google ignored a cease and desist order, though Google counters that it has opt-out procedures which AFP could have followed but did not. Google has since ceased aggregating AFP's stories.

Google News provides searching, and the choice of sorting the results by date and time of publishing (not to be confused with date and time of the news' happening) or grouping them (and also grouping without searching). In the English versions, there are options to tailor the grouping to a selected national audience.

Users can request e-mail "alerts" on various keyword topics by subscribing to Google News Alerts. E-mails are sent to subscribers whenever news articles matching their requests come online. Alerts are also available via RSS and Atom feeds.

Users can customize the displayed sections, their location on the page, and how many stories are visible with a JavaScript-based drag and drop interface. Stories from different editions of Google News can be combined to form one personalized page, with the options stored in a cookie. The service has been integrated with Google Search History since November 2005. Upon it's graduation from beta, a section was added that displays recommended news based on the user's Google News search history and the articles the user has clicked on (if the user has signed up for Search History).

5
Media in Libraries

Historically, the library has been the home of books. The introduction of photographs, audiotape, videotape, DVD, and other materials have expanded our thinking about the things that are housed in libraries. No longer is information confined to shelves in a building. The walls of the library are becoming transparent as we see the library as a place where both local and remote collections of information can be accessed. The role of the physical library is changing as it becomes a "think-tank" for the general public where information and ideas can be shared face-to-face or through technology. Some libraries are viewing their patrons as collaborators who share in the evolution of the collection by providing suggestions or making contributions in the form of historical photographs, works of poetry, artwork, and other information and resources.

When printed books for the masses became common people felt that they would lead to idle workers and destroy memory. Live storytellers were much more interesting and dynamic than static books. The same has been said of audio and video technology. For decades people have debated the threat of television and technology to thinking and learning.

It seems that all new ideas take time to find their place. Harry Potter books have motivated many children to read, but they also have led kids and their parents to watch the movies too. There does not seem to be a corresponding reduction of interest in media technology as people continue to buy and discuss their books online.

EMERGENCE OF MEDIA LIBRARIES

Media started accumulating in libraries as a distinct form just over 100 years old, not much younger than sound and moving image recording technologies themselves. Over the course of the past eight decades, the profession has witnessed and dealt with a steady and often bewildering progression of new media forms and formats, as well as a rapidly expanding content universe. The impact of these media, particularly film, video, and television, on almost every aspect of world culture and life has been inestimable. Media collections and services in libraries, as well as the practice of media librarianship, have also continued to evolve at a rapid pace. With this evolution have come changing perceptions of the field, changing expectations, new roles, and new demands.

The place of media collections has historically been a precarious one in libraries of all types. The persistent biases against "non-print media" in libraries have been abundantly documented, described, and debated in the professional literature over the past 50 years. The "books vs. audiovisual controversy was a particularly hot-button issue in the 1970s and 1980s, a period which saw the advent of home videorecording technology and a boom in both home and institutional media use. While the general public and institutional enthusiasm for both old formats, such as video, and new digital media technologies, such as DVDs and web-based media, may have softened some of these biases, media librarianship and media collections are still seldom on solid footing in libraries. The frequently minimal support for media collections in libraries, and the marginal role and limited physical space often assigned to these operations, is an eloquent testimony of this fact.

Given the historical and continuing biases and misconceptions mentioned above, it is not surprising that training for media librarianship has been rare and inconsistent over the course of the 20th century. What is

surprising is the persistence of this gap in professional training despite the central social and cultural role that film, video, and television have come to occupy in contemporary life. When media matters are included in library school curricula, they are increasingly approached from a systems and technology angle rather than from a content or user angle. With the rapid development of digital media and ongoing changes in information technologies over the last several decades, media literacy has become of paramount importance in libraries. Yet, approaches to teaching critical literacy and other skills related to media librarianship are something most media librarians learn on the job and not in the classroom, nor in professional development courses.

Media librarianship today is at a crossroads, just as media technologies and media content are at a crossroads. As a way of providing a framework for looking toward the future of the profession, the following discussion will look at the birth and evolution of media librarianship in the United States. The inclusion of media materials in libraries began at the end of the 19th century and the beginning of the 20th century with the development of academic slide libraries, motion picture and music libraries, and phonorecord collections in public libraries. Melvil Dewey laid the visionary groundwork for later pioneers by stating in 1906 that 'library' has lost its etymologic meaning and means not a collection of books, but the central agency for disseminating information, innocent recreation, or, best of all, inspiration among the people. Whenever this can be done better, more quickly, or cheaply by a picture than a book, the picture is entitled to a place on the shelves and in the catalog" (quoted in Loucks-DiMatteo, 1985, p. 76).

In 1914, the first instructional film library was established in a city school system – the Chicago Bureau of Visual Instruction. In 1916, the University of California Extension Division established its Bureau of Visual Education to make photographic slides, motion pictures,

and other visual aids available to faculty. The first catalog of the Bureau enthusiastically sang the praises of these new media: "The partial substitution of the picture for the printed word marks an epoch in educational work comparable with the introduction of machine power as a partial substitution for hand work". In 1924, the American Library Association (ALA) formally recognized the importance of non-print materials in libraries by establishing the Visual Methods Committee and appointing a committee on Relations Between Libraries and Moving Pictures. Interestingly, these actions were inspired by a figure outside the ALA, Ben Howe, a representative of the motion picture industry. In 1940, the Visual Methods Committee merged with the long-established Radio Broadcasting Committee to form the Audiovisual Committee.

Formats evolved, non-print collections in libraries grew, and from the late 1940s through the 1960s, Louis Shores crusaded for unity between two largely segregated professional camps: print librarians and audiovisualists. Shores not only helped bring these two groups together, but he also advanced the notion that various types of media, print, and non-print should not be segregated because of format. He believed, instead, that they should be integrated in libraries. In the 1950s, he developed the idea of the generic book: "The media specialist is concerned with all channels of communication. He is involved with what I have called the generic book – all of the media in all of their physical forms. By this definition, a motion picture is as much a part of the generic book as is last week's issue of Newsweek. In brief, the generic book is the sum total of man's communication possibilities; it is his evidence of life.

Through the 1960s and 1970s, traditional library services and media services continued to merge and develop into the "instructional resource centers," "learning resource centers," and "media centers" still found in libraries today. Professional organizations responded to the defacto

acceptance of media collections by devising guidelines and standards. In 1968, the Association for College and Research Libraries published "Guidelines for Audio-Visual Services in Academic Libraries," the first of three sets of such guidelines, most recently revised in 1999. The American Association of School Librarians and the National Education Association's Department of Audiovisual Instruction jointly published the "Standards for School Media Programs" in 1968. In 1970, the ALA published "Guidelines for Audiovisual Materials and Services in Public Libraries." Throughout the 1970s video formats evolved from U-matic, to Beta, to VHS, to videodiscs. Congress established off-air recording guidelines—the Kastenmeir Guidelines—and reviews of video titles regularly appeared in the professional literature. While libraries included video, films, and other moving image and sound media in their collections, these materials were generally segregated from print.

In many library circles, the 1980s brought the "video revolution." Indeed, the video market exploded. Media librarians gained more of a foothold in all types of libraries, and in both public and technical services positions. Despite this revolution, however, AV—and video in particular—did not enjoy the same respect as print in collection development or budget planning. In a late 1980s column for Video Librarian, Pitman shrewdly observed that "librarians are very much print-oriented creatures [and therefore] video is still not considered a basic library service but rather as a kind of 'loss leader' – a frill that brings new patrons into our libraries, thereby increasing circulation, which, in turn, guarantees support for the library – which ultimately means more money for the essentials: books and reference services. ALA members, however, recognized the importance of video in libraries, forming a video discussion group in 1988. This group received formal recognition, by petition, as the Video Round Table (VRT) in 1989. Older media-related groups in ALA, such as the Public Library

Association's AV Committee, grew stronger than ever during this period.

THE DIGITAL REVOLUTION

The 1990s ushered in the "digital revolution" in libraries. "The years between 1987 and 1999 marked a revolution in media resource collections and services. During this time media librarians grappled with a major technological development, the introduction of multimedia CD-ROMs. Just as media librarians were beginning to deal with questions regarding where these materials fit into library collections, the Web changed everything". While media librarians in the 1990s still needed to provide traditional audiovisual resources such as analog video and slides, the end of the 20th century saw media librarians becoming expert in emergent delivery methods for such digital media as the web and satellite systems. In addition to acquiring or licensing media content, some media librarians at the beginning of the 21st century are also responsible for creating unique media content.

One clear indicator of the uneasiness created by the inclusion of media in traditional library settings has been the struggle over facility or service names. The basic question of naming library media departments and positions has resulted in long discussions that generally add to existing confusion about services and resources. Is the proper term "audio-visual" or AV? Is it "media," "multimedia," or "instructional resources?" Not only are these terms vague, but they also have had various meanings over the years.

The definition of core media services in various libraries and the assignment of staff to administer or perform these services have been more varied and inconsistent. Except for the fairly rare instances in which video collections were built upon established 16mm film lending or programming collections, public libraries that made the plunge into video in the 1970s and 1980s found

themselves faced with the often daunting problem of incorporating radically new services and new collections into existing facilities. The models used to address these new media collections and public services have varied widely, depending on the commitment of the library to the new format, the resources available, and the public reception of these new services. Approaches have ranged from segregated media centers to collections integrated with books and other media; from large, broadly based collections of documentaries and feature films to small recreational viewing collections; and from fully-cataloged to perfunctory or minimal bibliographic access.

In some instances, film, video, and sound recordings have played a central role as teaching and learning resources and self learning materials for many years, although media centers on these campuses are frequently administered by departments external to the library. In other cases, for example, large research institutions, newer media such as video have often been incorporated as a concession to undergraduate services and have thus served as an adjunct to reserve-book operations. It has often been the case that such services and collections have been developed more as an afterthought or as a curricular expedient than as well-planned and integral parts of the larger library collections and services.

The range of functions performed by academic library media centers ranges from collection support to classroom equipment support to production and instructional technology design. It is increasingly common to find old-line academic library media centers evolving into convergence points for new services and resources related to digital media and instructional technologies. It is equally common to find media operations within the library caught up in broader campus discussions regarding instructional technologies and classroom resources.

The organization and staffing of basic media services in libraries has often reflected the general misconceptions

and biases about media mentioned previously. Much of the misunderstanding of and ineffective planning for media services in libraries is related to a continuing confusion and/or blurring of the line between media content and media delivery mechanisms. The very fact that the newest formats and equipment are often in the media librarian's domain has ironically been a professional detriment in some cases, at least in terms of the image of the profession and expectations placed upon it. In many instances, because media libraries function in equipment-intensive operations, any medium that requires a plug, a lens, or a specialized disc drive falls (or is thrust) into the media librarian's lap. In many libraries, for example, the microform collection is housed together with moving image and sound recordings simply because library users need equipment to view and copy the medium.

The advent of the web has only served to further muddy the distinction between content and content delivery. Nevertheless, video either on a cassette or on a computer is still video. The same is true of print. Unfortunately, in an attempt to consolidate resources and live within tight budgets, libraries all too often tend to forget that each medium has a complex and unique set of content characteristics and uses.

New digital technologies are changing the fundamental nature of collection development and reference services in libraries. Virtual collections and online library resources are taking their place next to artifactual collections. Reference librarianship is also being widely redefined as an occupation no longer tied to a physical place. In this new digital environment, the work of media librarians will take on a new and expanded meaning. The blurring of the line between media content and media delivery, the convergence of entertainment and information, and the ability to easily create and/or manipulate visual and sound resources are among the key factors influencing changes in the jobs of media librarians.

In the digital environment, a collaborative working model with non-traditional partners will become increasingly important for media librarians and librarians in general. Such partnerships may include work with community and business organizations, teaching faculty, scientists, and other professionals in a variety of fields. In 2000, for example, seven dental schools across the United States participated in a project that provided incoming students with a DVD that contains all of the materials that they will need for four years of dental school. Each DVD has 2.2 million pages of text and images, 300,000 other images, and 20 hours of video, includes complete textbooks, course syllabi, handouts, faculty manuals, and slides. The expansion beyond traditional library functions and traditional library clientele has a definite impact on library collection development practices, reference services, and the library budget. These directions also signal an opportunity for librarians to collaborate with faculty and publishers in new ways in order to create and facilitate the use of digital materials.

In addition to fostering new and creative partnerships, the new digital media environments offer unique opportunities for creatively using basic collection development skills. The incorporation of print images, video, audio, and text is occurring with the creation of innovative web-based collections. Examples of such projects include the American Memory Project of the Library of Congress (http://www.memory.loc.gov);/); the Vincent Voice Library (http://www.lib.msu.edu/vincent);); and The Health Library Video Collection at Stanford University (www.med.stanford.edu/healthlibrary/videos.html). Digital video delivery is the subject of research at several institutions. Three examples are: The Informedia project (http://www.informedia.cs.cmu.edu/);); the Video Streaming site at the University of Wisconsin-Madison (pocahontus.doit.wisc.edu); and the University of California-Berkeley Multimedia Research Center (http://

www.bmrc.berkeley.edu/). Although projects such as these are typically administered by engineering and computer science departments or specialized research units, libraries have much to learn and benefit from these endeavors.

MEDIA LIBRARY PROJECTS

Memory of the World Programme number of regional and inter-regional projects with flagship character has been launched for demonstration and promotion purposes. Some of these projects are presented herewithin the Memory of the World Programme. The national libraries of twelve countries (Brazil, Chile, Colombia, Costa Rica, Cuba, El Salvador, Mexico, Nicaragua, Puerto Rico, Peru, Portugal and Venezuela) are taking part in the project on the nineteenth-century press. It has led to the drawing up of a computerized inventory of some 6,000 newspaper titles and other press organs. The second phase of the project is to arrange for the conservation of the listed collections and their transfer to microfilm and digital form with a view to exchanges between national libraries, the organization of exhibitions and special publications.

The historic postcards chosen for this project constitute a pictorial treasure and are related to the 16 countries of the Economic Community of West African States (ECOWAS). These postcards are very rare because they are scattered in many countries, mostly in Europe. Only their presentation on a CD-ROM or a Web Site could bring them together, at least partially, under one theme or in an historical and geographical framework. The CD-ROM, prepared in collaboration with the Association Images et Mémoires and ICG-Mémoire Directe, features 3.000 postcards, which represents only a small part of the 50.000 which exist for the same period (1890-1930) and the same countries.

NATIONAL LIBRARY VENEZUELA

The huge number of photographic collections scattered around the world led the promoters of this project

to limit its scope, in a first stage, to Latin America and the Caribbean and to public collections of the XIXth century held in national archives and libraries.

Through the prints stored in the stocks, often in inadequate preservation conditions, it is the whole life of the nations which resurges with its important moments and the portraits of those who have influenced the course of history.

A CD-ROM containing more than 3.000 prints illustrating the main stages of the history of some ten countries of Latin America and the Caribbean and a presentation on the Web of a representative sample of images (video quality) with comments in English, French, Portuguese and Spanish, will enhance the value of this fragile heritage, in danger of disappearing. It is hoped that this will then help libraries and archives to ensure that preservation of their photographic collections is a priority

UNESCO has launched the Slave Route Project and set up an International Scientific Committee for the Slave Route Project with the mandate to examine the whole question of the slave trade and its impact on the prevailing economic and political situation in a number of countries as a means of promoting intercultural dialogue based on the history of the Atlantic slave trade. This Committee has stressed the importance of archival materials as the basis for the study of the slave trade. The feasibility study of the Slave trade archives project will be carried out in close co-operation with the broad guidelines set out by that body. The study will be carried out within the framework of the 'Memory of the World' Programme of UNESCO in close co-operation with the International Council of Archives (ICA).

The feasibility study will identify national archives and related institutions in six African countries (Angola, Benin, Ghana, Mozambique, Nigeria and Senegal) and in Brazil, Haiti and St. Croix to upgrade their facilities and services in order to ensure adequate preservation of

original records; obtain copies in appropriate formats of records held elsewhere; and ensure training of technical staff as a means of improving access to the records and other documents pertaining to the slave trade and slavery held in Africa and elsewhere. The feasibility study will identify the direct beneficiaries of the project and also all those who will benefit from the project as they will be made more aware of the common bondage of history.

The interest in the archives of the Dutch East India Company (Verenigde Oostindische Compagnie - VOC) has grown steadily in recent years. UNESCO, within the framework of the Memory of the World programme, now co-operates with VOC to make these archives more widely available. Attention focuses particularly on material remains from the period in which the VOC formed the largest commercial enterprise then operating in the world. Considerable interest has also been directed at the historiography of how different cultures interrelated. In many places the VOC's presence is seen increasingly to be a significant aspect of that country's history. The VOC is gradually losing its image as an organisation of pre-colonial domination. The tendency now is to incorporate the company as a seminal influence on the development of the country's identity and its historical self-image.

UNESCO will co-operate within the framework of the Memory of the World in the project of making electronically accessible the VOC archives which represent a unique source of information about the 17th and 18th century history of many countries and cultures of Europe, Africa, Asia and Australia. The history of the East India Company is not merely that of a large Dutch business conglomerate symbolized by many architectural monuments such as warehouses, meeting halls or ship wharves. The records of this Company deal with its operations in Asia, and thus shed considerable light on Asian history as well. The aim of the project is safeguarding the extensive material heritage this trading company has left behind in the

Netherlands and Asia, and how this mutual heritage can made be accessible and available for further use.

CARNEGIE MELLON DIGITAL LIBRARY PROJECT

As we approach the twenty-first century, accessing information quickly and accurately has become indispensable in everyday life. The information superhighway has revolutionized our concept of information, bringing us into the realm of digital information. Digital libraries have been developed to organize the mass of information on the Web. The Carnegie Mellon Digital Library Project (Informedia at CMU) (http://www. informedia.cs.cmu.edu/) aims to allow access to science and mathematics materials from a video library system. To this end, they are developing technology that will allow the use of speech, language, and images to accomplish the search and retrieval of information.

The primary sponsors of the project are the National Science Foundation (NSF), Advanced Research Projects Agency (ARPA), and the National Aeronautics and Space Association (NASA). There are also commercial sponsors, some of which include the Boeing Company, Intel Corporation, and Microsoft Corporation. The page contains links to the project's publications, sponsors, staff, and other Digital Library Initiative (DLI) projects, administrative information, and resources.

The publications of the Informedia project include:

1 reports and proposals;

2 papers online; and

3 media coverage.

The reports consist of periodic updates, and the papers share completed findings on the various aspects of the Informedia project. The progress reports of the NSF are some examples. In May 1996, the NSF issued its sixth quarterly report which focused on video skimming, face and name association, colour image similarity matching,

and spoken query interface, among other things (http:// www. informedia.cs.cmu.edu/html/subl_may96. html). Some of the finished papers are readily accessible; but most of them have to be downloaded for use with Adobe Acrobat.

The Resources page (http://www. informedia.cs.cmu. edu/resources/) contains links to text, audio, and video collections. The text and audio collections are under construction. Among the videos available are those produced by the Bureau of Mines, Federal Emergency Management Agency, National Oceanic and Atmospheric Administration, and the Smithsonian Institution. Like the reports and papers of the project, they are all accessible through downloading.

The Experience-on-Demand link (http:// www. informedia.cs.cmu.edu/eod.html/) provides slide presentations that discuss processes by which sensory experiences are translated into information recall. An example pertains to the ability to view an object then recognize it in a number of different contexts. Another element is that of speech recognition and natural language processing. Some issues relating to this area are noise filtering, a speaker's non-verbal cues, unlimited vocabulary, sentence structure, and topic shifting. The objective is to create a complete, retrievable history "of personal memor(ies) and experience(s)" and share these experiences with others. This transfer of information leads to questions regarding full or selected access and how a common understanding can be reached among a number of different people.

In addition to the Informedia Project at Carnegie Mellon, there are five other Digital Library projects which focus on specific areas of the sciences. These include the University of Michigan (earth and space), University of Illinois at Urbana-Champaign (engineering), University of California-Berkeley (environmental information), University of California-Santa Barbara (geographical and spatially referenced information), and Stanford University

(general sciences). From my browsing of these sites, they seemed to be well organized and informative. Two topics being researched are information analysis of cancer literature and interoperability issues for geographic access.

The Carnegie Mellon Digital Library Project is an excellent resource for librarians since it is well organized, efficient, and informative. Navigation of the site posed no problems even when dealing with graphics; also, I reached no dead ends. One element I was unable to test was the downloading capability. Other than that, I have no real criticisms of this site.

TOWARDS THE FUTURE

Reality may end up being a mix of all the given responses. Media libraries are in a good position to establish their future roles in the profession. They will need to master all the basic skills that media librarians have today, with an increased focus on media literacy. The present trend toward 24 hours and 7-day access to all things and services is already bringing changes to the traditional library. Demand for immediate service no matter the time of day will work hand-in-hand with media convergence. It will become even that much more important for librarians to be media literate. Video and media libraries may become involved in new modes of access, requiring innovative and interesting negotiations with distributors for licensing agreements. The popular library jargon "access vs. ownership," which conjures up images of electronic journals, is likely to include media formats when media librarians find themselves licensing programs from distributors for delivery via the web.

Creative methods of promoting media literacy will also likely develop within existing print literacy programs. The Information Literacy Competency Standards for Higher Education (www.ala.org/acrl/ilcomstan.html) adopted by the ACRL are moving in that direction. Survey responses and job advertisements mentioned above

indicate that flexibility, communication skills, technology skills, and media literacy skills are vital tools that all media librarians should possess. The importance of media archiving, media cataloging, metadata, and media indexing will grow as more resources are available in more formats and delivery modes. The key to the future will be professional open-mindedness and a diversity of approaches to building collections and services.

Media librarianship has evolved over the last century and will continue to do so well into the future. Shores' fight for media unity and his concept of the generic book in the 1950s is close to becoming a reality with the creation of multimedia products and the web. As Gray observes, the notion of "cutting edge" is much more problematic than it appears at first glance. Slide shows with synchronized audiotapes, the instruction multimedia of the 1960s, evolved into the use of 16mm films and educational television by the 70s. Videotape, the multimedia of the 80s, constituted one of the first forms of multimedia that truly put production capabilities in the hands of typical teachers, who were eventually challenged in the 90s with new technologies like CD-ROMs, video games, and the World Wide Web. Currently, cutting-edge multimedia consists of all the elements of the past enhanced by extremely high-quality digital visuals and audio in an interactive package that invites user involvement."

It is a challenging time for media librarians. What remains constant in this era of intensified change is the need for media librarians to develop meaningful and useful collections for clients, regardless of what shape and form these "collections" take. Media librarians are straddling the rapidly changing digital landscape and traditional delivery and presentation formats. The prognosis for the imminent demise of analog tape formats is more an advertising fantasy cooked up by the purveyors of broadband networking and chip builders than reality. After all, the technological hurdles and the economics of the film

and video industry present big hurdles to realizing the dream of universal and on-demand digital media. On the other hand, media librarians must prepare for a future filled with revolutions.

6
News Libraries Today

Information is a vital resource for every human activity. It is said to be the currency of journalists. It is the basic resource for a news reporting. The vast amount of information gathered in varied forms of documents is the raw material for a production. It should be used with great care. The media producers should have firm control over all the resources in order to avoid any confusion as the arrangement and presentation of information in an imperfect way can lead to convey different meanings.

A news media library holds the collection consisting of newspapers, magazines, news broadcasts, cable wire or Internet -based news organizations. The modern news reporters adopt a multi-media approach to understand the gist of the intended news item to be prepared. They need information in varied forms and at different stages of work. The ideas are needed for selection of the production themes.

News media libraries are dominated by newspapers and magazines. They manage information resources stored in files, on tape or microfilm or in computers. They are used by news and editorial staff in publishing establishments, such as newspaper and magazine publishers, and in broadcasting establishments, such as radio and television stations; directs activities of workers engaged in clipping, classifying, cataloging, indexing, storing, editing, and retrieving library information, or performs these activities as needed. Researches, retrieves, and disseminates information in resource library or commercial data bases in response to requests from news or editorial staff, using knowledge of classification system

or computer data base. Maintains records and statistics on use of data bases and information services provided.

A large number of libraries manage in-house data base of news information, assign classification terms to news articles, input news articles into data base, and research news information for in-house data base. May develop databases for data storage and retrieval, according to needs of news staff. May hire, train, schedule, and evaluate library staff. May prepare library budgets. May promote and market library products and services to public. May coordinate activities of library with activities of other departments. May select and purchase reference books for library collection. May manage graphics library, assign classification terms to graphics, and research graphics and be designated Photo-Graphics Library.

Newspapers enjoy the status of mass communication media in the society on wider plane. The story of establishment of newspaper libraries is very long and ful of doubts. There is no clear indication of the foundation of the first newspaper library. There is not only this confusion but the further problem of definition also comes in the way. A dicision of establishment of the news media libraries may be taken on the basis of the date of the library's founding with the date of the first clipping retained, the date of the oldest reel of microfilm, the date of the first reference book purchased, or when the first librarian was employed.

The earliest newspaper collections were not organized by librarians. By the 1850s, managers of the largest newspapers begin to designate space, money and staff to build news libraries. Newspapers were discovering that they could no longer rely upon unverifiable human memory. Haphazard methods of information gathering and fact checking were frustrating, time consuming and dangerous. The value of accurate, complete and convenient access to information was beginning to be recognized as crucial for reporters and editors. It took time, but newspaper

publishers were awakening to their deepening public responsibilities as well as their corporate ones.

Competition among papers for subscribers led to the recognition of readers' increasing need for accuracy, fairness, and authoritativeness. An increasing demand for more analytical writing rather than just reporting took hold. Broader conceptions of the scope of news led to coverage beyond simply the affairs of state, commerce, sports and politics. Newspapers developed or acquired writers who could skillfully cover complicated topics such as economics, science, medicine and law. Fact checking, backgrounding and analysis increased. Still, professional librarians and information specialists were typically not in charge of these morgue operations even in large newspapers. Recognition of their value as prime contributors to the entire publishing enterprise would not come for several decades.

Most early newspaper libraries originated by collection of reference books (atlases, dictionaries, encyclopedias, local histories, and so on) and later added clippings and photos. Sometimes these clips and photos were selected from their own papers. Occasionally newspapers acquired these collections from other papers.

The New York Herald started to build a library of books in. Clippings were not saved systematically until 1860, the beginning of the Civil War. An index to the Herald was started in that year and continued until 1919. It was considered so valuable that an effort was made to retrospectively index to 1835, the date of the founding of the paper. Other newspapers followed the New York Herald's lead in building in-house libraries. The New York Tribune, founded in 1841, began its library of books in the late 1840s. Its clipping collection, which at first included only biographical material, was started in 1860. The Tribune also started a news index in book form in 1875, went retrospective with it to 1841 and continued indexing until 1906. The New York Times, founded in 1851, began

a handwritten index at approximately the same time. Clippings, some dating from as early as 1869, were primarily biographical. Subject headings were not started at The New York Times until 1914, when a growing collection of war material formed the nucleus of the subject clip files. The New York World started its reference department in 1889 with clippings dating back to the 1870s.

The early clips were subsequently discarded because they took up too much space, a move typical in many newspapers since then. Subsequent collections of clips, reference books, bound newspaper volumes, photographs and engravings were rarely held in one centralized location. Frequently these collections were distributed among various departments within the newspaper building. Clips were in the "biographical department." Books were in the "library." Photos and cuts were in the "art department." Decades later there was a strong trend toward centralizing the collections. Even so, complete newspaper library clipping collections are rare.

The New York Daily News, established in 1919, started its library by purchasing a collection of clippings covering events from 1908 to 1923. These clippings, dealing with New York City government, crime and civic affairs numbered nearly 320,000 and were estimated to have cost $100,000. The News also bought a collection of more than 100,000 photographs of prominent persons during the nineteenth and early twentieth centuries.

Most of the early newspaper libraries were developed in New York. Subsequently, The Boston Herald established its library in 1876. It added substantially to its collection when it acquired the Boston Traveler's clippings dating back to 1825. When the Boston Journal merged with the Herald, it contributed a collection of clippings from the Civil War period, including biographical material about Union officers. Few of these early newspaper library collections survived. The current location of those that did is unclear. Efforts at preserving these remaining collections are

affected by conflicting interests, money and technology. The Boston Globe launched its library in 1887 with reference books dating to 1852. A collection of clippings about prominent persons was donated to the library by an editor.

Systematic clipping of the Globe did not begin until 1890. The library was reorganized in 1922 by William Alcott, who succeeded the first Globe librarian, Edson W. White. The Massachusetts Springfield Republican began its clipping collection in 1888, supplemented by a valuable collection from the Springfield Union that it had purchased. This is one of the earliest examples of newspapers selling or merging their in-house libraries. The San Francisco Chronicle established a complete library in 1879. The 1890s saw the establishment of the St. Louis Post-Dispatch and the Detroit News libraries. The latter was reorganized in 1917 when the News entered its new building.

Regardless of when news libraries were founded, their survival was not assured. As with most organizations, they went through cycles of decline, neglect and subsequent rejuvenation. Some news libraries endured gaps in collections and services; others were simply discontinued. Still others went through substantial overhaul with little regard for early collections. To find a newspaper library with a complete collection stretching back to its earliest origins is extremely rare. The Library of Congress has an important newspaper collection that is both current and historical. A different approach involving newspaper preservation was taken by the U.S.Newspaper Project launched in 1981. Funded by the National Endowment for the Humanities with technical support from the Library of Congress, it is involved in cataloging and microfilming early newspaper editions, but not clippings. Perhaps with a coordinated effort by local institutions and newspaper publishers, the files and artifacts from once-great, dead dailies could continue to serve their communities. The unavoidable questions continue, however. Who could afford the money, space and time to undertake such a project?

Other large-circulation newspapers, not described here, started their morgues by the end of the nineteenth century. The search for accurate, comprehensive access to a wide variety of information was beginning to move ahead, albeit slowly. Several more decades would pass before high-quality information storage and retrieval services moved into high gear in news organizations.

Newspapers frequently receive important pieces of news that lack the necessary details for presenting them with due dignity of length. It becomes necessary to supply the missing materials in the office. In many cases this can be done with the aid of the "morgue" or cabinet of biographical and obituary materials that is maintained in every wide-awake newspaper office. Sometimes books of reference will supply much of the needed information. There is no mention of the need for more than a simple collection of materials. No suggestions were made on where to find materials or on which materials should be collected. There was no mention of the need for a professional, a librarian, who would collect, organize and manage the materials.

Publishers and editors of smaller newspapers began publishing on shoestring budgets. A secondhand press and a news staff doubling as reporters, typesetters, carriers and ad takers characterized the typical turn-of-the-century community newspaper. Uncertain revenues and economic hard times caused more than a few publishers to fold their operations. A premium was placed on holding down all costs. That these publishers for the most part did not invest in in-house libraries is quite understandable.

Most of the smaller newspapers did not have their back issues indexed or clipped. Early issues of these newspapers were rarely saved or preserved systematically. It would be the mid-1930s before microfilming of newspapers became commonplace. Usually the bound editions of newspapers served as the morgue. Lack of competition among papers in smaller communities and the

philosophy that newspapers were interested only in today's news, never yesterday's history, served reporters and citizens poorly. Time and effort would be needed to convince publishers from smaller newspapers about the values of preservation and in-house libraries, even on a modest scale.

Situation was different for larger newspapers. In the first decade of the twentieth century, the following large metropolitan newspapers launched in-house libraries. A larger economic base, a more diverse population and greater competition for readers are some of the reasons for expansion of newspaper libraries in the early decades of the twentieth century. World War I, natural disasters, political upheavals, economic recessions, business closings, crop failures and weather catastrophes have been cited as the impetus for editors and publishers to examine the adequacy of their libraries and to press for better, more responsive ones, but there may have been other reasons. Reliable in-house news libraries can provide the means and methods for quick fact checking, thereby offering a vital competitive edge among fiercely combative large metropolitan dailies. Also, newspapers needed to do more than spotlight events; they needed to illuminate them with in-depth analysis. News libraries were beginning to perform the backgrounding function vital to this type of reporting. The arrival and growing influence of national/international wire services (the Associated Press in 1848 and the United Press International in 1907) further fueled the fierce competition for timely, accurate, comprehensive news gathering.

As a result of ensuring standards in the library services, the utilization of a library increased, as one might expect it to, precisely in proportion to its demonstrated value. A staff inured to disappointments soon learns not merely to expect nothing from a newspaper library, but to seek nothing in it. The staff also, and rightly, demands instant service, since the exigencies of newspaper

production do not permit the leisure so well known in public libraries.

Complementing these first steps toward professional news library standards was an early outline of a professional mission statement. It is generally agreed among veteran news librarians that to be worthy of the name, a newspaper library should offer efficient, high-quality reference service. Its mission is to support the entire publishing enterprise. Further, to perform at the highest possible level, it must be endowed with at least five basic elements:

* Accurate, current, accessible files of news clips, photos, graphics, maps and newspaper microfilm
* A core collection of reference books and serials
* Space and equipment to house and maintain the collections
* Qualified staff to manage the collections and provide reference services
* Money to support the expanding operation

By the 1930s the tewspaper librarians were turning away from being wardens of clipping collections toward becoming information specialists. The change came in part from the news industry itself and from the emerging newspaper library profession. The Newspaper Division was taking a leadership role in this evolution. Over the years its continuing education seminars, conferences, workshops and publications became the foundation for the highest standards of professional newspaper librarianship:

One of the earliest technological applications in news libraries involved microfilming projects. Leading the way in microfilming U.S. newspapers was New York Herald Tribune librarian David G. Rogers. In 1932 he worked with Eastman Kodak on the possibility of adapting a microfilm camera to film newspaper files. After several years, Eastman Kodak staff developed a camera that filmed

newspaper pages rapidly and displayed them in full-page format. Newspaper preservation was a growing concern to news librarians as well as their archivist colleagues.

Whatever motivated newspapers to establish in-house libraries, it was soon discovered that firstrate libraries contributed significantly not only to the accuracy and preservation of the papers but also to the total publishing effort. News management finally recognized that the public relies upon its newspapers as its most vital source of current events and historical records. News organizations began investing in better information storage and retrieval methods to guarantee authoritativeness in their publications.

The 1950s and 1960s began a period of decline for newspapers. Newspaper readership gradually waned. The competition for advertising revenue increased. Large, metropolitan newspapers merged or closed. The collections of these defunct dailies faced an uncertain future. Some collections were donated to public or academic libraries; others were discarded or lost. But the news organizations remaining were developing more effective in-house libraries.

The shift in the mass communication industry from print to television news broadcasting was under way. Network news broadcasters came, in large part, from print as well as radio journalism. This broadcast staff was discovering that the demand for data on deadline was strong regardless of the medium. Information from newspapers was now being read, marked and filed for television news broadcasts. While competition between print and broadcast media escalated, so did the recognition of good reference and research. Network in-house news libraries were attracting professionals to build and index their valuable collections of tapes, scripts and film.

As a group, newspaper librarians were discovering newer professional responsibilities. Professional standards

were explored, continuing education programs were started, and professional publications were launched. Newspaper librarians were recognizing their own professional identity and developing the strength to become modern information managers.

One of the significant changes of these midcentury news libraries was the consolidation of several in-house collections within newspapers. In earlier decades there has been a tendency to separate the storage of certain materials according to departmental proprietorship. While some of this division and departmentalism was the result of the physical layouts of the newspaper plants, more was due to factionalism and turf wars. This separation and division was confusing, wasteful and costly. News clips and photo engravings were kept in the morgue, reference books were shelved in the library, photo prints and negatives were filed in the photo department, and map engravings and graphics were stored in the art department. Multiple copies of serials went everywhere; back copies could not be located when needed. Coordinating collections varying in format as well as content was particularly challenging. News librarians demonstrated that centralization through well-managed library procedures reduced these problems while enhancing the overall effectiveness of library services.

During the decades of 1950s, newspapers, much like other businesses were started, stopped, merged, and bought and sold. When a newspaper closes, it leaves behind a veritable mountain of information. The millions of clips and photos stored in thousands of boxes and cabinets became the residue of defunct dailies. The problems created were large and difficult to solve. For example, what is the value of these collections? Who wants to use them? How can they be preserved? Should they be preserved? Who will become the caretakers of the collections? How will access be arranged? What about copyright protection? Finally, what has happened to these news library collections?

Some newspapers donated these collections to university libraries, historical societies or public libraries, usually for a tax advantage. Undoubtedly, newspaper library collections have intrinsic value. For example, the San Francisco Examiner donated its entire clipping collection (after microfilming the clippings) to the San Francisco Public Library upon establishing its professionally appraised tax valuation at an estimated several million dollars.

Making these huge newspaper collections available to the public is costly and time consuming. The original plans to do so are not always successful. For example, at the University of Missouri, 60 million clips from the New York World-Telegram, which ceased publication in 1967, and other defunct newspapers were headed for a landfill until publicity prompted the university to reconsider. At the time it was costing over $1,000 per month to store these clips in an elaborate records/archives center.

However, when a surviving newspaper acquires the morgue of its deceased rival, the public generally does not get access to those files. The library receiving the materials is faced with a large problem about how to merge the collections. Ron Larson, librarian with the Wisconsin State Journal, described in a winter 1988 issue of News Library News how he managed the monumental task of integrating the Capital Times library collection into the Journal's. He was given just one month to complete the task.

The availability of the morgue files to the public does not mean that they are heavily used. The enormous cost and time involved for the university and public libraries to index and organize dead newspapers' collections delay convenient access for the public. Only the largest newspapers have published indexes. Currently, fewer than 150 newspapers are online full-text. These databases, available to the public for online search fees, rarely reach back further than the early 1980s. The information access gap, as far as newspapers are concerned, is widening.

The lesson of this experience is that practical alternatives to the storage of older, fragile, space-consuming clip files are available. These methods include converting news clips to microfiche, undertaking news indexing and abstracting services, or automating the clipping files. The next step involves distribution to publicly accessible places such as local libraries. These alternative systems vary in cost, but when compared to the value of the entire collection and the need for preservation of, and convenient access to, unique historical records, the costs appear to be justified.

THE NEWS LIBRARIES OF TOMORROW

The decade of the 1990s began with a reversal of fortunes for many newspapers. A stagnant economy, further declining readership, rising costs and eroding advertising revenues resulted in a downward spiral for the press and networks as well. Top management responded in a businesslike fashion with downsizing and restructuring. Some newspapers folded or merged. Many news libraries took cuts in budget, staff and space. However, news libraries were not the only departments to take the cutbacks. It was a struggle to guard against a siege mentality. The clarion call seems to be to do more, work harder and manage better with less of everything but dedication and enthusiasm. As might be expected of professionals, news librarians responded well. Not in recent memory had there been such an opportunity to understand clearly the importance of working together to help the profession and the industry. Articles describing how news librarians are surviving this neorecession filled News Library News. It is generally agreed that this situation is not yet over and, in fact, may deteriorate before it improves.

In 1993-94 the News Division of the Special Libraries Association celebrated its 70th anniversary. Newspaper libraries existed long before the introduction of the News Division. It took world wars, civil conflict, national disasters

and journalistic competition before newspapers realized the importance and value of investing in their own in-house libraries. News librarians are part of a larger journalistic heritage, one that is deeply embedded in our country's convictions as well as its Constitution. They are part of this country's commitment to freedom of the press and the concomitant goal of freedom of information. This commitment is part of the excitement and responsibility of the news library profession.

On the periphery, but still of concern, is the need for developing a wide-ranging information policy for our profession and country. Typically, news librarians have been too absorbed in their daily routines, escalating technology and developing professional identities to address these broader concerns. As they secure their positions in news organizations, members of this new breed of information specialists must look beyond their parochial and corporate interests. Preservation and archiving of historical newspaper collections, videotapes and photographs demand attention. The ethics of information selling concern everyone. Defining public access to information, determining the value and accuracy of information, and establishing its cost must be part of the news librarians' future agenda.

Information storage and delivery systems will dominate news librarians' agenda, but other topics affecting the growth and development of the news industry deserve careful study. There are several ways to undertake this study, but a good place to begin is with The Freedom Forum Media Studies Center's 1992 report titled Media at the Millennium. In it are highlights from a symposium covering such crucial topics as "The Future of the Media," "The Future of Media Studies," "Converging Technologies," "Free Expression in the Information Age," "Media and the Political Process," "Affirming Diversity—Multicultural Media," and "International Communication." The Baby Bells' entrance into electronic information selling has

profound implications for the news industry.

Likewise, desktop publishing, compact disk technology, optical imaging, hypertext, and multimedia are already stimulating changes across broad spectrums of society. Issues of open access to public-record's laws and the corresponding right to privacy will continue to confront us. Who will train and educate the journalists of the future? One journalist recently invented a new, multimedia computer, called Reporter's Workbench, that packages journalists' varied news resources into one handy PC system. Are news libraries a part of this new technological development? Are news librarians even aware of what is happening, let alone what might be happening in their industry? If so, how will they respond to these new and different demands on their time and talents?

Managing information resources is just part of what news librarians do. The bigger task will be not only finding the answers to questions, but discovering what questions need asking and then packaging the data and analysis in ways to be most effectively used. News library managers of the 1990s must continue, more than ever before, to read, study, learn, plan, experiment, cooperate, communicate and evaluate. There are few other professional organizations better prepared to lead news librarians into vital contributions to the media in the twenty-first century than the News Division of the Special Libraries Association.

Today, most of the United States' daily newspapers have some sort of news archive/library. It is rarely, if ever, referred to as the morgue. This development is matched by network broadcast news organizations. However, fewer than one-third of these news organizations have librarians who are represented in the membership of the only professional organization prepared to promote high-quality news library service. No longer can this competitive industry tolerate the morgue of yesteryear. It is just too costly to continue operating a poorly arranged,

inadequately staffed, space-wasting, time-consuming, out-of-date, impossible-to-find-anything warehouse.

Newspaper librarians will need to prepare themselves for an expanding news role. The effort will require not only new skills and knowledge, but a willingness to actively participate in the development of new technology. Times and methods have changed, and so have the news industry and its libraries. Regardless of whether the tools of the twenty-first century news librarian remain scissors, file cabinets and telephones, or become computers, optical discs and satellites, the vital ingredient will always be the individual's professionalism and enthusiasm. One element that has remained constant is the news librarians' prime directive. It is still "Information, please, and make it fast, accurate and comprehensive."

During the next few years it is possible for us all, with large newspaper collections on microfilm, to digitise our collections, to build "Digital Newspaper Libraries" for our users. Periodicals, journals and newspapers, have turned out to be a target that has a great demand on the Internet from researchers as well as the public in large. For curators in libraries this is a great challenge. Libraries should take the responsibility of digitising these collections, to build up digital libraries, to ensure that the cultural heritage is available for all. Librarians should be aware of the advantage and knowledge we have acquired from preservation microfilming of newspapers over many decades. Much of the needed infrastructure is already available. Now we have to combine our knowledge and experience into a fruitful combination - we have to improve the long-term survival of valuable documentary resources, as well as to improve access to these collections.

In The Electronic Media and the Transformation of Law, M. Ethan Katsh discusses the changes in access to information for attorneys and the public. His perceptions and analysis can be transferred easily to the news media. Katsh asserts that traditional notions of what the rule of

law is, which cases and concepts are the most important and controlling ones, and other historical notions of the law are changing due to access to information in electronic format. No longer are judges, attorneys, citizens, librarians and others merely relying on the information in the print format; they use information in all formats. The implications are that all types of information must be considered; it is no longer necessary, or possible, to rely exclusively on the printed word, such as the printed reports of cases.

The obligations and rights of the media and private citizens are clouded by the electronic information dissemination. Electronic formatted information is more difficult to control, and it is disseminated more widely to more people and potentially to persons who might want the information for less-than-admirable reasons. Use of the computer to access various files can make finding information for journalists easier because it provides many access points. For example, it is relatively easy for reporters and other journalists to search online versions of standard publications such as the Marquis Who's Who titles and request results arranged in many ways, such as all individuals with certain common characteristics. One recent example was an analysis of a file that established which individuals were members of an all white country club. Other illustrations might be for the electronic resource to provide the names of all who are attorneys or journalists. Electronic access makes the manipulation of data easier, but it also carries an obligation to use the services effectively and ethically.

Privacy law, long considered an important part of American society, is an area that can be changed drastically because of access to information in electronic formats. Katsh argues that "large parts of privacy law punish the communication of information in print or on television but impose no restriction when the same information is transmitted" in other ways, such as orally and via electronic

communications. Privacy law then becomes dependent somewhat on the publication of the information in the newspaper or magazine, and a violation is more difficult to prove when information is transferred electronically where it can be used and manipulated, but then deleted or removed. In a recent Taking Sides issue paper, "Can Privacy Be Protected in the Information Age?" the authors argue that the information age has created substantial problems for Americans. The selling of individuals' names, addresses, phone numbers and other data to companies who wish to market their products or to target a specific group is commonplace. The conclusion is that American society must create sophisticated encoding devices that restrict unauthorized individuals from misusing the information that has been stored to ensure privacy rights. The authors outline some difficult political and ethical questions raised by computerized databanks, including the almost-impossible task of controlling the flow of personal information that they contain and the persons who have access to the information.

The other side of the issue, however, is that some information should be available to journalists and media personnel. "Unlike some early predictions in the news trade literature, journalists do not have unlimited access to electronic technologies," conclude the authors of a study concerning the use of computers and electronic information resources by news organizations. They report that the newspapers in their study allow journalists access to their own newspaper's electronic library, but most do not provide journalists with unlimited access to commercial information systems. Thus the news librarians become the crucial players in this environment. They must play the role of gatekeeper or mediator when it comes to access to electronic database information. The librarians' roles in the dissemination of information entails not only an information-distribution role, but also an ethical role in determining whether the journalist is a permitted user of

the system, whether the information in the system should be provided to outsiders, and whether the data is "dirty" or ready for interpretation and use.

NEWS LIBRARY SERVICES

A news library supports by providing information resources in the production process of news. There are three stages in the news production process where the librarian's role is essential. These three stages are news-gathering, news production, news packaging and delivery. Here we discusses the librarian's changing role and the importance of the traditional skills and knowledge of the information professional. Earlier research skills were needed more but the reporters, editors, and graphic artists had now acquired computer-assisted reporting skills and the tools to collect and process most of the information themselves.

The fundamental role of the news librarian had radically changed. It is a change that must be hitting all media libraries as we, as a society and as organizations, move from an industrial age model into the information age. What does this mean for the work of the news library and the role they play in their news organizations? Looking back at the history of information access in newsrooms and the roles the news library played can help us understand the profound changes that we will need to make in our roles and relationships. It can be quickly seen that the type of information available and the form in which it was available has been a powerful determinant of the role that the news library played.

In the pre-digital days, when the library primarily contained single copies of paper-based information resources, the role of the librarian was cataloger, circulation agent and custodian. The location of the copies had to be determined and accounted for, requests for their use had to be controlled, the copies had to be carefully returned to their location after use. For the most part, librarians were information gatekeepers, controlling the

flow in and out and back again of the information resources in the library.

This set up a view of the librarian as a clerical assistant, concerned more with putting information away carefully and controlling it's accessibility than with truly being a partner in research and reporting.

As newspapers moved from hot type to cold type production systems and the ability to capture into databases the text of the news product was realized, news librarians became the information intermediary, the keyboard jockey who knew, because of their training and the role they had in building the databases, how best to retrieve the information from the databases. And as the database superstores became invaluable, but expensive, information resources, the librarian acted as the intermediary for economic reasons, their knowledge of the convoluted search engines made for more efficient searching. That and the fact that funding for database access was usually in the library's budget made the librarian an economic gatekeeper through which the newsroom had to access information.

This created, in some ways, a sense of the librarian as an obstacle to access to information. Reporters had to go through the library to get to the information they needed. Economic concerns often made the librarian more stingy with information retrieval than the reporters might have liked, having to cue up to get access to the librarian who had access to the information was frustrating.

THE IMPACT OF INTERNET

Ours is the age of the end-user information consumer. As search software became more intuitive and, reporters have started to search the database themselves. The growth in the number of tremendous information resources on the Internet and it's availability on reporter's computers has created a newsroom full of information end-user searchers. Not needing an intermediary, someone who will lay hands

on the keyboard for them, end-user searchers need the "consultants, advisors, trainers, coaches. Freed from the hands-on searching of routine information requests, done now by the end-user / reporter or editor, the library has time to be the scout locating the best information resources on the Internet.

This evolutionary change in role between the library and the newsroom will result in an information partnership where the librarian's skills as evaluator, tracker and trainer of information will work with the reporter's role as interpreter, explainer and compelling writer. Together, the news reporting will be more accurate, contain more perspective, bring in more voices and provide different angles than possible in the past.

The news librarian, with their training in understanding, evaluating, cataloging and compiling information will be the key partner in helping reporters know how to form and master the material as his command. This is not to say that the research role will be totally abdicated to the reporter. In a partnership, those with the greatest skills do the part of the job they can best get done. In a reporting crunch or for research requiring detailed and in-depth searching, the librarian / researcher's role will be an important contribution to the newsgathering.

As the production line of the newsroom changes from an assembly line to pagination systems, the news librarian's role as overseer of all departments' data processing needs is essential. The output from any new production system will have to make it's way into the text archive. The opportunity to capture full-page representations of the news product has great potential for searching and researching. The digitization of photos and graphics as page elements will bring in other challenges for archiving. The librarian must be a key participant in the development and planning of pagination systems or for any major changes in the production process. Their overview of newsroom needs and their perspective

on the various uses to be made of production output is essential.

A further role is in coordinating the aspects of research and data retrieval into a new production system design. Ensuring that the needs of researching and retrieval are recognized and incorporated in the proposal stage can help prevent costly mistakes when systems which do not provide the full range of capabilities are selected.

One of the ironies of late 20th century newspapering is the development of the online news product in decidedly offline newsrooms. In too many newsrooms where a daily web news product is packaged, the majority of the employees know little or nothing about the medium to which their work is contributing. As more newsrooms provide the material for websites and explore more imaginatively what this medium can do for the form, function and scope of their journalistic output, the need for greater understanding of the medium itself will grow. Here's where the coach / trainer role of the librarian will be essential. In the training on how to use the web as a research / information tool the understanding of the web as a packaging / delivery medium will grow as will the understanding of how this medium of three dimensions (length / width / depth) is fundamentally different than the two-dimensional newsprint page.

The growth of electronic newsproducts will also create a great appetite and need to "feed the beast". Here is where the librarian's traditional role of information packager will grow. Many news librarians are contributing to the content of the newspaper's website through the creation of special information packages, backgrounders, and chronologies. Often, these were initially created as a research aid for reporters and made available on the newsroom's intranet (internal Internet site). Many should find a useful outlet on the newspaper's website as a way to enhance the news site as the one spot for unique and complete local news and information. The librarian is also contributing to the

website through the creation of lists of links to quality information resources that users of the site might want to be aware of. As the form and function of online news becomes defined, clearly the "give me more" aspect whereby readers are led to additional information of high quality on outside sites would need the librarian's searching and evaluating skills involved.

In the changed information scenario of the 21st century, the news libraries should make the following provisions of rendering their services in a better way:

* The databases or clipping files, which is often the best collection of information for an intial search on a local issue.
* Database fron news and business information aggregators, such as LEXIS-NEXIS, Dow Jones Interactive, Dialog and Northern Light.
* Online Public Record Sources, such as LEXIS-NEXIS, CDVB-Infotech, AutoTrack and selected websites.
* Reference Book Collection
* The publications staff photographs aand other graphics collections
* Wire services and stock photograph houses
* Web resources.

It is hopefully expected that the role of the information professional will expand and grow. Building on the traditional skills they have always brought to the function of information managers, they will be the best suited to refine and redefine their roles in a newsroom which will increasingly rely on their professional strengths of location, evaluation and education of how to use information resources.

BROADCAST AND MAGAZINE NEWS LIBRARIES

In the 1980s special-interest groups were formed with the goal of attracting new members among the media partners. Programs and workshops designed for these

special news librarians appeared at annual conferences. The division acknowledged this growing trend in membership from broadcast and magazine news organizations and in 1987 changed its name from the Newspaper Division to the News Division of the Special Libraries Association.

These broadcast and magazine librarians joined their newspaper comrades in tackling the technological challenges of the decade. Advanced technology such as computer-output microfiche, optical disks, computerized indexing, automated full-text retrieval systems, digital photo archiving, online database searching, spreadsheets, computer-assisted reporting, and media polling appeared on the scene. News librarians were going to be ready with the professional skills and talent to select, manage and master such electronic wizardry.

ELECTRONIC NEWS LIBRARIES

The explosion of the information age has special meaning for news libraries. It is sort of "Goodbye, Gutenberg; hello, Mr. Chips." In the late 1970s and early 1980s, many newspapers went from hot type to cold type, that is, to electronic front-end typesetting. Even smaller newspapers could amortize multi-million-dollar computerized typesetting investments in a relatively short period of time. Sadly, this technological advancement eliminated long-time newspaper craftsmen, typesetters. As a result, within a few years, newspapers were able to reduce the number of their employees significantly with a substantive improvement in productivity. That meant dollars saved and profits increased. Some have speculated that newspaper libraries were able to reap some of the benefit of this increased corporate savings. By the end of the 1980s, over 150 United States and Canadian newspapers had electronic full-text storage systems operational or in the development stage. That number is constantly increasing.

A brief history of automated newspaper library systems acknowledges that The New York Times' Information Bank led the way in 1971. The original Information Bank consisted of a computer index and abstracts of articles in the Times and other selected publications, with coverage extending back to 1969. This pioneering system was the first newspaper database to become publicly available in online form. Full-text capacity was added to The New York Times Information Service in 1981. In 1983 the marketing and distribution rights to the Information Bank were sold to the Mead Data Corporation and NEXIS was born.

Other newspapers experimented with different approaches to automating their libraries' clipping files. The Detroit Free Press began using a system called Miracode in 1971. This system used a numerically coded index to the microfilmed full text of articles stored in 16-mm roll microfilm cassettes. These cassettes could be searched using an automated microfilm reader-printer. A system designed for internal use only, it was not installed at any other newspaper and it was replaced in the early 1980s by VU/TEXT. In 1976 the Louisville Courier-Journal installed INFO-KY with DEC PDP computers for an online index and microfiche storage. The system allowed a user to search the index and to control reader-printer display and reprinting from the keyboard. The Toronto Globe and Mail introduced the first full-text, online electronic newspaper library system in 1977 using the QL software. David Rhydwen's 1977 article in Special Libraries gives the first account of a full-text computerized storage and retrieval system.

From the early 1980s, other full-text electronic news library systems evolved, including VU/TEXT, DataTimes, Mead Data Corporation and ELS, to mention just a few of the over 20 systems on the market. Currently the trend is away from huge, mainframe computers to smaller, but still-powerful computers equipped with modems and a variety

of database-management software packages to enhance, annotate, analyze, print, download or transmit information. Integrating text and graphics in electronic storage and retrieval systems is on the horizon.

In 1985 newspaper libraries had reached a watershed year. More than 50 papers were using commercial electronic systems for full-text storage and retrieval of newspaper stories. Start-up costs were high and remained so for several years. Dedicated full-text hardware-software packages still range from $50,000 to $400,000. The advantages, however, seem to be overcoming the costs, at least for large-circulation papers. Besides offering convenient in-house and remote access, these systems are encouraging news libraries to explore potential revenue from the general public.

Access to full-text news databases, such as NEXIS, VU/TEXT, DataTimes, Dow Jones News Retrieval System, BRS and DIALOG, is becoming more frequent in larger news libraries. Since Knight-Ridder's purchase of DIALOG in 1989, DIALOG has been mounting an increasing number of full-text newspaper databases on its system. Tapping into these electronic sources is costly but justifiable when compared to more costly and less fruitful alternatives.

A study of information technology changes in large newspaper libraries was an important contribution by Hansen and Ward. The study researched 105 newspapers with circulations of over 100,000. Newspaper librarians and newsroom managers described the availability of electronic news libraries, commercial database subscriptions, fax and other information technologies. Sixty-seven percent of newspapers had an electronic library, and 90 percent had commercial database subscriptions. The authors also discussed the implications electronic libraries have on public access. They speculated that online access to large municipal newspapers seems to negate the preparation of locally prepared newspaper indexes. The impact of this technological development on

public access to information in newspapers is beginning to have a profound effect.

Larger, better-financed newspaper libraries have obviously led the way in the development of electronic libraries. Smaller news libraries have had a struggle. Unlike their colleagues from larger newspapers, these news librarians lacked budgets for computers, books and travel to professional seminars. Without management support, money, education and training, these librarians were struggling to meet the information needs of their newspapers. A descriptive study by Hegg compared information storage and retrieval methods in 20 smaller newspapers (under 52,000 circulation) located in several states. The author discovered on her visits that not only was there a paucity of automation, but 6 of the 20 newspapers had no library at all. Significantly, the status of the library increased with newspaper circulation size.

But librarians from smaller newspapers have been discovering ways to incorporate this electronic technology, albeit on a smaller scale, in their libraries. Working with in-house computer systems and data-management staff, librarians were getting space on the front-end electronic typesetting equipment to establish news indexes, ready-reference directories and subject-authority files, to mention just a few information tools. The division newsletter, News Library News, was filled with path-breaking accounts, usually in the column, written for librarians of smaller newspapers, titled "Small, but Good!"

This was also a period when smaller newspapers were awakening to the possibility that not just the big, metropolitan papers could have a quality in-house library. Investigative reporting required a skilled information support staff. Recognizing that the journalistic function of "watchdog" could not be left to large papers exclusively, midsized and smaller papers were beginning to invest in the talent and the tools to support their own news staffs. They were hiring professionally trained librarians

knowledgeable about database searching and information management. The trend was for news libraries to be expanded, upgraded, and improved.

An eloquent statement of the mission of strong, effective, professional newspaper libraries was prepared by James Scofield, former librarian with the St. Petersburg Times. His keynote speech, originally delivered at a 1984 regional seminar of North Carolina news librarians, was reprinted in Editor & Publisher. An oft-quoted remark from that speech is "Newspaper managements must remember, and perhaps be reminded occasionally, that excellence costs, but in the long run, mediocrity costs far more." Joseph Kwapil, the founder of the Newspaper Libraries Division, made a speech 64 years earlier with a similar theme. "At a conservative estimate I should say that every dollar judiciously spent on the morgue will add at least ten to the physical valuation of the newspaper property on the whole." Kwapil went on to say that the morgue, when conducted on a modern basis, is an indispensable department of any well-regulated newspaper.

DIGITAL NEWS PHOTO ARCHIVES

Just about any technological change in a news organization has an impact on the news library. Witness the advent of the electronic darkroom in the 1990s. The arrival of digitized photos via AP's Leaf System is a prime case in point. This advanced technology arrived on the scene without electronic or computerized archiving capability. That meant that if any of the hundreds or thousands of photos streaming across a newspaper photo editor's computer each week needed to be saved for subsequent access, the desired photos had to be printed and filed in cabinets. There had to be a better way.

In 1991-92 the News Division, under the direction of then chairman Lany McDonald, created a task force of selected members to research the problems of digital photo archiving. Further, the division would seek opportunities

to discuss these problems with the Associated Press and the inventors of its Leaf System. McDonald was placed on an AP advisory committee, and the task force went to work.

Well-researched reports on the electronic darkroom and digital photo archiving appeared in News Library News by Mary Ann Skinner from the Newsday library, George Schlukbier from the Sacramento Bee Editorial Library and other members in 1990-91 detailing the process and its impact on news libraries. The archiving system is not yet defined, but a proposal by Kathy Foley, librarian with the Washington Post, is making headway in charting the territory. News librarians are taking their rightful place as knowledgeable information managers in this newest area of technology.

NEWS INFORMATION MARKETING

Newspaper managements are interested in a return on their investments from departments that hitherto had not been sources of revenue. News libraries, with their growing research collections and electronic access expertise, began to look promising for news information packaging and marketing possibilities. The early beginnings were small and limited.

David Hughey in 1983 referred to newspapers meeting the challenge of electronic publishing and commercial profitability via the special collections in news libraries. The need for providing to the newspaper's public retrospective local information, well categorized, conveniently located and attractively priced, is compelling.

Documenting news library practices in information marketing started with a survey in 1982-83. Shirley Mooney Aabjerg, now retired from the Pacific Press, Ltd. library, undertook a survey of newspaper library information marketing practices by Newspaper Division members. Although the response rate was low, she found a wide range of these activities, everything from charging the public $.10 for a clip photocopy and $3.00 for a microfilm

print to an hourly fee for research. She reported that a few newspapers, mostly large circulation ones, operate a special in-house service, usually separate from the library, to accommodate public requests for photos, back issues and other information published in their papers. This charge for service came about in some newspaper libraries as a way of managing the flood of requests. While possibly acceptable in metropolitan areas, it usually meets with publisher and public disapproval in smaller cities and towns. The library in these cases is supposed to provide the service as part of maintaining the paper's good will.

Not until the establishment and acceptance of electronic news databases did news library revenues surge. The advent of online full-text news databases opened publishers' eyes about other possibilities for revenue. Early on, database service vendors tempted newspaper management with the possibility of revenues from public use, thereby offsetting the heavy financial start-up and maintenance costs. For large metropolitan newspapers, news database revenue can range from a few thousand dollars annually to hundreds of thousands of dollars. Royalties from subscription sales of newspaper microfilm have generated returns ranging from modest to significant. Librarians now are making efforts to boost revenues by actively demonstrating microfilm's value for other libraries, even to the point of negotiating royalties so that a better bargain can be had for budget-minded clients. In-house newspaper indexes marketed to the public usually yield only modest revenues due to the labor-intensive costs.

A few of these libraries advertise their commercial services. Income ranges from a few hundred dollars per year to thousands dollars. This income usually goes directly to the newspapers' general revenues. Sometimes such revenue is credited to the libraries' budgets. In hard economic times this bottom-line approach becomes a potential standard to measure the library's value, which is fine as long as the contributions continue to increase.

One wonders about the librarian's position when such monies diminish.

Another problem is emerging in this area of information marketing, the ethics of selling it. Nora Paul, formerly director of The Miami Herald library, addressed the issues of information selling. The Miami Herald advertises its library reference services to the public. The revenue generated is substantial. But Paul discovered potential conflicts of interests between revenue and satisfied customers. The Miami Herald's lawyer counseled that confidentiality of information requests could not be guaranteed to public clients. The problems centered on how librarians can balance the interest of the news organizations with the privacy rights of the public clients. Tips from research requests could be passed on to the news staff. While this is not a concern to some clients, others might legitimately feel otherwise. Newspaper libraries considering getting into the public information business can expect situations to arise requiring a delicate balancing act between the needs of the clients and the needs of the newsroom. Guidelines need to be clearly established and followed.

ONLINE FULL-TEXT NEWS DATABASES

Newspaper Databases

In recent years, online full-text news databases of nearly 100 large metropolitan newspapers, several dozen smaller newspapers and numerous national and international wire services have been made available at a price. While this number will continue t o grow, the reader should bear in mind that there are over 1,600 daily newspapers and over 9,000 nondaily papers in the United States. Even as the number of online newspaper databases continues to grow, it is small in comparison to the total number of new spapers published in this country. It is doubtful that all, or even the majority of, papers will be in electronic retrieval format accessible by the public in the

near future. Also, full-text databases do not include everything published in the paper. Thi s is-yet one more reason for realizing that the need for local newspaper indexing does not diminish with these online full-text news databases. If anything, the need grows.

Some online vendors offer gateways to news databases. H & R Block's CompuServe, for example, provides access to 850 databases, 48 newspapers including AP wires and a specialized "clipping service." The principal database vendors are Mead Data Central with NEXIS/LEXIS, Knight-Ridder's VU/TEXT and DIALOG, DataTimes and Dow Jones News/Retrieval. DIALOG offers full-text access to over 80 newspapers and magazines. We can expect to see a merging of DIALOG's newspaper files with VU/TEXT as a result of VU/TEXT's purchase of DIALOG in 1989. VU/TEXT currently offers over 70 newspapers full-text. NEXIS/LEXIS provides more than 16 wire services, dozens of magazines and newsletters, plus over 100 newspapers and business journals. In short, these database vendors suppl y an extraordinary amount of information, most of it since mid- to late 1970s. There are other online services. Check with Gale Research's Computer-Readable Databases: A Directory and Data Sourcebook for an up-to-date list.

For discussions about the early status of online news retrieval systems, consult works by Stephen Smith,42 Carol Tenopir, and Reva Basch. A very useful and recent article about full-text, online newspaper databases was written in 1991 by Dorothy Ingeb retsen and Thomas Lutgen. The authors compared and contrasted varying strategies for searching the Los Angeles Times on DIALOG, VU/TEXT and NEXIS. Anne Mintz and Reva Basch offer valuable insight into searching and quality control of full-text datab ases.

The authoritative source for online, full-text newspaper databases is a guide prepared by the News Division of the Special Libraries Association. It is designed

to guide news librarians, their managers and data-processing staff in the development of in-ho use electronic clipping files. For an update consult Judy Metcalf's chapter in this book on electronic news libraries.

BROADCAST NEWS DATABASES

Radio and television stations are awakening to the value of convenient access to information previously published and/or broadcast. For in-house indexing operations, check "Television News Libraries" by Jeannette Kopak later in this book.

Printed indexes to broadcast news are few, but they are available in larger academic and research libraries. The Television News Index and Abstracts: A Guide to the Videotape Collection of the Network Evening News Program in the Vanderbilt Television News Archives reaches back to 1968. A monthly publication with quarterly cumulations, it has author, title and subject indexes for the combined coverage of ABC, CBS and NBC. There was no weekend news recorded until May 1970. Local preempting of the evening ne ws for other programs, which occasionally occurs, causes some unavoidable gaps. The Macneil/Lehrer Report: Broadcast Review and Index has been available since 1979.

Recently, commercial databases have begun to include the full text of news and public-affairs programs from television and radio. One of the vendors, Burrelle's Broadcast Database, offers timely, comprehensive access to ABC, CBS, NBC and FNN as well as Na tional Public Radio. Network shows are not included. Unfortunately, there is not yet indexing for personal or company names. Searching is further complicated by the current limitations of the User Guide and its lack of a thesaurus. If Burrelle's Broadcast Database does well in the marketplace, doubtless these problems will be properly addressed. Other broadcast databases include NEXIS's full-text transcripts of Public Television's "The Macneil/Lehrer Newshour" and

DELPHI's full-text transcripts of "Nova" and "Frontline."

Online searchers have several sources for keeping current with the increasing number of electronic newspaper abstracts and full-text news databases. Access to such journals as Database Searcher, CD-ROM Librarians and Computers in Libraries is the mark of the true information professional.

While a number of indexing case studies have been reported in the literature in recent years, including newspaper indexing projects, there has been little in the way of research on the topic. Most of what has been done focuses upon postcoordinated indexin g or interactive searching done online. Two helpful articles, one by Tefko Saracevic and the other by Louis Gomez, Carol Lochbaum and Thomas Landauer, include valuable bibliographies.

OTHER PUBLICATIONS

Guidelines for Newspaper Libraries was first published in 1974 by the American Newspaper Publishers Association. It was updated in 1976 and completely revised in 1983. Chapters on newspaper library policies, procedures and practices were written by veteran division members. It is still available from NAA in Reston, Virginia; the price is $25. The editorial board for the 1974 edition included Anne B. Jennings, owner of the consulting firm Newspaper Library Services; Ernest Perez, librarian with the Houston (Texas) Chronicle; Agnes Henebry with the Lindsay-Schaub Newspapers; Rex Schaeffer from the Gannett Rochester Newspapers; and Gayle Thompson from the Miami News library. The 1976 edition was in reality a supplement that included three new chapters. Alison Oppedahl, librarian with the Detroit Free Press, was the editor. For the 1983 edition the editorial board included Ellen Wood Brisco, formerly with the Contra Costa Times; Michele Kapecky and Chris Kucharski from the Detroit Free Press Library; Kathleen Trimble with the U.S. News

& World Report; and Shirley Mooney, Lindsay Corbett and Barbara Valle from the Pacific Press, Ltd. library.

Basic Specifications for a Full-Text On-Line Automated Newspaper Library System emerged from the Newspaper Division's Automation Committee in 1979. The specifications were the result of the joint efforts of a wide range of newspaper automation experts including newspaper librarians, data-processing personnel, and systems vendors. The specifications were approved by the division membership in 1979. The publication was highly successful in terms of readership and revenue for the division. It has been superseded by the division's 1987 publication Automating Newspaper Clipping Files. The editorial board included James S. Scofield from the St. Petersburg Times library, Andrew V. Ippolito with Newsday's library, Kathleen Trimble from the Toledo Blade library, Ernest Perez with the Houston Chronicle library and Beverly Russell from the Seattle Times library. Additional contributors were Shirley E. Mooney, formerly with the Vancouver Sun and Province; Barbara Newcombe, then with the Chicago Tribune; Sandy Hall, formerly with the Arizona Daily Star; and Harish Trivedi, formerly with the Dayton Journal Herald.

The 60th Anniversary Commemorative Publication of the Newspaper Division of the Special Libraries Association, 1924-1984 was printed by the St. Louis Post-Dispatch in 1984. It was distributed by the Newspaper Division. The 44-page edition is now out of print, but is located in the News Division's archives. The commemorative editor was Nan Stoddard, librarian for the St. Louis Post-Dispatch. Yvonne Egertson, librarian with the ANPA Foundation, Judy Grimsley from the Orlando Sentinel, and Joan Stern, formerly with the Los Angeles Times assisted.

Newspaper Libraries: A Bibliography, 1933-1985 was compiled by Celia Jo Wall and published by the Special Libraries Association in 1986. The author, a former

newspaper librarian, recognized the need for a bibliography when undertaking research in the area. She discovered that the professional literature of newspaper libraries had not been well documented. This was the first comprehensive treatment of newspaper librarianship. The body of the work is organized into several categories, including history, administration, classification, indexing, microforms and automation. Author and subject access is available, but no annotations are offered. It is still in print. The price is $35.

Automating the Newspaper Clipping Files was edited by Mary Jo Crowley, library manager for the Philadelphia Newspapers. It was published by the Special Libraries Association in 1987 and is still in print. As with the guidelines publications, chapters were written by division members knowledgeable in the field of automation. The Newspaper Division Automation Committee involved with this publication included Kathy Foley, librarian with the The Washington Post; Anne Legett, librarian with the State-Times (South Carolina) Morning Advocate; Homer Martin, Jr., librarian for The (New Jersey) Record; Shirley Mooney, librarian with the Pacific Press, Ltd.; Ernest Perez, librarian for the Chicago Sun-Times; Judy Sall, librarian with the Dallas Morning News; and Kathleen Trimble, librarian for U.S. News & World Report.

THE UNITED STATES NEWSPAPER PROGRAMME

The Unites States Newspaper Programme (USNP) is a coordinated national effort to locate, catalog, preserve on microfilm, and make available to researchers newspapers published in the United States from the eighteenth century to the present. The program is supported by funds from the National Endowment for the Humanities (NEH), and with technical and management support provided by the Library of Congress (LC). USNP project teams in each of the fifty states, territories, and the District of Columbia locate and inventory newspaper collections held in repositories in their state in an attempt

to discover all extant issues; conduct a detailed inventory of holdings to assure completeness and to evaluate the physical condition of the papers; make bibliographic and holdings data available to researchers via an international database; and select appropriate files for reformatting onto microfilm which is produced and stored in accordance with national and international preservation standards. Information about titles and holdings is converted into machine-readable form and made accessible through a database managed and maintained by the OCLC Online Computer Library Center, Inc. (OCLC), an international library network with more than 25,000 participating libraries worldwide. Microfilm copies are held and made available through state agencies.

The origins of the United States Newspaper Program can be traced to the mid-1970's, when a poll of historians determined that bibliographic access to newspapers was one of their highest research priorities. The National Endowment for the Humanities initiated funding for the national program in 1982. If funding continues at current levels, it is expected that the final USNP grants will be awarded by NEH in 2006. All fifty states, two trust territories, and the District of Columbia are currently involved in or have completed their role in the national newspaper program.

The Library of Congress and New York Public Library began microfilming newspapers in the late 1930's. The life-expectancy of early film, however, was less than a generation. More recent developments and improvements in film stability and environmental controls, combined with refinements in high-resolution photographic equipment, provide assurance that microfilm that is produced, processed, and stored in adherence to appropriate national and international standards will serve historians and researchers for hundreds of years

Recent improvements in the quality of preservation microfilm can be directly credited to the support provided

by the National Endowment for the Humanities Division of Preservation and Access. Participants in the NEH Brittle Book Microfilming Program and the USNP have served as a laboratory for refining practices and procedures. Guidelines; documentation; training workshops; and consultancies provided during the past decade by diverse groups such as the Research Libraries Group (RLG), the New England Document Conservation Center (NEDCC), SOLINET, AMIGOS, and research support from the Image Permanence Institute at the University of Rochester all have been funded in large part by the Endowment. In addition, many of the same preservation professionals who developed these guidelines and workshops have been very active in standards work under the National Information Standards Organization (NISO), the Association for Information and Image Management (AIIM), and their international coordinating body, the International Standards Organisation (ISO), and have contributed their preservation expertise to the standards development process.

The primary audience for the guidelines that follow is intended to be staff of agencies and institutions participating in the United States Newspaper Program; vendors contracted by those institutions to perform preservation microfilming services; and libraries, archives, historical societies, and publishers seeking guidance in performing high-quality newspaper preservation microfilming.

This manual is intended to direct the attention of participants in the USNP - and others concerned for the reformatting of large files of newspapers - to the appropriate standards and recommended practice, and to offer additional guidance and options in the following areas: selection of materials for preservation; technical standards and specifications; physical and bibliographic preparation of newspapers for microfilming; microfilm inspection and

quality control; and contractual negotiations with microfilming agencies.

The guidelines represent the collaboration of many participants in the USNP, and are the product of experience and expertise shared among participants both formally at USNP conferences and workshops, and informally in correspondence and problem-solving.

7
Indexing and Clippings

The information has no value unless it is organized to retrieve for right user at right time. The basic principles of organization and managements of the news media in libraries are almost the same as in case of the other libraries. The management of media collections to a great extent depends upon the schemes of classification, cataloguing codes, assignment of proper subject headings and the other library techniques that are employed for organization of the print based media but with certain modalities required as per the special needs of the collections.

Audiovisual materials are difficult to scan without the aid of machinery. Invention of machinery is necessary between a user and information, which is a time consuming task hence, these non browse able material requires detailed classification Books are generally arranged on shelves in a classified order. But tapes are arranged according to the Accession Numbers with the reason that each tape contains programmes on different subjects. Same tapes are also sometimes reused for recording another programmes on a different subject.

INDEXING

Indexing is a major function of the news media libraries. It is needed because the contents of media programmes are not organized in a logical sequence as in case of the other media resources. Index is defined as a list of citations to journal articles and/or books arranged by subject, author, or title; indexes may be in print format, electronic format, or both. Also, a list of subjects covered

in a book, usually published at the end of the book.

An index is a specific kind of tool for finding information. Whether an index is used by a human being or by a machine, its essence is a list of index entries. Each index entry leads to an indexed item somewhere outside the index; for instance, to a record in a database, to a folder in a file drawer, or a book on a library shelf. The entries are in some recognizable order, usually alphabetical. A back-of-the book index is alphabetical by subject and points to a page number(s) in the work with information about that subject.

Indexes organize the literature so that a specialist can identify documents of interest more easily. This is particularly important in scientific and technical fields of endeavor, but it is also becoming increasingly recognized as essential in the social sciences and humanities. An appreciation of the decisions necessary in the compilation of abstracts and indexes is essential not only to the intending indexer but also to the information professional devoted to information work in whatever setting.

Traditionally, the subject approach to document retrieval is solved by a two-step process. First, each document is analyzed by an indexer according to its subject matter and assigned to one or more concept classes. These concept classes are represented by index terms. In the second step, the indexer chooses the appropriate index terms to represent the concepts identified in the document.

For all practical purposes, subject cataloging is a form of pre-coordinate subject indexing. Subject headings and index terms reflecting the concepts are surrogates for the physical documents. With subject headings, the relationships are established at the time the list is created. However, online catalogs with Boolean search capabilities allow a measure of post-coordinate indexing since the user can specify new relationships by the use of Boolean operators. A file of index terms may thus be arranged,

rearranged, manipulated, and searched. As each index term is associated with unique document numbers, documents may be identified. Indexes are not restricted to indexes of subject terms. Index files of authors, titles, report numbers, chemical formulae, and social security numbers may provide other access points if they are useful for retrieval for the users. However, the greatest challenge in document representation is in the creation and maintenance of subject access to documents.

Effective indexing involves deciding what a document is about and how the document is likely to be of interest to a particular group of users. For example, an article may be indexed in several different indexes with different descriptors or terms based on the interests of the targeted group of users. An article on computer imaging of a particular organ of the human body might be idnexed in Index Medicus and in the Engineering Index, but the particular aspects of the article brought out in each index would be different. In the Engineering Index the technical aspects of how the computer technology works would be stressed in the terms selected, while in Index Medicus, the medical aspects would be emphasized.

NEWSPAPER INDEXING

A newspaper index should not be confused with a book index. Book indexes usually index the content of individual monograph publications. Typically they appear at the back of the book and are alphabetical, including subject and name terms. Books are separate, discrete entities with a unified approach in content and style. Newspapers are ongoing publications with episodic coverage of people and events written in varying styles. The most significant difference is the frequent and ephemeral nature of newspapers. That newspapers are short-lived, fast-paced, linguistically fluid and overfull with small and seemingly insignificant information is testimony to their function as a mass medium. Philip Graham, former

publisher of The Washington Post, referred to newspapers as the first rough draft of history. Obviously, the final edition is not yet written.

A newspaper index, because of its extreme usefulness, must be made to fit the time, the place and the occasion. It must be made to suit the needs of its creators and it must meet the demands of every type of user. To be accurate and comprehensive, and, more important, to be objective in a scientific sense, the newspaper index should not interpret news and opinion according to the beliefs of its creators-it must reflect only what actually exists.

Quick, reliable, comprehensive access to information in newspapers has long been a recognized need. Libraries, historical societies and news organizations have attempted to meet that publicly expressed need in a variety of ways over the years, from bound ledgers, loose-leaf notebooks and card files to keypunch sorters, mainframe computers and personal computers. The major change in the last decade has been the advent of online full-text newspaper databases. Although most of these formats are still in use today, the trend is toward computer-assisted indexing.

With the exception of a relatively few large metropolitan newspaper indexes published and distributed to subscribers, most indexes to local newspapers are not published. They are usually one-of-a-kind projects stored in public or academic library file drawers, notebooks and even shoe boxes. Increasingly they are stored on computer disks. The quality and continuity of these indexes vary considerably. Patron usage and satisfaction with these local newspaper indexes have not been well documented. Factors affecting the success and longevity of newspaper indexing efforts include understanding the fundamentals of newspaper indexing, defining a mission, obtaining qualified staffing, purchasing and maintaining the appropriate equipment, securing sufficient and ongoing financial support and, finally, marketing the index.

INDEXING IN NEWS LIBRARIES

A good deal of indexing of books and periodicals preceded newspaper indexing. Newspaper indexing, while not an ancient art, is hardly new. Still, there remains some difficulty in differentiating this process from book or periodical indexing. What is noteworthy about these indexes is that they have survived. In this current era of high technology, when the equipment required to retrieve or display retrospective information is occasionally malfunctioning and costly to repair, it is satisfying to be able to refer to the simple written record.

Sometime in the 1850s, newspaper indexing actually began to expand and develop along the lines of modern indexing. For more than 100 years, attempts had been made to index the press of the period. The Spectator and Tattler, London's literary gossip and sa tirical newspapers, were indexed as early as the turn of the eighteenth century, and, of course, the London Times has been indexed as far back as 1790. Robert Desmond's book, Newspaper Reference Methods, contains a chapter with useful information about e arly newspaper indexes in the United States. Since then, other newspapers have been indexed for varying periods of time. These indexes also vary in scope and format. Some are handwritten notebooks or ledgers with just a listing of obituaries. Others are on typed catalog cards and include articles on local events as well as personalities. Some include annotations. A few index national and international events. Photos, however, were rarely indexed.

The most prominent and perhaps most widely used newspaper index in the United States is The New York Times Index. Established in 1851 as a handwritten guide to the contents of the newspaper, it continued in this form (with the exception of a missing index for 1859) until 1860, when the first printed index, only two pages, was issued. A three-year interval elapsed before the next issue of the

index, but it continued without interruption until 1905, when the printed index was suspended. In 1913 the present The New York Times Index started and continues to the present date. Online periodical abstracts and selected full-text articles were offered to the public via The New York Times Information Bank in the mid-1970s. In 1983 marketing and distribution rights to this online service were sold to Mead Data Corporation, which gave birth to NEXIS, a full-text online news database companion to Mead's law database, LEXIS.

As early as 1893, the American Library Association expressed interest in and the need for newspaper indexes, particularly a national newspaper index. However, R. R. Bowker, an advocate of newspaper indexes, saw substantial difficulties in developing a national newspaper index. Nevertheless, the Annual Literar y Index followed the next year under Bowker and William I. Fletcher. The plan was to index eight to ten newspaper dailies covering news of general interest that would be indexed by dates and not as references to any one paper. The index was to be planned as a cooperative venture, the actual work being done by librarians in the designated cities. The next step was to forward these indexes to a central site where a composite index would be created. The Annual Literary Index was issued at regular intervals u ntil 1904.

The concept of a news index that would serve as a key to all the newspapers of Michigan was conceived in 1920 by Stuart H. Perry and J. S. Gray of the Adrian Daily Telegram. There is the mistaken concept by many not directly affiliated with the newspaper industry that all newspapers are somehow alike. Further, it is assumed that it would be more convenient to use the identical subject headings and the same article selection policy to index a dozen or more papers. Not only is such an approach naive, it turns out to be impractical and unrealistic. Even if by some chance such a project could be launched, the resulting index would be too unwieldy to g ather into a composite

volume, particularly for the annual cumulation. On the other hand, a logical attempt by the indexing committee to control the index size by severely restricting article selection and relying upon only the most general subject terms would defeat the major purpose of an index. Library patrons would be disappointed and frustrated with such ineffective access to material published in their local paper.

A more difficult-to-anticipate indexing problem, especially for composite projects, is the decision-making process for adding new subject terms, deleting old ones, dividing subject terms and selecting cross-references. The communications problems emerging from these daily occurrences would boggle the mind and overwhelm the spirit of even the most dedicated indexers. The alternative of having one central indexing operation undertake the task of indexing several newspapers simultaneously reduces the procedural problems somewhat. Nevertheless, costs, quality and timeliness remain difficult to manage on multiple-newspaper indexing projects, even given the advantages of high-powered computers and effective indexing software.

A far better approach for librarians interested in launching a newspaper indexing project would be to treat local newspapers individually and index appropriately for the users in each paper's circulation area. Scholars and other patrons eager to search a topic through several of a state's papers may have to adjust to different terminology. That problem can be mitigated with abundant cross references, useful scope notes and a clearly expressed article selection policy. Foremost in the mind of indexers shou ld be the eternal questions, "What types of articles would the public seek?" "How would someone, anyone ask for this information?" "What terms would they use?" To avoid these questions is to discover that the public will not use what is not useful.

Prior to card indexes, which could be easily updated

with new entries, libraries relied upon loose-leaf ledgers with handwritten or, occasionally, typed entries. The problems with expanding subject and name headings while maintaining chronological order were manifest. A better system had to be found.

The origin of newspaper card indexes is unclear. One of the chief claimants is the San Francisco Chronicle, which started its index in 1864 and continued until the disastrous fire of 1906 destroyed all its records and files. Partial substantiation of the Chronicle claim is contained in a newspaper report of the dedication of the newspaper's building in 1879. A reference was made to seeing "in the three hundred tin pigeon holes along the blank wall of a narrow room what was doubtless the germ of the index card system.

In 1927 a questionnaire about newspaper libraries was prepared by the Newspaper Group of the Special Libraries Association. The survey was mailed to 380 newspapers. Seventy replies were received. Among the questions asked was one about indexing. Twenty-nine librarians reported indexing their newspapers, 15 on cards and 4 on long sheets. The remaining ones were apparently too closely allied with the clipping files to be called true indexes.

With the advent of the Works Progress Administration in 1935, newspaper indexing enjoyed rejuvenated interest. The WPA was called upon to provide funds for the digesting and indexing of newspapers. More than 20 newspapers from across the United States lau nched projects covering editions from 1728 to 1940. In addition, some collections of newspapers owned by historical societies and schools were indexed and microfilmed. Friedman's book on newspaper indexing lists some nineteenth century newspaper indexes. Most are incomplete and many have long been discontinued, but some can still be consulted by checking newspaper archives

in large public and research libraries.

The Lathrops, Norman and Mary Lou, created the Newspaper Indexing Center in Flint, Michigan, in 1969.18 They wanted to create the first comprehensive, descriptive bibliography of all published and unpublished newspaper indexes in the United States and Can ada. The couple's efforts resulted in The Lathrop Report on Newspaper Indexes, first published in 1979.

A detailed listing of valuable newspaper archives, including indexes, can be also be found in the 1991 publication Untapped Sources: America's Newspaper Archives and Histories prepared by the Gannett Foundation Media Center for the American Society of New spaper Editors. The interested reader should also consult several excellent journalism bibliographies, notably Jo Cates' 1990 Journalism: A Guide to the Reference Literature and Eleanor Blum's and Frances Wilhoit's 1990 Mass Media Bibliography: An Annotated Guide to Books and Journals for Research and Reference.

At one time, early in the development of full-text news databases, it was thought that additional enhancing or indexing was unnecessary. After all, one could search not only on the headline, dateline and byline, but the entire article. Surely that was bet ter than an abstract or simple bibliographic entry. In short, what more could be needed? The passage of time, expanding news coverage, investigative reporting and the vagaries of news reporting styles have revealed how wrong that assumption was. Some addi tional intellectual effort and news article analysis are necessary to link appropriately all the myriad, fleeting and unstated associations among a never-ending stream of stories about people, events and institutions. News librarians were discovering that as their databases grew and reporters came and went, a high level of information retrieval precision was difficult to maintain. The quality control of online full-text databases is definitely improving with enhancement of effective indexing techniques, a

dditional costs notwithstanding.

Generally, newspaper libraries do not index their papers for their own staffs. The few that do are exceptions. Traditionally, reporters, editors and photographers have relied upon their libraries' clipping files and photo collections rather than published indexes. These files are arranged by personal name and subject and usually contain all that is needed.

Indexes are time-consuming for news staff to use, requiring several steps before the information is captured. Immediate, full-text access (clip files or online database) is preferred. However, not all newspapers have in-house libraries, or, if they do, they are so lightly staffed that maintaining a labor-intensive, space-devouring clipping file has too many disadvantages. Local news indexing in these circumstances is a reasonable option.

Among smaller and midsized newspapers, the number of newspaper libraries preparing, publishing, marketing and distributing their own indexes to public subscribers is small indeed. Notable among these few is a relatively long-term index to three small (com bined circulation 65,000) Southern newspapers. It is IND-EX, published by the Durham Herald-Sun, Inc. From April 1981 to February 1990, the Herald-Sun library with a staff of two to three indexers prepared monthly newspaper indexes and annual cumulations for 15 paid subscribers. This indexing project was initiated following research undertaken by a Herald-Sun library intern, Gloria Colvin. When the project was launched in-house, additional library staff were employed to maintain the index. It was a sepa rate project from the in-house clipping file operation. The news staff did make regular and frequent use of IND-EX, particularly for byline reports, but, as expected, it was the clipping files, complete and in date order, that the news staff turned to for faster response time. After nine years the Herald-Sun Index was reluctantly discontinued as a

result of company-wide budget cuts. A procedure manual of this new indexing operation is available from this chapter's author.

Public and academic libraries have a long history of starting to index local newspapers (on cards or in ledgers) only to become overwhelmed by the enormity of the task. The investment of money, the need for managerial support, the twin problems of staff shortage and training, the questions of whether to market the index or not, the difficulty of maintaining consistency and currency, and the tribulations of selecting and keeping up-to-date with equipment modifications and software enhancements combine to frustrate even the most dedicated public librarians. Hence news indexes may be started but are quickly found to be costly, time consuming and difficult to maintain. As a result, they are likely to be just as quickly discontinued. However, even such incomplete indexes continue to be valuable.

Many, but not all, state libraries have printed guides to their newspaper indexes. Public and academic libraries in the states make every effort to keep as current as possible with their newspaper indexes. A more recent description of a college library computerized newspaper indexing project was delivered in 1992 paper by Candace Peterson.

Occasionally groups of libraries have banded together to undertake news indexing projects in anticipation of sharing responsibilities and costs. Interestingly, this approach seemed to complicate matters rather than simplify them. Questions about newspaper indexing policies and procedures proved difficult to identify and resolve over time and distance. The policy and procedural considerations start with determining the best computers, peripherals and software available and then spiral into a myriad of other decisions. How long can the project continue without maintenance and upgrades? Will the equipment invested in be superseded by newer versions? What is the cost of conversion to newer computers? Bear in mind that

the handwritten or printed news indexes of 250 years ago are still usable. Can we forecast that the indexes, thesauri and authority files stored on the computers using the software purchased on today's market will be available even in ten years time? How will the vocabulary be controlled? What a bout updates and cumulations? What will be the marketing approach? Who will train and supervise data-entry staff? The questions seem endless, the answers elusive.

Until 1982 there were no indexing programs for microcomputers. In the past decade there has been a marked increase in the number and quality of indexing software programs. For the most part, however, they have been targeted for the "back-of-the-book" ind exer rather than for newspaper or periodical indexers. A few of these innovative programs can meet some newspaper or periodical indexing requirements. Experimentation with demonstration disks offered from these indexing vendors will help in selecting soft ware.

Linda Fetters prepared A Guide to Indexing Software for the American Society of Indexers. Essentially, there are two kinds of indexing programs available. The first is a text-embedded style designed to work with word-processing files. The second type works like electronic index cards. It is possible, with some accommodation, to create newspaper indexes with existing software. Currently, there are no software programs designed exclusively for newspaper indexing available at a moderate price. The full-text online systems offer some indexing capability, but they are usually attached to a newspaper's front-end electronic typesetting system. Fetters's guide provides authoritative descriptions with illustrations of such software programs as Cindex, IndexAid2, Indexer 's Assistant, Indexit, INDEXX, Macrex Plus, wINDEX and Micro Indexing System. She also includes a publications list from the American Society of Indexers covering indexing bibliography, proceedings and where to find advice for

selecting a computer for ind exing. Many of these programs have demonstration disks available for interested clients at nominal cost.

Hypertext is another type of indexing. It was first developed on mainframes and minicomputers in the 1960s and 1970s. It was not until about 1987 that it appeared on microcomputers. Examples include Apple Computer's HyperCard, IBM's Textbank/PC, Houdini f rom MaxThink, Software Garden's KnowledgePro and Eastgate's Hypergate. There is debate about what are so-called true hypertext programs. A full discussion of this topic is beyond the scope of this chapter. Information is readily available in local libraries.

On the cutting edge of experimental indexing software there are topics as automatic indexing, artificial intelligence and expert systems. The interested reader is invited to explore these topics in other sources than this chapter. At this time we can report that expert systems are intended to capture human expertise and encapsulate it within a computer system. The American Petroleum Institute in the 1980s designed an expert-like system for automatically indexing abstracts for the API database. A thesaurus developed over 20 years of indexing was used. The goal was not only to reduce the cost of indexing but to increase the efficiency of searching the database.

The library literature offers several creative examples using word-processing programs and database-management software for indexing newspapers. These programs may have been modified or superseded. Fetters's guide to indexing sof tware is more recent and comprehensive.

The advent of personal computers and relatively easy-to-use indexing software packages has made newspaper indexing more attractive, but not without costs and continued support of top-management support. Indexing local newspapers is not something librarians can do in their

spare time. Relying upon volunteers, eager and inexpensive as they are, presents special problems in training and scheduling. Consequently, widespread, convenient, accurate, timely and comprehensive access to loca l news published in local newspapers is rare. However, newer, simpler computer-assisted indexing of newspapers is making the long-term objective possible and even economical.

While corporate and research libraries make extensive use of costly online full-text news databases, other major libraries as a rule do not. How to pass on news database search fees to students, faculty and scholars who are accustomed to no-fee access is a severe problem for public libraries and even large academic libraries. As a consequence, there is still heavy reliance by these libraries upon the relatively low-cost published newspaper indexes. Typically The New York Times Index, The Washington Post Index, The Christian Science Monitor Index, the Atlanta Journal-Constitution Index, The Wall Street Journal Index, USA Today Index, as well as international newspaper indexes are standard news reference tools.

Not to be overlooked among published newspaper indexes is the Index to Black Newspapers, which started in 1977. It is compiled quarterly from the final editions of at least eight prominent black newspapers. The current list includes Afro-American (nationa l edition), American Muslim Journal (Chicago), Amsterdam News (New York), Call & Post (Cleveland), Chicago Defender, Daily World (Atlanta), Michigan Chronicle (Detroit), and Sentinel (Los Angeles). The index covers local, regional, state, national and int ernational news with subject and personal-name access. Also in the area of special newspaper indexes is the Alternative Press Index, started in 1969, which covers purportedly alternative and so-called radical publications.

The Canadian News Index is another published newspaper index. Started in 1977, it continues with monthly indexes and annual cumulations. Coverage

extends to the Calgary Herald, Toronto Globe and Mail, Halifax Chronicle, Montreal Gazette, Toronto Star, Van couver Sun and the Winnipeg Free Press. The subject index covers governmental and corporation names, while individuals appear in the personal-name section. References are arranged chronologically. Online searching for articles appearing in several of thes e newspapers since 1981 is available on several database services.

In 1992 the United Kingdom daily paper, The Independent, announced a new monthly official index. The Independent Index for the first six month of 1992 to be available in two paper-bound quarterly cumulative issues from July. Subsequently, the monthly is sues will be cumulated annually into a cloth-bound volume. "The index is prepared by a team of indexers of Research Publications International based in Reading, UK. The aim is for a three-week turnaround from keying to customer, with access to news, edito rials, features, financial information, captions, letters, and obituaries." Research Publications International also publishes indexes to The Times, Financial Times and Le Monde.

News digests such as Editorials on File (from 1970) and Facts on File (from 1941) provide useful access to national and international news. Editorials on File reprints leading editorials from over 150 newspapers. It is indexed by subject. Facts on File of fers factual summaries of national and world news. The advantage of this weekly index is that it provides access to the contents of newspapers before their own indexes are published. It is also available online.

CD-ROM products such as Newspaper Abstracts and the full-text ProQuest Newspapers Ondisc are alternative methods of gaining subject access to newspapers. They are not cheap. While the hardware costs are declining, the updates on discs are not. With a larg e clientele these products can be useful and cost-effective.

Information Access produces InfoTrac with automated bibliographic recovery. InfoTrac contains indexing to nearly 800 periodicals, including a year of The Wall Street Journal and two months of The New York Times. The information is on optical disc and is etrieved by patrons using PCs. While InfoTrac fills in the lag-time gap from printed indexes, it does have some retrieval problems. One current drawback is that search terms cannot be linked by Boolean operators. For large libraries, the big investment costs of CD-ROM products may be manageable.

NewsBank offers libraries a package of newspaper articles on microfiche with indexing. Articles are selected and microfilmed from selected newspapers published in all 50 states. Access is through rather broad index subject headings. Almost 100,000 items are added annually, but no one paper is completely indexed. NewsBank indexes are available on an automated, self-contained system, NewsBank Electronic Index.

The availability of these indexes in varied formats, while useful, does not diminish the urgency for subject access to local newspapers. Printed indexes to local news continue as a vital information need.

PRESS CLIPPINGS

For more than 100 years an enormous number of libraries, archives, companies, NGOs and governmental institutions have been collecting newspaper clippings and maintaining clipping archives. With the emergence of online-editions of newspapers and networks of such electronic editions some of them have closed their paper-based collections. The newspaper publishing houses themselves have ceased to clip their newspapers. But most of the other institutions still maintain their paper-based clipping collection, and they will continue to do so in the future. The reasons for this are simple: their users are not only interested in the pure text of a newspaper article but

demand a higher level of authenticity. The typography, the layout, the pictures that come with it, the impression of the whole page - all this information is lost in the full-text database.

As long as print editions are the main distribution media of newspapers, it will make sense to collect clippings of the print edition, because they have this added value of information - either by cutting them out manually, or by scanning them and cutting them electronically. But this is not the only reason why we are optimistic about the future of clipping archives. Another reason lies in the general role research libraries will play in the near future: The information society of the future will not suffer from a lack but from a surplus of information. Distinguishing relevant from non-relevant information will, therefore, be one of the main tasks of librarians in the future. Since the very beginning it has been the job of archivists to select from a wide range of newspapers specific articles related to the subject of the collection.

When accessing a clipping archive one can be sure that the archive has recorded every important article on politics, culture and contemporary history from all newspapers - and this simple fact gives the user an enormous amount of confidence. He can be sure that, in principle, all of the important articles have been selected by specialists. This argument becomes even more important if we do not think in months or years, but in decades. Searching a database containing the full text of newspapers from 1990 to 2010 will produce a huge number of hits that working with such a database will be a task for information specialists only. The majority of users, who may be able to use a database but who are no specialists, will prefer a system where librarians have reduced complexity to a degree which allows non-professional users to access relevant information in a comfortable way.

These considerations have been the starting point for any effective exercise on press clippings. It has been

initiated in order to equip paper-based clipping collections with the main tools for doing their job in a digital environment

1. To develop tools and software in order to facilitate the scanning, clipping, indexing, OCR-processing, storing, and accessing of newspaper clippings.
2. To build up the prototype of a network of clipping archives. The user will gain access to the collections via an OPAC, and he will be able to download the desired articles - within the bounds of copyright restrictions, of course.
3. To work out a business model for a successor of a network. Clipping archives from all over are welcome to join the network, thus securing a constant increase of data and the technical advance of system.

When considering clipping collection that are still growing, however, we are confronted with a completely different situation. This is particularly due to the new role of newspaper articles after the digital revolution.

It is only recently that, under the influence of the Internet, newspaper articles have become a completely new product. Not too many years ago they were just written for the day, and their value diminished after a very short time. By contrast, the Internet permits various kinds of re-publication of electronic newspaper articles. Especially online editions of newspapers, online archives, networks of newspapers, homepages of electronic bookshops, companies, and information services, appreciate the availability of news articles. Obviously, the writers and publishers of these articles are fascinated by the new possibilities and have a strong interest in the exclusive exploitation of the new value of newspaper articles. On the other hand, the "new" newspaper article and the possibilities of its dissemination through the Internet are more akin to the broadcasting of music songs on the radio than to the traditional form of paper publishing. And what

would Radio be like if songwriters had to exploit their songs without the support of collecting societies? It is quite likely that collecting societies will play an important role in the retrodigitisation of clippings, and they might play a similar role in the case of current articles, too. There is a strong need to compare various possibilities in order to solve this problem.

The articles can be accessed locally, and they are delivered as paper copies by snail mail to off-site users. The standard workflow of an electronic clipping archive will be organised in a similar way and will consist of the following steps:

* scanning
* clipping
* pasting
* prime and bibliographic indexing
* filing
* content indexing final storing

STOCK SHOTS

News media libraries support in the production process at different stages of production with varied types of library materials. They provide ideas on the topics of programme through subscriptions to periodicals or the press-clipping services. The idea can be further elaborated with the help of books, films and periodicals. The topic of production is usually finalized keeping in view the financial capability, availability of subject experts and the feasibility of shooting. But what we do not take into consideration is the amount of feedback already available in the libraries in the form of Stock-shots.

Normally, every producrion agency possesses some programmes which be can comfortably use the shots since being their own productions copyright is not a problem for them. The shots from other agencies' productions can be used up to certain duration free of charges. One particular

shot can be used in a number of programmes and in different perspectives, thus conveying different meanings. 'Stock-shot' literally means a shot from the library collection. They are visuals or a combination of audio and vision already available in the library. They can be identified from slide/tape programmes, films or videos. Some of the stock-shots have been used in innumerable productions. The reuse value is directly proportional to their archive value. The live coverage of dropping the atom bomb at Hiroshima and Nagasaki, man's landing on the moon and various expeditions undertaken by mankind have a high archive value. But there arc some stock-shots which saved mankind from a possible disasters too or rather by seeing the impact of these bombs (SCUD 'missiles, etc.) could be a deterrent in future. It could even advocate in preventing the production of these weapons for all times to come. This would depend on how effectively these events arc originally recorded and preserved.

Stock-shots can be divided into the following four categories

1 Recordings of Historical Events
2 News Stories
3 Shots listed out of Complete Programmes
4 Rough Cuts.

Historical events may include visits of dignitaries, launching of new programmes, seminars, international meets and even the events, which seem to be common today but may obtain significance in the time to come. In West Bengal, the government has decided to withdraw the tram service from the city of Kolkata. This might be overlooked being an ordinary event day but is fact significant for a person having futuristic outlook. In the time to conic shots on trams will certainly be needed by anyone who attempts to write the history of Kolkata or of the modes of transportation. It will always be better to fulfill the arising requirement in advance. Gandhi and Nehru are no more

with us but they are still needed to inspire the generations.

New stories are usually available on video or in 16 mm film with combined or separate magnetic sound tracks. They form a valuable source of material for reuse not only for strictly news purposes but also provide a wider range of themes, which can be incorporated for teaching and learning purposes. In fact, every significant event is news at first which goes down slowly into the ages of history. The reusability of the coverage depends upon its news values and also its non-availability. There are news stories, which can never loose their value at any point of time. Even if there are no financial constraints involved in special shooting, the producers may come across difficulties leading to delay in programme production; one cannot wait for the whole year to cover a shot of heavy rain or snowfall. Just imagine waiting a full day to shoot rising sun which may disappoint further if covered with clouds the time of sun rising. In a case like this, the stock-shot is the best answer.

Stock-shots can be identified from complete film and television programmes available in a library or a group of libraries for resource sharing purposes. Producers use shots from their early productions or from the current productions of others they preview but such use is generally based on the personal memory of the producers or their diaries if maintained by them properly. A computerized information retrieval system can provide an easy access to a vast amount of audio-visual resources. This is slowly becoming inevitable.

8
Preservation Techniques

Newspapers are more fragile unlike books. Their preservation poses greater problems than the other media of communication. The contents of newspapers are also not organized according to the subject hence they need to be preserved in full, whether physically or on the electronic media.

The first and the foremost requirement in preservation of newspapers is to save them from physical and environmental threats. Natural calamities destroyed valuable collections of libraries in the past. No one knows when disaster will strike. An important first step is the formulation of a disaster plan. Every news operation and every news library should have one. Disaster plans range from the very general to the very specific. Here we will discuss the many perils a library may face and also some basic principles required for the news libraries in preparing for the unpredictable.

The most common disasters in libraries almost always involve water damage-often in the course of fighting fire. Early warning and careful placement of fire-fighting equipment constitute the first order of business. To a library, water is a friend as well as a foe. While computer rooms have the luxury of expensive Halon gas systems to fight fire, most libraries must make do with water sprinkler systems placed in the ceiling. Sprinklers usually stop the total loss by fire, but the resulting water causes a host of new problems.

To provide some protection from both fire and water, there should be some special plans for materials of greater value to your news operation: the publisher's papers, for instance. Some cabinets have limited fire and water resistance and may be used to protect materials in the case of a minor fire. If valuable materials are not actively used, off-site storage by storage specialists may be the ticket.

Although the process of putting out fires is a frequent cause of water damage, it is not the only one. Broken pipes and floods have inundated many a collection. Basement libraries or storage areas are at particular risk. Making sure that nothing is stored directly on the floor is an important first step.

The most common method of handling wet books and papers is freeze-drying or vacuum drying. There are companies in most areas that specialize in this relatively common process. Some have specially outfitted trucks that can dry the materials. Freezing wet materials, even in a local meat locker, stops mold and gives time to make difficult decisions on the preservation of library materials, the weeding or the destruction. A note on microfilm: it should not be frozen but stored in cold water until arrangements can be made with the manufacturer for drying and reprocessing. But when considering the problems of water-based glues, ink stains or photos stuck together, it is better to figure out ways to avoid the whole catastrophe.

Structural collapse caused by improper building engineering is fortunately a relatively rare occurrence and, given qualified architects and engineers, should not be of great concern. Floor loads must not exceed the designed strength of the building, or the floor must be rebuilt to handle a larger load. Structural collapse caused by earthquakes, tornados and other natural disasters is beyond our prediction and control. Again, these types of disasters are relatively rare.

If there are ways to create duplicates of collections to store off-site, consider them carefully. Cost may be prohibitive in many cases. In microfilm clipping collection, it is probably worth making a duplicate copy to store in another loca tion. It might make sense to store negatives in a separate location from photographs. With the advent of electronic libraries, storage of the library database in off-site locations has become part of the routine. The cost and size of backup tapes make the procedure relatively easy and inexpensive. The arrival of electronic photography and storage should also make off-site storage possible, although the tremendous cost of storing photographs digitally will not make this an easy decision.

Here we will discuss some of the problems of formation and implementation of disaster plans. The disaster plan for a news operation is a bit different than for the average business. A news operation is more concerned with how to continue the operation of the business in spite of all odds, since disasters are something news people do not want to miss.

There are four basic areas that need to be addressed in a disaster situation.:The leader: Who will be in charge? Have a mechanism to determine that and have materials and procedures for guidance.

* **Personnel:** Who will direct emergency medical needs, organize the staff and look after their general welfare? This is the first team in action, and it has top priority.
* **Facilities:** Who will survey the facilities, systems and equipment? You must know their safety and their usability.
* **Newsroom operations:** How will the news operation work, taking into consideration the previous three factors and various scenarios?

Some other disaster preparedness topics to consider are the following:

* Setting up a disaster preparedness committee
* Electrical backup and generators
* Telephone systems, cellular phones and two-way radios
* Medical supplies and provisions
* Staff orientation and training
* Disaster plan responsibility
* Mutual aid agreements and off-site facilities
* Emergency instruction, booklets and wallet cards
* Insurance coverage

STORAGE

Back issues of newspapers are generally not arranged and kept properly in houses for future use. Most people discard and recycle their papers, but some editions that are considered special may be worth preserving and retaining. Preserving the newspapers of today presents a challenge, however, because they are printed on paper that is inherently unstable. Prior to the mid-1800s, most newspapers were published on paper made from cotton rags. Many of these surviving papers are in excellent condition today, and show little sign of discoloration or brittleness. But producing paper from rags was expensive and, as the century progressed, the supply became insufficient to meet increasing demands.

In the later part of 1980's, wood was introduced as an alternative fiber. Trees were in great abundance. The wood pulp industry grew quickly, which produced a less expensive paper that was also smooth and absorbent,desirable properties for the highspeed printing presses that were growing in popularity.

Newsprint is not a permanent-quality paper because of the wood impurities that remain in the paper after processing. These include resins, tannins and lignins. Lignin represents the largest percentage of impurities, 16-

35 percent, depending on the type of tree. Lignin is an amorphous substance found in and around the cell walls of the fiber and may be thought of as the cement that glues the plant fibers together. Lignin itself is not an acid, but when exposed to light, high humidity, and atmospheric pollutants, it promotes acidic reactions in the paper. Acidity causes the fibers to weaken and break, and is the major culprit in causing paper to deteriorate and become discolored and brittle. Lignin can be extracted if the paper pulp is processed chemically and fully bleached. But most modern newsprint contains a mixture of wood pulp from chemical and mechanical processes. The mechanical process involves grinding the wood to form a pulp, but it does not remove lignin from the fibers.

When newspapers or clippings are valued most for the information they contain, and not as artifacts, reformatting the information on to a more permanent quality medium may be the best preservation option. Archivally processed microfilm will work.

For long term storage, it is necessary to store papers in a dark, stable environment of 60-70° F and 40-50 percent relative humidity will slow the rate of deterioration. A central location in one's home is usually recommended for storage, not the attic nor basement or garage. An attic can become quite hot and basements and garages are often damp. Excessive dampness or humidity,bove 65 percent is conducive to mold growth. It is also important to store papers flat and in contact with materials that will not contribute to further damage. A chemical transfer called "acid migration" can occur in papers in contact with one another: The more acidic sheets transfer acids to less acidic sheets. To prevent this damage, the quality of cardboard boxes or paper storage folders should meet the permanence specification, and materials within the enclosure should be interleaved with permanent quality paper.

Newsprint may also be protected by polyester film encapsulation or in plastic sleeves. Encapsulation was

developed and tested by the Library of Congress to protect fragile and brittle papers. This process involves placing the sheet of newsprint between two clear sheets of a polyester film and sealing the film to itself, not to the paper. The film is sealed around the edge with a double-stick tape, or by machines designed to bond the film. Encapsulation is preferred to lamination, which melts plastic into the paper and is difficult or impossible to reverse. In addition, often we do not know the long- term aging effects of the plastics or adhesives used in lamination. The encapsulation process allows one to reverse the procedure without damage to the paper. Safe plastics for paper storage include pure polyester, polypropylene and polyethylene. These materials have no additives or surface coatings that can adversely affect the paper over time. Permanent-quality paper boxes and folders, plastic sleeves and encapsulation materials can be purchased from the conservation suppliers. However, even papers that are encapsulated or placed in plastic sleeves will generate acidic gases that are trapped inside the envelope and cause deterioration. These gases need to be neutralized; there is an additional procedure that can chemically stabilize the acidic gases.

This procedure, called deacidification, is designed to neutralize the paper's acidity and leave an alkaline salt behind to absorb future acids. This chemical treatment does not stop future deterioration or restore the paper's original color or strength, but it will slow the rate of deterioration, and extend the useful life of the paper three-to-five times. Deacidification is recommended for all papers that are encapsulated or placed in plastic sleeves. If deacidification is not possible for a sheet that requires physical protection, it will be beneficial to place a sheet of permanent-quality paper inside the capsule or sleeve. Deacidification is best performed by a conservator who can assess the paper's condition and provide the most appropriate treatment.

Newspapers are threatened by deterioration because of the high content of acid in the paper used. This makes it

necessary to transfer the newspapers to some other medium. So far, the preferred method has been microfilming. Microfilm has the advantage to be a rather stable medium, and it may form the basis for a subsequent transfer of the newspaper to digital format. Digital media for storage have not the same stability as microfilm. Digital technology, however, presents better possibilities for providing access to the newspapers. For this reason a transfer to digital formats is considered in many libraries.

There are several approaches for the preservation of valuable, old, deteriorating newspapers. A limited number of pages of a newspaper can be preserved by deacidification procedures. The procedures involve deacidification followed by either lamination or encapsulation. One home remedy involves treating materials by soaking newspaper sheets in a solution made with milk of magnesia and club soda. Another uses diethyl zinc gas. A third technique involves soaking in two calcium solutions, drying in any acid- free environment and then encapsulating or laminating in mylar. With lamination, a "sandwich" is made with the document between two sheets each of mylar and acid-free tissue paper. Heat (300 degrees) and pressure is applied for a period of time to this "sandwich." Laminating a newspaper page may take one week to process. The bonding is supposed to last more than 100 years stored under archival conditions. Encapsulation is a process where a deacidified document (or newspaper page) is placed between two sheets of mylar or other similar chemically inert plastic and the edges are sealed with a heating element. Before the last seal is made, air is removed from the "pocket." Each page can be bound and prepared into a volume for archival storage.

Without archival storage conditions, high temperatures can speed the decomposition of materials and cause excessive drying and brittleness. High humidity encourages mold growth, as does poor air circulation.

Bright light causes fading of colors and browning of paper and other materials.

BINDING

Binding of the printed editions is anothert way for providing durability to the library collections. This goes well for newspapers as well for the last many decades as a continuous process for most of the reputed libraries. While the problem of preservation is often overlooked, the binding of newspapers has been, and indeed still is, a central concern of librarians, who are firmly convinced that both operations make an important contribution to the protection of the originals.

In the case of binding, there is an evident tendency to equate newspapers with books, even though their origins and use are quite different. Among other things, it should not be forgotten that the binding of a codex was devised in an era when volumes were laid horizontally on shelves. The change to a vertical position led to a series of unforeseen effects that endangered even the most robust and functional of bindings. For the larger sized books structural features closely resembling those of medieval bindings (wooden boards of considerable thickness, spine bands of cow hide, metal clasps, etc.) remained in use up to the 17th and 18th centuries, as they appeared to offer the only guarantee of assured durability. This could, however, only be assured in the case of horizontal storage. The switch to vertical placement, which has been customary in all libraries since the 16th and 17th centuries, presented structural dilemmas for bookbinders, which have never been satisfactorily solved. It is no coincidence that most large-sized books now display very serious damage to their bindings, even when structured by means of techniques closely resembling those of the Middle Ages.

The binding materials and processes for books and newspapers are quite different. The bindings of ancient books were designed to ensure a certain solidity, but this

cannot be said of those now produced for newspapers. Though comparatively expensive, newspaper bindings offer no guarantee at all of the physical preservation of the contents.

Moreover, the binding of newspapers could be described as "unnatural," given that dailies are produced as separate sheets and their assembly is rarely justifiable except as a deterrent to theft. It is not clear however, how effective a deterrent it is. Given the great fragility of the paper used, it is by no means rare for larger or smaller portions of sheets to be removed (either deliberately or accidentally).

Regarding the binding of newspapers, the only advantage (protection against theft) is of negligible importance, and numerous disadvantages persuade that the practice of binding newspapers should be discontinued as soon as possible.

MICROFILMING

Microfilming, also called microphotography, consists in the reduction of images to such a small size that they cannot be read without optical assistance. This amazing photographic compression often results in a ninety-nine percent saving of space. The microfilming service is one of the most extensively used and common practices in modern reprographic science. With the advancement in the field of documentary reproduction, the function of the library is not only restricted to classification, and handling of printed materials but to documentation, in the form of microfilm, which is becoming a major factor in library science, particularly where reproduction is essential for preservation purposes. The remarkable increase in microfilming activities is due to the recognition that a large portion of books, periodicals and newspapers are deteriorating because of the poor quality of paper and print. The use of microfilming for almost seventy years has provided an excellent reproduction method for recording

photographic images of library materials.

Preservation of rare and deteriorating documents is considered one of the most important purposes in microrecording. Valuable rare documents are now being microfilmed to preserve them from loss and destruction. Although the principles of microfilming have been known for over 150 years, it is only after the Second World War that the use of microfilming methods became very popular as a technique for reproducing the printed page. In the case of valuable documents, which might become damaged by constant use, a microfilm copy of it may be made and stored separately. It must be protected against loss, which would be irrecoverable in the case of valuable documents, records or rare books. The film used is safety film and if properly processed it will last longer than the originals. If possible, the microfilm copy may be given to the reader for reference purposes which not only prevents the original from damage by constant use but will also protect it from danger, such as fire, natural disaster, etc. For additional security, negatives and positives can be stored in different places; being of small bulk, it can be specially protected. Scientific estimate indicates that a negative with careful handling and storage could be preserved for about 500 years.

Although treated as a novelty until the 1920's, microforms originated much earlier. John Benjamin Dancer, an English scientist, known as the "Father of Microphotography," began to experiment with and manufacture microproduced novelty texts as early as 1839. In 1853 he successfully sold microphotographs as slides to be viewed with a microscope. Utilizing Dancer's techniques, a French optician, Rene Dagron, was granted the first patent for microfilm in 1859. He also began the first commercial microfilming enterprise, manufacturing and selling microphotographic trinkets. Dagron, in the fall and winter of 1870-71, during the Franco-Prussian War, demonstrated a practical use for microforms when carrier

pigeons were used to transport microfilmed messages across German lines to the besieged city of Paris.

Two significant events in 1938 hastened the use of microforms for archival preservation in American libraries and institutions. Because of rapid deterioration of the newsprint original and the numerous difficulties in storage and use of newspapers, Harvard University Library began its Foreign Newspaper Project. Today this project continues and the microform masters are stored at the Center for Research Studies in Chicago. This same year also saw the founding of University Microfilms, Inc. ('UMI') by Eugene Power. He had previously microfilmed foreign and rare books, but in 1938 his work became a commercial enterprise as he expanded into microfilming doctoral dissertations.

The improved technology of today also increased computer output microform applications. Microforms produced directly from a computer are being used to produce parts catalogs, hospital and insurance records, telephone listings, college catalogs, patent records, publisher's catalogs and library catalogs. Although this technique is widely used, the permanence of microfilm masters on film is the standard for most libraries and those applications where preservation is an issue. Microforms will have a future not only in the short term but probably in the more distant future as well.

In the light of the foregoing, and while the digital reproduction of newspapers should in any case be commenced as soon as possible, microfilming remains a positive method of preservation despite all its limitations. Though unquestionably in need of improvement, it provides a starting point in most cases for transfer from traditional to electronic media without subjecting the originals to any further stress.

Finally, and despite widespread notions to the contrary, the durability of microfilm depends on a series of steps, such as the creation of a master, the provision o

at least one copy for current use, and preservation of the master in a controlled environment. It is essential to have two copies because the film undergoes a series of traumas every time it goes through the reader. The preservation of the master copies (when they exist and are of acceptable quality) is also greatly neglected. While this point is important for all items of cultural heritage, it is particularly so in the case of photographic material, whose average lifespan can be halved by exposure to relative humidity of over 50%.

It is possible to get as good full text search from scanned microfilm as from scanning the originals. The resolution of 35 mm fine grain microfilm reduction ratio is equivalent to 12.5 million pixels, which gives the user a good platform for years to come. However the possibilities of the film is not always sufficiently used because of lack of good laboratory practise during preparation and microfilming procedures. Improving the quality needs a quality program that can be implemented in the ongoing processes. It is important to rise the awareness of the personnel.

The quality of the originals is crucial for their future use. In preparing the newspapers it is essential to sort out pages of bad quality and replace them with other copies if possible. In the case of torn and brittle material the pages have to be conserved especially on the information area. Wrinkles have to be flattened.

The identification of the newspaper numbers, pages, editions and supplements is important. Also the refilming of pages would be important to point out. This procedure could be prepared at this stage and implemented during the microfilming. If the library chooses to index the substance of the film the future use of the scanned images will be much more easy to handle.

There is lower or more sophisticated levels to acknowledge the needs of the scanning process. Usually

the microfilming scanners have problems with the identification of many varying page sizes on the film. This is because the scanners usually recognize a new frame at an indicated place, at its left corner or margin. Identification problems occur when the format changes of the newspaper or its supplements. The supplements can also be filmed in another direction than the original newspaper. In filming doublepaged newspapers the change of newspaper number can cause problems if the first page of a new number is filmed separately. In this case the scanner cannot recognize the frame where the left side is empty and hence black. This concerns microfilms without blip. To identify each image on the film the camera table can mark the left side of the frame area with a 2-3 cm broad white tape strip, which will indicate the beginning of a frame for the scanner. A more sophisticated way could be to place a white bar on the left side, which would include one or more of the following information:

* information about the size of the item (in cm or inches)
* bar codes for fixed symbols for the following information: change of newspaper number, (page), new edition (if changed editions are filmed), new supplement, page repetition, defect original and so on. This information could to some extent also be indexed by the blip-functions in some cameras.
* a grey-scale indicator

Different library materials are sensitive to these conditions in different ways. Microfilm, which is very stable, may react to chemicals in paper with which it comes into contact, while newspaper clippings are innately a preservation time bomb. Since about 1860, most manufactured paper has contained alum, which produces sulfuric acid when exposed to normal atmospheric moisture. The acid then makes the paper brittle. Deacidification of a clipping collection would be

prohibitively expensive. Most libraries interested in preservation of their clippings and in reducing their bulk as well, have turned to microfilming. The advent of CD-ROM technology also holds promise for a high-resolution product that can be retrieved and viewed from a computer terminal.

It would be unusual for the typical news librarian to have professional training and experience to qualify for archival responsibility of visual and audio collections. Nevertheless, managing the photo and graphic collections over a period of time does raise questions about who and where to find expertise in this area when the need emerges. Extensive discussion of preservation and restoration techniques for photographs, videotapes and audiotapes is beyond the scope of this chapter, but mention should be made of at least a few of the approaches and resources currently available on these topics.

Although computers and electronic data are also sensitive to the environmental factors listed in the preceding section, the advent of computer technology in news libraries has brought a whole new list of cautions to the forefront. Probably the most important rule is to back up software and data on a regular basis and store these backup disks or tapes off-site. Many people have lost days, weeks or months of work by not having appropriate backup procedures.

Password security for computers and files will keep the hacker from getting into your system and causing problems. Security software allows for levels of access that can control the authority of the user. There is also software that will block the use of computers by unauthorized personnel.

Computer viruses are another major problem. These viruses are hidden computer programs designed by hackers often as proof of their ability. It spreads from computer to computer when a machine "boots up" from a floppy disk. The results range from a mild, brief interruption to

wholesale devastation of data.

Few organizations with growing numbers of microcomputers can afford to ignore the spread of computer viruses and other contaminants. The news library cannot operate independently of other departments regarding computer safety; the entire organization must be committed to institute and follow safety measures.

Computer users who never copy software, data or games from other computers, who never download files from electronic bulletin boards and who never lend their floppy disks to a friend should be safe. A good rule is to avoid shareware and unauthorized copies of software and use virus-checking software to check new software. Consult with local computer vendors for anti-virus programs and how to install them. Symantec, Microcom and McAfee Associates are among several vendors offering reliable, reasonable cos t programs.

New viruses continue to infect and reinfect computers, so the best computer disaster prevention advice is to minimize opportunities for contamination and keep current with anti-viral protection.

Accessibility of the electronic media and the long life expectancy of microfilm is a good combination. Preservation microfilm should last for 500 years, which give the brittle collections transferred to this medium a future of archival safety.

The preservation microfilms have advantages and disadvantages relating to future digitisation. High-contrast microfilms have a limited dynamic range, which in many cases is a good thing. This is a good feature especially if you compare the scanning result of the originals and the microfilms of grey text on brittle and brownish paper. Smaller shades, spots or wrinkles in the paper are also eliminated. The text is clearly extinguishable from the base. It favours fulltext search possibilities of the newspapers, which uses Optical Character Recognition (OCR)-software

on bitonal images. The resolution quality needed of the films are quite sufficient including 16x reduction rates and favours a Quality Index of 8. On the other hand photographic material will never be as good as digitising in greyscale from the original. But there is also a clear difference between the different kinds of copies, while the negative direct duplicate gave the poorest results for the photographs in the newspapers.

There are many possibilities to combine microfilming and digitisation today. It is possible to microfilm first, and digitise from film. Another choice is to digitise first and preserve the content on film by COM (Computer output on microfilm). There is also the possibility to use hybrid microfilm-digitisation cameras for simultaneous microfilming and digitisation. For newspapers the first option is by far the most used.

In this guidance we are focusing on the microfilming first aspect according to the IFLA Newspaper Microfilming Guidelines and aiming at high quality film to satisfy the image quality and advanced search needs for the users of digital newspaper libraries. The newspaper originals have to be of high quality to enable fulltext search of the collections. The aim is to get sufficiently high-level images – to microfilm collections once, avoiding the expense of refilming even when technology requires better images. The better the quality of the digitised image and fulltext search possibilities and the less conversion expenses.

This guidance will try to give some suggestions for the libraries to make their own production plans and guidelines for future digitisation of microfilms. With microfilm as the platform it is possible to convert the collections whenever needed into the technologies of the future centuries.

Policy decisions regarding selection criteria and copyright will not be dealt with here, these matters belong to collections management. Bibliographic requirements,

indexing of newspaper editions, supplements, quality control and choice of agency have been discussed in the IFLA Guidelines.

DIGITIZATION

Digitization refers to the process of translating a piece of information such as a book, sound recording, picture or video, into bits. Bits are the fundamental units of information in a computer system. Turning information into these binary digits is called digitization. This digitization process can be accomplished through a variety of existing technologies.

Digitisation offers easy access to the collections of newspapers. It is possible to combine these processes in a more economical manner when the aspects of digitisation are considered already in the microfilming process. There are problem in converting newspapers in the electronic form for all kind of media. A newspaper is a composite work consisting inter alia of articles and paragraphs written by the staff reporting all kinds of news, contributions by free lance writers e.g. feature articles, letters to the editor, advertisements &c. They usually also contain artistic pictures, e.g. drawings or caricatures and photographs illustrating the articles.

Digitization is one of the hot topics in librarianship today. To build a digital collection requires that the content of a collection be available electronically. The rhetoric of the Information Highway has provided the impetus to convert many existing paper-based (or sound and video) collections into new digital media. The assumption is that digital collections will be more accessible to a broader range of users, presumably through networking technologies, and that there are new efficiencies to be gained in resource-sharing and for preservation.

It should be noted that libraries have already undertaken some of the most significant digitization initiatives in the past 25 years — most notably, the creation

of searchable OPACs. There are also many digitization projects and initiatives which provide digital information in a variety of formats, such as CD-ROM and locally-mounted databases. There are many private digital collections already being maintained by DIALOG, Mead Data, and Micromedia. This background document examines some of the basic digitization concepts and issues. The focus will be on the digitization of paper-based artifacts and associated data-capture technologies.

In general, many of the technological challenges to the digitization of paper-based materials have been met. Microform digitization still poses a number of challenges. Digitization technologies for library- based applications, rather than business applications, are still relatively new and much of the hardware and software should be considered as first generation products] In all cases, the effective retrieval of digitized data remains a significant challenge.

The concepts and technologies connected with digitization are complex. There is a basic process which involves different sets of hardware and software technologies at each step. Determining the appropriate technology is directly linked to the anticipated use and purpose of the material being digitized.

Artistic pictures, like caricatures have always been covered by copyright. Photographic pictures, however, have in the Nordic countries, except Island, been covered by special rules, until they were included in copyright law at the great revision of Nordic copyright law in 1995. The new law distinguished between photographic works and photographic pictures. Photographic works are the result of the independent creative effort of the photographer, whereas photographic pictures are not the result of an independent creative effort. A photographic work is protected 70 years after the death of the author. Photographic pictures are protected 50 years after the

production. Norway deviates a little from the other Nordic countries. Here the term of protection for photographic pictures is 15 years after the death of the photographer, though at least 50 years after the production of the picture.

The newspaper as a whole, as a composite work, is protected. A person, who creates a composite literary or artistic work by combining works or parts of works, has copyright in the composite work. But the copyright in the composite work shall be without prejudice to the rights in the individual works. Not only the editorial work, but also the layout of the newspaper enjoys independent protection.

THE COPYRIGHT PROBLEM

Copyright implies that the author has the exclusive right to control the work by making copies of it or making it available to the public, whether in original or amended form, in translation, adaptation into another literary og artistic form or into another technique. The transfer of the work to a device which can reproduce it, is considered as a reproduction. This implies, that others, e.g. libraries, may not without the permission of the author or special warrant in the law transfer the newspaper or the works it is composed of, to a device which may reproduce it. When digitizing the newspaper, this is what one is doing.

The major part of the contents of the newspaper is produced by regular employees on fixed salary or correspondents or photographs on a free-lance basis, paid for their occasional contributions. The newspaper also receives many uninvited contributions: Feature articles, which the author is paid for, letters to the editor involving no payment and lastly advertisements, the printing of which you have to pay for.

The terms for employees or free-lance contributors are regulated either by collective or individual agreements, and the right to use the works is expressly transferred to the newspaper. That the newspaper has the right to use uninvited contributions follows from the fact, that the

author usually requests the newspaper to print it. The author may accordingly transfer his rights in the work. His droit morale, however, may not be transferred.

The author may also transfer future works, future rights and future forms of exploitation. If a given form of exploitation, however, is not known at the time of agreement, it is assumed that the author has not transferred this particular form of exploitation.

The employers right to exploit the copyright of employees is limited to the usual activities of the establishment, and if nothing else is stipulated in the agreement, only those rights are transferred which are necessary for the performance of the normal activities of the newspaper. What is considered normal activities is judged either from the time, when the works were produced, or the terms of employment were made or last revised.

This is of importance for the question concerning the right to publish digital versions of the newspapers. Not before the development of the Internet within the last five years, digital publishing can be said to be a normal activity of newspapers. Now the activity is usually covered by the agreements between publishers and the regular staff and the contracts with free-lance correspondents. One must assume that other contributors must at some time during the nineties have realized, that digital publishing either actually was or was at the point of being a normal activity parallel to the traditional printed edition.

So far we have been concerned with the authors transfer of rights to the publisher. The conclusion is that digital publishing not before at some time during the nineties can be claimed to be a normal part of newspaper activities. Publishers may therefore not claim to have a right, without the consent of the authors, to re-publish newspapers produced before this time in digital format, e.g. in a database.

Finally, and this may be the most important point in

relation to libraries, the transfer of copyright does not give the new rightsowner the right to change the work or to transfer the right further, unless this further transfer of rights is normal or evidently presupposed.

The conclusion, therefore, is that even if publishers may have acquired the right also to publish the newspaper in digital format, it does not follow that they may further transfer this right to libraries. This would only be possible, if this further transfer were either contained in the agreement between authors and publishers or normal or evidently presupposed. And neither is the case. The implication of this is that the reproduction implied in the process of digitizing either requires an agreement with the authors or must be warranted by law.

COLLECTIVE AGREEMENTS

It is natural to start with the publishers the development of digital collections in libraries. The permission of publishers is important, as they have the rights to the newspaper of a composite work. But concerning the specific works contained in the newspaper, the publisher has only the right to use the works in the usual way. Further ways to exploit the works remains with the authors.

Journalists and photographers are normally organized in trade unions. It is the normal job of trade unions to negotiate agreements concerning wages and working conditions, including remuneration for the exploitations of members' copyright. But not all journalists or photographers are members of trade unions, and as there does not exist a possibility for extended collective license agreements on this field, one must make individual contracts with those authors, who are not comprised by the collective agreement made by the union.

Many of the other contributors are most likely to men of letters, authors of fiction and special literature and the like. They are often organized in authors unions, who

normally are authorized to negotiate agreements concerning remuneration for the exploitations of members' copyright.

Another important group is authors to advertisements. Many of the advertisements, printed in newspapers, are produced by the professional staff of advertising agencies. Design, layout and drawings will normally have such creative quality that they are protected by copyright. Within advertising branch transfer of copyright is accepted to a larger extent than within journalism. The transfer in question, however, concerns transfer of the product and use of it to the customer. The transfer of copyright to a library with a view to digital use of the products is not a part of the normal activity of an advertising agency, and therefore still belongs with the authors, i.e. the staff. Some of these are probably members of a trade union, who may be authorized to make copyright agreements on behalf of their members.

Finally, there are many individual contributors whom it may be difficult to categorize, e.g. authors of letters to the editor &c. They are not likely to make claims of remuneration in case their contribution is digitized together with the rest of the newspaper. It is, however, quite possible that some of these authors would not like to see his contribution re-published by being digitized – for perfectly legitimate reasons.

The conclusion is that the unions or organizations of journalists and photographers, professional authors and advertising staff are possible partners in agreements concerning digitizing their members' works. However, there will still be many contributors, who for some reason or other, will not be covered by such agreements. This problem may in certain cases be solved by extended collective licensing.

Bibliography

1 Allen, Susan. ed. 1994 Media Anthropology: Informing Global Citizens. Westport, CT: Bergin & Garvey.

2 American Society of Newspaper Editors. "Newsroom Employment Survey." Published 2003. Web site: http://www.asne.org.

3 Amjad Ali Computerization of media libraries. Jl. of Information Sciences 3 ,19; 1993: 119-127.

4 Amjad Ali Computerized information retrieval system for stock shots: the experience of a media library in Librarianship and Information Technology, 1992. Indian Library Association, New Delhi.

5 Amjad Ali. Information management in film and television libraries. Lib. Herald 32, 1-2; 1994.

6 Annette Lewis. Survey of Journalism Libraries," Special Libraries, vol. 34, no. 9, November 1943, pp 454-456.

7 Arbitron, Inc. "Radio Today: How America Listens to Radio," various editions, 1998 through 2003. Web site: http://www.arbitron.com/study/grt.asp.

8 Arbitron/Edison Media Research. "Internet and Multimedia 11: New Media Enters the Mainstream, 2003." Published 2003. Web site: http://www.arbitron.com/downloads/Internet_Multimedia_11.pdf.

9 Association of College and Research Libraries (ACRL). Media Resources Committee. (1999). Guidelines for media resources in academic libraries. Retrieved August 30, 2000, from http://www.ala.org/acrl/guides/medresg.html

10 Audiovisual Committee, Public Library Association. Guidelines for Audiovisual

11 Audiovisual handbook. 3rd Ed. 1954. Department of Public Instruction, Oklahoma.

12 Audit Bureau of Circulations. "Audit Reports," various magazines, 1991-2003. Web site: http://www.accessabc.com.

13 Audit Bureau of Circulations. "Newspaper Publisher's Statement," March 30, 2003.

14 Bahr, AH. Video in libraries: A status report 1979-80. 2nd Ed. 1980. Knowledge Industries Publication Inc.

15 Banks, Marcus. 1994 Television and Anthropology: An Unhappy Marriage? Visual Anthropology 7:21-45. 1994b Interactive Multimedia and Anthropology: A Skeptical View. Anthropological Multimedia 1:1-6 (electronic journal at http://www.rsl.ox.ac.uk/isca.marcus.banks.02.html)

16 Becker, Gay. 1995 Editorial: Medical Anthropology in a Time of Change. Medical Anthropology Quarterly 9(1):3-5.

17 Behr, R., & Iyengar, S. (1985). Television news, real-world cues and changes in the public agenda. Public Opinion Quarterly, 58, 479-508.

18 Big browsers are watching you...January 1993 Library Association Record David Nicholas and Kevin Connolly

19 Birkhead, Douglas. 1989 An Ethics of Vision for Journalism. Critical Studies in Mass Communication 6:283-294.

20 Boyd-Barrett, Oliver, and Peter Braham, eds. 1987 Media, Knowledge and Power. London: Croom Helm.

21 Boyle, D. (1977). In the beginning was the word...libraries and media. In D. Boyle (Ed.),

Expanding media (pp. 3-11). New York: Neil-Schuman.

22 Briyant, Eric Thomas. Music librarianship: a practical guide. 1959. James Clarke & Co., London.

23 Brosius, H., & Hans Kepplinger, M. (1992). Beyond agenda-setting: the influence of partisanship and television reporting on the electorate's voting intentions.. Journalism Quarterly, 69, 893-901.

24 Brosius, H., & Hans Kepplinger, M. (1992). Linear and nonlinear models of agenda-setting in television. Journal of Broadcasting and Electronic Media, 36, 5-23.

25 Brown, Jane Delano, C.R. Bybee, S.T. Wearden and D.M. Straughan. 1987 Invisible Power: Newspaper News Sources and the Limits of Diversity. Journalism Quarterly 63:45-54.

26 Brundin, Robert. "Changing Patterns of Library Service in Five California Junior.

27 Bryant, Jennings, and Dolf Zillmann, eds. 1986 Perspectives on Media Effects. Hillsdale, NJ: Lawrence Erlbaum Associates

28 Burkett, David Warren 1986 News Reporting: Science, Medicine and High Technology. Ames, IA: Iowa State University Press. 1965 Writing Science News for the Mass Media. Houston: Gulf Publishing.

29 Cabecairas, J. The multimedia library: Material, selection and use. 1991. Academic Press, New York.

30 Case, Tony. 1994 Newspapers as Community Boosters. Editor & Publisher 11/26:11,35.

31 Center for Media Literacy. Retrieved August 31, 2000, from http://www.medialit.org/

32 Chiball Bernard. The National Film Library and its cataloguing rules. The Jl. Of Documentation. 112; June 1955. 79-82.

33 Chisholm, Margaret E., and Ely, Donald P. Media Personnel in Education: A Competency Approach. Englewood Cliffs, N.J.: Prentice-Hall, 1976.

34 Christian, Harry, ed. 1986 The Sociology of Journalism and the Press. Totowa, NJ:Rowman and Littlefield.

35 Clement, Evelyn G. "Audiovisual in Libraries; the Past." Paper presented at the 95th ALA Conference, ISAD Audiovisual Section Program, July 1976. ERIC document #ED 129 328.

36 Cobociars James. The multimedia library. 2"1' Ed. 1982. Academic Press, New York.

37 Colleges." PhD. Dissertation, Stanford University, 1970.

38 Collision. RL. Ed. Libraries for television. Library World. 59, 781; July 1965; 3-7.

39 Comenius, John Amos. The Orbis Pictus. Syracuse, N.Y.: C.W. Bardeen, 1887.

40 Commentary. 1992 Making use of the Press. Practicing Anthropology 14(4). Features several articles from applied anthropologists about dealing with the press, including a helpful "how to" by G. Alfred Hess, Jr. (27-31).

41 Competency and Task List for Specialists and Technicians in Media Management, Media Product Development, and Instructional Program Development" Audiovisual Instruction, November 1974. pp. 22-69.

42 Covering the Persian Gulf War: The First 72 Hours at ABC News Library May 1991 American Libraries. Carolyn Schade

43 Craig M. Allen. News Is People. Ames, Ia.: Iowa State University Press, 2001.

44 Crawford, W. (1999). Being analog. Chicago: American Library Association.

45 CT: Bergin & Garvey. Features chapters on television, radio, newspapers, magazines, etc., by anthrpologists who have worked in the mass media.

46 Dahlgren, Peter, and Colin Sparks . 1992 Journalism and Popular Culture. London: SAGE Publications

47 DAILY (J. E.) Organizing non-print materials. 1986. Marcel Deckker, New York.

48 Dale, Edgar. Challenges to Librarianship. Tallahassee, Fl.: Florida State Uni

49 Dalip Singh. Newspaper libraries. In JAIN (MK). Ed. Fifty years of library information service in India. 1998. Shipra, Delhi, 136-145.

50 Dalton, R. J., Beck, P. A., Huckfeldt, R., & Koetzle, W. (1998). A test of media-centered agenda settings: Newspaper content and public interests in a presidential election. Political Communication, 15, 463-481.

51 'Day, Dorothy L. Film in the library. Library Trends 4, 2; October 1955,174-181.

52 De Kieffer, RE and Cochran, Lee M. Manual of audiovisual techniques. 1966. Printice Hall, New Delhi.

53 Dewey, Melvil. Detvey Decimal Classification and Relative Index. 16th ed. Lake

54 Dhir, BM. Types of media and its selection. 1987. TTTI, Chandigarh.

55 Does the Web Threaten the Sanctity of Electronic Archives?. April 11, 1996, E&P Online

56 Doss, Milburn Price, ed. Information Processing Equipment. New York: .

57 Dunn, Fannie W., and Schneider, Etta. "Practices in City Administration of

58 Duprey, Trevor N. Ferment in College Libraries: The Impact of Information

59 Eason, Tracy. "A Selected Bibliography of AV Media in Library Literature, 1958

60 Effects of the Electronic Library On News Reporting Protocols. 1988 Journalism Quarterly, vol. 65, no. 4. Kathleen A. Hansen, Douglas M. McLeod, and Jean Ward

61 Eiselein, E.B. 1976 Applied Anthropology in Broadcasting. Human Organization 35(2):165-172.

62 Ellison, J. (1985). Media librarianship. New York: Neal-Schuman. Ensor, P. (1999, October 15). Multimedia to the people. Library Journal Net Connect, 34, 15-16.

63 Enroght, B). Non-book/media materials in the library: a note. Library Association Record 72, 12; 1970; 368-69.

64 Entman, R. M., & Paletz, F. L. (1980). Media and the conservative myth. Journal of Communication, 30, 154-165.

65 Erbring, Lutz, & Godenberg, E.N. (1980). Front-Page news and real-world cues: A new look at agenda-setting by the media. American Journal of Political Science, 24, 16-49.

66 Flemingl Bennett. "Audio-Visual Services in Colleges and Universities in the

67 Forging a Professional Relationship with the Newsroom. October 1997, Speech given to the AUKML conference. Nora Paul

68 Forman, Sidney. "Innovative Practices in the College Library." College and

69 Gerber, Gloria S. "Occupational Task Inventory for Media Specialists." Unpublished paper, State University of New York at Buffalo, 1980.

70 Ghorpade, S. (1986). Agenda setting: A test of advertising's neglected function. Journal of Advertising Research, 26, 23 27.

71 Gilbert, 1 and Wright . Non-book materials: their bibliographic control. 1971. NCET Working Paper 6.

72 Gray, S. (2000). Multimedia across the disciplines. Syllabus, 13, 9, 14-18.

73 Grove, Pearce S. Nonprint Media in Academic Libraries. Chicago: American Librarv Association. 1975.

74 Guernsey, L. (2000, March 2). Bookbag of the future. New York Times, G1.

75 Guidelines for Newspaper Libraries. Published by American Newspaper Publishers Association, 1974.

76 Hamman, Frances. "Bibliographic Control of Audiovisual Materials: Report of a Special Committee." Library Resources and Technical Services Bulletin 1 (Fall 1957): 180-89.

77 Hart, Roderick P. 1996 Easy Citizenship: Television's Curious Legacy. Annals of the American Academy of Political and Social Science 546:109.

78 Hessel, Alfred. A History of Libraries. Metuchen, N.J.: Scarecrow Press, 1950.

79 Hester, B., & Gibson. R. (2003). the economy and second-level agenda setting: A time-series analysis of economic news and public opinion about the economy. Journalism and Mass Communication Quarterly, 80, .

80 Hobon, Michi S. Sound recording cataloguing: a practical approach. Cataloguing and Classification Quarterly. 17, 2; 1990.

81 Holbrook, R. A., & Hill, T. G. (2005). Agenda-setting and priming in prime time television: Crime dramas as political cues. Political Communication, 22, 277-295.

82 Hostrop, Richard W. Education Inside the Library Media Center. Hamden, Conn.: Shoe String Press, 1973.

83 Hume, Margare.) Searching for Media in the online catalogue. MC Jl. Of Academic Media Librarinship. 3 (1) 1995 pi-18

84 Information Strategy in Newsrooms: New Emphasis on Traditional Roles for News Librarians. July 1997, NetMedia conference paper. Nora Paul

85 Information Technology Changes in Large Newspaper Libraries. Fall 1991 Special Libraries. Kathleen A. Hansen and Jean Ward

86 Intranet Management, Content Development, and Digital Gift Shop: the Cutting-Edge Library at the Atlanta Journal-Constitution Nov/Dec 1998 Online, vol. 22, no. 6. Thomas Pack and Jeff Pemberton

87 Iyengar, S. (1979). Television news and issue salience: A reexamination of the agenda-setting hypothesis. American Politics Quarterly, 4, 395-416.

88 Iyengar, S. (1991). Is anyone responsible?: How television frames political issues. Chicago: Univ of Chicago Press.

89 John L. Nolan, "Audio-Visual Materials." Library Trends 10, (October 1961), p. 262.

90 Johnston, W. Dawson. "Symposium of Music in Libraries: St. Paul Public Library." Library-Journal 40 (August 1915): 574.

91 Kane, Joseph Nathan. Famous First Facts, 4th ed. New York: H.W. Wilson, 1981.

92 KAPLAN (DON). Television and the classroom. 1986. Knowledge Industries Publications.

93 Ken Auletta, "Vox Fox." The New Yorker, May 26, 2003.

94 Kidwell, Ronald E., Jr. 1991 Key Factors in Changing a Newspaper's Culture. Editor & Publisher April:60, 51.

95 Kim, S-H, Scheufele, D. A., & Shanahan, J.(2002). Think about it this way: Attribute agenda-setting

function of the press and the public's evaluation of a local issue. Journalism & Mass Communication Quarterly, 79, 7-25.

96 Kujoth, Jean Spealman. Readings in Nonbook Librarianship. Metuchen, N.J.: Scarecrow Press, Inc., 1968.

97 Lancaster, F. Wilfred. Information Retrieval Systems, 2nd ed. New York: John Wiley and Sons, 1979.

98 Latrobe, K. (1998). Chronology of significant events in school librarianship. In K. Latrobe (Ed.), The emerging school library media center. Historical issues and perspectives (pp. 279-283). Englewood, CO: Libraries Unlimited.

99 Laurien Alexandre and Henrik Rehbinder, "Separate but Unequal." Columbia Journalism Review, November/December 2002, pp 99 - 101.

100 Lenz, Linda. 1992 Commentary: Notes from Journalism 101. Practicing Anthropology 14(4):35-36.

101 Lett, James. 1987a Commentary: An Anthropological View of Television Journalism. Human Organization 46(4):356-359.

102 Library lecturer found on moon. 1993 Library Association Record, vol. 95, no. 2. Richard Whitey

103 Lieberman, Irving. Audiovisual Instruction in Library Education. New York: Columbia University School of Library Service, 1955.

104 Lindstrom, R. (2000). How pictures are taking over the world. Presentations, 14, 44-54.

105 Loucks-DiMatteo, A. (1985). The history of media librarianship: A chronology. In J. Ellison (Ed.), Media librarianship (pp. 72-89). New York: Neal-Schuman.

106 Mackuen, M. B. (1984). Exposure to information, belief integration, and individual responsiveness to agenda change. American Political Science Review, 78, 372-391.

107 Materials and Services for Public Libraries. Chicago: American Library Association, 1970.

108 McBride Commission. 1987 Many Voices, One World in Media, Knowledge and Power, Oliver Boyd-Barrett and Peter.

109 McCleneghan, J. Sean. 1994 The 1993 Newspaper Science Reporter: Contributing, Creative and Responsible. Social Science Journal 31(4):467-477.

110 McCombs, M. & Estrada, G. (1997). The news media and the pictures in our heads. In S. Iyengar & R. Reeves (Eds.) Do the media govern? Politicians, voters, and reporters in America (pp. 237-247). Thousand Oak, CA: Sage.

111 McCombs, M. (1997). Building consensus: The news media's agenda-setting roles. Political Communication, 14, 433-443.

112 McCombs, M., & Gilbert, S. (1986). News influence on our pictures of the world. In J. Bryant & D. Zillman. (Eds.), Perspectives on media effects (pp. 1-15). Hillsdale, NJ: Erlbaum.

113 McCombs, M., & Shaw, D. (1977). The agenda-setting function of the press. In D. Shaw and M. McCombs (Eds.), The emergence of American political issues: The agenda-setting function of the press (pp. 89-105). St. Paul, MN: West Publishing.

114 McCombs, M., & Shaw, D. L. (1972). The agenda-setting function of mass media. Public Opinion Quarterly, 36, 176-187.

115 McCombs, M., Einsiedel, E, & Weaver, D. (1991). Contemporary public opinion: Issues and the news. Hillsdale, NJ: Earlbaum.

116 McDonald Gerald D. Educational Motion Pictures and Libraries. Chicago: American Library Association, 1942.

117 McDougall, Lorna. 1992 Commentary: Communicating With the Press. Practicing Anthropology 14(4):33-34.

118 Media libraries and new media

119 Milet, L., & Albright, M. (1997). Media centers in transition: Results of a 1997 CCUMC member survey. College & University Media Review: A Look at Practices, Trends & Research, 4(1), 11-41.

120 Miller, J. M., & Krosnick, J. A. (1997). Anatomy of news media priming. In S. Iyengar & R. Reeves (Eds.) Do the media govern? Politicians, voters, and reporters in America (pp. 258-275). Thousand Oak, CA: Sage.

121 Miller, M. (1998). Anticipating the future: The University of Michigan's media union. Library Hi Tech, 16(1), 71-83.

122 Miltenoff, P. (2000). Integrating streaming media into Web-based learning: A modular approach. Syllabus, 14(1), 58-61.

123 Mim, Y. (2004) Media agenda-setting and its electoral consequences: A study of political advertising, the news media, and the public in the 2002 primary election for texas governor. Dissertation Abstracts International, A: the Humanities and Social Science, 64, 4609-A.

124 Modern News Library: Documentation of Current Affairs in Newspaper and Broadcasting Libraries. 1978, Gaylord Professional Publications.

125 Morgue' as a Factor in Journalism, Library Journal, vol. 46, May 15, 1921, pp. 443-446. By Joseph F. Kwapil.

126 Morgues No More. July/August 1994 American Journalism Review. Jacques Leslie.

127 Mullins, Lynn S. "The Rise of Map Libraries in America During the 19th Century." Bulletin 63 (March 1966).

128 National Telemedia Association. Retrieved August 31, 2000, from http://danenet.wicip.org/ntc/NTC.HTM

129 New Media Sends Some Librarians to the Late Shift. March 25, 1996, E&P Online

130 News Libraries in Crisis. University of Minnesota's Institute for New Media Studies and the Minnesota Journalism Center. Kathleen Hansen and Nora Paul

131 News Media Libraries: A Management Handbook. 1993, Greenwood Press. Edited by Barbara P. Semonche

132 Newspaper Libraries 1952, The Library Association Joseph LewisThe

133 Newspaper Libraries, their History, function and Methods: a Symposium by Librarians in Various Parts of the Countries," Special Libraries, vol. 15, no. 1, January 1924. [Note: includes papers presented by Joseph F. Kwapil, William Alcott, Maurice Symonds, among others.

134 Newspaper Morgues become Libraries of Value," Special Libraries, vol. 18, no. 10, December 1927.

135 Newspaper Number," Special Libraries, vol. 17, no. 9, December 1926.

136 Newspapers in the Library: New Approaches to Management and Reference Work

137 Nolan, John L. "Audio-Visual Materials." Library Trends 10 (October 1961): 261 -67 .

138 OLSON (Nancy B). Cataloguing of audiovisual materials. 4'" Ed. Media Marketing Group, Dekalb.

139 Olson, C. (2000, January 8). The year in video 1999. Billboard, 87.

140 Palmer, Joseph W. "Surveying the Future of Public Library Film Service." New York Library Association Bulletin, 30 (April 1982): 1-8.

141 Pan, Zhongdang, R.E. Ostman, P. Moy and P. Reynolds. 1994 News Media Exposure and its Learning Effects during the Persian Gulf War. Journalism Quarterly 71(1):7-19

142 Parker, John Austin. "A Brief History of the Picture Collection." Wilson Library Bulletin 30 (November 1955): 257-58.

143 Parsons, Edward Alexander. The Alexandrian Library. New York: Elsevier Press, 1959.

144 Pearce S. Grove, Nonprint Media in Academic Libraries. Chicago: American Library Association, 1975, p. x.

145 Pierre Key's International Music Yearbook, 1928. New York: Pierre Key, Inc., 1928.

146 Pitman, R. (1992). The video librarian's guide to collection development and management. New York: G.K. Hall.

147 Placid Club, N.Y.: Forest, 1959.

148 Post War Standards for Public Libraries. Chicago: American Library Association, 1943.

149 Post, Richard. "College and University Functional Learning Resource Program Evaluation." Unpublished paper, Ohio University 1980.

150 Pringle, Eugene A. "Films in Public Libraries." Drexel Library Quarterly 2 (October 1961): 261-67.

151 Processing Audio Visual Materials. Bloomington, Ind.: Indiana University, 1948.

152 Qualter, T. H. (1989). The role of the mass media in limiting the public agenda. In M. Margolis & G. A.

Mauser (Eds), Manipulating public opinion: Essays on public opinion as a dependent variable (pp. 139-152). Pacific Grove, CA: Brooks/Cole.

153 Quinly, William J. "Audio-Visual Materials in the Library." Library Trends 5 (October 1956) 294-300.

154 Ralph J. Shoemaker. Weeding and Other Space-Saving Methods," Special Libraries, vol. 47, no. 8, October 1956, pp. 357-360.

155 Reinhold, 1955.

156 Research Libraries 29 (November 1968): 486.

157 Richard W. Hostrop, Education Inside the Library Media Center. Hamden, Conn.: Shoe String Press, 1973, p. 3.

158 Richardson, Ernest Cushing. Classification: Theoretical and Practical. 3rd ed. New York: H.W. Wilson, 1930.

159 Robert Luce.1913 "The Clipping Bureau and the Library," Special Libraries, vol. 4, Sept./Oct. 1913, pp. 142-157., President, Luce Clipping Bureau.

160 Roberts, D. (1976). 'Printism' and non-print censorship. Catholic Library World, 48, 223-224.

161 Role of the Newspaper Library in the Production of News. 1987 Journalism Quarterly, vol. 64, no. 4

162 Rufsvold, Margaret. Audio-Visual School Library Service. Chicago: American Association of School Librarians, 1949.

163 Saettler, Paul. A History of Instructional Technology. New York: McGraw-Hill Book Company, 1968.

164 Schleuder, J., McCombs, M., & Wanta, W. (1991). Inside the agenda-setting process: How political advertising and TV news prime viewers to think about issues and candidates. In F. Biocca (Ed.), Television and political advertising: Vol. 1 (pp. 265-309). Hillsdale, NJ: Lawrence Erlbaum.

165 Schmeckebier, Laurence F., and Eastin, Roy B. Government Publications and Their Use. Rev. ed. Washington, D.C.: Brookings Institution, 1961.

166 Scholtz, J. (1995). The video industry – history and evolution. In J. Scholtz (Ed.), Video acquisitions and cataloging: A handbook (pp. 3-15). Westport, CT: Greenwood.

167 SCHRAMM (Wilbur) Big media little media. 1985. Sage Publications, London.

168 Schudson, Michael. 1989 The Sociology of News Production. Media, Culture and Society 11:263-282.

169 Schudson, Michael. 1995 The Power of News. Cambridge, MA: Harvard University.

170 Science 79 (February 23, 1934).

171 Shane, M. Lanning. "Audiovisual Aids & the Library." College and Research Libraries 1 (March 1940): 143-46.

172 Shores, L. (1973). Audiovisual librarianship. The crusade for media unity (1946-1969). Littleton, CO: Libraries Unlimited. Slide, A. (1992). Before video: A history of the non-theatrical film. New York: Greenwood Press.

173 Shores, Louis. Audiovisual Librarianship. Littleton, Colo.: Libraries Unlimited, 1973.

174 Small Newspaper Libraries: The Libraries That Time (and Automation) Passed By. Fall 1991 Special Libraries. Judith L. Hegg

175 Smith, Joel. 1995 Understanding the Media: A Sociology of Mass Communications. Cresskill, N.J.: Hampton Press.

176 Smith, Josephine Metcalfe. A Chronology of Librarianship. Metuchen, N.J.: Scarecrow Press, 1968.

177 Soloman, William S. 1992 News Frames and Media

Packages: Covering El Salvador. Critical Studies in Mass Communication 9(1):56-74.

178 Soroka, S. N. (2003). Media, public opinion, and foreign policy. Harvard International Journal of Press/Politics, 8, 27-48.

179 Special Library Association, Geography and Map Division, Directory Revision Committee. Map Collections in the United States & Canada: A Directory. 2nd ed. New York: Special Library Association, 1970.

180 Stone, C. Walter. "The Place of the New Media in the Undergraduate Program." Library Quarterly 24 (October 1954).

181 Stone, Sharon D.

182 Strabo. The Geography of Strabo. New York: Putnam, 1917.

183 Survey of Large Newspapers Studies Information Practices. Fall 2003 Newspaper Research Journal (vol. 24, no. 4) Kathleen Hansen, Nora Paul, and Betsey Neibergall

184 Taglang, K. (2000). Universal service update. Digital Beat. Retrieved August 31, 2000, from http://www.benton.org/db022900.html

185 Technology. Washington, D.C.: Communication Service Corporation, 1968.

186 The Electronic News Library: An Online Revolution Takes Shape. 1996 American Libraries, vol. 27, no. 9. Ron Chepesiuk

187 The History of Media Librarianship: A Chronology 87

188 The History of Media Librarianship: A Chronology 89

189 The Joys of Being a News Librarian. American Journalism Review. Joanne Meil

190 The Newspaper Library in the Information Age: a Personal View from WithinNovember 1989 Online. Ellen D. Briscoe and Kathy Foley

191 The Virtual Library: Yesterday's paper will provide tomorrow's revenue through digital access. September 1995, Presstime. David Cole

192 Thompson, James Westfall. Ancient Libraries. Berkeley, Calif.: University of California Press, 1940.

193 Thompson, Oscar, ed. The International Cyclopedia of Music and Musicians. Rev. ed. New York: Dodd, Mead, 1958.

194 Tipton, I., Haney, R. D., & Baseheart, J. R. (1975). Media agenda-setting in city and state election campaigns. Journalism Quarterly, 52, 15-22.

195 To cut or not to cut...and who does the cutting? 1993 Library Association Record, vol. 95, no. 2. Anonymous

196 Tsfati, Y. (2003). Does audience skepticism of the media matter in agenda setting? Journal of Broadcasting & Electronic Media, 47, 157-176.

197 Wanta, W., Stephenson, M. A., Van Slyke Turk, J., & McCombs, M. E. (1989). How president's State of the Union talk influence news media agendas. Journalism Quarterly, 66, 537-541.

Index

Preface

The Indian Banking scenario is passing through a dynamic phase of unparalleled metamorphosis.

Particularly since nationalisation, this banking system got increasingly involved in the process of economic development for attaining the twin objectives of growth and social justice. Banks have grown tremendously, both geographically and functionally. Managing the change and particularly its speed has been a challenge for the banking system. Phase of expansion has given place to phase of consolidation.

In the years to come, apart from increasing involvement in catering to the needs of the masses in rural and semi-urban areas, particularly in the context of Service Area Approach, banks will have to meet the challenges of emerging trends. Financial sector reforms, globalisation, diversification, securitisation, disintermediation, faster telecommunication and computerisation and mechanisation have already made their impact on the functioning of banks. In the years to come, these factors will accentuate and with the competition becoming fierce, customers' demands would be more exacting.

For meeting this challenge, banks will have to evolve an appropriate organisational structure and manage their resources, for ensuring efficiency and effectiveness of their functioning.

Evidence across the globe, from the developed North and the developing South, suggests that such of the banking and other organisations which have devoted proper attention to the area of human resources development will have an edge in this millennium over others in over coming their operational problems, extending better/ efficient services and ensuring viability profitability of the organisation. Training is one of the important sub- systems of human resources development and has to play its role effectively. So the HRD and training efforts of the Indian Banking sector (along with concurrent operational/ infrastructural support) will have to be geared up to meet the challenges not only of the emerging global banking scenario but also to address the imperatives of sustainable Rural Development and the concerns of disadvantaged segments as the poor and women.

It is in this background, in realization of the pivotal role that responsive/ responsible/ effective HRD and Training systems fan play in ensuring the healthy effectiveness of the Indian Banking Sector (and so of the Indian economy), that this study has been undertaken. Under financial sector reforms/ globalisation, the Indian Economy/ Banking Sector is passing through a period of rapid and significant change and only a radical action plan for reengineering the Human Resource Development, HRD(including Rural Human Resource Development,RRD and Gender Resource Development, GRD) systems of the Indian Banking scenario can ensure its promising/healthy/bright long term prospects. RRD and GRD—Specialised components of HRD, are innovative concepts introduced by this book. Based on the backdrop of eminent publications in this field (many of which are listed in the Bibliography/Chapter Notes), consultation with specialists, organisational, family and academic support and the global perspective acquired by the author through his exposure/ visit to the international/bilateral/national developmental and commercial banking systems in the United States of America, Canada, United Kingdom and some Third World Nations including India, this book is a pioneering attempt to work out the modalities of this Integrated Reengineering Action Plan, Model through HRD, RRD and GRD interventions. This plan, it is hoped would provide ingredients of the Reengineering blue print for the Indian Banking Sector in this Millennium.

The Author is indebted to several organisations (IDRC, World Bank, UNIFEM, CIDA, SICI, ADB, USAID, DFID, NDC, National Bank, IIMs etc.) for their valuable inputs. However, the opinions expressed are his own and do not in any way reflect organisational perspective. Finally, for the errors/omissions that remain (despite efforts), the author seeks the reader's indulgence.

1

Introduction: Objectives, Scope and Plan of the Study

Overview : In this introductory chapter, we define and explain the research task which has been undertaken in this study "Re-engineering the Indian Banking Sector for the Millennium: HRD, RRD and GRD Interventions", to get an idea of the objectives, need and rationale of the study.

The dynamic phase through which the Indian Banking scenario is currently passing through under the influence of globalisation and financial sector reforms is examined. Then we discuss the role of the Human Resource Development (HRD) and Training Systems in the functioning of the complex/ varied organisational machinery of the Indian Banking Sector, the inadequacies in these systems in meeting the challenge at hand and the need to determine/propose the structure and modalities of a more effective HRD/Training System(which accords the requisite importance to Rural Human Resource Development, RRD and Gender Resource Development, GRD) through this study. Thereby we arrive at the rationale for the study.

This is followed by a discussion of the significance and applications of the proposed study, the Research Methodology to be followed and an outline of the Book through a Study Plan.

Objectives, Need and Rationale of the Study

Dynamic Indian Banking Sector and Its Challenges

In the last decade of this century, the Indian Banking Industry has been passing through a dynamic phase of rapid changes. It underwent a transformation from 'class' banking to 'mass' banking and 'social' banking in the post *nationalisation*[1] era. Now it is undergoing another radical restructuring while implementing financial sector reforms which stress improved profitability, viability, mechanisation etc. in a 'liberalised', deregulated, modernising and increasingly competitive environment (notwithstanding the continuing onerous obligations of social banking and rural development).

Indian banking industry in decades to come will have to face a number of new challenges which can be met only by professional bankers of high competence and qualified, yet committed bank officials. With the anticipated change in the growth environment of our banks, the human resources need to be developed in such a fashion that they are able to produce workers who are fulfilled, authentic, caring, competent and well adjusted to the stresses and demands of the banks and the outer value system.

Indian banking has recorded unparalleled growth and tremendous diversification in the past decades since nationalisation. While the growth in the number of branches and the volume of business has been spectacular, the ever-changing environment in which the banks function today has thrown up several challenges in the areas of diversified business activities and customer satisfaction. There is also the growing realisation that growth and diversification have subjected the banking system to severe strain on all fronts such as house-keeping, customer service, credit management and profitability.

Some of the major challenges Indian banks will be facing in the 1990's would cover several expanded as well as new areas. They should expect fierce competition with respect to deposit mobilisation not only among the banks themselves but also from non-banking investment companies, from government saving organisation and from the corporate sector, Bankers will have to seek the patronage of customers and demonstrate to them their innovative abilities in providing need-based banking services. The credit scenario for banks in India is likely to be much more challenging. The demand for credit from various sectors of our economy as also for anti-poverty programmes will be rising and more diversified. This change will require new types of skills to effectively manage the banks' credit extension functions. Again, with our industrial sector undergoing important structural changes, the banks will have to build up necessary expertise for financial and technological appraisals as also to strengthen their monitoring mechanisms which alone can help them to identify potentially sick borrowing industrial units. In the context of rising quantum of agricultural/rural credit and intensification of coverage especially of small and marginal farmers and of members of weaker sections, banks will have to improve credit delivery system and improve their recovery position. Unless banks succeed in making priority sector financing a viable proposition, their own viability will remain in doubt. In order to improve their profitability position, banks have been trying to increase their revenues by diversifying into new areas such as, merchant banking, portfolio management, mutual funds, factoring, leasing, housing finance etc.

The deepening and widening of the financial markets, growing disintermediation process, adoption of modern technology in banking operations, rising customer expectations, introduction of innovative financial services and schemes, globalisation of financial services, national priorities, etc. are presenting tremendous challenges to the banking industry-calling for further improvements not only in organisational structure but also in developing and sharpening of human resources skill. Recent years have also seen promotion of new development activities in the rural sector (e.g. innovative, hitech, export oriented projects, non-farm sector etc.) and innovative modes of credit delivery (as through self help groups) and stress on factors like gender/ecological issues in Rural Development Banking.

Thus Indian Banks are going to witness a sea-change in the type, quality and composition of their business which in turn requires appropriate changes in the original structure of individual banks, improvement in work technology and efficiency, requisite training and orientation of staff. The new responsibilities Indian banks are expected to shoulder in this millennium indicates the broad contours of their HRD needs. The task is immense and requires changes in the management style not only in banking operations but also in new areas like career planning, long range planning, performance budgeting, work technology. The crux of the HRD problem lies in reorienting the basic attitudes and behaviour of the bank staff and to develop specific skills through training and retraining at different management levels.

We need most today to introduce appropriate changes in the basic character of Indian banking so that it becomes a truly professional, market-oriented and service-efficient system. It is necessary for banks to initiate appropriate measures to improve overall efficiency, reduce operational costs and increase productivity. In addition, banks should try to develop an aggressive marketing approach, particularly in rural and semi-urban sectors, identifying and satisfying effectively various customer needs.

For a service industry like banking to remain vibrant in a dynamic and competitive environment and to continue to survive and grow, it has necessarily to be futuristic in its orientation, taking stock of the challenges ahead and the opportunities in store. For this, it is a prerequisite for the banking sector to have appropriately responsive operational and HRD/training policies and programmes.

Compact Analysis of the HRD & Training Programmes of the Banking Scenario under Financial Sector Reforms: The optimum management of this dynamic Indian Banking, its exacting requirements calls for acquisition of new skills and capabilities, an expanded knowledge base, reorientation in attitudes/work culture and enhanced commitment from the Indian Banking personnel for effective marketing of banking services. To achieve this desired state of human resource development a sophisticated, strong, scientifically planned and executed HRD system and training programme, based on a rigorous and methodical assessment of training needs for meeting these banking challenges, has to function on a continuing basis.

Need for HRD : HRD is very relevant in result oriented organisations like banks which are not only service organisations but also considered as wheels of social change. The HRD approach assumes relatively greater importance in the banking industry for several reasons. One, it is essentially an industry in which considerations of personalised customer service are paramount, which depends on the quality, work attitude and performance of the employees. Secondly, following recent growth and diversification of the banking industry, it has to consider adoption of appropriate changes in work technology, particularly by way of computers and mechanisation. Thirdly, being an industry which provides wide-ranging services, both financial and non-financial, it requires appropriate training and other development programmes to develop requisite professional skills among its employees.

Traditional banking is undergoing sweeping and phenomenal changes all over the world. The three great gates of change, viz., deregulation, technological innovation and globalisation, have shifted the focus from security-orientation to market-orientation, thereby making manpower the key factor. In an age of speed, creativity, productivity, risk-taking, capability and shock-absorbing capacity are becoming the fundamental criteria for success. To be able to compete successfully and achieve results in this complex environment, banks have to make determined efforts to develop the capabilities and commitment of the staff. Banking is a service industry characterised by white-collar jobs and knowledge-workers whose productivity is related to their education and elbowroom in operation. Human resource thus occupies a unique and sensitive position and should therefore, be managed in such a way that it is developed and not demoralised.

HRD in some banks has gained some achievements. The components of HRD for banks may broadly include areas like manpower planning and personnel inventory, personnel policy, career planning, selection and organisational development of employees, system of workers' participation and motivation, performance appraisal system and research studies in human areas. However it is true that HRD functioning in a majority of the banks is far from satisfactory. There are also cases of the banks where the HRD is carrying out only the routine personnel administration functions of recruitment, transfer, promotion training etc. But Training though important, is only a part of HRD and not the whole of it, because the HRD concept is much more wider as it embraces almost all areas of an organisation and places emphasis on allround development of individuals. *So a discussion of Training has to be within the context of overall HRD system of the Indian Banks.* (as will be *attempted in this study)*[2].

Need for Training : In the context of growth of nationalised banks, the need for training arises because of unprecedented. quantitative and qualitative changes, which continually exert pressure on the bank personnel. This task cannot be achieved without proper and adequate training of the new personnel in the job. The need for training also arises on account of new areas of banking operations such as agricultural finance, small scale industries, leasing, merchant banking, export finance, new methods of credit appraisal such as cash flow analysis of new projects, requirements of technology changes, financial sector reforms and globalisation. In a service-oriented industry like banking, manpower is the key input and sharper focus has therefore, to be given on human resource development so that the banking system can successfully meet the emerging challenges in the coming years. In equipping the personnel to accomplish the future tasks ahead, the pivotal role of banking education and training is evident and hardly needs any emphasis. But keeping in view the future challenges, the education and training systems have to play still greater and more effective roles.

Training has come to be recognised as an integral part of the process of growth of any organisation. Several studies have shown that even in industrially advanced countries, of North America, Europe & East Asia the major factor contributing to economic growth has been the quality of labour. In some countries, the contribution of this factor is even greater than that of capital. In almost all organisations, improved customer service and higher productivity depends on the quality of the people employed. This is all the more so in service organisations like banking. Training is concerned with helping people to acquire the knowledge, skills and attitudes necessary to do the work for which they are currently employed. It also prepares them for their future roles in the organisation. Many organisations in the past used to emphasise on structure, strategy and systems as the lever to success. But more recently it has become clear that a truly successful organisation must emphasise equally skills and style of the staff — that is strategy and structure can become effective only if the staff have the right skills and attitudes. It is in this context that training as a means of improving the skills and changing the attitudes becomes very significant.

Banks realised the need for setting up their own training institutions to cope up with the heavy demand for the development of their human resources in the context of these far reaching changes in their operating environment. Presently there are about 247 Training establishments run by 28 Public Sector Banks. Besides training colleges and centres, some banks have also established specialised training institutions with focus on rural development. In addition there are national level training institutions such as National Institute of Bank Management and Bankers Institute of Rural Development (BIRD). However, the task of updating the operational and managerial skills of the large existing manpower of the banks is in itself a very gigantic one-beyond the ability of the inadequate training infrastructure in many banks.

In the financial sector, as commercial banks have been dominating the scene (particularly since nationalisation) and with the changes now being introduced in the financial systems through liberalisation policies, more changes in structure and functioning of commercial banks are expected in future. The rapid changes in information technology, introduction of computers and various financial innovations during recent years have transformed to a great extent the contours of manpower required to handle the growing volume of operations as well as new financial products and services. Emergence of various new financial intermediaries such as mutual funds, factoring organisations, venture capital funds, and subsidiaries of commercial banks to handle several other financial services has posed new challenges for effective development of managerial manpower.

Need/Rationale for the Study : Against this backdrop, training and developing the skills needed among the future managers of banking system gains special emphasis. Following the acceptance world over of 'Universal Banking' and India moving forward to freeing the banking system from controls and making them market oriented, even while fulfilling the social/developmental obligations specially for rural development, the HRD and training systems for banks have accordingly to be attuned to address the new challenges. The present training procedures and need assessments at the training institutes are largely oriented to traditional banking. As would be evident from this study, the aspect of dynamic nature of banking sector today, the changes in HRD policies and practices it requires to implement successfully the financial sector reforms, and the specific/unique requirements of Rural Banking and due emphasis to crucial concerns like Gender issues are not adequately reflected in these endeavours.

This is the rationale of this study: *"Reengineering the Indian Banking Sector for the Millinneum: HRD, RRD and GRD Interventions"*

The study proposes to formulate a long-term action strategy based on HRD/Training interventions for equipping the dynamic Indian Banking sector with the necessary competencies required to face the challenges of financial sector reforms/globalisation. It would thereby be tackling this critical problem area of the Indian Banking sector. It would hence be covering a new territory as existing works have not attempted an *integrated/practical*[3] treatment incorporating the latest developments/advances in the HRD and Training fields, as related to the banking sector, with particular reference to Rural Development Banking and Gender and Development.

The institutional arrangements of Indian Banks required for providing training facilities is also an area which needs attention. In a training institution which is part of a commercial bank, the faculty is usually drawn from the bank and training is not their primary vocation. A good manager is not necessarily a good teacher. Training has to be viewed as an investment and in that sense it has to be carefully planned, properly operated and suitably monitored. Available training facilities must be fully utilised. Programmes must be such as evoke spontaneous response from the participants. Teaching methods must change with the type of programmes offered. Also if training is to be meaningful, it should be closely integrated with HRD policies, manpower planning and placement. Training cannot operate in a vacuum. It must be in tune with the organisational culture even while making an effort to change the culture where necessary. An integrated treatment of these critically important requirements which the HRD and Training systems of the Indian Banking sector should possess in the dynamic phase of financial sector reforms was very much needed today. This study is an attempt to meet this need and to offer a pragmatic remedial action plan.

Significance/Applications of Proposed Study : The proposed study would endeavour to access the current HRD/training systems of Indian Banking organisations (with special emphasis on Rural Development Banking/Gender and Development issues) in the context of globalisation/financial sector reforms/liberalisation/rural development/women and development imperatives, identify the gap that exists vis-a-vis the prevalent training practices and subsequently suggest the consequent reengineering/innovations required in the HRD and Training strategies for closing this gap. (e.g. increase of training capacity, qualitative improvements, innovative strategies like computer based training/interactive video/ multimedia pedagogy etc.).

The findings of this research investigation would be useful for the Indian banking organisations, to their training network including apex level institutes like Bankers Institute for Rural Development (BIRD), College of Agricultural Banking (CAB), and regional/cooperative training institutions) in gearing up to meet these current training needs.

The proposed study would hence make a original and important contribution to the field of Training and Human Resource Development as applied to the national endeavour of financial sector modernisation by incorporating the specialised training implications for the rapidly changing Indian banking sector, which has not been attempted in other scholarly endeavours. The implementation of the research findings will contribute towards the optimum management/ marketing of Banking services in India, enabling them to play a more meaningful role in India's economic transformation under the process of globalisation/liberalisation/financial sector reforms.

Research Methodology and Book Plan

The Research comprises of data collected from primary and secondary sources (visit to banking institutions at head office and bank levels, discussion with training faculty at apex and state level training institutions (BIRD, CAB, Staff Colleges etc.) development/management professionals at the IIM's, ISTD, NIBM etc.). Inputs from concerned international institutions as Institutes of development finance/training/ gender research in such countries as U.K., Canada, U.S.A to acquire a broader/comparative perspective, data from sources as WORLD BANK/ASIAN DEVELOPMENT BANK/GOI/ NABARD/RBI, and bilateral international development cooperation agencies (as Department for International Development, UK, United States Agency for International Development Canadian International Development Agency) their reports and statistical compilations were also consulted.

After this introductory chapter (Chapter 1) the study will take an overview of the Indian banking scenario and it's changing state (Chapter-2) and appraise it's current HRD and Training machinery (Chapter-3). It will analyse important national/international evaluations/view points/seminar proceedings etc. on the HRD and Training systems of Indian Banks and of other equivalent organisations to estimate the gap in their HRD/Training mechanisms (Chapter-4). It will determine the Re-engineering interventions required in the areas of macro HRD policies—Strategic Human Resource Management (Chapter-5) and Training delivery machinery related innovations (Chapter-6). This investigation would then assess the role of training in the context of certain critical areas (keeping in mind the strategic HRM requirements) as computerisation, customer service, productivity, management development etc. (Chapter 7). Special emphasis will be accorded to the thrust area of Rural Development Banking (Chapter 8), and Women & Development issues (Chapter-9), since they have a vital role to play in our national priorities while operating in a very difficult environment. The study will also propose a Re-engineering Model which will incorporate these various intervention strategies to formulate a multidimensional, integrated corrective Action Plan (Chapter-10).

Notes

1. The nationalisation of 14 public sector commercial banks took place in 1969. In 1980, 6 more public sector commercial banks were nationalised.
2. A discussion exclusively focussed on the Training sub-system of the Indian Banking Sector would not have provided the comprehensive, three dimensional view possible by consideration of Training within the overall Human Resource Development/ (HRD) system.
3. An integrated/concerted/practically oriented Action Plan is called for, since piecemeal/theoretical measures and adhoc remedies will not bring the radical improvements required to meet the immense challenges faced today by the Indian Banking Sector.

2

Restructuring of the Indian Banking Sector under Globalisation and Financial Sector Reforms

Overview : The Banking sector in India comprises of a vast and diversified network operating at several tiers, linked operationally to the international/multilateral financial organisations, national government machinery and other sectors of the economy at various points. It is not a static body, but a dynamic conglomeration which has evolved from humble beginnings to its present state of complexity. Even now it is undergoing changes while adjusting and adapting to meet the needs and demands of globalization and financial sector reforms. In this chapter we shall initially attempt an understanding of the structure/composition of Indian banking and its rural wing. Then, we shall analyze the restructuring it is presently undergoing by firstly getting a global feel of the banking trends in developed countries, and then study the changing national banking trends, growth phases of the Indian Banking Sector. We shall take a comparative view of the pre- and post liberalization status of Indian banks. And since, to keep with these changing trends, the functions performed by Indian banks were also required to change, we shall consider both their traditional and innovative functions. Furthermore, in keeping with the special emphasis in this study on Rural Development Banking, we shall consider this area in detail: the concept and progress of rural development endeavours in our country, World Bank/Asian Development Bank guidelines, the role of rural banking, the restructuring it is undergoing, its problems and innovations, current issues and challenges confronting it. This will give us an idea of the immensity of the challenge before the HRD and training systems, in equipping the banking sector's manpower with the capabilities for performing these multiple functions and coping with the rapid pace of organizational change in an effective manner.

The Structure of the Financial System: Indian Banking Sector

The financial system of India comprises of the system of borrowing and lending of funds or the demand for and the supply of funds of all individuals, institutions, companies and the Government. It includes the institutions and the mechanism which effects the generation of savings by community, the mobilisation of saving and the effective distribution of the savings among all these who demand the funds for investment purpose, i.e.

— The banking system, the insurance companies, mutual/investment funds and other institutions which promote savings among the public, collect their savings and transfer them to the actual investors and,

— The investors in the country composed of individual investors, industrial and trading companies and the government—these enter the financial system as borrowers.

— Apart from these there are certain other essential institutions of the Indian financial system the facilitators. For example, the New Issue Market which facilitates new savings to flow into new issues of stocks and shares.

The Indian financial system consists of two parts, viz., the Indian Money Market and the Indian Capital Market. The Indian money market in which short-term funds are borrowed and lent—does not deal in cash or money but in bills of exchange—trade bills and treasury bills—and other instruments, drawn for short periods. The capital market in India, on the other hand, is the market for medium tern and long term funds. The Indian Money Market comprises of unorganized and organized sectors. The unorganized sector consists of indigenous bankers and money lenders catering to the credit needs of a large number of persons in the country side. This study will focus on the organized banking sector component of the Indian financial system's money market, with special emphasis on rural development banking and related gender issues. Firstly we shall understand the composition/ structure of this system and then examine it's changing face.

The Composition of the Indian Banking System

The organized banking system in India can be broadly divided into three categories, viz., the Central Bank of the country, known as the Reserve Bank of India, the Commercial Banks (including Regional Rural Banks) and the cooperative banks. The Reserve Bank of India is the supreme monetary banking authority in the country. Commercial Banks which have been in existence for many decades, after the 1969 nationalization, are broadly classified into nationalized or public sector banks and private sector banks. The State Bank of India and its associate banks along with another 20 banks, are the public sector banks. The private sector banks include a small number of Indian scheduled banks which have not been nationalised, and branches of foreign banks operating in India.

The Regional Rural Banks (RRBs) which came into existence since the middle of 1970s as low cost organisations with the specific objective of providing credit and deposit facilities particularly to the small and marginal farmers, agricultural labourers and artisans and small entrepreneurs are essentially commercial banks but their area of operation is limited to a few districts. Primary Co-operative Credit Societies (or Co-operative Banks) were originally set up in villages to promote thrift and savings of the farmers and to meet their credit needs for cultivation. To support them, Central or District Co-operative Banks and above them State Co-operative Banks were established.

We shall now discuss the Indian Rural Banking System and its changing functions/trends/associated issues.

Rural Banking System

The rural banking sector consists of three institutions, viz., cooperative credit sector, commercial banking sector and Regional Rural Banks (RRBs): Primary Land Development Banks, branches of State Land Development Banks, Primary Agricultural Cooperatives, large sized adivasi Multipurpose Societies, Farmers Service Societies, branches of RRBs and branches of commercial banks located at rural and semi-urban centres and also some of the branches set up at urban locations. The cooperatives, commercial banks and RRBs respectively account for about 47, 40 and 8 per cent in the total rural credit disbursed and about 31,53 and 8 per cent respectively of the credit outstanding in rural areas. There is the complimentarity in the roles played by different banking sectors in the rural area and weaknesses of either of these constituents of rural credit will have severe repercussions on the availability of the right kind of credit support for the rural economy. Even after so many years of directed credit there is a huge gap between the demand and supply of rural credit in India.

In order to support, nurture and guide rural credit institutions in respect of planning, policy making, institution development and refinance operations, *National Bank for Agriculture and Rural Development (NABARD)* was formed in July 1982 as an apex level developmental financial institution. It took over the agricultural credit functions of the Reserve Bank of India and the refinance functions of the Agriculture Refinance Development Corporation (ABDC). Thus National Bank serves as a refinance institution for all production and investment credit needs in the spheres of agriculture, rural small scale and village industries, handicrafts and allied economic activities. It coordinates the activities of Planning Commission, Central and State Governments, other national/ state level organisations and voluntary organisations in the field of agriculture and rural development. It has been entrusted with the responsibility of inspecting cooperative banks and regional rural banks, and is also engaged in the rehabilitation/strengthening of primary agricultural credit societies in order to build a viable and strong grassroots level cooperation credit structure.

Rural Branches: Banks have created specialised branches to discharge their responsibilities in the field of rural credit eg. the State Bank of India's organisational innovations viz., Agricultural Development Branch (ADB) and Agricultural Banking Division in branches (ABD). ADBs are specialised branches handling agricultural credit extension with adequate field staff and technical officers and equipped with suitable vehicular support, whereas ABDs were created as non-specialised branches to handle agricultural lending. The Agricultural Banking Divisions are mini ADBs with a complement of field and technical staff. Other Banks have also evolved suitable organisational innovations.

However, no uniform pattern of rural branches has so far emerged. Not only are there bank-to-bank variations, but there are variations with the same bank as well from the simplified Accounting Branch (with one officer and a very small complement of supporting staff of 2-3 persons) to the specialised Agricultural Development Branch. Between these two there are non-specialised branches of various patterns such as branches without on Accountant, branches without Accountants but with a Field Officer/Technical Officer etc. In banks like the State Bank, Branch Managers have been delegated adequate powers to sanction practically all direct agricultural loans. The Field Officers and R.D.Os (Rural Development Officers as the Technical Officers (Agri.) are known) have also been given limited sanctioning powers. The R.D.Os also perform practically the same tasks as a Field Officer and other banking officers. One man branches (i.e. branches with only one 'passing' official) pose a problem in rural areas as the branch manger has little time to move from village to village for processing/supervising loans or accept fuller responsibilities implicit in Service Area Approach.

Restructuring: Changing Trends in Banking System

The composition of the Indian banking system discussed is not static, but passing through a dynamic phase of rapid growth and restructuring. Many significant changes taking place in India, especially in recent years, in response to changes in the national and international economic environment have also affected the financial sector and are forcing it to move towards a deregulated and more competitive environment. In the historical context, a fast pace of change has occurred in the financial systems of developed countries and more particularly in the U.K., Canada and the U.S.A in the last two decades. It is frequently referred to as constituting a "revolution of financial services". A number of major interlocking trends have changed the institutional characteristics of the financial system. Since the forces of globalization are making us move towards `one world', we shall consider firstly the banking trends in developed countries and then discuss them, as also the growth phases and changing functions in the Indian context.

Banking Trends in Developed Countries: Globalization Forces

Important changes have taken place in the activities of commercial banks in the developed countries resulting in removal of barriers between banking and non-banking activities, commercial banks undertaking functions which were traditionally handled by security houses and investment banks and these non-banking institutions are undertaking banking functions. Banks have expanded their activities into specialised areas like leasing, mortgages. The financial services industry has become market oriented with innovation of new services and development of new instruments--euro-currency markets, certificates of deposits, commercial paper, zero coupon bonds, option markets, disintermediation, wherein corporate borrowers go directly to the savers for funds instead of bank acting as intermediary. This trend has been characterized by what is known as securitisation of debts, that is replacement of traditional bank loans with issuing of and investment in securities. Technological developments and improved communication network have further facilitated the financial sector to provide improved, efficient and speedy services.

Banking Trends in the Indian Context

The objective of planned economic development in India and social orientation of banking led to bank nationalization in July 1969. In order to discharge their obligation of social banking banks moved into rural areas and lent increasing proportion of credit portfolio to priority sectors of the economy, margins on loan and advance narrowed down and their profitability affected. The Indian Banks Association has identified following *six factors* which have contributed to the *declining profitability of public sector banks*. These include:

1. Persistant increases in lending to priority and preferred sectors at conessional rates of interest resulting in narrowing down margins.

2. Large preemptions of lendable resources through continuous increase in Statutory Liquidity Ratio (SLR) and Cash Reserve Ratio (CRR).

3 Increasing incidence of industrial sickness with interest accrued on bank advances locked up in sick industrial units.

4. Rapid expansion of branch network, particularly in rural areas, which take about five years to break even.

5. Growing incidence of financial disintermediation by corporate sector in directly entering the capital market to raise funds, which has also affected the profitability of banks.

6. Administered interest rate for deposits, credit and refinance, disadvantageous to banks, unfavourable change in deposit mix.

So the viability of the banking system was under a grave threat and if the system was to continue to serve the social objectives, banks had to take steps to improve their productivity and profitability. That was how in the eighties, the beginning of liberalization of economic policies was followed by financial liberalization and on-set of paradigmatic shift. In the *first phase* interest rate structure of bank deposits and lending was administered, investment and credit of banks were directed. Branch expansion was based on RBI's branch licensing policy, performance evaluation was mainly in terms of deposit mobilisation, priority sector lending etc., and good banking practice like maintaining quality of assets etc. were not emphasized, risk management and profitability were not stressed, Balance-sheet of banks based on their accounting practices did not properly reflect financial strength of the banks.

Since the mid 80s *(second phase)* banks changed towards flexibility and freedom, with diversification into new business areas. However, there was no perceptible change in the overall environment as weight of controls was greater than that of few liberalization measures. Assets of the banking industry, such as knowledge, innovative capabilities etc. were not exploited fully. Manpower planning and development received little attention, concern for profitability and productivity was less. There was leakages on account of weaknesses in housekeeping and internal audit system. The phase after 1992, the *third phase*, reflects a move towards *paradigmatic shift* in the banking industry in response to implementation of *financial sector reforms*. It was in this phase that the report of the *Narasimham Committee* set up by the Government of India to examine all aspects of the structure, functions and procedures of the financial system, was tabled.

Narasimham Committee Recommendations[2]

Some of the *major recommendations* of this committee related to the banking sector are:

(1) Progressive reduction of Statutory Liquidity Ratio (SLR) and Cash Reserve Ratio (CSR) in line with the Government's intention to reduce its fiscal deficit.

(2) Rationalization of interest rates.

(3) Limiting priority sector lending to small and marginal farmers, the tiny cottage sector of industry and other weaker sections.

(4) Strengthening other prudential regulations relating to income recognition, loan loss provisions.

(5) Revamping the structures of the banking system.

(6) Allowing entry of new private sector banks and permitting foreign banks to open branches under terms and conditions applicable to domestic banks.

(7) Improving operational autonomy and concomitant accountability of bank managements with regard to internal management, credit and investment decisions and opening and closing of bank branches, speeding up banks computerization.

(8) Removing duality of control over banks by Government and the RBI in favour of the latter.

Changing Functions of Indian Banks

In keeping with the changing trends and phase of growth, the functions of Indian Banks have also changed over the years in response to the needs of the economy and the government policies. We shall first discuss the traditional banking functions which the banks continue to perform. Then we shall take up the innovative functions which the banks are being called upon to perform due to the demands of liberalization, especially in the period after 1992. This will give us an idea of the tall task before the HRD/Training Systems of the Indian Banks to enable their personnel to cope with the demands of these rapid changes.

Traditional Banking Functions

Banking traditionally is concerned with the acceptance of deposits from the customers, the lending of surplus to customers and the transmission of funds. Banks nowadays also provide a wide range of services for financial and non-financial needs to all types of customers. These functions of banks can be categorized as:

Financial Intermediation: Banks act as financial intermediaries between savers (lenders) and investors (borrowers) by accepting deposits and then on lending to those who wish to borrow. In a developing country like India, capital scarcity makes banks the key agents of mobilizing/channelling resources. Banks will, however, have to face increasing competition in savings mobilization. The banks have also been assigned poverty eradication, employment generation and rural development related responsibilities.

Payment Mechanism : The transfer by cheque, standing order or credit transfer etc. is one of the most important method of debt settlement and distinguishes banks from other financial institutions.

Ancillary Services : The ancillary services offered by banks cover a wide range of financial and advisory services that cater to the individual needs of the customers and can be divided into (i) traditional services; and (ii) non-traditional and innovative services. Most of the traditional services like collections, remittances, safe deposit values etc. are being provided by banks since long.

Innovative Banking Functions

Having discussed the tranditional functions we shall now take up the innovative banking services which have been added to the banking arena, mostly in the third phase of growth of Indian Banks during the nineties. Significant among those are housing finance, hire-purchase, leasing, factoring, merchant banking, mutual funds, consumer loans and venture capital finance being provided by banks on their own or through special subsidiaries. Also there is unfolding of the computer revolution and many other important innovations such as introduction of new financial instruments like certificates of deposits, commercial paper and credit cards to cope with the emergent competitive environment. Besides, investment management including investment counselling and tax services are also creating innovative packages to meet consumer demands. Further, in view of the growing equity culture in the economy, banks may have to become active in distributing stock and shares, debentures and bonds even to their own depositors. Several banks have expanded their overseas operations and have undertaken financing of the import-export business. The international banking scene has undergone drastic changes, with the introduction of computer and telecommunication technology, which have led to integration of international financial market. Responding to changes in the international environment commercial banks in India have also being trying to diversify in such areas as consumer credit, credit cards, travellers cheques etc. In keeping with the *requirements of liberalization, globalization and financial sector reforms*, Indian banks are diversifying their business and providing many *new services* to their clientele, as elaborated below:

Merchant Banking : The merchant banking activity includes areas such as managing of public issues, loan syndications, financial and management consultancy services, project counselling, project appraisal and arrangement of technical consultancy, mergers and amalgamations, management of NRI investments, portfolio management etc. It is estimated that there are about 75 merchant bankers in India, of whom not more than 15 can be considered as active merchant bankers. Major merchant bankers like SBI Capital Markets Ltd., Can bank Financial Services Ltd. are mainly concentrating on management of public issues, underwriting, portfolio management and leasing.

Leasing : Many industries prefer to take lease than buying. Separate leasing division by Commercial Banks have started gaining ground in India.

Factoring : A financial service under which the factor undertakes collection, accounting and management of clients debts and also finances the clients. Beginning has been attempted by a few banks in factoring business e. g. SBI Factors and Commercial Services Pvt. Ltd.

Portfolio Management: Banks have been undertaking portfolio management of surplus funds of their corporate customers directly or through merchant banks and assisting their clients to invest their funds to achieve the twin objectives of liquidity and optimum yield.

Mutual Funds : Mutual funds are collective investment schemes conferring benefits of diversified portfolio and expert investment management to a large number of investors, through institution alised risk pooling mechanism e.g. SBI Mutual Fund, Canbank Mutual Fund.

Venture Capital : The Technology Development Fund set up by IDBI, The Equity Development Scheme set by SBI Capital Markets Ltd. are some of the venture capital institutions set up.

Housing Finance: Considering the acute housing shortage and inadequate funding, the commercial banks have recently entered this arena—SBI, Canara Bank and PNB have set up separate subsidiaries for housing finance.

Consumer Credit and Credit Cards: Commercial banks have been expending consumer credit for financing consumer durable and some have also entered the credit card business with a linkup with international networks such as VISA.

Stock Invest: Under the stock invest an investor's account gets debited only upon the finalisation of the basis of share allotment. The investors parts with his money only in case of successful total or partial allotment.

Off Shore Banking: Banks deal in foreign currencies and with foreign countries in various internationally reputed instruments in a free trade zone. India's first open-ended off shore fund has been launched by Indbank Merchant Banking Services Ltd.

Diversification of Customer Services: Commercial banks are rendering multifarious services to the customers-Safe Deposit Lockers, Credit Loans, Traveller's Cheques, Teller System, Credit Cards, ATMs, Gift Cheques, Consultancy Services extending guarantees, collection of cheques, demand drafts, bills of exchange, promissory notes etc. Various banks have made positive contribution in providing community services support for a variety of cultural activities, exhibitions, sporting events, services like payment of income tax and insurance premium on the basis of standing instructions of customers.

Furthermore, measures like phased reduction in statutory Liquidity Ratio (SLR), prudential accounting, partial deregulation of interest rates, allowing of private sector commercial and foreign banks in a bigger way and increased computerization of banking operations are also likely to go a long way in imparting competitive efficiency in Indian banks. This would also 'improve their operational efficiency and strengthen the financial position of banks which is a prerequisite of their exposure to the globalized banking environment.[3]

Restructuring: Changing Face of Rural Development Banking

Concept of Rural Development: Rural Development is very significant in the Indian context-about 74 per cent of our population lives in rural areas, and nearly 80 per cent of the estimated population (1989-90) living below the poverty line is from the rural areas. Since the inception of planning in India, various development programmes have been implemented for raising the quality of rural life through raising their income levels and providing them access to employment, education, health care etc. But the activities of the bankers have largely focussed on rural disbursement of credit rather than the development of the rural poor, which has wider connotations.

World Bank's Perception: The World Bank looks at rural development 'as a process through which rural poverty is alleviated by sustained increase in productivity and increase in the income of rural workers and households.'[4] The World Bank's rural development (RD) strategy sought to expand development efforts and resources for alleviating poverty in rural areas of less developed countries. The rural development strategy enabled the Bank to shift the focus of development efforts towards smallholders, whose productivity and efficiency had previously often not been well recognized. The earlier pattern had been one of supporting mainly large-scale agricultural production. This change in emphasis influenced a similar evolution among other donors and borrowing governments and was a notable achievement of the rural development strategy. Though the results have been encouraging some institutional development, training and policy aspects of RD projects were often wanting, even when physical implementation was successful. Project benefit may be difficult to sustain in many cases.

Asian Development Bank's Perception : This public international development finance institution is engaged in promoting the economic and social progress of it's Developing Member Countries (DMCs). It provides loans, equity investments and technical investments. The Bank's strategy in the agriculture and rural development sector is to enhance the management and development of the natural resource base of DMCs, improve productivity and sustainability of conventional agriculture, and catalyze a self-sustaining rural development process. The strategy emphasizes linking natural resources, agriculture and rural development assistance with a DMC's overall programme of solving economic, social, and environmental problems, and ensuring that the Bank's investments are supportive of the macroeconomic framework of the country.

The Bank has identified five strategic objectives in it's medium term framework : promote economic growth, reduce poverty, improve the status of women, develop human resources and help bring about sound environment/natural resources management.

Other Perceptions : Other authorities have defined rural development differently e.g. *Miller*[5] sets four tasks of development programmes which are as follows:-

— development of human resources

— expansion of physical resources

— extension of the community's own control over its physical environment as a result of the expansion of physical resources and;

— correspondingly bringing more permanent changes in relation to the external environment.

The *seventh plan*[6] laid special emphasis in the area of human resource development (HRD). HRD in achieving targets of the Seventh Plan connoted:

— a drive to eradicate illiteracy totally
— provision of safe drinking water to all habitations.
— drive to wipe out the major diseases afflicting the health of people.
— preventive health care and higher nutritional standards; and
— determined perseverance with the programmes for fertility control and reduction in child mortality.

Thus, the focus of several schemes as well as development strategy for the recent five year plan is on the Development of Man. Consequently, the emphasis of banks' contribution in rural development has to be essentially in the context of 'Development of Rural Client'. This is possible if only banks are able to develop their own human resources to do rural development work.

However, despite plethora of rural development programmes during five decades of planned development since independence, the rural areas continue to have low productivity in agriculture, high population growth, poor infrastructural facilities, and dependence on agricultural sector for livelihood. There is hence urgent need to redesign the strategies for accelerating rural development in the country.

Progress of Rural Development Programmes/Endeavours

Institutional credit for rural development was introduced in the country with the legislation of the 1904 Cooperative Credit Societies Act. Primary Agricultural Cooperative Societies (PACs) were organised at the village level to meet the farmers' short-term credit needs and were linked with the District Central Cooperative Banks (DCCBs). The Cooperative Land Mortgage Banks were founded for long-term loans to agriculturists. The cooperatives have subsequently diversified their activities to include general banking input distribution, agro-processing, warehousing etc. But the cooperative credit agencies, have become less effective due to constant interference, dependence for their sources of fund and neglect of the principle of cooperation, viz. thrift and self-reliance by the ground level credit institutions. The 1969 nationalisation of commercial banks saw the expansion of the branch network and improved the access of farmers to institutional credit. This with the establishment of the Regional Rural Banks in 1975, led to low-cost banking for the poor.

After independence, the government endeavour to bring about rural upliftment started with the launching of the Community Development Programmes (1952) and National Extension Services (1953) for creating awareness about the development potential and the major technological advancements. Decentralisation efforts through the establishment of Panchayat Raj Institutions at the village, block and district levels had limited success due to the denial of adequate financial support from the state governments. During the third five year plan period, programmes like Intensive Agricultural Development Programme (IADP). Intensive Agricultural Area Programme (IAAP), High Yielding Variety Programme (HYV) were launched.

But the benefits of these programmes went to economically better off. This led to special target oriented programmes through agencies like the Agency for the Development of Marginal Farmers and Agricultural Labourers (MFAL, 1969) and Small Farmers Development Agency (SFDA, 1969) so that the benefits could reach the target group. Integrated Rural Development Programme (IRDP) was introduced in 1978 to enable the rural population get sufficient income by utilising the local resource potential and to bring them above the poverty line. It replaced some of the ongoing programmes like SFDA, MFAL etc. To upgrade the skills of the rural unemployed Training of Youth for Self-Employment *(TRYSEM) was launched as part of the IRDP.*[7]

Due to the poverty alleviation and other rural development programmes, the rural population below the poverty line has come down from 51.2 per cent to 28.2 pe rcent as per government statistics. The foodgrains production which was a mere 50.8 million tonnes during 1950-51 had reached a level of 176.2 million tonnes during 1990-91, an increase of about 250 per cent. However, the country continues to be a net importer of edible oils and the per capita consumption of oils and fats is below the world average. The production of pulses has almost stagnated. The "Green Revolution" was followed by the "White Revolution" for increasing milk production in the country.

Problems of Rural Banking: Operational Areas

Credit institutions have played an important role in supplying production and investment credit to the neglected rural weaker sections. The share of institutional credit agencies in the total rural borrowings increased from a mere 7 per cent in 1951 to 63 per cent in 1980-81. But about half of the rural households are still outside the purview of formal credit. Some of the problems of Rural Banking are :

1. The achievements of rural development programmes have largely not kept pace with a rapidly growing population. With land available for agriculture and allied activities getting reduced, deforestation is on the rise leading to ecological imbalances, rural unemployment continues to rise leading to migration. The increased pressure on agriculture sector led to more sub-division and fragmentation of the land holdings.

2. *Credit Access:* More than half the rural households still do not have access to institutional credit system. Large number of tenants will have no access to the institutional credit unless the state governments implement the land reforms. The emphasis under credit dispensation is on achieving the targets set under various programmes rather than having a strong commitment to rural poor upliftment.

3. Evaluation studies reveal that the factors adversely affecting the productivity of credit are under financing, leading to incomplete or infructious investments, non-adherence to technical parameters,

non-availability of linkages, failure to perceive the total credit needs of the borrowers, poor support from the extension agencies and poor credit supervision.

4. *Infrastructure:* Inadequate development of physical, and social infrastructure by the government has resulted in low productivity of credit because of inadequacy of forward and backward linkages.

5. Loan recovery essential for recycling of credit, has been poor. Problem of overdues continues and restricts the eligibility of borrowers for fresh loans. It places a serious constraint on the lending capacity and solvency of the credit system.

6. *Women's Role*: The Indian rural women are largely employed in the unorganised sector in low skill areas, are comparatively low paid, are more disadvantaged in their access to employment than men. With regard to credit women are handicapped by their inability to provide collateral for loans as they do not generally possess any assets worth pledging to the banks. These, together with lack of skill and organised approach have rendered it difficult for poor women to gain access to institutional credit, though they can take up enterprises which can provide gainful employment and economic independence, given proper training and opportunities— *Gender Training* component of the 'Women & Development' field (discussed in chapter 9).

7. *Inadequate Entrepreneurial Skills:* The development of human resources in rural areas which is a crucial input has not received due attention due to lack of proper educational and training facilities. So the entrepreneurial skills required to make an optimal use of the available resources and make the credit supported activities financially viable are not well developed.

Innovations in Rural Banking

A long-term strategy for rural development to be effective must take cognizance of the fact that the rate of transfer of people out of low productivity agriculture and allied activities to non-agricultural activities/pursuits has been slow, widespread poverty in the rural areas still persists and rural areas have abundant labour, but limited land resources. Available capital, if mobilised properly, could help in improving the quality of life. Credit institutions could promote rural development by channeling their resources for increasing production/productivity in the given agro-system, shifting population from agriculture to non-agriculture activities and improving and activity specific infrastructural facilities.

The Eighth Five Year Plan document has indicated that the thrust areas for which institutional finance is to be directed are (1) minor irrigation, (2) animal husbandry, dairy and fisheries development, (3) livestock improvement, (4) soil and water conservation measures, reclamation of water logged, saline, fallow lands, etc., (5) agro-processing, (6) promotion of high yielding plantation crops in traditional and non-traditional areas, and (7) provision of financial and technical support to the non-farm sector and encouraging rural artisans and small rural enterprises.

We shall now discuss some important innovations in rural banking in relation to these thrust and other areas:

(1) *Innovations in Credit and Planning— SAA & PLP :* Planned allocation of scarce credit resources among different sectors of economy in accordance with plan priorities is essential, given the natural tendency for credit to move towards sectors and activities capable of yielding high rewards. The service area approach (SAA), introduced by the RBI and Potential Linked Credit Plans (PLPs) undertaken by the National Bank together form the new strategy for credit planning in the rural sector in India. Under SAA the emphasis is on planning from below with village as a unit, and this approach should contribute to the orderly and

planned deployment of credit in the designated area. Instead of the earlier limited involvement banks are now entrusted with more intensive promotional and developmental responsibilities —a group of about 25 villages is assigned to the service area of each rural branch. To enhance the productivity of rural credit through planning and monitoring, NABARD has initiated the process of preparation of Potential Linked Credit Plan (PLPs). These plans reflect the resource endowments, infrastructure availability and provide estimate of institutional credit requirement.

2. *Dryland farming* : The assessment of irrigation potential indicates that even if the potential is fully exploited, about 50% of the net cultivated area will still be dependent on rainfall for crop production. The country will continue to depend on dryland areas for much of its requirements of coarse cereals, pulses, oilseeds and cotton. One of the strategies to increase the productivity in dryland areas is an integrated watershed based approach covering aspects like soil and water management, crop management, etc. An operation research project envisages promotion of Self Help Groups (SHGs) to ensure active involvement of villagers in the transfer of technology and provision of common items.

3. *Biotechnology* : Biotechnology (genetic engineering, tissue culture, etc.) has the potential of raising the productivity of the field crops, forest plants and livestock. It is acknowledged as a lifeline for Indian agriculture, offering opportunities for increased sustainability profitability and global competitiveness.

4. *Non-Farm Sector* : Banks are providing financial assistance for development of handlooms, handicrafts, coir, seri-culture, khadi & village industries, tiny industries with a view to promoting an integrated rural development. The functions of

Banks in the area on non-farm sector can be classified into credit supported and development oriented programmes.

5. *Group Lending Experiments* : Though the banking institutions have been able to provide increased credit access to weaker sections, the poorest of the poor are still forced to meet their credit needs from informal sources like moneylenders, who exploit them. In recent years several voluntary agencies who are working for the development of weaker sections through social organisation, non-formal education, skills improvement, etc., have sought to improve the access of rural poor to formal credit institutions so that they can improve their production base. Recognising the importance of such Self-Help Groups, the Indian Banking Sector has devetailed in its credit strategy the group approach in improving the access and acceleration rating the lending to rural poor.

6. *Innovation in RRBs and DCBs* : Revamping of the problem ridden Regional Rural Banks and District Cooperation Banks had been undertaken by formulation of Memorandum of understanding (MOU) and Development Action Plan (DAP's) to improve their operational efficiency, productivity and financial viability. This is with the involvement of NABARD, state government and sponsor Commercial Banks etc. Besides, the RRBs have been granted relaxation in respect of several banking functions (which was earlier in the domain of only Commercial Banks) in order to increase their profitability as part of the Financial sector reforms.

Current Issues in Rural Banking

In the context of this discussion on Rural Development Banking we can discern "the basic issues in the days ahead is in the developmental role of the banking sector not being diluted, viability aspects not being ignored and rural banking system being viewed as banking proper instead of being treated as an institutional arrangement for providing cheap credit." The banking sector will have to be viewed as a total developmental system which aims at improving the quality of life in rural areas. Its credit delivery system will have to be effective in reaching the target group at the right time with right type of package of services. The cost of playing the developmental role will have to be shared by all the three partners in the development process, viz. credit suppliers, credit users and the credit facilitators, instead of the major burden of the cost of giving banking services by the credit supplier only, as this has eroded the financial health and morale of the credit supplier.

Because of the high magnitude of rural poverty and increasing pressure on land it is imperative that diversification of the rural economy be resorted to more systematically. Attention is required to be given to the industrialization of the rural areas by development of agro-based industries in general and food processing industries in particular. While the banking sector has been expanding its coverage in the rural areas in quantitative terms there is much to be done on the qualitative dimension of rural banking. Effective follow-up and supervision, improving the quality of loan, etc. strategy of Self-Help Groups (SGHs) and involvement of Voluntary Agencies (VAs) for improving people's participation in the development process etc. could strengthen the rural banking activities.

Desirable changes in systems and procedures in rural banking have not been undertaken. Achievement of the financial viability and the developmental role by the rural banking system simultaneously presupposes the creation/existence of the right type of structure. Contributing to the creation of the structure is the branch licensing policy related to rural banking. The branch licensing policy (BLP) in the post-nationalization period is related to expansion of banking facilities in deficit areas and the reduction of inter-state and inter-district disparities. It is based on the multi-agency approach with emphasis on coordination between the three financial institutions, viz. commercial banks, cooperatives and RRBs to avoid wasteful competition and duplication of effort.

Rural economy is on its way to diversification through activization of non-farm sector and also programmes such as wasteland development, afforestation, dryland farming within the agricultural sector. This may call for some kind of credit and banking support which has not been required/offered so far. While giving specialized banking services to the traditional rural economy this dimension should not be lost sight of. The Rural Financial Institutions (RFI's) face a hierarchy of constraints which dilute their effectiveness in reaching the rural poor and women (as per findings of a World Bank study which has been elaborated upon in chapter 4). The issue of Rural Development Banking catering for Human Resource and Social Development has been illustrated through the case study of 'Women in Developemnt' (in chapter 9).

Notes

1 According to the Reserve Bank Governor., "The Indian Banking is at the start of what seems a banking revolution". Dr. Rangarajan. C.: "Imperatives of Banking in India", *Reserve Bank of India Bulletin*, Vol. XI-VII, No. 9, pp. 1059.

2. Narasimham Committee, *Report of the Committee on the Financial System*.

3. Roy A.K.,"Turning Phase of Indian Banking—Need for Strategic Planning, *IBA Bulletin*, September 1993.

4. Pareek, Udai, *Education and Rural Development in Asia*, New Delhi: Oxford & IBH Publishing Company Pvt. Ltd. 1982.

5. Miller, E.J., *Towards a Model for Integrated Rural Development in Latin America;* Linkage 1977.

6 Seventh Plan Approach Paper.

7 Integrated Rural Development Programme and Allied Programmes of Rural Youth for Self-Employment (TRYSEM), Department of Rural Development, Ministry of Agriculture, Government of India, New Delhi 1988.

8. *Ibid*.

3

Analysis of the Existing HRD and Training Systems in the Indian Banking Sector

Overview: The Indian Banking Sector has a complex structure and is undergoing a dynamic process of restructuring under financial sector reforms. Consequently it's various systems (HRD Systems, Operational and Planning Wings) and policies (economic/corporate/HRD related) are also in a state of flux. However, in keeping with the focus of this study, in this chapter we shall analyse only the present HRD and Training Systems in this sector.

We shall understand the concept of Human Resource Development, its subsystems, evolution of HRD in Indian Banks, followed by case study of HRD in Canara Bank (which is one of the better public sector banks with progressive HRD policies).

Subsequently we shall focus on Training subsystem of the Indian Banking Sector within the context of total HRD intervention , it's evolution and set up both for general banking and rural development banking. We shall also acquire an overview of the existing Training machinery/methodology of Indian Banks, the various steps involved in the training process (Training Needs Assessment/Techniques Used and Evaluation). These aspects will be illustrated through the case study of Training System in the State Bank of India, which is the country's largest public sector bank and has a better training machinery than many others.

Human Resource Development (HRD): Concept and Definitions

In the background of the discussion of the structure of the Indian Banking System and the changes it is undergoing. we shall proceed to understand HRD and Training mechanisms in the Indian Banking Sector. For this we have to acquire a clear understanding of the concepts.

Development is acquisition of capabilities—capabilities that are needed to do the present job or the future expected job well. Unlike other resources, human resources have an unlimited potential capability. The potential can be used only for creating a climate that can continuously identify, bring to surface, nurture and use the capabilities of people. Human Resource Development Systems aim at creating such a climate.

In the past, organizations were content with 'training' as a mechanism of developing competencies. As organisations started realizing the limitations of training and the need for creating a 'development climate' that can develop and harness the human resources, they began exploiting other mechanisms. In fact it was this need for paying attention to other mechanisms of development that led many organizations to set up new departments of Human Resource Development.

So the need for paying attention to other mechanisms of development contributed towards the growth of the HRD movement.

Human Resource Development (HRD) programmes help to ensure that the organisation has the people with the skills and knowledge it needs to achieve its strategic objectives. They aim to train new employees to the level of performance required in their jobs quickly and economically and to develop the abilities of existing staff so that performance in their present jobs is improved and they are prepared to take on increased responsibilities in the future.

The approaches used by HRD in achieving these aims have been defined as follows :

— The identification of needed skills and active management of employee learning, for the long-range future in relation to explicit corporate and business strategies. *(D.Hall)*

— These learning experience which are organized, for a specified time, and designed to bring about the possibility of behavioural change *(Nadler)*.

Rao (1985)[1] describes the HRD concept as follows : "HRD in the organisation context is a process by which the employees of an organisation are helped, in a continuous, planned way, to :

— Acquire or share capabilities required to perform various functions associated with their present or expected future roles;

— Develop their general capabilities as individuals and discover and exploit their own inner potential for their own and/or organisational development purposes;

— Develop an organisational culture in which superior-subordinate relationship, team-work and collaboration among subunits are strong and contribute to the professional well-being, motivation and pride of employee."

The HRD concept varies across cultures/nations. In our context, the main characteristic of HRD efforts in India, both the concepts and the practices, form a value-anchored system (SILVERA, 1988). HRD efforts are based on certain values (openness, confrontation, authenticity, trust, proactivity, autonomy and collaboration or OCTAPAC). Prof. T.V. Rao underlines the importance of an organizational climate conducive to development of human potential having the following 'OCTAPAC culture[2] ' elements :

1. Employees are action-oriented, willing to take initiative and show a high degree of proactivity (Proactivity).

2. Employees feel free to express their ideas and the organisation is willing to take risks and experiment with new ideas and new ways of doing things. (Openness and Risk taking).

3. Employees collaborate with each other and have a feeling of belonging to the same family and working for a common cause. (Collaboration).

4. Employees, departments and groups trust each other and can be relied upon to 'do' whatever they say they will. (Trust and Authenticity).

5. Employees face the problems and issues squarely without hiding them or avoiding them for fear of hurting each other.

6. Employees have some freedom to act independently within the boundaries imposed by their role/job. (Autonomy)

7. Employees are continuously helped to acquire new competencies through a process of performance planning, feedback training and creation of development opportunities through training, job-rotation, responsibility redefinition and other similar mechanisms. (General Development Climate).

PAREEK (1990) says that even the concept of "Human Resource" is not value free. Three aspects in the concept of HRD are that persons working in organisations are regarded as a valuable resource, implying that there is a need to invest time and effort in their development. Secondly, they are human resources, which means that they have their own special characteristics, therefore, cannot be treated like material resources. This focuses on the need to humanise organisational life. Lastly human resource does not merely focus on employees as individuals, but also on other human units and processes in the organisation.

Training System as a Component of HRD System

The targets of HRD form one axis. The other axis is formed by HRD systems and activities. These two axes make the HRD matrix. The HRD systems are :

1. *Career Systems* : are concerned with the advancement of the individual employees in their careers in the organisation e.g. ITC prepares career development plans for each employee within the frame work of the organisation's business plans.
2. *Appraisal Systems* : There are three main appraisal systems: performance appraisal: potential appraisal; and performance coaching counselling—of these, much more attention has been given to performance appraisal. An interesting experience of disciplined management through employee counselling has been reported from Indian Hotels (Silvera, 1988).
3. *Training System* : Inspite of being the oldest element of HRD, training is inadequately treated in most Indian organisations. Greater attention to identification of training needs, preparation of training strategy, development of training systems, curriculum designing to meet specific needs, follow-up and evaluation and post-training support would be needed. Innovative training programmes like the use of video programme material for process change have been tried in HDFC.
4. *Cultural Systems* : are the most neglected parts of HRD. Cultural Systems are concerned with development of appropriate organisational culture, improving communication and evolving effective reward systems.
5. *Work Systems*: Generally, work systems which have not attracted much attention in HRD efforts in India include task analysis, quality of work life; productivity and role stress.
6. *Self-Renewal Systems* : An organisation needs to diagnose its problems from time to time, and take

steps to develop new competencies to cope with the various problems through effective organisation development. Planning of implementation is as important as, but more difficult than, designing HRD systems. Implementation is rather neglected.

Human Resource Development components in practice relate to training and development. Training fills the gap between what someone can do and what he should be able to do. It ensures that, as quickly as possible, people can reach an acceptable level in their jobs. Training then builds on this foundation by enhancing skills and knowledge as required to improve performance in the present job or develop potential for the future. Development can be defined as the modification of behaviour through experience. It provides for people to do better in existing jobs and prepares them for greater responsibility in the future. It builds on strengths and helps to overcome weaknesses, and ensures that the organisation has the expertise it needs. Development operates at all levels. For shop floor and more junior supervisory, office, technical and professional staff it should be programmed to provide the right training at the right time and to broaden people's expertise and abilities by giving them new tasks to carry out. At a higher level, management development programmes aim systematically to identify talent, improve skills, widen experience and help people to grow in their ability to accept greater responsibility. Dr. Lynton and Pareek[3] writing on issues of training contend that "training cannot increase the effectiveness of people unless it emphasizes the human aspect: the dignity of people. We have to increase the culture of openness and confrontation. All this later came to be called OD... for training to be effective it is necessary that it should be part of a strategy and not be viewed in isolation."

Evolution of HRD System in the Indian Banking Sector

At present Indian Banks by and large are pursuing only one or the other of the HRD components, and not all of its essential subareas. For instance many banks do undertake the personnel functions but without developing them as an integral part of the human resources basket. In the pre-nationalization period, the recruitment policy followed by most of the banks was based on local considerations. Following the assumption of an all-India character by the major public sector banks, they have become heterogeneous and diverse. The values and culture possessed by qualified young persons who are now joining the banks is substantially different from their older colleagues. This has naturally led to a 'clash of values' between the two groups of bank employees. Again, with the slackening of the growth process in banks, particularly in the last one decade, the opportunities for promotion have consequently slowed down, causing an increasing degree of frustration at the middle and senior levels coupled with a growing alienation at the lower level of employees. Almost every bank resorts to the exercise of performance appraisal but this is done more by way of an administrative necessity rather than as a tool of human resources development. Not many banks have introduced the systems of performance feedback or career planning. Again most of the banks base their promotion decisions, not on the worker's potential merits but, on the candidate's seniority and past work appraisal. This has resulted in a mismatch.

Among the several HRD sub-areas, the one in which some individual banks have done relatively better is the training function. But still only about 20-25 per cent of the bank staff is covered under the various training programmes every year. So, the urgent need in the area today is to formulate a comprehensive training policy.

In short, Indian banks are not yet adequately equipped in the important areas of HRD. Since it is ultimately the employee who lies at the crux of a banking system, it is high time that Indian banks now concentrate on developing their human resources in a serious manner so that they are able to effectively meet the new challenges.

The human resource development movement in India is of recent origin. The term gained currency only in the early seventies. In the area of management sciences, the decade of 1980's is known as the decade of computers and HRD. The term HRD was first applied in 1968 in George Washington University. In the opinion of Prof. Udai Pareek, the term was first used in India in 1972 by the State Bank of India. By the late seventies and early eighties this professional outlook on HRD caught on to a few Public Sector Undertakings and Indian Banks. HRD systems vary across the banks in sophistication/effectiveness. Canara Bank has a more promising HRD system and we shall illustrate it through the following Case Study. (IJTD).

Overview of HRD Systems of Canara Bank : Case Study : The following is a brief account of the various HRD systems in practice, at Canara Bank:

System	***Objectives***	***Target Group***
Entry interview	Introduction of the new entrant to the Institution : its culture tradition, ethos and work ethics.	New entrants
Training	To induct the employees, develop skills and impart knowledge in functional and behavioural area.	Employees
Job Rotation	Provides an opportunity to the employees for being trained in various functions of the Branch/Office.	–do–
Staff Meeting	A participatory forum at unit level for exchange of ideas, improving communication skills and involving people in the effective functioning of the Branch/Office.	Branches & Offices
Study Circle	A forum in which employees share knowledge/individual experiences and invite guest faculty for educational lectures etc.	Employees/ Branches
Quality Circle	Gives an opportunity to the employees to use their potential and creativity to solve work-related problems through voluntary participation. Promotes team spirit and leadership development.	Employees

Contd..

System	***Objectives***	***Target Group***
Effective Communication	To improve the public speaking skills/ communication ability of employes and utilise their talent for educating the public on the bank's schemes and services.	Identified Employees
Brain-storming Sessions	To elicit ideas/views/suggestions from a cross section of employees, on subjects of importance to the Bank. The topic is advised from Head Office in advance every quarter. The broad based feedback generated by the Brain-storming sessions is found valuable in shaping bank's systems and procedure in various functional area.	HO, COs & DOs, Branches
Performance Appraisal for Officers	An open - system linked to promotion process for objective evaluation of performance counse lling and career- planning.	Officer
Skill inventory & talent bank	Identification of skills talents, proficiencies of the employees and creation of Data Bank.	Employees
Welfare Officer	An executive posted exclusively for the purpose of employee development, grievance handling,counselling and close liaison provides the management with feedback relating to employee morale, motivation and problem areas.	Circle Office
Branch visit and interface by executives	To review and monitor the Branch performance and to interact with the personnel. Participation of teams from Branch and Controlling Office in across-the-table discussion.	C.Os
Circulation of	To educate the employees about the changes taking place in the internal and	–do–

Contd..

System	*Objectives*	*Target Group*
communications	external environment, sharing of information on organisational goals and strategies.	
Branch Management Board	A branch level team for tacking the day-to-day problems of the Branch.	Branches
Division Management Board	To formally review and monitor all aspects of functioning of branches of the Division- a training ground for Managers to take on higher responsibilities in course of time.	C.Os
Suggestion Scheme	Involving employees in Organisation Development, encouraging thinking process for contributing constructive ideas/ suggestions.	Employees
Exit Interview	To obtain free and frank feedback from the employee who is retiring/resigning from the services of the Bank, on the policies and practices of the Bank, suggestions for, improving performance, support expected at operational levels and so on.	Exit Employees

As would be observed from this Case Study, the HRD systems of Canara Bank have several innovative features and attempt to cover the banks functioning at different operational levels; though, of course, the scope of improvement remains (as per other new features covered in this study). And we can say that this bank's relatively better HRD system has contributed in giving it a top place in the Indian Banking Sector.

Evolution of the Training System in the Indian Banking Sector

Institutional Setup: The importance of training has been recognized in the banking sector for a long time. The Reserve Bank of India established the Bankers Training College in 1954 to teach sound banking as it was understood in Britain. At about the same time, the Imperial Bank of India also set up a training school in Calcutta to train probationary assistants and opened two more schools in the other two circles namely Bombay and Madras.

The State Bank of India Act in 1955 enjoined the proposed bank to carry out its banking activities on the principles of business efficiency having due regard to public interest. However, very little was done, in the initial stages, to ensure indoctrination of the operating staff at the field level through training, since it was believed that the best method of learning banking was to apprentice a novice to a veteran on the job. But the extraordinary change in the social context of banking needed a new kind of banking, for which apprenticeship training was hardly appropriate.

The establishment of the Staff Training College in December 1962 at Hyderabad constitutes an important landmark in the history of training in the State Bank and in the banking industry. In the mid-sixties, the Bankers Training College offered for the first time, a progrmame for middle and senior levels of management. The State Bank also started offering short duration courses on general management for its middle level managers. Earlier banks had been sending their middle level officers for participation in general management programmes of the Administrative Staff College of India.

In the meantime, other banks were realizing the need for providing training facilities to their employees. A few banks set up join staff colleges. A few more established their own institutions/training centres.

All nationalized banks have set up residential staff colleges and training centres to train officers and work-men staff. There is a training infrastructure of 7 institutes, of which 3 have a capacity of 100 to 120 participants. The other three institutes are on a smaller scale-one catering to the needs of the banks in the north-eastern region and the other two to training needs of smaller banks in the northern and southern India and the fourth training institute looks after the training of RRB personnel. The institute are: the National Institute of Bank Management (NIBM), College of Agricultural Banking (CAB) North-Eastern Institute of Bank Management (NEIBM), Northern India Banks Staff Training College (NIBSTC), the Southern India Banks Staff Training College (SIBSTC), the Bankers Institutions of Rural Development (BIRD), Bankers Training College (BTC). These institutions each offer 40-100 programmes in all aspects of banking, including conferences, workshops, seminars and courses. Of these, BIRD at Lucknow and the College of Agricultural Banking at Pune specialize in management of rural credit.

At the individual bank level, there are staff colleges and training centres where the college is recognized as an apex institution and is meant for training junior officers. SBI has two staff colleges and two specialized staff colleges—one for rural development and one for information technology. Central Bank of India has a rural development institute. Central Bank of India and Dena Bank have a joint staff College, so have Bank of Baroda and Bank of India, apart from their separate staff colleges. Canara Bank has a Central Staff College and four regional colleges. Punjab National Bank has its central staff college in Delhi. There are about 30 colleges in the banking industry which concentrate mainly on training officer staff and the training centred on workmen staff. There are about 150 Staff Training Centres in the country; of these, the State Bank Group has about 70 STCs and the remaining serve the needs of the 20 public sector banks. They offer courses on various aspects of the general banking, branch management and credit discipline, though a few specialized courses in agricultural financing or small industries financing are also offered.

Only the rural development institutes offer exclusive courses in agricultural financing and allied subjects—their number, however, is very small. So the existing colleges will have to take up the increasing responsibility of handling training required for equipping officers for their new role under the Service Area Approach and other important developments/concerns like gender issues.

Adarkar Committee: Establishment of NIBM

Appointment of a working group by the Reserve Bank of India in 1968, on training facilities for higher level bank personnel under Adarkar[4] as a sequel to the debate on nationalization was a landmark. For the first time, this committee took a comprehensive view of the training process and training was seen as an important tool and an integral part of human resources and an organisation development process. For becoming effective, all elements of human resources development and manpower planning had to be integrally linked up. The committee lamented that no effort was made in this area. Lack of systematic action had created succession gaps, dilution in the quality, low motivation and very low development of professionalism. In the banking industry, training had been interpreted to mean job training and vocational education. The committee emphasized that the main purpose in training was to develop decision-making skills and qualities of leadership through management education, covering a broad range of management and social sciences. The committee recommended that a new national level institute—*National Institute of Bank Management* (NIBM) had to be created for the provision of training research and consultancy services to the banking industry. It was expected to focus attention on problems of the banking industry and organize seminars and conferences. Soon after its establishment, NIBM organized a seminar on management development for top level and senior level executives in 1970. The participants felt that mere institutional training by itself was not enough, unless it was linked with on-the job training and proper post-training placement. Procedures for selection, recruitment, performance appraisal, and promotion had to be modernized and made more systematic and scientific.

As a followup to this seminar many banks created manpower planning cells in their personnel or staff departments. A few banks created management development units. From 1972 to 1974 NIBM held annual seminars on manpower planning and development (HRD) with the specific objective of imparting skills and techniques to enable these cells to undertake various tasks and sub-tasks of manpower planning and manpower development. From 1972, NIBM also held annual conference of the principals of staff training colleges. NIBM held a number of trainer training programmes on teaching methodology, performance budgeting, credit management, lending to priority and preferred sectors, research methodology with a view to mdernizing class-room teaching in training institutions of banks. Thus considerable efforts were made by NIBM to improve awareness and to upgrade the knowledge of bank officers at various levels in these specialized areas. NIBM also took the lead in setting up task forces, comprising bank officers and NIBM faculty to evolve schemes for implementation. Thus tasks forces were set up on manpower and skill inventory, career path planning.

In 1971, the Department of Banking, Ministry of Finance, Government of India, set up a committee of direction for training in public sector banks for monitoring the functioning of the training and HRD systems. As a result of this, banks took steps to improve these systems and their functioning. The department of banking also formed subcommittees of the committee of direction to study specific issues. During 1969 to 1977 NIBM held a number of short duration programmes for middle and senior level managers. The programmes for middle managers were in functional areas such as credit monagement, management of human resources, rural development and seminars and courses on general management.

Raj and Kasbekar Committees

In addition to NIBM, two other industry level institutions, the Bankers Training College, Bombay and the College of Agricultural Banking, Pune continued to offer programmes for middle and senior level executives in functional areas and banks took advantage of these programmes. Banks also took advantage of similar programmes offered by the Administrative Staff College of India and the Small Industry Extension Training Institute. Several middle and senior level managers benefitted from participation in these programmes.

But the banks did not derive commensurate benefit in terms of improved performance. The programmes' participants couldn't address themselves to the task of developing a uniquely Indian banking tradition and style-since the courses were of too short a duration and nothing was expected of them as a result of their having attended a training programme, the selection of these courses was mostly the result of ad-hoc decisions-not the result of careful planning for training and manpower or management development. During this period, banks sought consultancy help from NIBM, IIM and other consultants in the area of training and HRD. NIBM established a full fledged institute of bank personnel selection. Despite all these efforts, all was not well with training and HRD in banks. The *James Raj Committee*[5] in 1978 recommended the appointment of a committee to make an in-depth study and the setting up of a high powered monitoring authority under the chairmanship of the Reserve Bank Governor. Consequently the Reserve Bank of India appointed a committee under the chairmanship of *P.D. Kasbekar*[6] which found that staff training colleges were not adequately staffed and equipped with all the necessary infrastructural facilities, there were gaps in the structure of courses and in many cases the course contents had not been fully worked out, the courses were not standardized and rationalized at the industry level.

After 1977 NIBM questioned the effectiveness of the strategy of short-duration courses and offered its first long duration programme in 1978—the bank management programme of nine months duration covering systematically various areas of specialization required in the banking business and supporting disciplines such as statistics, management accounting, behavioural sciences, operations research and research methodology. Some banks launched projects of installing the LRP (Long Range Planning). NIBM followed up this programme by launching another 10 weeks programme on management education for senior executives.

An idea of the broad range of NIBM courses today is apparent from a representative Calendar of Programmes.

NIBM: Calendar of Training Programme (Extracts)

International Programmes: e.g. Programme on Project Appraisal and Follow-up (National Development Bank, Sri Lanka).

General Management: e.g. Conference of Chairman of Private Sector Banks.

Computers and Systems : e.g. Programme on Relational Data Base Management System.

Finance: e.g., Programme on Merchant Banking and Financial Services.

Human Resource Management : e.g. Programme on HRD: Systems and Processes.

Money and International Finance: e.g. Programme on International Finance, Trade and Banking.

Sponsored/Incompany Training Programmes: e.g. Trainers' Training Programme on Maharasthra Rural Credit Project.

Types of Trainings Imparted in Indian Banks

As the training requirements differ at different levels, various types of trainings are given to meet the desired objectives by the training institutes of Indian Banks:

Subordinate Staff: This category of staff includes peons, messengers, drivers, watchmen, guards, cleaners etc. training for this category of staff, given for a period between three days and fifteen days includes introduction and history of bank, the type of behaviour expected of them, routine performance of their jobs, brief idea about bank deposit schemes etc. This type of training is given immediately after their placement on permanent basis.

Clerical Staff: This Category of staff includes cashiers, clerks, godownkeepers, typists, stenographers etc. After the placement of the employees of this category, they are imparted some training in order to familiarize them with their job and work environment. They undergo training in these courses:

— *Induction Course* : This training, given to new entrants before they take up their job, is of two to three weeks duration. It aims at introducing them to the job, the organisational objectives and work environment.

— *Refresher Course* : This course is organized for senior clerical staff who have completed a minimum of five years of service to acquaint them with the latest developments and techniques in their respective fields. This course can be conducted through a series of lectures, seminars, panel and group discussions with the help of audio-visual aids.

— *Specialized Training* : This training can be organized for specialized fields such as cash statements, foreign exchange, non-resident accounts, small business and agricultural finance etc. These courses are of short duration between there to seven days.

Officers Grade Staff: This category includes all officers who undergo several courses such as:

— *Induction Course* for Probationary officers for two to three weeks followed by 'on the job' training.

— *Management Course/Seminars* for Senior officers of one/two weeks duration on the latest management techniques.

— *Specialized Courses* conducted in fields like Merchant Banking, underwriting and in technical areas e.g. Industrial loaning.

We shall now consider in some detail the existing training and development machinery for rural banking.

Training and Development for Rural Banking: Evolution/ Setup

Human Resource Development being an integral part of institutional development, for institutionalizing the rural credit, training of personnel has been emphasized. The RBI set up the Co-operative Bankers Training College at Pune (named as College of Agriculture Banking) to train the senior and middle level personnel of co-operative banks and has continued to train the personnel of RRBs as well as the rural branches of commercial banks. Since it's inception, NABARD devoted special attention to the training needs of Rural Financial Institutions (RFIs). While continuing to collaborate with the CAB in the training of rural bank functionaries, the National Bank independently set up the *Bankers Institute of Rural Development (BIRD)* at the national level and the *Regional Training Centres (RTCs)* for training of a large number of rural bankers in general and RRB personnel in particular. National Bank also continued its support both academically and financially, the training of personnel of land development banks in the Junior Level Training Centres (JLTCs). Thus, training as a part of the institutional development has been supported, in RTCs, CAB of RBI, BIRD and JLTCs of SLDBs with financial and other support from National Bank. The BIRD and the two RTCs which were training exclusively the personnel of RRBs till 1992 have taken a new role in the context of reorganisation of the BIRD as an autonomous society-national level apex training institute of excellence. The reorganized BIRD has been given the responsibility for training of trainers, conducting high quality functional programmes, diversifying into action research, consultancy services, adoption of innovative approaches such as seminars for senior executives, client specific training programmes with regional focus, constructing live case studies as an instrument of effective training and organisational development initiatives to change the mindset of the personnel for effective functioning.

National Bank also encourages the SCBs and DCCBs to develop their human resources by extending support for training programmes in the Agricultural Co-operative Staff Training Institutions (ACSTIs), supporting/formulating HRD plan alongwith the business development plan of the Development Planning exercise both for short-term and long term co-operative credit institutions.

HRD Policies in RRBs : The Human Resource Development (HRD) policies in RRBs, based on the systems obtaining in their respective sponsor banks and instruction of GOI, NABARD and RBI, differ from bank to bank due to variation in the policies of sponsor banks and also the interpretation of official guidelines.

In most of the RRBs the HRD functions performed by a Senior Manager in Personnel or General Administrative Department at head office are maintenance or reactive rather than proactive. These activities are such as sending relievers to branches, transfers, dealing with legal disciplinary cases, handling industrial relation cases rather than proactive/ preventive actions like improving motivation levels among staff, team work, leadership development etc.

Training : Initially in RRBs when recruitment was done at a massive scale, fresh recruits were posted to branches without proper training-adversely affecting their business and image. Management recognized the need for training of the staff as a part of RRBs HRD efforts though no systematic efforts were made to assess the staff's training needs. Sponsor bank's support in this matter was also not adequate, although some of them established training centres for the staff of their RRBs.

Since in RRB's, deputation for the training was generally considered as a reward this activity has also become another 'hygienic' factor like (perks) whose absence leads to demotivation. Further inability of the management to not post the person after training in the relevant department also leads to reduction in training effectiveness. Most of the training facilities were for officers and it focussed more on skill development rather than attitudinal/behaviour/orientation change.

We shall now take a detailed overview of the presently existing HRD and Training practices in the Indian Banking sector and consider some illustrative Case Studies.

Existing Training Systems in Indian Banking Sector

Parameters of the Training System : Planning training course in the Banking Sector would begin with clarifying training needs and then setting training or learning objectives. Having set objectives then, the following are decided by the training establishment:

— The *content* of the course, as established by job and task analysis and information from performance appraisals.

— Training *techniques.*

— The *location*, which can either be:

Off-the-job where training can be concentrated, planned without distractions, and given by qualified trainers.There are, however, disadvantages, including the problems of transferring knowledge and skills from what is sometime called the learning situation to the place of work.

On-the-job where the advantages are that it should be practical and immediately relevant, but the quality of instruction may be poor, the training programme may not have been properly planned.

— The *duration* of training, which depends upon how much learning has to take place. An induction course for freshly recruited officers might involve a prolonged course mixing theoretical, practical, on- and off-the job training. Or the training could comprise a short course—like technical courses on fisheries, minor irrigation etc.

— *Responsibility* for training: a professional training or a designated manager who is given the task as part of his other responsibilities. Full time faculty members are nominated from a panel.

— *Evaluation:* the methods used to assess the result of training. These start from the definition of training objectives and then attempt to measure how far these objectives have been achieved. Basic skills effectiveness can be measured first by classroom tests, followed up by analysis of the extent to which these skills have been applied successfully at work. Management training may be more difficult to evaluate because it is not always easy to measure the effect of what has been learned. There are a number of levels at which such training can be evaluated.

Training Needs Assessment System: Training must be relevant. Often it is not. So because the content of adhoc courses may have little or nothing to do with what the trainees really need to learn-learning objectives are not set, inappropriate methods are used, the trainee finds it difficult to relate what he has learnt in the classroom to what he actually has to do, and it is next to impossible to evaluate results. This problem can be solved if the training course is based on an analysis of what people have to do and need to know.

The identification of training needs starts from job analysis, which describes the tasks that are carried out. From this is derived the training specification which sets out the characteristics that the employee should have in order to perform these tasks successfully:

— *Knowledge*: what the employee needs to know-professional, technical or commercial knowledge e.g. about the basis of technical and financial appraisal of projects, the products to be sold.

— *Skills*: what the employee needs to be able to do if results are to be achieved and knowledge is to be used properly—manual, intellectual or social skills.

— *Attitudes*: the disposition to behave or to perform in a way in accordance with the work requirements.

Task analysis techniques define for each task:

— Its relative significance to the successful performance of the whole job.

— The level of skill or knowledge required to perform it; the typical faults that can occur, how they should be recognized, what causes them and what can be done to remedy them.

— The instructional techniques and the type and length of experience required to become proficient.

Although the starting point is job analysis it is necessary to go beyond this. A results oriented approach compares achievements with agreed targets or standards of performance for each task. A performance appraisal system should identify individual training needs. If the results of the whole scheme are analysed, information should be obtained on collective training needs which would be satisfied by organisations courses. The training department of an organisation prepares a proforma to facilitate the collection of essential data about the training needs of each officer—the information collection to be made keeping a three year perspective in view. The proforma collects data related to:

— Educational/Professional Qualifications.

— Work History: Past experience (period & nature of work at different centres and department)

: Present desk/seat-period and nature of work.

: likely work responsibilities in 2-3 years.

— Training already received-details of training institutes/training programme/course coverage.

— Estimate of the nature of training needs—training required by the employee in the context of both present and future work responsibilities.

Training Techniques : The following training techniques in various combinations are used:

Probationer's Training : a combination of on-the-job and off-the-job training, it requires the cooperation of the employer, trainers at the work place and in training schools, government agencies (e.g. in relation to field visit). The newly recruited probationer commits himself to a period of training involving both formal classroom learning and practical on-the-job experience. A modular scheme of integrated training for newly recruited officers at NABARD is in operation.

On-the-job training : The widely used method of training (formal and informal) is on-the-job training where the employee is placed into the real work situation and shown the job and the tricks of the trade by an experienced supervisor. If it is not handled properly there can be lack of practical awareness of grassroots realities, unsatisfied customers, and poorly taught workers. So trainers must be carefully selected and should use effective training techniques in instructing the trainee. For example trainers of IOP (Inspection Oriented Programmes) of NABARD have been imparted on-the-job training by associating them as under study in the inspection of a cooperative bank under supervision of an experienced Inspecting Officer.

Simulated Training: The trainee learns the job in an environment that simulates the real working environment as closely as possible.

Off-the-job training : It is done in organisation, classrooms, vocational schools etc. The frequently used methods for off-the-job training are the lecture/discussion, programmed computer based and simulation approaches.

Lecture/discussion approach: This frequently used training method is for a trainer to give a lecture and involve the trainee in a discussion. Effective classroom presentation supplements the verbal part with audiovisual aids such as slides or lectures videotape or audio tapes are used, allowing the trainer's message to be given in many locations and to be repeated.

Programmed/Computer-assisted instruction: One of the newer methods being used in organisational training is programmed instruction where material is presented on teaching machines or in text form and learning principles are followed. It is a useful method for self instruction. It is a learner-centered method of instruction, which presents subject-matter to the trainee in small steps or increments, requiring frequent responses from him and immediately informing him of the correctness of his responses.

Other/Manager Oriented Methods: Other methods used to present materials are more frequent in *management development programmes* than in employees training programmes:

The Case method: In the case method, a case (a written description of a real decision making situation) is presented to trainees to study and propose solutions and implement the best solution. One variation of this method is the incident method, wherein the bare outlines of the situation are given initially, and the students are assigned a role in which to view the incident.

The in-basket technique: In the in-basket technique the trainee is given a box of material which includes typical items from a specific manager's mail. The trainee is analyzed and critiqued on the number of decisions made in the time period allotted, the quality of decisions, and the priorities chosen.

Role Playing: In this method each participant is assigned a role in a training situation and asked to play the role and to react to other players.

Audio-Visual Aids: In the off the job training particularly for sepecialised programme (e.g. technical areas like Minor Irrigation, Fisheries Development etc.) use is made of slide projectors, Film Projectors, overhead Projectors, which are instrumental in improving the receptivity of the trainees.

Evaluation Tests: The trainee officers on probation are subjected to evaluation tests during the training period to ensure their active involvement and to gauge as to what extent they have assimilated the inputs given during the different phases of the training process.

Training Evaluation: The assessment of the total value of a training system, training course or programme in social as well as financial terms. It is assessment of the success of the training under *criteria* which can include.

— does the course satisfy its stated objectives to a major extent?

— Is the course cost-effective to the organisation?

— do the participants put the learning into effective action on work condition?

The satisfaction of these criteria can vary-technical/procedural training is often the easiest to assess—the learning is straight forward and direct testing of skill and knowledge will show whether learning has been achieved. Less specific forms of training such as human relations training can be very difficult to assess.

Levels of Assessment/Evaluation: Various levels of assessment can be identified:

— Immediate: Progressive validation during the training event.

— Immediate outcome : an end-of-course validation of the course by the participants in terms of individual sessions activities.

— Intermediate outcome : an assessment of the retention and application of the learning some time following the end of the course, say three to six months.

— Ultimate outcome : a longer-term assessment after say a year's interval of retained learning and application and the organisation's long term benefits.

Alternatively the *processes* occurring as a result of a successful training programme are viewed as being divided into *levels — evaluation* can be carried out at any of these:

— *The Reactions Level*: Trainees react to the training (form opinions/attitudes about the trainer, the presentation).

— *The Learning Level* : Trainees learn (acquire knowledge, skills and attitudes about the subject matter).

— *The Job Behaviour Level*: Trainees apply this learning in the form of changed behaviour on the job.

— *The Functioning Level (Efficiency & Costs)* : This changed job behaviour affects the functioning of the organisation. The "Learning", "Job Behaviour" and "Functioning" levels are referred to by some experts as the "immediate", "intermediate" and "ultimate" levels respectively, referred to earlier.

Reactions Level: Information about trainees' reactions to training may be obtained during training, immediately after training, or some time later, by the use of rating scales for sessions-trainees are asked to place a tick on a number of seven-point (or five-point) scales.

Learning Level: Evaluation at this level obtains information on the amount of learning that trainee acquire during the training programme, irrespective of whether they go on to apply the learning on the job. Learning can be divided into knowledge, skills and attitudes. Knowledge learning can be evaluated by various forms of tests and examinations. Skill learning can be evaluated by practical tests in which the trainee is given the opportunity to demonstrate his skill. Attitude learning is an objective of most training programmes to measure changes in attitudes, we can use attitude scales.

Job Behaviour Level: The purpose is to discover whether trainees have applied their learning in the form of changed behaviour on the job. Trainers should actually involve themselves as far as possible in the job situation of their trainees to obtain a large amount of systematic information about their job behaviour. Among the techniques that can be used are: activity sampling (for discovering the percentage of time spent by the trainee on different aspects of his job), observer diaries (for obtaining a continuous record of the trainee's pattern of activities), self-diaries (the trainee keeps a record of his own activities over a specified period) and appraisal by superiors.

Functioning Level: Evaluation consists of any attempt to measure aspects of the effects of trainee's job behaviour—whether on the productivity or efficiency of the trainee's department, or on the morale of his subordinates. The main difficulty is determining to what extent changes are the result of the training rather than of other factors.

Some Prevalent Training Evaluation Methodology: The evaluation techniques being currently used in institutions like NABARD utilize questionnaries, rating scales, as well as evaluation tests to evaluate the effectiveness of training at reactions and learning levels.

— *Evaluation Tests*: The trainee officers on probation are subjected to evaluation tests during the training period. These tests ensure better involvement of the participants in the training. The participant's performance in these tests has been largely found to be satisfactory, indicating assimilation of the knowledge inputs of the learning level imparted during different training phases.

— *Participant's feedback*: On the various core training programmes and technical programmes etc. participants are asked to provide feedback towards the close of various courses covering such aspects as:-

–programmes utility to the participants

–adequacy and relevant of programme material/ content

–extent of achievement of programme objectives

–extent of effectiveness of the training methodology.

This feedback would be consolidated and discussed with the participants on the concluding day of the concerned programme. The participants views are also sought as to nature of additional inputs that could be incorporated in the programme and suggestions for improvement of the programme.

This general discussion of the Training System of Indian Banks shall be now illustrated through the Case Study of State Bank of India (IJTD), which has a better record in this area as compared to other Indian Banks—though the scope for improvement remains.

Case Study: Training Sub-system in the State Bank of India (S.B.I)

Training in State Bank, which dates back to 1950s is regarded as a vital and critical component of Human Resources Development. "Training Philosophy" of State Bank of India has been expressed as: "Training in the State Bank is a proactive, planned and continuous process as an integral part of Organisation Development. It seeks to impart knowledge, improve skills and reorient attitudes for individual growth and organisational effectiveness."

The training function in the State Bank is divided into the following:

— Institutional training

— On-the-job training

— Distance learning.

Institutional Training : The Institutional training network in State Bank is recognised as one of the best in the country. The Training network comprises 4 apex level Institutions/ Colleges and 55 Staff Training Centres spread throughout the country. Institutional training focuses on imparting knowledge, sharpening skills and developing appropriate attitudes towards people and task. The Staff Training Centres cater to the needs of job-related requirements pertaining to Key Skill Areas (KSA) in respect of clerical, sub-ordinate and junior level supervisory staff. The apex-level institutions concentrate on role-related requirements, pertaining to K.S.A in respect of officers in middle, senior as well as top Executive Grades. While the Staff Training Centres conduct programmes for imparting basic job knowledge, the apex level institutions devote more attention in developing managerial competence among the critical levels of officers in various grades. Post-nationalisation period in Banking industry saw unprecedented growth in branch network enormous recruitment of staff and a number of problems. One of the painful consequences of this period was indiscipline and apathy of bank staff toward customers.

In this emerging scenario, State Bank initiated efforts to revitalise and develop its human resources to create a new work culture. Towards this, intensive inputs on 'Behavioural Science' were introduced in the training programmes. At present, the State Bank has a work force of nearly 2,25,000 employees on its establishment, spread over more than 8,800 branches. With a view to catering to their training needs at various stages, the existing training network has been strengthened with the capacity to accommodate as many as 2715 trainees at any given point of time (399 at apex level institutions and 2316 at STCs).

All the training institutions are well equipped with the latest audio-visual and other technological aids available. The apex level institutions, besides, conducting uni-level and multi-level management development programmes, also organise specially designed programmes in areas like: Credit Management, International Banking, Personnel Management, Merchant Banking, Marketing etc.

Visiting Faculty Scheme: In addition to the programmes conducted at training institutions, S.B.I has also evolved an innovative approach to institutional training, under which the faculty from STCs visit the branches as per predetermined schedules and impart training in specific job-related areas to employees working in rural and semi-urban areas at the doorstep of a Branch.

Evaluation of Training: To achieve the twin objectives of ensuring transference of learning and assessing impact of training, S.B.I has also developed suitable models to evaluate training programmes conducted at various Centres/Colleges.

Training Consultancy: S.B.I has also been extending training consultancy to Banks situated outside India; particularly in the developing Afro-Asian countries, for whom it has been conducting tailor-made programmes.

On -the- job Training : Besides institutional training, S.B.I lays emphasis on learning through doing. This approach is particularly adopted in helping the directly recruited officers to appreciate intricacies of systems and procedural complexities of different Banking operations, which they would be required to supervise, guide and co-ordinate, in their role as members of the managerial cadre, after confirmation.

Distance Learning: This is another innovative intervention introduced in State Bank to enable the otherwise busy group of executives, to update themselves on various aspects of operational Banking, academics concerning a professional Banker, as well as major developments. Under this project, undertaken at S.B.I. Staff College at Hyderabad, two vehicles for distance-learning, the transcriptional journal "Chayanika" and "Educational Briefs" are utilised. "Chayanika" contains condensed versions of selected reading material on various topics and subjects concerning a professional banker, the "Educational Briefs" gives reading material on specific subjects of relevance, to enable the Bank's staff to acquire the much needed perspective on economic environment. This helps in bringing about an economic orientation in the thinking of Bank's officials necessary in these days of globalisation in diverse fields.

Summing Up: Despite considerable efforts by the Indian Banking sector, HRD and Training system have not taken root to the required depth due to various reasons. Rates of recruitment and promotion have fluctuated, creating bulges-career stagnation for some age bands and undeserved early promotion opportunities for others. The performance appraisal system, despite efforts at improving it, is still not functional. It should be such as would generate reliable data for taking posting, promotion and training decisions. No work is being done in career path planning. A good HRD system should provide every opportunity to every employee to reach the highest level of responsibility, which he is capable of reaching, while providing the right man with the right capability for the right job, at the right place and at the right time. Such a situation has not been reached and if the present situation and present practices continue, it will never be reached.

Despite all policy pronouncements and hard work on the part of banks, they still do not have fully functioning and effective training and HRD systems, since training and HRD systems have been moving in their own orbits. It is unfortunate that HRD is getting equated with training though progressive Banks do like not to be limiting the HRD activities to training. The line manager still does not consider training and HRD as his business. Since nothing is expected from trained men, the trainers too have no incentive to optimise the efficiency of the class room learning process. The true purpose of training and HRD is to create a youthful forward looking result oriented organisation which is capable of thinking originally, having its ears to the ground and at the same time looking to the horizon. Training alone cannot create the new banker as it is only one mechanism of human resource development. Total HRD efforts require conceptual understanding of what HRD can achieve in the successful performance of banking business. As a followup to this general critical overview of the state of the HRD and Training Systems in the Indian Banking sector, we shall now examine (in the following chapter) the findings of some important studies/seminars to identify the present gap in these systems.

Notes

1. Rao, T.V. and Pereira, D.F. (1985), *Recent Experiences in HRD,* New Delhi: Oxford and IBH.
2. Rao, T.V., Paper in *The 1985 Annual: Developing Human Resources,* edited by Leonard D. Good Stein and J. William Pfeiffer (CA: University Associates Inc. 1985).
3. Lynton, R.P. and Pareek, Udai, *Training for Development* (Sage, New Delhi 1990).
4. Report of the Working Group appointed by the Reserve Bank of India in 1968 on Training facilities for Higher Level Bank Personnel under the Chairmanship of B.N. Adarkar.
5. Report of the Committee appointed by the Reserve Bank of India on Functioning of Public Sector Banks under the Chairmanship of James S. Raj, 1978.
6. Report of the Working Group appointed by the Reserve Bank of India to review the Training arrangement in Banks, under the Chairmanship of P.D. Kasbekar, 1980.

4

Operational Problems–HRD and Training Gap in the Indian Banking Sector : Need for Re-engineering

Overview: The concern with improving the productivity of the Indian Banking Sector by improving the quality and quantity of HRD and Training inputs has been the subject of several studies, seminars and conferences. In these, eminent bankers and HRD professionals have endeavoured, on the basis of scientific data, to diagnose the areas of concern and suggest remedial measures. We shall briefly review these studies and view points to get a realistic picture of the prevailing state of affairs, the various gaps and lacunae in the H.R.D and training systems. These studies are :

(1) National Institute of Bank Management (NIBM) study on 15 Nationalized Banks.

(2) Recommendations of the Reserve Bank of India (RBI) seminar on `Emerging Training Needs of the Banking Industry in the 1990's'.

(3) Proceedings of the conference of Principals of Training Colleges of Commercial Banks.

(4) Recommendations of the National Workshop on Cooperative Training.

(5) World Bank Study on Financial Services for the Rural Poor and Women in India.

(6) Other miscellaneous viewpoints.
   (i) Limitations of HRD efforts in Indian Banks.
   (ii) On Rural Training.
   (iii) New Training Areas.
   (iv) The Price Waterhouse Cranfield Project.
   (v) The Laurie International Report (1990).
   (vi) Current Global Training Challenges.

This will provide a base for examining the need for restructuring and reengineering efforts necessary to improve the HRD and training delivery mechanism of the Indian Banking Sector generally, and the Rural Banking Sector specifically.

Evaluation Studies/Viewpoints on the HRD Training Gaps

In this book, we shall be considering the findings/ recommendations/excerpts of the following studies and viewpoints on the HRD & Training Systems of the Indian Banking Sector:

(1) National Institute of Bank Management (NIBM) study on 15 Nationalized Banks.

(2) Recommendations of Reserve Bank of India (RBI) seminar on `Emerging Training Needs of the Banking Industry in the 1990's'.

(3) Proceedings of the conference of Principals of Training Colleges of Commercial Banks.

(4) Recommendations of the National Workshop on Cooperative Training.

(5) World Bank Study on Financial Services for the Rural Poor and Women in India.

(6) Other miscellaneous viewpoints:
   1. Limitations of HRD efforts in Indian Banks.
   2. On Rural Training.
   3. New Training Areas.
   4. The Price Waterhouse Cranfield Project.
   5. The Laurie International Report. (1990)
   6. Current Global Training Challenges.

Appraisal of these studies would give an idea about the existing lacunae in the HRD and Training Systems of the Indian Banking Sector so that we shall be in a position to identify the gap in these systems and work out the requisite remedial measures.

We shall now discuss these evaluation studies in some detail :

(I) *NIBM Study*[1]: A study was conducted by National Institute of Bank Management (N.I.B.M.) Pune in 15 Nationalised banks on management functions i.e. planning, organising, staffing, directing and controlling, to analyze their training systems. Methods of questionnaire, personal interview collection of records and formats were employed. Analysis of the data collected by the N.I.B.M. study revealed the following features of the state of the management system related to Banks' training :

(i) The various documents on planning on psychological preoccupations of the functionaries, indicate an excessive concern for the volume: number of people trained, percentage increments over the last year, the capacity utilization rate etc. Rarely there is any interpretation of what these numbers mean in terms of employee performance and organizational achievements.

(ii) The psychological climate in the banks regards the training function as a "paid holiday", not a serious matter. Related to this is the widespread feeling that being posted as a trainer is "dumping" i.e. being sidelined, though some really competent people are in the training function for a while. The belief is that in the final count, training is not very useful or necessary for "practical" functioning. It is dispensable. Instead of sending competent employees to a training programme, incompetent employees are nominated.

(3) The belief that decision making in the field of training is "anybody's business" for which 'neither

professional expertise nor much of effort is required' is strongly established. There is simplistic approach to decision making in this area-assessment that simple common-sense conclusions are good enough and that instead of measurable and specific information for deciding training matters impressions are enough. Commonsense in place of professional expertise, and impressions in place of hard information.

(4) *Organizing:* Training cannot be a line function; it has merely to serve the operational wings. In the banks, however training is more like a line function than a staff function where the Zonal Managers and the Regional Managers hardly play any significant role in this matter. They do not exercise any real decision-making authority in the training matters. Another major structural weakness pertains to the relationship between the zonal Training Centres and their centrolling officers which violates the principles of unity of command as the former are required to take instructions or approval from HRD or Personnel Department at H.O., the apex Staff Training College, and the Zonal Office simultaneously. Another problem arises from the lack of clearly defined limits of authority and responsibility between the apex Staff Training College and the Personnel Department at H.O. leading to conflicts. The degree of formalization of the structure is scanty-organizational chart, job descriptions, the limits of authority or the reporting relationships amongst the various organs related to training is not adequate, impeding smooth execution and coordination as well as organizational learning from the experiences.

(5) *Planning:* The weakness in the planning process is the absence of a set of clear and comprehensive policies on all aspects of human resources development, the policies being implicit in the practices followed or written piecemeal in different circulars. These are not comprehensive: important aspects like evaluation of

training or training for individual development lack policy statement. There is lack of objective information systems, planning does not depend on objective data about performance deficiency (for which training is a remedy) or performance expectation but on the number of employees (in various categories). This rule out the possibility of assessing whether training has made any contribution.

(6) *Staffing*: Bank's pool of qualified personnel are not appropriately placed in the training function due to lack of a defined career path in many banks-being placed in training might mean 'parking'. The training of the personnel assigned to look after the training function (Principal, HRD Manager, Instructor, or Faculty Member) is haphazard and unplanned. Principals and other trainers, mostly operational bankers, are seldom given exposure to modern educational administration, so are unable to supervise the training institutions in a professional manner. Though for faculty members most banks have recognized the need for some training, the approach continues to be unsystematic.

(7) *Directing*: The climate of value is not conducive to training-all concerned do not value the training activities and the 'paidholiday' notion of training prevails. The incentives to the personnel are not adequate to motivate them strongly. Requisite non-monetary, incentives like opportunity to do important and prestigious work, deputation to prestigious institutions, social recognition etc. are lacking. Autonomy granted is not very high-adequate delegation with explicit accountability for results is lacking, though training is a function which can be performed meaningfully with freedom for all the concerned matters.

(8) *Controlling*: The effectiveness of any management is ensured by its control system-training in banks is

characterised by the weaknesses in its control system. The fundamental weakness of the control system lies in the lack of a set of clear objectives which are specific, observable and measurable due to lack of proper management information system for training (MIST). There is the lack of a comprehensive evaluation system to assess the efficacy of the training process at various stages before, during, and after training. This makes the whole training activities act of faith or a "shot in the general direction of the enemy". There is lack of meaningful review and analysis of the training activities. Presently the only measurable parameters have been the number of employees trained and the amount of money spent, reviews limited to the analysis of such parameters in terms of efficiency measures (e.g. capacity utilization, per trainee cost etc.) The appraisal system for the training personnel is not purposive enough to ensure the right kind of performance. A managerial system needs to be audited periodically., assessed for rational and empirical adequacy. In the training area no comprehensive audit is noticed. Thus, the control systems pertaining to training continue to be very primitive–to be expected from the way planning is carried out, because execution and control cannot exceed the efficacy of planning.

As the comprehensive NIBM study shows, almost all aspects of management of nationalised banks–planning, organising, staffing, directing and controlling need to be revamped. Many of these observations apply to other Indian banks as well. The remedial measures we shall be taking up in our discussion of reengineering interventions.

(II) *RBI Seminar*[2] *on `Emerging Training Needs of the Banking Industry in the 1990s'*: some recommendations :

(1) *Organisational set up* : Banks have a long way to go as it is estimated that bank training in India works out to less than 2 days in a year as compared to 15 days

in USA and 51 days in UK. Further, while at present the infrastructure is generally adequate, though it varies as between banks, capacity utilisation still needs to be improved as it is estimated that the utilisation is generally between 75 per cent and 80 per cent of the capacity as advance planning at various levels in regard to drawing up a calender of programmes and preparing the list of staff to be nominated is not being adequately done.

(2) *Faculty Selection/Development:* While in some banks, applications are invited for faculty posts, in some others officers are nominated to serve as faculty,. It is desirable to call for applications for faculty posts as that would, at least to a large extent, ensure that only those who are eager to serve as a faculty, would be applying for the posts. There could be a few cases where some other considerations, such as avoidance of transfers or difficult work situations, would prompt the staff members to apply for faculty posts. Selection should be based on aptitude/proven competence or potential. Some degree of professional status should be attached to the post and it should be perceived as such. There should be a better rapport between the operations departments and the training establishments. Such inter-action will facilitate better appreciation of operational problems by the faculty which would help them in modifying training inputs and the utility of training would enhance. Although in some banks faculty are also engaged in research work, this is not a common feature in all the banks. The emerging trends demand that training should be research oriented.

(3) *Training Methodology*: Though training aids like overhead projector, cassettes, films, etc. are being increasingly used, more audio-visuals, will have to be prepared having bearing on conditions obtaining in India. In years to come greater sophistication in

the methodology as also teaching aids would become necessary. Emphasis will have to be laid on selecting appropriate methodology for training in the area of leadership, time management, marketing of services etc. Indiscrimination in the use of aids has to be avoided; otherwise the aids would supplant training instead of supplementing it.

(4) *Programme Design*: The designing of the programme for new areas would need a good deal of discussions, imagination and innovative approach. Programmes have to be need based and future oriented. In the context of the emerging trends, banks will have to create a cadre of specialists for undertaking various new activities, either from within or partly by induction from outside. The technological changes envisaged will demand designing of special programmes. It would also be necessary to bring about a change in orientation and for this purpose different types of training will have to be arranged according to the hierarchical levels of staff.

One of the important areas in years to come is going to be the Management of Information which would emerge once computerisation/mechanization become fully operational. Management of the decision making process would then assume as much importance, if not more, as the decision making itself. All this would mean change in orientation and knowledge and skill to use the information/data. Appropriate training programmes will have to be designed for this purpose.

(5) *Preparation of Course Material*: In developing programme material by individual training establishments, there seems to be some avoidable waste. This can be taken care of by the individual bank's various training establishments using the same materials, particularly in the standardized programmes. Efforts made so far for exchanging

course material, particularly the case studies, have not borne the desire result.

(6) *Identification of Participants*: The system of identification of trainees varies, as between banks proper stock has to be taken of the organization's need and participants selected accordingly. Discussions at various forums have revealed that while some improvement has taken place in this area, a lot more remains to be done.

(7) *Award Staff Training*: Award Staff comprises clerical, typists, stenographers, special assistants and the sub-staff, including the security personnel. In quite a few banks till recently hardly any training was imparted to sub-staff. The first contact point of the customers is the sub-staff of the bank and his behaviour towards the customers often paves the way for the eventual relationship between the banker and the customer. There is, thus, an imperative need to impart training to this category of staff, which may be of a short duration, where in addition to the customer service, the other inputs like up-keep and maintenance of records and bank premises, inculcating sense of belonging to and pride for the bank discipline, etc. could be included.

For some time now banks have been conducting various programmes for clerical staff. These are mainly job oriented for explaining what, how and why of the job contents. Capacity utilisation of the training facilities is not quite satisfactory. These programmes are run on a non-residential basis and the participants find it difficult to make arrangements for stay within the cash allowance admissible to them. Where banks have their training establishments run on residential basis, the attendance in generally satisfactory. Roving Faculty concept introduced by some banks helps to tackle this problems to some extent. If the funds position permits, it would be desirable to have the training establishments even for clerical staff on residential basis.

(8) *Training/Career Planning*: Little work has been done to link training with career planning. It is high time that the banks take up this work in the right earnest. In the context of the emerging challenges, banks should identify the officers with necessary aptitude and potential and expose them to requisite training.

(9) *Post Training Placement*: Experience has shown and certain studies have confirmed that there is no satisfactory linkage between pre-training selection and post-training placement.

(10) *Training Evaluation*: A good deal of money is being spent on Training. It is, therefore, necessary that it is evaluated. There is generally a practice to have a course and review, either formal or informal, for ascertaining the trainees' reactions to the programme conducted. Such responses are mainly impressionistic and some times participants want to play safe and do not comment on unsatisfactory aspects of training.

(III) *Proceedings of Banks Principals Conference*[3]: The conference of Principals of training institutions of Indian Banks has indicated the following major constraints in the training system of the banks:

(1) In most banks training does not receive due attention from the top management.

(2) Training need identification is not systematically done; as a result training system and operational sides tend to move in different directions.

(3) Undue interference with training system regarding duration, levels, contents etc.

(4) No systematic selection of faculty and lack of equal opportunity for promotion of faculty, which naturally leads to frustration.

(5) The training system does not have much powers to exercise.

(6) Lack of residential facilities in colleges and centres.

(7) Reserve Bank's insistence on the number of programmes becomes counter productive.

(8) Post-training placement is not appropriately done.

(9) Excessive demands on the training system from BSRB, Defence Personnel training, Hindi language workshops, Security measures etc.

(IV) *Recommendation of the National Workshop on Cooperative Training (Excerpts)*[4] :

(1) *Cooperative manpower planning*: Recognizing that manpower planning is the crucial aspect in the effective functioning of any enterprise including cooperatives, it was felt that steps should be taken to introduce manpower planning in the cooperative sector with the responsibilities and unit as envisaged below:

Type of Cooperatives	***Unit of planning***	***Responsibility***
Primary agricultural service cooperatives	District	District Cooperative Bank
Primary Land development banks	State	State Land Development Bank
Primary agricultural marketing cooperatives	State	Apex State Federation
Urban banks	Individual Unit	Individual Unit/Apex Federation wherever exist.
Large-sized processing units	Individual unit	Individual Unit
Consumer cooperatives	District/State	Federal Organisation
Industrial Cooperatives	District/State	State Federation Registrar of Cooperative Societies
Other type of Societies	State	Registrar of Cooperative Societies

(2) *Responsibility for implementation, coordination and review* : The workshop recommends that a special Committee for Manpower Planning and Development should be constituted in each state under the chairmanship of the Registrar of Cooperative Societies with the Chief Executive of the State Cooperative Union as convenor and the chief executive of various sectoral federations and one or two experts as members. In order to service these committees, manpower planning committees should be set up at the level of federal organisations in each state.

(3) *Reorganizations of cooperative training structure* : Keeping in view the diversified growth in conformity with the national planning policy, priorities and objectives and imperatives of manpower planning, the existing training facilities and arrangements need to be reviewed and adequately strengthened in term of physical and academic improvements. A time-bound programme should be made to strengthen the facilities. The workshop recommends revamping and restructuring the entire cooperative training structure on the following lines:

— The status of Vaikunth Mehta National Institute of Cooperative Management should be raised to the level of a university.

— One cooperative college in each region should be raised to the level of regional management institute to meet the growing regional requirements.

— Cooperative training colleges should be strengthened by providing more specialized faculties to undertake research, consultancy and techno-education.

— The number of cooperative training centres should be suitably increased so as to meet the training requirement of junior personnel and the existing training centres should be adequately strengthened.

— Effective working links should be established between the three-tier structure so as to evolve an integrated national cooperative training system.

(4) *Development of Training Institutions* : The workshop appreciated the vast requirements for training of various categories of personnel involved in the cooperative movement in the country and inadequacy of the existing training institutions and facilities. It was unanimously agreed to formulate a National Plan in regard to cooperative training. While doing so, the workshop experienced the need for:

(a) A comprehensive state wise survey of the training needs at various levels (junior, middle and senior levels);

(b) An assessment/review/survey of the facilities at the existing institutions in the State;

(c) An assessment/survey of the available training facilities, besides those available in the States.

— The above survey could help in working out the gaps and inadequacies of the training needs and the available facilities. The state surveys so formulated could be integrated into a National Plan for projecting the overall requirements. The National Plan should project adequate facilities, (requirement of faculty and its development, building, auditoriums, libraries, hostels, audio-visual equipments, other teaching aids, etc.) as well as financial component. This task for formulating the plan could be entrusted to National Council for Cooperatives facilities.

— The faculties of Cooperative Training Institutions should be properly equipped with the latest training materials and techniques so as to effectively impart necessary knowledge, skills and attitude to the participants based on their job requirements.

— The Vaikunth Mehta National Institute of Cooperative Management, should take steps to evolve necessary training programmes for faculty development for the benefit of the Cooperative Training Colleges on a regular basis.

— For Junior Cooperative Training Centres, the National Centres for Cooperative Education and Cooperative Training Colleges should organise such programmes.

(5) *Job related training* : The Workshop was of the opinion that there is a need for management training for different categories of personnel i.e. (a) Senior level, (b) Intermediate level or middle level, and (c) Junior Level. Although the basic management training, in essence, will be generally similar, there has to be specialized training keeping in view the need of the sector concerned, for example, Agricultural Credit, Training, who would elicit necessary information/ data from the states after circulating a comprehensive questionnaire to be drafted by them on the subject. The workshop also considered the question of streamlining and strengthening the cooperative training arrangements presently available under NCC/NCUI/State Cooperative Unions. It was agreed that:

— The Cooperative Training programmes should continue to be supervised/conducted under the overall umbrella of NCC/NCUI so as to enable conduct of the training programmes in an integrated manner.

— In addition to general cooperative courses, the cooperative training centres/institutions should also undertake need based specialized courses.

— Any additional training facilities to be developed by other institutions/agencies should be only after taking into account the existing facilities available with NCC/NCUI to avoid duplication.

— In view of the immediate requirements the workshop felt the need of setting up/upgradation of Regional Cooperative Management Institutes in the country for training the Intermediate level functionaries. These Regional Training Institutes should be Marketing, Consumers, Processing, Fisheries, Dairy, Handloom etc. The job specialization and training need of personnel of each sectoral cooperative should be identified. Employees of all the three categories stated above should be exposed to training programmes depending up on their job responsibilities. Within the sectoral cooperatives, there are two broad categories of societies. One category is the societies at primary level which normally employ one or two persons only who have to perform all the functions of the society. The second category comprises of large-sized primary societies and societies at district level or above in different sectors where senior, middle level and junior categories of employees work. In respect of personnel of primary societies falling under the first category, separate comprehensive programmes based on the job skills should be provided.

(6) The training capsule should comprise institutional (classroom) learning and on the job training. Practical job assignment will depend upon the type of trainees and their training needs. Classroom learning should adopt participation learning methods to the maximum extent possible in addition to other teaching methods. Classroom training should reflect the working in the type of organisation through case studies, research studies, management cases in such

institution where practical assignments are to be given.

(7) For the production/procurement testing, adoption and distribution of training materials, it is very necessary to establish National/State level resource centres. The National Resource Centre will design suitable training materials after conducting necessary research and field studies to meet the requirements of various training institutions, based upon the needs of the various sectors of the cooperative movement in the country. The National Level Cooperative Federations, Government of India, I.L.O., I.C.A as well as international agencies could be approached by the National Cooperative Union of India with a detailed proposal for financial as well as technical assistance for the proposed National Resource Centre. These State Cooperative Unions will be the nodal agencies and act as the state level resources centres for production and distribution of training materials. These centres will produce good quality materials including training packages, audio-visual aids such as films, slides, video film cassettes, etc. in collaboration with specialized agencies such as the National Federation of Film Producers Cooperative.

(V) *Financial Services for the Rural Poor and Women in India: World Bank Study*

A study commissioned by the *World Bank,*[5] reviewed the performance of Indian financial institutions in providing services to the rural poor and women and examined the key issues facing policy makers and institutions as the country moves forward on financial sector reforms. The study posited two sets of causal variables for institutional performance: (1) Internal Practices Attitudes (IPA's) of bank officials who deal with the rural poor and women as clients; and (2) mechanisms for client interface that either enhance or tharwt access by the rural poor and women (MEAs). Both of these variables are largely within the control of the financial institutions. The study sought to identify changes in these variables that could improve access to financial services by the rural poor and concluded that rural financial institutions (RFI's) are faced with a hierarchy of constraints, largely beyond their control and any attempt at developing workable and sustainable approaches to improved access of the rural poor to financial services will need to address a whole range of macro-policy issues.

The study findings suggest that RFIs are today faced with a hierarchy of constraints in providing services to the rural poor, particularly rural women and IPAs and MEAs are at the bottom of this heap. The study team's *formulation of constraints* in ascending order of what an RFI can do about those are as follows:

— the chronically income deficit nature of the target group and the inadequacy of livelihood opportunities which would generate a living wage and an income surplus.

— the erosion of the repayment ethic, particularly with respect to loans from formal institutions.

— the erosion of the banker-borrower relationship of mutual trust. This has been a major negative consequence of linking up poverty alleviation programmes with bank credit. There has been a spread of corruption in selection of borrowers, and sanction of loans. This has also bred cynicism among the bank officials about the poor as credit worthy clients.

— the rural branches of the nationalized commercial banks, the regional rural banks and the co-operative banks can be reorganized or converted into more effective financial institutions with difficulty by overcoming pressures from trade unions and from political lobbies of the land-owing borrowers etc.

— there is a system-wide dependence on low-cost capital, operating subsidies and periodic capital infusions to make up for loan losses. The commercial banks are subsidizing the operations of their rural branches and in turn receive a subsidy for rural lending in terms of concessional refinance from the apex institution, which itself survives on low-interest, no-risk capital. Further banks get reimbursement for bad debts through a credit guarantee programme.

— the erosion of the RFI's autonomy: this arises from 1) the political view of the banks as an instrument of state policy, 2) fully government ownership of banks, 3) job security consciousness among the staff and at the operating level and 4) increasing tie-ups of banks with government development programmes–which in turn, leads to further erosion of a commercial ethos and incursion of the ills of the public bureaucracy.

— restrictive nature of regulations concerning the operation of the banks. These include high statutory liquidity and cash reserve requirements etc. which cum ulatively erode profitability and make rural bank operations unviable.

— failure of the RFIs to adopt institutional practices and attitudes (both internal and on the customer interface) to address the requirements of the rural poor as a customer through policies, products, structure, systems and people. The study concluded that many of the higher level constraints must be addressed before institutional performance (access and sustainability) can be improved by appropriate changes in IPAs and MEAs.

A review of the steps taken by the Government and Reserve Bank of India as part of the financial sector reforms shows that, so far, these have been focussed on the regulatory framework within which FIs operate and the adoption of prudent accounting norms. While these are steps in the right direction, the potential gains for the rural poor from these initiatives are likely to be small unless these changes are accompanied by:

— depoliticizing of rural credit (e.g. no blanket loan waivers).

— increasing the autonomy of RFIs professional boards, freedom to select borrowers, freedom in staff matters etc.

— allowing multiple private sector RFIs to come up even as existing government sector RFIs are given incentive to improve performance.

— revamping the recovery system.

— increasing the accountability of RFIs (prudent accounting, explicit subsidies, market-based funds and credit guarantee costs etc.)

Finally, there is a need to provide incentives for the existing RFIs to become customer–oriented through behavior appropriate to the rural poor market, development of new products, channels and promotional methods based on–the ground market research and a reorientation of policies and systems.

The study team's formulation of the required (new generation) behaviour to improve access of the rural poor in a sustainable manner can be summarized as the *Seven I'S (Ingredients) of Successful Micro Finance Programme for the Rural Poor:*

Attribute	***New Generation Behaviour***
Image of the poor	Not see them as beneficiaries, but as entry level customers.
Independence	No political interference, such as loan waivers, no bureaucratic control.
Interest rates	For deposits: high enough to attract savings. For loans: high enough to cover costs of funds, cost of operation, cost of loan losses.

Contd..

Attribute	New Generation Behaviour
Incentives	For staff; to ensure good customer service but prudent lending. For customers : to ensure deposits come in and loans are repaid on time.
Increased Capacity	Larger scale; broader scope of services to include savings, consumption and production credit and insurance.
Integration	With social intermediation (e.g. by Self-Help groups) and technical assistance (e.g. by NGO's and government bodies).

(VI) *Other Miscellaneous Viewpoints*

1. *Limitation of HRD efforts in Indian Banks* : In the matter of designing and implementing HRD the experience of Indian Banks throw up a number of issues. Some of the main limitations of these HRD efforts in the last one decade are identified as under (Khandelwal):

    1. *Systematic Orientation* : In many banks the initial focus of HRD has been on introducing new systems like Performance Appraisal etc. with the assumption that the innovative systems themselves can bring about change in the culture of the organisation. This unfortunately has not happened. Research has revealed that the organisational culture in our banks and configuration of shared beliefs and values do not seem to be conducive to HRD (Amsa, 1986). Too much initial emphasis on introducing systems without creating HRD spirit can be counter productive.

    2. *Structural Inadequacy* : The HRD function in the banks is housed in the Head Office which is not adequate to percolate the HRD message. In view of the uniqueness of banking, HRD functionaries need to be available nearer to the field, through structural placement of HRD function in regional offices.

    3. *Lack of Conceptual clarity and role ambiguity* : The introduction of HRD in banks lacked conceptual clarity in terms of its linkages with the overall

personnel management function. HRD came to be identified as a cosmetic function incapable of handling complex issues of man management in banks. It came to be identified only with training and appraisal which have been the activities of personnel function and therefore, the perceived promise of HRD to channelize the latent energy of employees remained more a hope than a reality. The lack of conceptual clarity also created problems of role ambiguity for HRD functionaries.

4. *Lack of interconnection between HRD and other sub systems of personnel management*: HRD and Personnel/IR in banks have been operating as two separate and distinct functions without much linkages in the work undertaken by these two departments. This not only deprives each of these departments from the contributions of one to the other but in some cases have also created misunderstandings.

5. *Lack of focus on critical groups*: Most HRD efforts in the banks in the last one decade is focussed on officers' cadre and that too limited to middle management cadre. Two important significant groups viz. senior management and award staff (front line staff) and line managers have not been covered through any major intervention of HRD. So there is a lack of overt support of top management and involvement of the operating staff. There are also critical groups like women, SC/ST and religious minorities groups which have their own problems of development. HRD effort has not focussed to a desirable extent on these groups.

6. *Appraisal and Training: Main Focus of HRD*: The focus of efforts in HRD in banking has been on initiating a new appraisal system and handling training function. Appraisal is a good mechanism for initiating HRD work but appraisal cannot be the only route to start HRD. It can create anxiety, fear and cynicism if relevant changes in the process such as process of goal

setting and feedback are not attempted. In some banks appraisal became a controlling tool and this severely stigmatized the HRD function itself. Similarly in some banks HRD is equated with training. No doubt training is an important tool of HRD but in isolation and absence of linkages with other subsystems, training can be a mere formality.

7. *Absence of union involvement in HRD work*: Available data from banks suggest that unions' involvement in HRD work has been quite limited. In most of the banks there are bipartite forums and issues relating to Personnel and IR are regularly discussed. However, issues relating to HRD have not found place in these forums. This has created cynics and in some cases even hostility amongst unions towards HRD efforts.

8. *Inadequacy of top management commitment*: Research has shown that there is a wide gap between the beliefs of the top management and their practices with regard to HRD in banks. Whereas the beliefs and philosophy are of the ideal order, the practices of it fall much below its expectations. Unless the top management develops conscious policy, creates necessary structure to implement the policy, develops the monitoring mechanisms, introduces accountability for HRD and provides resources, it is extremely difficult to institutionalize HRD even though there may be general enthusiasm at lower or middle level.

9. *Involvement of Line Managers*: Existing efforts in the banks in HRD are more focussed on doing rather than creating. For example, one of the challenging tasks for HRD is to create awareness amongst line managers about the potential of HRD and also to develop change a gentry skills in them by actual involvement of line managers in HRD projects.

2. *On Rural Training*: The condition of training in the banking sector, particularly the needs assessment aspect in regional rural banks, is also not very encouraging, Khandelwal

points out that in view of the inadequate infrastructure within the sponsor bank in relation to their own training requirements, the desired amount of attention has not been paid to R.R.B. staff training. He has emphasized the need to work out specialized training requirements of the R.R.B's staff. For this purpose he has also suggested structural changes in the training system. The fate of training in the cooperative sector is similar and the needs assessment is the most neglected area. Cooperative training structural networking consisting of one National Institute, 18 Cooperative Training Colleges and 92 Cooperative Training Centres, is not very methodical in identification of training needs of various categories of personnel working in different segments of cooperative institutions. Due to drawbacks in the cooperative training system, National Cooperative Development Corporation, a development financial institution, gave a new dimension and direction to cooperative education and training by establishing its own training centre called as Topic Training Centre. (Sah, 1986[6]).

3. *New Training Areas*: An illustrative list of the critical areas in which financial institutions need training for meeting the changing demands of the financial sector as suggested by an HRD banking specialist[7] is as follows:

    1. Costing and Pricing of Financial Products and Services.
    2. Risk-Management
    3. Recovery Management
    4. Monitoring Financial Performance of Branch Offices
    5. Capital Usage and Developing Ancillary Services
    6. Asset-Liability Management
    7. Treasury Management/Funds Management
    8. FOREX Management
    9. Foreign Exchange Business
    10. Financing Foreign Trade
    11. Off-shore Banking

12. International Banking (General)
13. Prudential Supervision and Inspection
14. Delivery vs Payment System
15. Market Intelligence
16. Merchant Banking
17. Funds Raising and Cash Management Methods
18. Structural Changes and Financial Innovations
19. Central Banking in the emerging scene
20. Internal Debt Management
21. Asset-valuation and Assets Management
22. Human Resources Development
23. Technology for Better information System/Customer Service and Innovative Banking.

4. *The Price Waterhouse Cranfield Project*: An important study[8] by the Cranfield School of Management (1990) and the consulting group of Price Waterhouse has been attempting to discover what human resource practitioners believe to be the main issues confronting them. Some 6,000 companies and public sector bodies in the United Kingdom., West Germany, France, Spain and Sweden have been examined by drawing upon the resources of leading business research centres in the countries concerned. As regards training and development, some important findings have emerged which have considerable significance for the Indian Banking sector gearing up to meet the challenges of liberalisation and globalisation. These are as follow:

* Organisations throughout the countries covered by the survey have increased significantly their investment in training although there is little evidence of the systematic training evaluation.

* Personnel responsibility is increasingly being delegated to line management.

* Although the survey reveals that between 60% and 90% of the responding companies systematically analyse their training needs, it also show up a lack of knowledge among human resource professionals of how much their companies are actually spending on staff development.
* Apart from the traditional reaction responses of trainees and their line managers to particular training experiences, the training validation and evaluation tends to be informal and unsystematic.
* Managers are currently being trained across a wide spectrum of what can be called 'people management' skills and it is 'people management' which is expected to dominate.

It is significant that although the majority of organisations are increasing their investment in training and systemtically identifying training needs, there is apparently no complementary system for evaluating training effectiveness and assessing its value for money. There is no virtue in training for its own sake but only in terms of profitability and efficiency.

5. *The Laurie International Report (1990)*[9] : This report identified as the most important and critical success factor for the successful management of training and development, that training and development objectives must be derived from business objectives. To promote this critical success factor it is essential that line managers are informed, committed to and actively involved in the training activity. Equally essential is that human resource professionals in general, and trainers in particular, become business literate and get involved. This can be achieved by moving trainers away from the traditional training role towards being internal consultants capable of contributing to organisational analyses, and it is a logical next step where attributes, performance and outcomes are inextricably linked with corporate competence and the achievement of organisational goals. This will not increase the trainers workload, but heighten their involvement, and

commitment in a true partnership with line management in the examination of the business objectives and the assessment, both short and long-term of the training implications. This is a effective means of ensuring that the training and development activities are truly congruent with corporate objectives. Such a process of involvement and shared ownership of the training activity will close the gap between what happens when people receive training and what happens when they return to the workplace. Since otherwise although the learning may have been excellent, the opportunity to practise what was learned does not exist and so the training is unjustly condemned.

6. *Current Global Training Challenges* : Based on reserach carried out for the Employment Department and the National Economic Development Office (NEDO) on the British labour market and on such reports as 'Workforce 2000. An Agenda for Action', Alan Davies[10] has provided a perspective on the global training challenges of the coming decade in view of certain key developments taking place. Key developments which are likely to have an important impact on European business have been identified as: International Developments and Competition (e.g. globalisation of world economy); new technologies and materials (e.g. Information Technology); environmental concerns; and population changes (e.g. an ageing population because of increasing longevity).

According to Davies, "Meeting the challenges of the 1990s will clearly require a wide range of different skills, but some of the broad themes emerging are increased need for :

1. A stronger base of general competencies at all levels in the workforce.
2. Increasing enterprise and initiative across the workforce.
3. Higher-level skills overall — more technicians, fewer operatives; more managers, fewer supervisors; more professionals.

4. Specialist skills in new or growing areas to implement new technology (correspondingly fewer in shrinking areas).
5. Wider management appreciation of potential of new technologies and techniques and the environmental challenge—especially the organisational implications.
6. Training for increased job flexibility (e.g. enabling operators to programme machines, or jobs covering several related skills).
7. Updating and upgrading within occupations (we face qualitative as well as quantitative skill shortages).

In short the whole labour force must become more highly skilled, more technologically competent and more innovative.

Under such circumstances *Employers* will need to adopt a flexible attitude to:

— Recruitment : They can no longer afford to approach recruitment with a stereotype 'idea' candidate in mind and give a chance to diverse/disadvantaged groups like women, ethnic minorities etc.

— Development and utilization of their existing employees since taking on new peple to get new skills will be expensive.

— Work patterns and conditions. Women will form over 90% of the increase in the labour force over the next ten years, and many of these will also have family responsibilities. Some employers are already offering a variety of flexible working options (such as part-time working) to attract them back.

Individuals will require the right incentives and motivation to:

— Accept the need for regular updating of skills/ retraining and responsibility for their own development.

— Operate over a wider range of skills.

— Consider a range of different types of relationship between themselves and business—since the permanent, full-time, life-time employee model is likely to ebb out with the advent of part-time/`home office' work trends.

Three main types of adjustment are implied (Davies) for training and vocational education, to allow for:

— New and growing requirements for skills (such as those outlined above).

— Changes in the nature of the labour force.

— Greater emphasis on continued development and retraining.

The HRD/Training Gap : Re-Engineering the Training Function in the Indian Banking Scenario

HRD/Training Gap : Concept/Components of Re-engineering :

The overview of the HRD and Training Systems of the Indian banking sector in the previous chapter and the analysis/ recommendations of the various studies/viewpoints on this area outlined above lead us to conclude that despite the progress made, several deficiencies remain and a lot still remains to be done to optimize the effectiveness of this sector. We observe that the considerable gap between the present and the potential effectiveness of the HRD/Training Systems of the Indian Banking sector exists, between what they are presently delivering and are capable of delivering in today's challenging climate of financial sector liberalization/globalization.

This gap has several dimensions stretching over all the HRD subsystems covering organisational HRD practices, and various facets of the training subsystem (organizing, planning, staffing, directing, controlling, faculty selection/development/ Training methodology, choice of critical Training areas etc.). As has been emphasized earlier, the Training subsystem is an integral part of the HRD system, and Training can be made more effective if changes in its machinery are complemented by simultaneous changes in other HRD subsystems (Career/ Appraisal/Cultural/Work/Self Renewal Systems).

As the HRD/Training Gap is considerable and since the crucial phase through which our economy is passing requires very effective and highly efficient banking sector within a short time span, *radical efforts are required to close the gap*. Few randon, uncoordinated changes here and there will not suffice and reengineering the Training function is the need of the hour to close the H.R.D and Training Gap in the Indian Banking system. *Reengineering* means a radical redesign and reinventing new ways of doing things. Re-engineering, again, means dramatic changes, not merely making marginal or incremental improvements. Re-engineering means a total transformation in our approach to training and a paradigm shift in our strategies. We will have to question the very fundamentals like — "Why do we do what we do?" "Why do we do it the way we do?"

Reengineering efforts have been seen to possess *four major components (Lowenthal)*[11]

— A greater focus on the organisation's customers (both internal and external).

— A fundamental rethinking of the processes in the organisations that lead to improvements in productivity and cycle time (known as process improvement or business process reengineering).

— A structural reorganization, typically breaking functional hierarchies into cross functional teams (team building and organisational development activity).

— New information and measurement systems, using the latest in technology to derive improved data distribution and decision making (for example, quality and information technology).

In this perspective *organisational reengineering may be defined as* : The fundamental rethinking and redesign of operating processes and organizational structure, focussed on the organization's core competencies, to achieve dramatic improvements in organisational performance. (Lowenthal) It is a process by which a company may redesign the way it does business to maximize its core competencies. In turn, this redesign results in dramatically or significantly higher profits, greater customer satisfaction, lower expenses, consolidated activities, and increased productivity. Organisational reengineering redesigns the way work flows through an organisation, which often leads to system and infrastructure changes. Further this process focuses the organisation on its core competencies (in addition to cultural aspects of change). An organization's core competencies are its collective knowledge, the systems that enable an organisation to identify and use-to the best competitive advantage—the knowledge embedded within its organisation.

Organisational reengineering involves reorganizing work flows, cutting works, combining process steps and eliminating repetitive tasks. It will not work within the typical corporate culture itself. Reengineering strives to break away from the old rules about how organisations are structured and the way they conduct business. It involves recognizing and rejecting old methods and finding imaginative new ways to accomplish work.

Organisational reengineering does not lead to incremental improvements, which are usually associated with traditional quality improvement programs. Instead, it produces breakthrough improvements in operational and financial performance. It rethinks the way work is done inside an organisation; it does not simply try to improve the existing processes. Organisational reengineering change processes completely, so that they are logical and efficient and driven by an organization's core competencies.

Issues for Reengineering : The following issues have to be addressed as part of the Re-engineering process to close the training gap and make training effective in the Indian Banking Sector.

Linking Up Training with other HRD Systems : Training will have to be linked with other HRD systems, such as Performance

Appraisals, Promotions, Compensation etc. As a policy, an organisation could decide that an individual has to go through comprehensive training in a particular field if he has to be promoted from one position to a higher position. Training could also be thought of where people are promoted from the officer cadre to Managerial positions, when certain management skills are called for. Training is only a part of HRD and not the whole of it, because the HRD concept is much wider as it embraces almost all areas of an organisation and places emphasis on allround development of individuals. Training cannot operate in a vacuum. It must be intune with the organisational culture even while making an effort to change the culture where necessary.

Training could also be linked with transfers, promotions of the organisation to facilitate a smooth transition of learning of the trainee in work like situations, providing all support and the right environment.

Training Technologies Innovation: The Trainer must use new training technologies which will facilitate active experimentation-oriented training in place of a mere "reflective and observation" oriented one. Practical work-life situations in the form of case studies would be very useful for better appreciation and learning. The technologies must blend with the culture, and suit the changing trends to promote learning.

Trainer Involvement/Accountability : A Trainer should be a facilitator of the whole process, both pre and post training. He should participate right from the time the training needs are identified till post - evaluation of training; also, in ensuring that there is a transference of learning to actual work life situation. A Trainer has to change his role from being a mere "Trainer" to a "Catalyst and change agent". He should continuously measure the training effectiveness in terms of parameters determined at the beginning of the training effort. The performance and the result of Training should be perceived in the form of observable changes in the individual behaviour, actions, skills, knowledge, attitudes and awareness or whenever there is a change in the job content or `role expectations' of any individual.

Training & Corporate Business Strategy : Training is to be integrated with Corporate business plans and strategies. A thorough analysis of strategic decisions of business would determine the kind of skills for which training is required throughout the entire organisation. Re-engineering undertaken in any organisation would again throw up need for skills to manage the change process, resulting in wider range of job elements, increased flexibility and ability to handle higher and additional responsibilities, consistent with few layers of management.

Tripartite Learning Contract : For any Training effort to be successful, the beneficiary should sincerely feel the need for training. Further, the process of training cannot be a mere "Trainer–Trainee relationship". It has to be a contract between all parties concerned, namely Trainer, Trainee, Trainee's organisation. There has to be clarity on the expectation from the Trainer. Therefore, an agreement entered into by all these parties would involve a commitment on the part of the Trainer to meet the requirements of the Trainee; a commitment of the part of the Trainee to learn, and to translate the learning into actions; and a commitment on the part.

So the challenges before the training system in the coming decade for bridging the training gap by re-engineering the training function in the Indian Banking Sector could be broadly viewed in the *following terms*:[12]

(a) Likely spurt in the physical quantum of training needs mainly due to:

 (i) additional intake of employees

 (ii) retraining of the large volume of existing employees for taking up newer responsibilities and/or for being conversant with the new work technology;

(iii) felt inadequacy of training exposure in Indian Banking in relation to other countries.

(b) To gear the training system towards catering simultaneously to the diverse skill needs of the personnel. While, on the one hand reinforcement of some of the traditional skills of banking would have to continue, new skills have to be developed amongst the staff for specialized functions, on the other hand. Training has to be imparted to facilitate the transition in work technology, due to likely changes in systems/ procedures or introduction of computerization/ mechanization on a large scale.

(c) To bring about, through training, attitudinal changes (in employees) — of distinctive kinds — required for rural banking interface with automation, innovation in new financial service etc.

(d) To achieve a good co-ordination between the training and other HRD efforts and to establish a meaningful linkage between (individual) career-path and training exposure.

(e) To strengthen the existing training system to enable it to cope up with the challenges described above.

In the backdrop of this discussion, we shall now propose in the following chapters the parameters which this reengineering of the HRD and Training systems of the Indian Banking Industry should take into consideration. We shall consider this Reengineering in the context of:

(1) Proactive HRD organisational interventions under Strategic Human Resource Management (SHRM) approach, (2) Training Delivery innovations, (3) Critical Training areas coverage with (4) special emphasis on Rural Development Banking and (5) Women and Development/Gender issues in Development Banking. Finally, we shall propose an integrated Reengineering Model taking all these parameters into consideration.

Notes

1. Barthakur, P.K., Management of Training in Banks. Working Paper of the National Institute of Bank Management (NIBM) Pune. *Indian Journal of Training and Development*, Vol. XX, No. 2, March-April, 1990.

2. Joshi, P.N. and Dingakar, B.N., *The Emerging Trends in Banking in the 90's—Their implications and challenges for Institutional Training in Banks*. Paper presented in Reserve Bank of India seminar at Madras on 'Emerging Training Needs of the Banking Industry in the 1990's.

   The Seminar discussed this theme issue under five sub themes:

   I. The emerging trends in banking in the 90's: their implications and challenges for institutional training in banks.

   II. Training Strategy for meeting the requirements of deeper involvement of banks in rural development.

   III. Training Needs in the context of innovative banking business and diversification of banks' activities.

   IV. Training Needs for bringing about attitudinal changes to improve customer service.

   V. Training Needs in the context of computerization and mechanization in banks.

3. Reported in Rao, Y.P., HRD in Commercial Banks —Role of Training — A Trainer's Viewpoint, *Indian Journal of Training and Development*.

4. Recommendation of National Workshop on Cooperation Training.

5. Mahajan, Vijay and Ramola, Bharti Gupta : Financial Services for the Rural Poor and women in India. JOURNAL OF INTERNATIONAL DEVELOPMENT, Vol. O, No. O (1996).

6. Sah, A.K., Cooperative Education and Training—A New Dimension. *The Consumer Cooperator*, March-April, 1986.

7. Angadi, Dr. V.B. Emerging Training Needs—An Assessment, Bombay: *BTC Bulletin* (Bulletin of Banker's Training College) Vol. 14, No. 1, January 1995.

8. Cranfield School of Management : The Price Waterhouse Cranfield Project on International Strategic Human Resource Management. Bedford: 1990.

9. Laurie International Ltd: *Training and Development—Top management issues for the New Decade*, London, 1990.

10. Davies, Alan: ,Demographic Change—Implications for the 1990's in John Prior (ed) *Handbook of Training and Development*. Hants: Gower Publishing Co. 1994.

11. Lowenthal, Jeffrey N. *Reengineering the Organisation*. New Delhi: Tata McGraw Hill, 1995.

12. Prakasan, Ṙ. and T.S. Ravisankar, *The Emerging Trends in Banking in the 90's* : their implications and challenges for *institutional training in banks*. Paper presented in Reserve Bank of India seminar on 'Emerging Training Needs of the Banking Industry in the 1990's.

5

Reengineering Training: HRD Interventions

Overview: The effective functioning of the Indian Banking Sector is dependent on internal factors such as suitable HRD, operational policies etc. as well as external factors like Government of India's policies, support from other government departments/bodies, national and international economic environments etc. The focus of this book being on the training subsystem within the context of the HRD system, out of the various HRD subsystems (Career/Appraisal/Cultural/Work/Training/Self Renewal) considered in the preceding Chapter 3, while outlining action points for various HRD interventions, we shall selectively focus in detail on only certain HRD aspects.

The latest research findings indicate that the success of HRD/ Training interventions is significantly related to the overall organizational culture and to the extent of support it provides to such endeavours. As seen in the section on evolution of HRD/Training in the Indian Banking Sector, it has been quite sometime since these systems became prevalent in this industry in a formal way. However, the HRD spirit is yet to permeate deeply into the banking sector, as can be observed in the dissatisfaction prevalent among the pesonnel of this service industry and the complaints from the public regarding inadequate customer service/low productivity of this sector.

To begin with, Indian banks have to provide a more conducive culture and create conditions for the HRD spirit to find nurturance and strength. For this, innovative measures are required to modify the bank's *organizational culture* in the requisite manner. Alongwith evolving the HRD spirit, certain action points are required to cope with the organizational lacunae/problems related to HRD (which were elaborated upon in Chapter 4). Another important innovative step would be to turn Indian Banks into *learning organizations* wherein training is not separate from day to day activities but an inherent part of the working environment. In such a learning organization, related HRD interventions as *Mentoring* (individual entering into a relationship with somebody to act as advisor/counsellor) and *Coaching* (some specific planned activity designed to improve the skilled performance of another) would also get established. Furthermore, since Indian banks today are functioning in a rapidly changing environment where new management/organization/housekeeping problems are arising, goals and strategies are having to be constantly reoriented, traditional HRD and Training interventions, though useful and essential in their own way, are not sufficient. We shall consider one approach to manage organizational change in a planned manner by taking a total view of the organization—called *Organization Development Initiative* (ODI). ODI is a process of planning and implementing systematic changes to improve organizational effectiveness, help the organization avoid decay, enhance its problem solving capacity and facilitate its renewal by an unleashing/ channeling of the creative energies of all employees.

To enable the Indians Banks to cope with the requirements of rapid organizational change, and be in a position to undertake innovations like Organization Development Initiative (ODI), traditional HRD, its training and other subsystems have to enlarge their vision/ reach, anticipate and prepare for changes. This proactive HRD, which will be subsequently analyzed, is *Strategic Human Resource Management (SHRM)*. Such reoriented HRM will have implications for various HRD Subsystems of manpower planning, recruitment, performance appraisal, changing the promotion patterns, enforcement of effective transfer policy, effective incentive system, training and development etc. However, since the focus of this study is on Training subsystems as related to the HRD system, we shall selectively focus on only certain key areas of SHRM for emphasis reengineering industrial relations, HRD and Training for workmen staff and managing human resource diversity. Serious attention to these areas will go a long way in improving the training effectiveness of Indian Banks.

HRD Related Problems in the Indian Banking Sector : Action Points

HRD in banks acquires special meaning in view of the current problems of the banking industry, associated with their size, geographical dispersion, business priority and heavy line orientation etc. Any HRD effort in banks has to be such which takes into account these problems and accordingly planned. Unless problem specified action mechanisms are conceptualized and implemented, the HRD effort cannot make the necessary impact (Khandelwal).

We shall now briefly discuss some possible action points/ solutions which will be useful in solving HRD related problems which routinely arise in the Indian Banking Sector. We shall then take up in greater detail recent innovations of Learning Organisation, Mentoring & Coaching Organisation Development Initiative, Strategic Human Resource Management etc. which are necessary to bring about the required reengineering for coping with the HRD challenges.

Problem of HRD	*Action Points*
1. Issues relating to development of top management/senior management pro-HRD climate at the top.	1. Exposure to the concept of HRD/OD. 2. Intensive training in institutional leadership.
2. Issues relating to middle management (Regional/Zonal Management): (a) Their interest in HRD.	1. Exposure to the executives in General Management with special focus on managing Manager. 2. Exposure in HRD/OD concept.

Contd..

Problem of HRD	*Action Points*
(b) Skills in initiating change. (c) Support to branch functionaries. (d) Initiatives for creating climate for performance.	3. Accountability for initiating HRD in zone/region. 4. Recognition for good HRD work by instituting awards etc. at these levels. 5. Providing necessary structure which facilitates availability of time to Zonal Manager/Regional Manager for HRD work.
3. Issues relating to Line Management: (a) Their interest (b) Business Priorities (c) Environment at the branch	1. Exposure of Line Management to HRD concepts. 2. Developing `Change Agentry' skills in line managers. 3. Initiatives in HRD to be part of appraisal process. 4. Providing resources and help for initiating HRD.
4. Size and geographical dispersion of banking makes introduction of HRD a difficult proposition.	1. Continuous HRD awareness programme needs to be conducted at different levels. 2. Decentralisation of HRD. The function should be decentralised and full-fledged department should be created at the regional level. 3. Visits of top executives to field more frequently for bridging the communication gap between the top and operating staff. 4. Continuous review of the existing means of communication and use of alternative means for effective communication.
5. Developing a person in HRD role.	1. Providing `processes' orientation and developing process facilitation skills. 2. Providing necessary technical exposure on HRD/OD

Contd..

Problem of HRD	*Action Points*
	methodology of initiating changes, technical aspects of appraisal system and other sub-systems. 3. Encouraging innovative overtures/initiatives for HRD functionaries.
6. Issues relating to unions involvement in HRD : (a) Their support for HRD (b) Their involvement in HRD (c) Their cooperation in creating HRD climate.	1. Joint periodic discussion on relevant HRD issues like job redesign, job enrichment and issues relating to greater responsibilities for staff. 2. Undertaking joint projects such as helping employees in self-development, helping employees to develop confidence for promotion tests. 3. Encouraging and providing support for undertaking HRD activities for employees.
7. Inter-face between HRD and other sub - systems of personnel: (a) Collaboration between HRD and other sub-systems of personnel administration. (b) Unity of purpose between HRD and personnel management.	1. Integrating of personnel and HRD through suitable structural linkages. 2. Mechanism of collaboration between HRD and IR through joint task force. 3. Job rotation between IR and HRD functionaries.
8. Issues relating to institutionalisation of HRD.	1. Top management task forces on HRD, wider discussion on HRD issues and development of strategy. 2. HRD task forces at Zonal/Regional level.

Contd..

Problem of HRD	*Action Points*
	3. Periodical review of HRD progress like Mid-Term Review of Business.
9. Issues relating to HRD Climate: (a) IR climate–a pre-requisite (b) Professionalisation of personnel function.	1. Developing competencies and confidence amongst managers to deal with IR issues. 2. Developing and ensuring basic minimum norms of working and behaviour at the work place and communicating the same across the organisation. 3. Creating forums for periodical assessment of quality of Personnel Management and IR.

Requirements/Conditions for HRD Introduction in Banks

HRD must be relevant to an organisation and hence must be designed and introduced in ways which are suitable for that organisation. Since banks are different from one another in many dimensions, a programme related to human systems cannot be a standard universal programme which can be introduced according to a blueprint in different organisations. So HRD cannot be introduced in the same way in all the banks. However, there are some requirements/issues[1] discerned on the basis of experience and studies, reported by HRD experts like Udai Pareek and T.V. Rao, which will now be discussed:

1. *Study the Bank's Organizational Culture Traditions* : Before introducing HRD in a bank it is necessary to study the culture and traditions of the bank–the OCTAPAC elements elaborated by T.V. Rao (Chapter 3). Some banks came from family ownership, while some others were set up by the government from the beginning. The banks developed their own identities, and even after nationalization these identities and uniqueness continue to differentiate one bank from the other, such as, the Syndicate Bank which even before nationalization, took lot of interest in

agriculture loaning operations and rural development. In some banks there was much more informal culture, much more openness. In others the culture was more bureaucratic, coupled with the system of confidential assessment reports etc. Obviously, we cannot introduce HRD in the same way in the banks with such diverse traditions and cultures. Being sensitive to the culture, may give ideas about the ways of introducing HRD.

2. *Create HRD Climate* : In the early stages before the introduction of HRD as a system it may be necessary to create a HRD climate. Rao (1986) has developed an HRD climate instrument to find out how much of a favourable climate exists in a particular organisation for accepting HRD. If the climate for introduction of HRD is low, ways may be adopted to create a suitable climate by stressing the importance of development of people, creating effective teams, working together to find solutions of problems, exposing most employees to the general HRD approach and helping them to understand what is involved in HRD. Individuals from other banks can be invited to share their experience in the appropriate forums.

3. *Develop HRD Strategy and have wider consultations*: Introduction of HRD may begin by inviting an external consultant to study the organisation and prepare a strategy of introducing HRD functioning. Once the external consultant has prepared an approach paper and a strategy of introducing the HRD function, it may be useful to have a discussion on the implications at various levels in the bank. Using the feedback, seminars may be conducted in which representatives of the unions and staff associations may also be invited. The fear that associations may come in the way of the introduction of HRD in a bank is unfounded and unions may make a significant contribution to some ideas of HRD, relevant for the bank, and may become partners in

the process of implementation of HRD. When a decision was taken in the State Bank of India about introducing HRD in one circle, a seminar was conducted and the circle staff representatives were invited who endorsed the introduction of HRD. If these people had not been invited, the bank would have alienated them from an important function.

4. *Introduce HRD Spirit* : For HRD introduction much more emphasis need to be given on the spirit rather than the ritualistic part of it. The introduction of structured systems like performance appraisal, by itself may not give any results unless managers are provided training in giving and receiving feedback or if other sub-systems of reward management/training/job rotation are developed, to make use of the output of performance appraisal. The spirit of HRD can be created before HRD systems are introduced in a bank by giving emphasis on the development of individuals through the help of their supervisors and by solving problems by working together and such problems may be emphasized. The first can be accomplished by introducing performance counselling before a formal system of performance appraisal is introduced so that the latter doesn't degenerate into a ritual and generate resistance on behalf of the employees. Organisation development (OD) activities may also be introduced as a way to look at and solve problems. The experience of introducing OD in one region of the State Bank of India was very encouraging. In this, selected branch managers, some selected faculty members and a few persons from the region identified areas in which OD work was needed and plans were prepared of doing something about some aspect. For example, some branches decided to improve customer service. Different plans were prepared for the same problems by different branches according to their own conditions and it became clear, that problems can be

solved by jointly studying their nature through collection of data, and then by jointly working out strategies of improving the situation.

5. *Reorganize the Training Function* : Training needs to move more towards organisation development and problem solving alongwith standardized training systems (some of these may be useful and necessary)-more and more training should be focussed on action to be taken for improving some parts of the functioning of a bank and its sub-parts.

6. *Introduce Appraisal Systems in Phases* : The spirit of HRD being internalized in the organisation for performance counselling and OD, formal systems of HRD may be introduced. For example, performance and potential appraisal may be introduced in a phased plan-introduce the system in one part of the bank (geographical phasing) and to spread the system to other parts of the bank. Another way of phasing is in the sophistication and depth of the HRD system. For example, when the performance appraisal system was introduced in the State Bank of India in the first phase, it was without any ratings and quantification as a parallel system for development of people and not for assessment for rewards and promotion which followed subsequently.

7. *Line Management/ Personnel Function Strengthening* : When HRD is introduced, the role of the banks line managers and the functioning of the personnel and industrial relations function in the banks needs to be strengthened. HRD is a supportive system which helps the line manager and personnel people to become more effective.

8. *Formal HRD Function Creation* : When such ground has been prepared the bank will be ready to have a distinct HRD function which may be placed independently or in some other group like personnel, depending on the performance of a bank. In the long-

run HRD must be a distinct function and structured, the HRD people alongwith junior line managers need to prepare long-term and short- term steps for strengthening the HRD activities in the bank.

As would be evident from this discussion, Organizational Culture plays a pivotal role in the success or otherwise of HRD interventions. A favourable climate would permit the HRD spirit to flourish and turn the banks into 'Learning Organisations where, apart from formal HRD machinery/ mechanisms, informal processes like 'Mentoring/Coaching' also emerge.

Realizing the importance of an appropriate Organisation Culture for improving the effectiveness of the banking sector, innovations like Organisation Development Initiative are being attempted to reengineer this sector. This we shall discuss in the following sections.

The Cultural Dimension of HRD/ Training:Role of Organizational Culture

Bank's Organizational Cultural appraisal being important for HRD Training must be conscious of the cultural ramifications of it's work. Many of our banking organizational inadequacies are due to outmoded management techniques that have created dysfunctional cultures. Little has been done to integrate the theoretical concepts of organizational culture into the mainstream of training practice though it has been shown by research to have a considerable influence on trainer effectiveness. Campbell (1984), defines corporate culture as 'the attitudes, values, beliefs and expectations of those who work in an organization', while Field and Davies (1984) refer to the 'behaviors patterns and standards that bind it (the organization) together'.

Characteristics of Organizational Culture: Trainers operate in rather different cultures according to the nature of their organization. Indian Banks are conservative service organizations peopled by highly educated 'knowledge' workers. Many things characterize organization culture, generally, as the following:

* The level of involvement of line managers in the training activity.
* The philosophy of the organization concerning education, training and human resource development.
* The nature and use of power in the organisation (e.g personal power versus positional power, autocratic vs. democratic management).
* The form and nature of technology and the work to be performed, extent of computerization and mechanization.

The 'ideal' culture would have all the following characteristics:

— A unifying philosophy and spirit emanating from top management.
— The provision of regular, positive feedback.
— Intense communications.
— Allowance for mistakes.
— Opportunity for learning throughout the service (as in a Learning Organisation) and availability of mentors/ coaches to facilitate that learning.
— Work would be given meaning through a emphasis on caring for people rather than mechanistic management.
— Sound human-resources management systems for adequate pay and benefits, fair appraisal, a management style promoting participation and accessibility.

Organizational Culture & Training Interrelation : Cultural activities have a significant effect on the training function. For example, there is no point in sending a supervisor on a human-relations course and then returning that same individual to an authoritarian work environment where 'theory x' is the dominant management style or sending junior managers to a communications course when the primary method of communication in the home organisation is top-down with little room for feedback.

Culture affects the introduction of new technology (e.g. introduction of Information Technology & Computerization in the Indian Banks) for cultural assumptions regulate employees receptivity to change. The trainer who works in a culture in which change is regarded as a constant rather than a threat, will not find the introduction of new concepts to be an onerous task. If an organisation is to flourish, however technical innovations must be accepted and utilized by both management and labour. How technology is introduced is increasingly seen as the key to workers' acceptance of it. People resist change that threatens them, because it has been sprung too suddenly or it is too big an effort for them to grasp other difficulties that must be overcome, include feelings of inadequacy and a fear by employees that they will be unable to cope with the training involved' (Kleinscheid, 1980). Desired changes in the organisation culture can be brought about by such methods of Organisation Development (OD) as ' success flagging'. In this, the instructor informs the student abouts the success of others (for example those personnel who have mastered computer skills in a short time) who have gone before and /or suggest ways in which the trainees' jobs will be made easier, more profitable or whatever has been used to tackle this resistance. Organisation Development will be considered in detail later.

Trainers who are not fully aware of the cultural milieu in which they work are doing only a partial job. Since training is itself a cultural phenomenon that must be inserted into an ever-changing and sometimes resistant work environment so as to become an intrinsic part of the organization's overall cultural mosaic. After understanding the culture in which they operate, the next task is to ensure that all training activity 'fits', the organization's cultural reality through application of support/ maintenance systems.

We shall now consider important *new and innovative parameters/ areas of Organisation Culture* as : Turning Indian

Banks into `Learning Organisations', Mentoring/ Coaching as HRD Interventions and Organisation Development Initiative for changing banks organisation culture.

Turning Indian Banks into Learning Organisations

An important strategy for restructuring the organizational culture of Indian Banks is by taking the steps required for turning them into Learning Organizations. In the learning organization training is not separate from day-to-day activities but an inherent part of the working environment. When people need to know or learn something, the information and the facilities to learn must be immediately available to them. As the learning organization learns from all sources and directions, change is accepted, welcomed. This reduces the impact of change and strengthens the organization's ability to cope successfully and to survive (Bentley, 1990)[2]. A learning culture where training and development became demand—led, rather than supply driven will ensure that organizations attract, develop and retain the people talent needed.

Focusing where the training is to hit rather than adopting the scatter-gun approach leads into using quality, as opposed to quantity, as an appropriate measure of how effective the training has been—looking at outcomes rather than input.' One shot training for life cannot be seen as appropriate in a world which recognizes constant personal/organizational development. Customer care and total quality management are means of keeping people involved in that process'.[3]

The learning organisation describes the bringing together of people to achieve some objectives, great or small, in conditions where they are all searching, all the time, for ways of doing whatever needs to be done in a better way. Feedback is crucial to this organization because it needs to know whether what is being attempted is working out. The ideal of the learning organization is never to take anything for granted, to subject everything to keen examination, and to respect everyone's view so that openness prevails, trust develops, the best ideas surface.

Learning about new things or innovations is the secret of competitive success: a better quality product, better service—these are the areas where the learning organization focuses. The learning organisation avoids the reactive kind of maintenance learning and engages in innovative learning for preparing individuals and societies to act in concert in new situations. The learning organization facilitates the learning of all its members and continuously transforms itself (Pedler 1988). The IBM motto "Our business is learning and we sell the by-products of that learning" sums up the whole theme of the learning organization. Whatever your job, when you are working the whole purpose is to learn by changing one's understanding and approach and producing goods or services acceptable to the customers (Hammond and Wille 1994).

A learning organization which facilitates the learning and development of its employees, and is in a constant process of transition and change has certain characteristics (Beck, 1989)[4] –these the Indian Banks have to imbibe for facing the challenges of the massive upheaval they are undergoing. Such *desired characteristics are enumerated below:*

* A recognition of personal effort and achievement.
* Designated periods in timetables and work schedules where the focus deliberately turns away from business requirements towards a consideration of team relationships and individual needs.
* Encouragement of teams to look wider than the single work unit and to expand their horizons by networking.
* The absolute commitment and open style of top management.

Mentoring and Coaching as HRD Interventions in Indian Banks

People develop by their own individual efforts and/or with help from somebody else. Many skills we acquire are learned by imitating which can be proved by exchange with somebody who has experience and can pass it on to speed up imitation or to cut down on mistakes i.e. accelerating or improving the application of skill or knowledge through a mentor or coach. Both terms address the development of on-the-job skills—specific skills such as coaching a subordinate to make a better presentation or holding a career discussion with a young graduate. These are HRD interventions to bring about changes on organizational culture in the direction of fan ideal culture.

Mentoring involves an individual entering into a relationship with somebody to act as advisor, counsellor or even role model e.g. a senior bank manager keeping an interest in the development of a probationer throughout his/her career instead of casual interaction only during the latters on the job branch training. The role may be informal, where a senior manager takes an active interest in the career development of a younger employee.

Coaching essentially involves some specific and hopefully planned activity designed to improve the skilled performance of another to get people to do things differentially and more cost effectively. Coaching could involve.

* boss coaching subordinate.

* coach coaching team e.g. a mobile job trainer coaching team of officers and staff of a rural branch on service area imperatives Coaching can be one-to-one or one to-many and hierarchically upwards, downwards or sideways in organizational level.

Advantages of Mentoring & Coaching : In periods of high rates of change (as being the witnessed in the Indian Banks in current phase of financial sector reforms) coaching and mentoring can be crucial for changing the organization's values and culture. Some of the *reasons behind individuals undertaking mentoring or coaching are* :[5]

— *standards* : Coaching leads to excellent performance by giving examples of the standards that individuals are expected to achieve.

— *reputation* : e.g. if a previously average bank branch comes to be known as successful, it reflects, well on the manager. So by getting the staff to work as a team through coaching the manager's reputation is enhanced.

— *achievement* : in order to get the best out of the staff personnel, the competent coach decides upon challenging task that help them to grow in competence.

Some of the *benefits* by the use of *coaching and mentoring* are:

— Better communication and understanding achieved with staff.

— More productive teams.

— Succession cover improved and manager's own promotion ensured as a result of the mentoring provided.

— Staff more self-reliant and able to deal professionally with unexpected events.

Mentoring/Coaching provide improvement in the placement, development and retention of high-feyers of the Indian Banking Sector which is at risk of loosing them to the foreign banks/private sector offer of better prospects and enumeration.

Changing Organizational Culture/Re-Engineering Training Through Organisation Development Initiative

Banks have made tremendous progress in the last two decades but the growth has not been without problems: house-keeping, organisation and management problems due to fast expansion and reorientation of goals. Adhoc strategies, and short-term perspectives have guided the development. New management interventions like Organization Development Initiative (ODI) are required to handle new managerial problems of the banks which are becoming large and complex.

Response to change could not be fully managed by the strategies, of reorganization, specialization and training and traditional HR development. One approach to manage organizational change in a planned manner by taking a total view of the organisation is' organizational development'. HRD by itself has limitations to solve some of these problems. HRD and conventional training focus more on competency development for performing jobs effectively which is necessary but not enough for creating mechanisms to sustain effective functioning in a changing environment. What is required is long-term planned changes in the culture, and management of the total organisation. Research shows that unless the problems of the organisation are diagnosed properly, the efforts to bring changes will remain unproductive. OD is an approach to plan change, to enhance problem solving capacity and renew organizational health.

ODI's Theoretical Frame Work : Organizational development is a process of planning and implementing systematic changes to improve the organizational effectiveness, help the organisation avoid decay and to facilitate its renewal. It involves a collaborative diagnosis of organization's problems, and a joint problem solving approach culminating in it's resurgence. It assumes peer-pressure to be the most powerful force for change. ODI assumes that most people desire and are capable of making, a greater contribution to the organisation than they are normally permitted to make. ODI attempts to unleash/channelise the energy and enthusiasm of employees. Task performance becomes rewarding only when the individuals' goals are consistent and compatible with organizational goals.

Methodology of ODI: ODI Methodology comprises of assessment, diagnosis and action research through the use of participants in the research process to solve his problems. Action research is a three-phase approach:

— Diagnosis

— Intervention (design)

— Evolution

Diagnosis calling for an analysis of the strength and weaknesses of the organisation is based on observation of interview with a cross-section of population representing various sub-systems, levels and functions in the organisation. It gives some understanding of the problem. The OD intervention is specifically designed to achieve the intended results through planned change. The interventions can be of two types: structured and unstructured. Structured interventions focus on structural changes using structured methods e.g. recognization of banks. Under this category are role based interventions such as role efficacy lab (Pareek) and role analysis techniques (Dayal) as well as MBO (Maheswari). The focus of role based interventions are to analyze the role and to make them effective. Different kinds of unstructured interventions that have been used in OD work in India are:

— Intergroup development.

— Confrontation meetings.

Mentioned below are some interventions in the context of the problems as identified by researchers, faced by the banking industry (Pareek):

Problems	*Intervention*
Fall in worker as well as management prosductivity.	Personal growth lab. Goal setting and team building.
Underutilisation of manpower.	Management by objectives. Work redesign.

OD is an ongoing process which requires on-line control. The new learning acquired through OD interventions can be transferred to work organisation, when there is better institutionalization of the interventions as a regular part of the process of organizational self-renewal. In order to institutionalise OD as ongoing activity it is proposed that banks should create an organizational development department. OD in banks can be introduced at any level be it the top, middle, lower, zonal and branch. There are several areas of concern in banks like the productivity of the training system. OD interventions for training are also worthwhile to diagnose the extent training can enable organisations achieve their corporate mission and also to design appropriate interventions to make training more effective. Banks' important area of concern is customer service where there is lot of potential at the branch level to initiate OD intervention to tackle the same.

There is a strong unionism in the Indian banks. Sometimes even goal employee benefit programmes are looked with suspicion, if employees unions are not consulted or taken into confidence. However, in our country there are some success experiences where unions have supported/ participated in OD programmes. Gupta in his action research study of a bank comments: "The role of Award Staff Union Secretary in supporting the participative work system redesign remains absolutely and overwhelmingly positive.unions may be willing to play a positive and collaborative role in OD, if approached from the base of trust and respect".

The State Bank of India — the biggest bank in the public sector is using OD for better productivity. It is reported that the work redesign efforts in the State Bank of India which included streamlining of lay out, simplification of procedures and involvement of staff, showed marked improvement in the customer service of the constituents. Banking industry needs renewal and a new image. Individual banks need to take a total approach to organizational rejuvenation process. OD has tremendous potential to help banks diagnose their present problems and imitate measures to tackle them, since banks with their highly educated work force would be ideal institutions to initiate changes.

For successfully implementing a measure like Organisation Development Initiative (ODI), it is essential that HRD and Training systems have to enlarge their traditional vision, anticipate and prepare for changes. This aspect of strategic Human Resource Management we shall now discuss in the following section.

Re-Engineering For Strategic Human Resource Management and Training

In organisations like Indian banks human resource management (HRM) remains in the periphery, HRM policies and practices are developed through reactive processes—trade union pressure or pressure from the legal system—with inadequate efforts being made by the bank managements to develop appropriate HRM systems'. 'Banking organisations, particularly in the past decade, have been facing major challenges from the environment: deregulation and liberalization, advancements in technological front, changes in the internal environment, change in values of the breed of employees who have entered the organisations in the 70s and 80s (who are highly educated, have scant respect for formal authority and are much more achievement oriented). In the contemporary society, knowledge has become the power of the individual and it is being contended that the triumph of the individual will be one of the major trend in the future.[7] When the internal and external environments of organisations become more turbulent the need is to develop effective organizational management systems. HRM has to be more proactive: This concern for proactiveness in HRM has led to the development of Strategic Human Resource Management (SHRM) approach.

Strategic HRM primarily deals with developing human resource systems which will be in tune the changing realities by reviewing the existing HRM systems for their effectiveness and developing better systems, evolving newer perspectives on HRM systems which will explain how organisations' external and internal environments are changing and how HRM can proactively anticipate and respond to the challenges emerging from these changes. The SHRM would then help the organisation to understand itself better, and assist it to prepare itself to meet the demands from the external environment. Such reoriented HRM will have implications in manpower planning, recruitment, performance appraisal, training and development etc.

With the new changes taking place Indian banks have to enter into newer areas of activities calling for innovative ideas and marketing skills. However, with the type of reactive HRM that exist in banks, it would be extremely difficult to enter into new activities effectively (which need proactive policies). There are certain *areas where proactive SHRM activities can be initiated* in Indian Banking Sector which will give a little more flexibility to bank managements such as injecting specialized knowledge, changing the promotion pattern, enforcement of effective transfer policy managing human resources diversity, HRD for workmen staff and reorienting industrial relations (IR). Over the years the industry has followed reactive processes in industrial relations. So attempting to bring about drastic changes in the area of people management systems in the industry may not be desirable. However, it would be possible to bring about changes in HRM/IR in banking by understanding the emerging realities and taking advantage of the opportunities thrown up by the changing IR climate.

Re-engineering Industrial Relations : Industrial relations are undergoing major transformation, trade unions are becoming less forceful. A recent study[8] of industrial relations in banking industry indicates that the stage is set for major changes. Most of the trade union and officers association leaders interviewed in this study feel that industrial relations should not necessarily be based only on conflicts. If they are accepted as true partners in the growth of the industry, they are also willing to extend their support. However, they fear that bank managements are not yet ready to accept this and according to them bank managements still look at employee organisations as negative forces. They feel that there should be a positive change in the attitude of managements towards unions and associations. In recent years even trade unions like All Indian Bank Employees Association (AIBEA) and Bank Employees Federation of India (BEFI) which were opposing computerization earlier to have softened their approach. There is a gradual change in the attitude towards mechanization. They do, however have certain concerns (e.g. regarding retrenchment etc.) about the introduction of technology in banks. Bank unions at the industry level are now prepared to look at changes with a positive mind and unions at the bank level are willing to cooperate on reasonably acceptable issue. Bank managements have to reorient their approach e.g. in stressing HRD/Training inputs for banks workmen staff.

Managing Human Resource Diversity in Indian Banks : The profile of organisation world over are undergoing transformations as a result of the demographic, technological and other changes bringing diversity in human resources. This has compelled many organisations to seriously examine their approaches in managing human resource diversity as the straight-jacketed Human Resource (HR) Systems which view employees as homogeneous entitles are failing organizations to achieve effective performance. 'Several countries such as Canada, the US, Sweden and France have even gone ahead with legislations to project work force differing in social/ gender/cultural background and have evolved innovative approaches to manage HR diversity,[9]. For example, Bank of Montreal (Canada) has a separate department looking after HR Diversity and Work place Equality. Most of the Indian Banks, prior to nationalization functioned primarily as regional banks employing people essentially from the same geographical regions. This led to the existence of some degree of homogeneity in the manpower. The heterogeneity got introduced in three ways as discussed below:

1. The first instance of diversity crept in when banks gave up their regional/community identity and went ahead recruiting from all corners of the country as they were to expand beyond geographical regions. New selection methodology helped banks to get highly qualified persons at clerical and officer levels with diverse educational backgrounds though bank jobs remained unmodified. This mismatch led to wide-spread employee frustrations.
2. The second instance was when banks had to be in line with the national policy and had to enforce job reservations for socially disadvantaged groups like scheduled castes and scheduled tribes. This group of employees adds an important dimension to HR diversity in banks in terms of the difference in

competencies and the social stigma and isolation they bring with them.

3. In the eighties, a new diversity got accentuated in the form of women employees— a reflection of the social changes taking place (detailed discussion of women employees/gender and development issues has been done in Chapter 9).

Management of Diversity by Indian Banks : Indian banks had been by and large reactive in their approach to HR management, initiating changes due to external forces. Some of the actions initiated with reference to these diverse groups are discussed

— For educational and cultural background related diversity measures like quality circle introduced in State Bank of India (S.B.I) having development of the `whole person' as its focus has brought about "improvement in industrial relations climate, better interpersonal relations and fostering of team spirit" (Agarwal : 1989) as it enabled some of the highly qualified bank employees to translate their cognitive abilities to practical use.

— For Socially Disadvantaged Persons the government issues, directives such as expecting banks to conduct special pre-recruitment and pre-promotion coaching classes to help these people, and giving due attention to their training and exposure to all types of assignments.

— The current concerns of women employees are in relation to their immobility and career orientations. Indian women are vulnerable due to lack of infrastructure facilities and the social disapproval when they are away from their homes. Banks should help them ease out their problems with respect to their transfers and other behavioural problem areas. An *N.I.B.M. Workshop*[10] revealed their apprehensions about making unconventional behavioural responses that might elicit social disapproval. There is a need for Women Development Training and gender sensitization training.

SHRM-HRD & Training for workmen staff of Indian Banks : Another important area for application of the principles of Strategic Human Resource Management is the mostly neglected area of giving HRD and Training inputs for the workmen/award staff of the Indian Banking Industry. Some of the issues involved in worker HRD have been highlighted by *Khandelwal*. "In service organizations like banking 80 per cent of first level officers come from the ranks. Thus development of workers assumes critical significance both for the present as well as the future. Several developments havinglong-term consequences which require increasing attention to develop all workers are :

1. Declining work ethic.
2. Declining trends in productivity.
3. Growing alienation of workers.
4 Increasing induction of special population like socially disadvantaged groups.
5. Change in value systems and motivation of employees.
6. New technology.
7. Complexity of organizations".

Technological changes leading to obsolescence of certain jobs in the future will make it necessary for organization to prepare workers with new skills and attitudes to cope with changes. Money alone is an insufficient motivator and work must be viewed as a source of satisfaction. Khandelwal views HRD for workers as a process by which the workers are helped in a continuous and planned way to develop occupational capabilities, self management skills intellectual, psychological, social and cultural aspects of his personality.

Athreya[12] also focuses on the more bothersome area of HRD for the workers since "in confining it to managers we are only scratching the surfaces. The only thing to be said for working with managers is that they may become better `leaders' and hence more effective instruments of industrial and economic development. HRD however is a total activity for the company and there is a strong need for reallocating the resources to people lower down". Athreya suggests a balanced triangle of manager-worker relations, member-trade union relations and management-union relations, which couple each other. The manager-worker relationship needs to be strengthened; the management-union adversarial relationship has to give way to realism; and the need of trade unions to maintain relations with members has to be appreciated.

Strategy for SHRM: In view of the above discussion on SHRM, specially as applied to the crucial areas of Industrial Relations. HRM of human diversity, HRD for workers etc. in Indian Banks, an integrated strategy for implementation of SHRM can be formulated. The effectiveness with which the Indian Banks will be able to respond to the challenges of the new economic policy depends on the efficient and proactive management of human resource though SHRM and moving away from the reactive process involving HRM policies. The existing and emerging diversities in human resource indicate the need for changed orientations in HRM. "The tasks for the Indian banks would be to work out alternatives specific to the diverse groups of employees in terms of their career progression and the required service conditions. Banks should evolve interventions whereby flexibility in HR practices is accepted by all in the organisation through extensive process work including training at different levels" (Mankidy, 1996).[13]

A thorough analysis of the existing HRM policies at the bank level needs to be carried out with a view to establishing their negative and positive impacts on banks in the present context and identifying areas where new changes can be brought in without much resistance. To prepare the necessary ground work for the future certain basic steps have to be initiated :[14]

(a) *Develop HRM Philosophy:* Bank managements have to start looking at people from a positive stand point by developing an HRM philosophy.

(b) *Develop Transparent HRM Policies:* We have to make our HRM policies as transparent as possible as lack of transparency in the name of flexibility/ discretionary power cause unfair practices causing frustration/conflicts.

(c) *Develop Career Path:* For as many types of jobs as possible so that people will know the possibilities of their career progression.

(d) *Training for Redeployment:* to prepare employees to meet the challenges, they need to be trained and redeployed. To this a detailed stills inventory has to be developed and compared with the skills requirements of the future. The identified gaps will be filled through a complete revamping of the training system.

Since for training to make a contribution towards establishing the proactive spirit of SHRM, it has to make use of more effective Training Delivery mechanisms and take up critical training areas. These aspects will be considered in the following chapters.

Notes

1. Pareek, Udai, Designing Human Resource Systems—Action research approach. In Somnath Chattopadhyay and Udai Pareek (Eds) *Managing Organizational Change,* New Delhi: Oxford and IBH Publishing Company, 1982.

2. Bentley, Trevor, *A Training Consultant at Work—Banking and Financial Training,* Vol 6, No-2 June 1990.

3. Parry, Hugh, Training for Quality in *'Handbook for Training and Developemnt* Ed. by John Prior, 1993, Gower.

4. Beck.M.(1989), "Learning Organization—How to create them," *Industrial and Commercial Training Journal*, Vol. 21, No. 3.

5. Moorby, Ed, "Mentoring and Coaching". In *Handbook of Training and Development* ' ed. by John Prior. UK: Gower, 1993.

6. Mankidy, Jacob, *Benchmark Study of Industrial Relations in Banking Industry*, National Institute of Bank Management, 1992.

7. Nasbitt, John and Aburdene, Patricia, *Megatrends 2000—Ten New Directions for the 1990's*, William Morrow and Co. Ltd., New York 1990.

8. Mankidy, Jacob, *Benchmark Study of Industrial Relations in the Banking Industry*, Opening citation.

9. Jain,H.L.and Verma, A. *Workforce Diversity and Competitive Challenges*. Paper presented at the H.R. Diversity Conference held at Mc Master University, Canada, 1994.

10. *Report of the workshop on the Role and Functioning of Women in Banks*, National Institute of Bank Management, 1987.

11. Khandelwal, A.K., HRD for workers. Role of Unions—Paper presented at the National HRD Network's Annual Conference, 1987.

12. Athreya,M.B., *Formal HRD Systems—Paper* presented at National Institute of Productivity Management (NIPM) Conference, Hyderabad 1984.

13. Mankidy, Jacob, Managing Human Resource Diversity: Challenges and Responses of the Indian Banking Industry, *Prajanan (Journal of NIBM*, Pune) Jan.- March 1996, Vol. .XXIV No. 4.

14. Mankidy, J : Human Resource Management and Industrial Relations in the Banking Industry, *Prajanan*, Jan.—March 1993, Vol. XXI, No. 4.

6

Reengineering Training: Training Delivery Mechanisms

Overview: The reengineering endeavour of turning Indian Banks into proactive 'learning organisations', practising the principles of Strategic Human Resource Management, requires a more vigorous and effective training support. For this, reengineering of the training delivery machinery is necessary, covering its various facets. It will encompass organisational restructuring, modifications at the head/corporate/field and other levels and also with respect to the training institution.

The reengineering strategies will have to intervene at various steps of the training delivery process: Training Needs assessment, use of innovative training methods (e.g. distance/open learning, computer based training, interactive video) in addition to imaginative usage of traditional training methods, enhancing Trainer effectiveness and proper selection of trainees. These aspects shall be discussed in this chapter.

The reengineering of training delivery would also require redesigning the curriculum/content of the existing courses and devising new courses to cover critical training areas. This aspect we shall cover in the following chapters.

Re-engineering the Training Delivery Function

Organisational Restructuring

The finding/analysis of the N.I.B.M. and other studies indicate that the banks need to revamp their management systems with regard to the training function. Training would not "pay" unless the present organisation is changed, since otherwise the desired improvement in planning and controlling would not be feasible. According to the comprehensive study of National Institute of Bank Management on 15 nationalised banks, `radical change in the existing structure is basic to any true improvement in the functional of the banks'—training systems would re-orient the existing roles drastically.

The role of the Head Office (H.O.) is to change the most. HO is presently involve in planning and controlling all significant aspects of the training activities, combining the policy formulation and the operational roles. This has to be changed— the Head Office will have to confine itself to policy formulation, control system design, resources supply and goal achievement monitoring. This change would change the role of the field offices (i.e., Zonal/Regional/Branch Offices) — they will have to assume full responsibility for improving the quality of the human resources as per the policies laid down by the Corporate office. They will have to collect and analyze data pertaining to the performance of 'the human resources, implement and monitor the strategies for enhancing the quality and performance of the human resources under autonomy of means to field·offices. The Head Office will not, as at present prescribe any strategy (e.g. every officer to be trained once in two years). This calls for a drastic reorientation at H.O. and field office levels, and in the role of the training institutions. Professionalization, flexibility in strategies and an organisation problem-solving orientation has to take the place of the routinized, number-oriented training activities as discussed below (NIBM).

Corporate Office's Role : The function of a Corporate office in decentralized organisation is to define goals, monitor environment and decide macro strategies, define standards of performance. In the area of training and development it would:

(i) Clarify Organisational Ideal and Values with respect to Human Resources Management so the actions are not adhoc and piecemeal. The Head Office is responsible for clarifying and communicating these values to all the sections by an organisational communication process.

(ii) Formulate and revise policies : Any specific training and development activity must be related to organisational ideals and goals and clear policies should be spelt out to relate the ideals and the goals to the appropriate and specific activities.

A list of some areas where policy statements are necessary to be formulated may be as follows:

— Induction Training

— Continued Personal Education

— On-the-job-Training

— Training Need Identification and Planning

— Evaluation of Training

— Selection, Assignment and Training of Principal, Faculty, HRD Manager

— Performance Appraisal and Training

(iii) Formulate Standards and Indices of Quality of Human Resources, operational criteria for measuring the quality and competence of employees expected to be developed. Unless we can define and measure what is sought to be achieved, neither planning nor controlling can be performed meaningfully. Management cannot get appropriate returns from its investment in training unless it is known what is the standard to be achieved. In its absence only the inputs can be controlled — i.e. no. of persons trained, amount of time and money spent. This does not guarantee any output. While there cannot be absolute measures there can be approximations:

— Values and Attitude Measures

— Skill and Knowledge Measures

— Organisational Climate and Quality of life Measures

— Productivity Measures

— Innovativeness Measures

Reliability and Validity of such measures are known to be problematic. Yet measurement problems are not absolutely unsurmountable, though difficult.

(iv) Provide Macro Goals and Corporate Performance Information: The field offices can plan effectively only if they are well informed about the periodic performance goals of the Banks and the various performance parameters of the Bank.

(v) Provide Resources and Environmental Information: certain resources e.g. heavy capital budgets, additional manpower etc. have to be provided by the Head Office. Information e.g. about the competitors, information about training resources, techniques crucial in making training effective and efficient may be collected by the Central Office economically and provided to all the field offices..

(vi) Monitor Achievement of Results : the Head Office should monitor not the inputs but the outputs (the quality of the human resources) at any given moment by different measures and indices. To achieve this purpose an information system has to be set up— the Management Information System for Training (MIST) —includes information about activities, inputs, employees performance and productivity unitwise and aggregated performance of the Bank, results of surveys on employee knowledge and skills, attitudes, values, organisational climate.

The Role of Field Offices : The present problem is that Managers don't develop subordinates. Therefore, structural changes are essential to make training and development of subordinates a prime responsibility of managers by delegating this function to them. No real involvement, and hence effective results can be expected from training unless the accountability (and the accompanying autonomy) on the part of the field managers are established. For this purpose the role of the field offices (as also of the H.O. Departments) has to change and `should include the following functions :

— To organise the supporting Training Structure(s): these field managers must have the authority to establish, modify the Training centres or HRD Departments, the establishment of a new Centre, enlargement of an existing Centre or creation of specialized centres (e.g. a Rural Training Centre).

— To collect information and analyze Policies and Information for identifying Training Needs : for the various groups of personnel. While the information system will be designed, and the policies formulated by the Corporate Office, it is the field managers who will be responsible for applying these for deciding concrete actions.

— To participate in the Design of Training Courses and Evaluation Systems : The soundness of a course design cannot be ensured by the trainers alone, they need the operational managers help. Such a participation would make the courses relevant, comprehensive and output oriented.

— To participate in Evaluating Programmes : Whether training is paying must be a concern of the operational manager. The pretraining and the post-training evaluation would require participation of the field managers.

— To monitor the Quality and Performance of the Human Resources in the Zone/Region/Branch or Department by using the systems designed by the Head Office.

— To provide feedback to the Head Office at fixed intervals on the quality and performance of the personnel responsible to them.'

The Training Institution's Role: The role of the training institution may get more enlarged with a greater degree of professionalization along the following role dimensions.

— To undertake systematic and scientific Course Design by first specifying the expected level of performance outcome and then specifying the inputs by an analytic process. At the moment no such work is undertaken.

— To Design Educational Techniques and Methods for Effective HR Development : Educational technology has undergone a change in the last few decades, with the developments in cognitive psychology and computer technology, along with expansion in the field of AV creations. These changes are far too radical to permit their adoption without fundamentally changing the established pedagogic assumptions.

— To Conduct and Evaluate Training Programmes : evaluation should be made an essential and integrated function of the training institutions.

— To conduct Seminars, Conferences for Different Target Groups. While training courses have specifically spelt out objectives to achieve, the seminar etc. are general purpose interactions with broader goal of widening consciousness or sharing views on a given topic e.g. sharing of policies would make their implementation more purposive.

— To conduct Surveys & Research : the problems and the type of research must be carefully chosen—Banks need more of action research on complex, real-life problems rather than abstracted, conceptual research. The training of personnel for conducting such research has to be undertaken and organisational policies streamlined to pursue such action research.

Thus, it is apparent that for reengineering the Training Delivery Function, extensive organisational restructuring has to be undertaken at various levels-head/corporate/field offices and also with respect to the Training Institutions.

Re-Engineering Strategies—Training Needs Assessment

Re-engineering of training needs assessment in Indian banks has to take into account the corporate mission, deficiencies in performance and the needs of the individual employees. Hence, the assessment has to be at *three levels*: the corporate levels, the operating level, and the individual level.

Assessment of Training Needs at the Corporate Level:

1. Banks are required to have a perspective training plan[1] which, in addition to quantifying the training needs, identifies the thrust areas of training (as being done at the head office of Punjab National Bank) such as:
   - — Human Resource Development.
   - — Upgradation of credit appraisal skills in the context of deregulation.
   - — Consolidation of service area approach.
   - — Technology and awareness training in the area of computerisation.
   - — Intensive training in foreign exchange, merchant banking and industrial rehabilitation.
2. Some other functional areas[2] consequent to the far reaching changes taking place in the banking sector that would need to be stressed upon in Training needs assessment at the corporate level are listed below:
   (a) Marketing of products and also creating new markets for their existing services through well planned marketing strategies is required. Marketing has to find wide acceptance as a core function in the banking system.
   (b) Project appraisal for new units requiring assessment of technology/market potential/management capability/financial capability. Risk assessment in all these parameters and appropriate pricing on the basis of riskcosts will be a specialized inter-disciplinary team function.

(c) Special cells at the corporate offices, large branches for helping the corporate sector in floating new instruments like commercial papers.

(d) Opening of specialised branches at key centres for providing financial/other support to agro based industries will have to be planned.

3. The problems face by separate autonomous bank functionaries when entering other business areas is another area where corporate level training needs assessment is essential. Appropriate training would be required to tackle the following problems[3]:

    (a) The service provided for a limited part of a bank's customer base is seen as expensive and elitist, creating problems of image and market positioning for the bank.

    (b) The market is competitive and fee income hard to generate.

    (c) There are difficulties in marketing a separate company's services through the medium of branches e.g. organisational and image problems associated with retailing 'subsidiaries' services and problems of selling extra and more complex products through the branch.

    (d) Legal problems in the relationship between the parent and subsidiary.

4. The annual training plan derived from the perspective training plan quantifies the training needs during the year. A top level training advisory committee would lay down the training policy, identify thrust areas, assess training needs and evolve requisite strategies. This corporate level assessment cannot confine itself mainly to the new training which is comparatively a smooth task. The committee has also to assess the training needs of a bank in the grey areas of the Bank's performance e.g. poor credit management. For

identification of deficiencies and to properly assess the training needs, various sources such as the proceedings of quarterly action plan, meetings of Chief Executives of banks with the RBI Governor, RBI/NABARD internal inspection reports etc. can be used. In addition, training needs of senior executives also should be taken not of at the corporate level, which is still a dark area.

5. In recent years, Credit Administration including quality of rural financing by banks is a source of concern due to its significant effect on economic development generally, as also on the bank's financial health. In the context of Rural Banking Training, Needs Assessment is required for making rural financing attractive by following certain important principles. The *important principle of rural finance* are :
   — Credit should be provide with a package of required services.
   — It has to be supervised with problem solving attitude.
   — Assistance be provided to the borrowers in respect of social aspects like education, health and training.

The services in these three areas could be provided by the banks as follow:

1. By encouraging the Self-Help Groups of the borrowers to obtain such guidance/assistance from NGO's etc. if necessary.
2. Organizing educational camps for a group of villages with the help of the existing government machinery.
3. By encouraging the borrowers to become aware by participation in the Kisan melas, exhibitions organised by the agricultural universities etc.
4. Inculcating regular saving habits in the borrowers to enable them learn to save and have regular contacts with banks.

5. Conducting bank clientele training on development credit, result of its proper/improper use as done vide NABARD's Volunteer Vahini programme.

Training Needs Assessment at the Zonal (operating) Level

Zonal Offices of banks being mini head offices, the Zonal Manager should have the autonomy to assess training needs of the attached personnel by classifying them into convenient and homogenous groups on the basis of management level and functional responsibilities. For this, *key performance areas* have to be identified for different categories of personnel e.g. for a credit manager in Zonal/Regional Office, the KPAs could be:

— Judicious exercise of loaning powers.

— Timely submission of statement relating to his department.

— Following up health of the financial units, nursing and rehabilitation of sick units etc.

KPAs would reveal the critical attributes required for effective functioning as a credit manager and a comparison of critical attributes required with that of capability level of the persons would help to assess the gaps in capability. The *profile of a more effective manager* (as delineated in this study by Rao) would give indication of the training needs of such a manager:

> The branches are the most vital organs of any bank, as they do the real business. Therefore, the effectiveness of a bank depends to a great extent on how effective its branches are. The effectiveness of a branch, in turn, depends on how effective the branch manager is. The effectiveness of a manager depends on his/her leadership qualities needing the various competences—knowledge skills and attitudes. The importance of knowledge and skills has been well recognized and taken care of to some extent by the existing training programmes of banks. However, the importance of the managerial and leadership skills has not been adequately recognized.

Very often the effectiveness of a branch is measured only in terms of certain quantitative parameters such as growth in deposits, advances per employee, business etc. However, there are certain qualitative dimensions such as customer service, staff development, and betterment of the bank's image in the area, which are important in determining the effectiveness of branches. The effectiveness of bank branches in its totality—both in terms of quantitative as well as qualitative aspects has to be viewed.

The findings of Rao's study[4] on 'Effectiveness of Bank Branches: Role of leadership behaviour of Branch Managers' indicates that *the more effective managers (MEMs) have the following characteristics* :

— *Hopeful and optimistic* : The MEMs are found to be very positive in their attitude, hopeful of achievements and optimistic in outlook.

— *Concern for customers* : They have genuine concern and care for customers; understand their personal problems and help them, ensure prompt service and impress upon the staff to know and understand customers.

— *Marketing Approach* : They look to the customers' needs and satisfy them to secure business and project the advantaged and unique features of the schemes and services to the customers and offer service.

— *Relationship Orientation* : They attach great importance to building up rapport/relationship with customers, maintain regular contacts with them. They create confidence among customers.

— *Responsive to Environment* : MEMs are very sensitive and responsive to the environment, for spotting the opportunities for new business.

— *Long -Term Orientation* : They have foresight and aim at long-term objectives and initiate certain activities at the branch even though they may not bear the fruits in the immediate future.

— *Total Approach* : MEMs feel that they can take care of not only the financial needs, but some of their customer's personal, psychological needs to the extent possible.

Assessment of Needs at Individual Level

The individual's voice is not being properly considered by the Trainers. His/her appraisal report on his/her training needs is generally given the go by though this can form a meaningful basis for assessment of the training need. Attention by the bank and regional manager to the perceived training need of the individual would be fulfilling a gap and also increasing the motivation levels.

Identification of training need-role of appraisal system

A good performance appraisal system would include :

— performance analysis to identify factors facilitating and hindering performance.

— identification of training needs.

— performance counselling.

— performance assessment on behavioural and managerial dimensions by the appraiser.

Need for a well developed mechanism to cull out the training needs from the information provided in the performance appraisal form exists. This is because in most banking organisations, performance appraisal is routinely used mainly for the promotion exercise, and not linked up in deciding upon the training of individual personnel.

Re-Engineering Training—Innovative Delivery Methods

Institutional training time should not be wasted on information, rules and procedure giving lectures but devoted to making the employees feel the need for information, to get them to realise the problems and the necessity of solving these problems to explore innovative ways of meeting the demands of the customers and take decisions. For these kinds of sessions we shall have to develop innovative methods to close the quality and quantity aspects of the existing Training Gap in the Indian Banking Sector. For this re-engineering by optimum use of imagination, technology and feasibility/utility analysis, the immense potential of the following *new/innovative training methods—open/flexible/distance learning, computer based training, inter active video* has to be harnessed. These methods we shall discuss here in some detail. In addition, increased emphasis on simulation exercises like case studies, role plays, business games is required. Also we may have to explose our employees — trainees to complex realities by making them participate in real problem solving under supervised conditions. For example, if possible we should send a mobile/ODI trainer or facilitator to a branch where he sits with the employees and helps in solving concrete problems. *(ODI has been discussed in Chapter 5*—organisational culture related intervention). Also methods as field related projects, Quality Circle, Team Teaching can be emphasised.

Open/Distance/Flexible Learning

Many organisations recently have turned to alternative training methods which do not rely on direct face-to-face contact between trainees and trainers-termed as open and distance/flexible learning "Distance Learning" means that the learner.

* "Is not continuously and immediately supervised by a trainer or tutor.
* Does benefit from the services of a training/tutorial organisation.
* Utilizes materials in a variety of media provided by the training/tutorial organisation.
* Concept of distance refers to a separation in space and time of learners and trainers, although the latter, do provide the learning opportunities".

"Open learning (also known as flexible learning) aims to offer/provide flexibility and autonomy to learner to decide:

* What is learned
* How it is learned
* When it is learned
* Where it is learned
* At what pace learning occurs
* Autonomy is given to learners in the training activity. Such autonomy may or may not be present in distance learning. Separation of trainer and learner may or may not be present in open learning. 'Open' and 'distance' are distinguishable though neither concept is an absolute. Both are continuous on which any particular method or training activity can be placed in comparison with any other.

Need for Open Learning : Necessity of introducing flexible learning in the present banking industrial context is inescapable, at the level of the individual, because it puts into practice what we know about successful learning. Reskilling/ upskilling as an ongoing process is becoming the norm due to technological advances. They are essential components of Strategic HRM approach desired by Indian Banks (vide Ch.5). Our increasingly information based society will need to have training available as a resource in exactly the same way as it has telecommunications systems available at will, with the right messages going to exactly the right recipient. The world we live in, with its demographic and technical change and the move towards total quality management, demands that all individuals should assume greater responsibility for their own learning with some structure to help them. Training has to become a common-place, daily occurrence for most adults. Flexible learning is the successful means by which we can meet the training needs of the working population into the twenty first century encompassing all the delivery methods known to training, from private study to group discussion, and from the new technologies of computer-based training and interactive video to the low technologies of text and face-to-face conversation.

The relevance of open learning is all the more in the context of the Indian Banking Sector where the banking personnel are dispersed over far flung branches, specially in remote rural areas where changes are rapid, the diversities are immense and the institutional training capacity limited.

Characteristics of a good open learning package: Open learning package may be in the form of text, video, audio, computer program, practical kit, or any permutation of these. The medium (or, often, mix of media) should be appropriate for the objectives to be achieved. It should meets the following criteria :

* Objectives, or competences to be achieved through use of the package are clear.
* Learners are required to be active in variety of ways i.e. the package is inter-active and to relate the material to their own experience.
* Learners can progress (through self-assessment question, activities).
* Pace and tone are appropriate to the target group (with material being appropriately divided into units that can be absorbed at a sitting).
* Style is lively, layout contributes to understanding of the material, with clear headings, good typeface, diagrams, with enough space in the workbook for learners to write responses.
* Any multi-media material is well integrated (so that, for instance, there are activities associated with a video).

Successful implementation of open training : Banking Organisations to have successful results with flexible learning, in terms both of cost-effectiveness and of user satisfaction, have to ensure that the following factors are present :

* Genuine interest by senior management.

* Resistance identified and dealt with.
* Learners are given clear guidance on
  — the purpose of the training;
  — self-management of learning, including: allocation of time; regular, short study sessions; systematically completing exercises; relating what they learn to their own situation; sharing ideas and experience with other learners; and consulting resource persons managers, colleagues, trainers, tutors;
  — their own progress; and
  — the overall schedule of the training, including any negotiable features, 'Flexible' does not mean saying to learners' finish any time you like', as this can lead to demotivation and drop out.
* The system is tested with a pilot group to assess its strengths and weaknesses.
* Results of the scheme are disseminated and learners visibly rewarded.

Implications of Open Learning for Organisations : Open learning is not necessarily an easy option — a number of critical issues[5] concerning it require closer examination :

Learner Support : It is often assumed by organisations that learners using open learning can be left to their own devices. But research evidence demonstrates that this is not the case for the vast majority of individuals. Tutorial support likely to be needed is technical support to provide help with the subject matter and content counselling and motivational support to help learners through difficult periods and to provide reassurance. An aspect of support is time and facilities — the organisation initiates and implements a compulsory open learning programme —it is unlikely to succeed on the basis of staff using their own time. Similarly, facilities such as rooms and equipment need to be provided.

Motivation of Learners : Learner motivation is a critical issue in open learning. Many organisations have experienced high dropout rates and low take-up in their programmes. The learner support services can be significant in maintaining motivation. There are in addition further considerations. The way open learning programmes are introduced and implemented is critical. Explanations of what and why and how are necessary to create initial interest and motivation of learners. Another factor is the existence or otherwise of some individual reward. The intrinsic reward of learning and development, is often not enough. The opportunity to acquire a qualification or credit towards one has been found to be a significant motivational factor. Formal recognition in the job also leads to increased motivation.

Managing Programmes: Monitoring and control are of critical importance-setting up systems that can record and track the progress of learners as they move through the programme. It also involves having policies and procedures for ensuring that real needs are identified and met through open learning and, as part of this, that appropriate individuals are entered on the programme(s). Methods of validation and evaluation also need to be designed and applied. All of this demands comprehensive administrative systems.

Resource implications: Open learning can often be more resource-intensive than trainer-delivered programmes. The resources required for learner support and for managing programmes will normally prove quite expensive. This is because of the high development costs of open learning materials and the need for high quality in presentation. In summary open learning is not an easy or cheap option for organisations and several factors have to be considered in utilising this approach for training.

Implications for Trainers : Open learning provides many new possibilities for training professionals in organisations-key points in this context will now be considered.

Open learning v. traditional methods: The first question will be whether or not open learning is likely to be appropriate to meet a particular need in a specific set of circumstances. The list below gives some general guidelines on this.

* The organisation is not satisfied with existing provisions.
* Small numbers are to be trained.
* Large numbers are to be trained, especially in a short time.
* There is a wide geographic spread of those to be trained.
* Training is for critical staff who are difficult to release for traditional courses.

Open learning needs to be well managed and the following factors need to be present or created if it is to be effective :

* Involvement of the organisation through managers, trainers and colleagues.
* Access to tutorial support, both technical and counselling.
* Opportunity for interaction with other learners.
* Quality in materials in terms of presentation and design.
* Confidence and learning skills in learners.
* Provision of reward and extrinsic motivation.

Assessing materials/programmes : The question that arises is which materials or programmes should be chosen. Criteria of assessing materials and programmes are listed below :

* Run a pilot and apply existing evaluation procedures.
* Run a pilot and assess against existing traditional courses.
* Establish the reputation of the providers.
* Assess the extent to which the material is general or industry-specific.

* Assess the cost against other providers and investigate discounts for bulk purchases.

Producing materials in-house: In deciding whether to produce materials in-house the following issues need to be considered :

* Is there a clearly identified need which can be met by open learning?
* Have available materials been thoroughly investigated and assessed?
* Does the organisation have the necessary expertise and skill?
* What is the estimated cost and can it be justified?
* What media will be used and does the organisation have the necessary equipment?

Computer Based Training

The use of computer-based training (CBT) adds a valuable dimension in speeding up decision-making and so compressing the training time-scale. In recent years, micro-technology has contributed to reductions in the cost of computer hardware, opening up opportunities for promoting its use in the training area. Many training applications have been developed which enable computer technology to make more significant contributions to organisational effectiveness, with the added benefit of economics of scale as listed below :

Management of training: The overall management of the training function planning, organising monitoring assessing, recording etc. are generally being implemented by manual systems which are time consuming and complicated. A computer can be a very useful tool in controlling and speeding up these activities, thus reducing the administrative burden. In a large organisation the planning of the department's activities and the management of all its resources, such as instructors, training rooms, equipment, can involve the control of a large number of variables which is not always handled as efficiently as it should be. Resources are allocated arbitrarily as the need arises and without regard for the effects such action create elsewhere. A properly designed computer program can take the guesswork out of such decisions, planning the disposition of resources and providing an instant appraisal of their availability. A trainee's progress through the system can also be more efficiently traced by the computer than by the more common manual means. Details of his educational and occupational background may be stored in the database ready to be received at any time they may be required. This record can also include reports on his training progress, whether as part of a continuing programme or resulting from single modules of training such as technical updating. His future training needs can be fed into the system and the program designed to provide information on the most suitable means of satisfying them.

Learning aid: Use can be made of computers in simulations and business games. In programmed learning with facilities for providing diagrammatic and pictorial displays in colour has simulated the pages of a book, with a provision for student responses and for revision where the answers given are incorrect. The statements made and questions asked are standard and inflexible. In the latest developments a more natural dialogue can take place between man and machine.

Information source for trainees: A computer as a source of information is capable of storing a considerable quantity of data. In the concept of trainee-based learning, learners carrying out training tasks are able to access the information they need through suitable programs in the training room and elsewhere.

Design of training programmes: Trainers can enlist the help of computers when designing their programmes. The system lends itself to a high degree of experimentation with various ideas and approaches, with the advantage of instant modification where necessary. Writing course material in the traditional way may make it unnecessarily unwceldy in the choice and use of language, making the process complicated, the trainees become bored and consequently demotivated. Furthermore, the use of graphical and pictorial representation may not normally be fully exploited, because of the time necessary to produce it. A computerized design system, goes a long way towards reducing these problems. An enormous amount of potential training data can also be stored for retrieval as and when required. Searching for specific information in the database takes fraction of the time needed to work through books and filing cabinets. Since the trainers can be knowledgeable about every aspect of the business likely to be encountered in training, course design has to be a team effort. Detailed information on the topics to be explored has to be obtained from the practitioners, a computer specialist converts that information into a suitable program and the trainer ensures that appropriate training principles are observed.

Testing: A use of computer programs in training is for test purposes for assessing a trainee's progress, that is, it can be employed to measure his performance against certain criteria. Those criteria can be incorporated into the program and the computer can carry out the laborious task of comparing performance of a number of trainees against them. The program can also be designed in such a way that it provides a means of selection for training, thus avoiding expensive mistakes in allowing trainees to embark on training programmes to which they are not suited. By entering appropriate data into the database, tests or exercise may be devised. The correct answers are identified in the program and the accuracy of the trainee's responses communicated either to the trainee himself or to the trainer. The flexibility of testing by computer is demonstrated by one of the more advanced forms of interactive testing, known as *adaptive testing*. Although the program may contain a large number of items designed to test a trainee's comprehension of certain principles, it is not necessary for him to work through all of them or even to satisfy them sequentially in order to demonstrated his understanding. His responses to a limited number of questions will tell whether or not he has grasped the appropriate concepts to satisfy given training objectives. The process of testing can thus be speeded up considerably and can prove less frustrating for the trainee.

Computer saves the training department's time, allowing the staff to undertake more important work. Simulations and business games are attempts to bring reality into training. The computer greatly assists this process and improves the interaction which is so necessary if business is to be accurately modelled in the training room by the graphical and pictorial representation that a computer program can provide. Whereas in traditional training systems, coping with change is time-consuming, computer programs lend themselves more readily to modification as and when required. The results obtained from a computer program will, of course, only be as good as the quality of the programming, which will consequently need to have inputs of a high professional standard. The high cost of such an activity cannot be ignored. Suitable hardware has to be available when it is needed. The trainer must be fully versed in the operation of the equipment and must be aware of the problems that may be encountered as a result of his delegating some of his work to machines. There must be a balance between the use of the computer and other methods or aids in training as there is a risk of de-humanizing the activity, which would be in direct conflict with the true training objectives allowing cross-fertilization of ideas between participants.

With this background, we now proceed to discuss Interactive Video/Multimedia/other hitech technologies which are advancements over CBT.

Interactive Video (IV)

Concept and Components: I.V. combines the advantages of computer-based training with video pictures and sound, producing a unique blend of audio, visual and textual databases which can be received simultaneously from one screen. The combination of these provides a dynamic, more interactive method of training which, while being easy to use, can hold the interest of and motivate the trainee. I.V. is predominantly a training delivery method. It attempts to overcome limitations to the interactive capabilities of computer based training in which computer's responses are limited by the programmer's ability, and the computers ability to recognize key words in typed text, trainees having to choose from a list of options, none of which may correctly reflect their views.

Interactive video offers the full facility of using video sequence during the programme. The video is stored on a laser disk and this is enclosed in a laser player during use. The computer has another two cards inserted into its expansion slots, and these control the video and digital signals before presenting them on the screen with accompanying audio. The computer and its internal program entirely control the use of the laser disk. It can be used to show full video and associated audio, still frame (no sound), and audio only (no picture), the computer itself delivering the text and graphics on to the screen. The user runs the programme using just the keyboard, all the equipment is electronically linked together when it is switched on.

A typical I.V. delivery station will employ the following components:

— *Video disk player* : This is usually a laser video disk (from which the name Laser Vision or Laserdisc are sometimes used for this form of technology). It is the source of the still and moving pictures, or video sequences, and the two audio tracks.

— *Computer power and software* : The computing power can come from an on-board microprocessor or an external computer. Generally, the computer program and video run in tandem. The computer manages the video and audio material recorded on the disk and also supplies computer-generated text and graphics, which may be mixed with the video signals or displayed separately.

— *Monitor* : This is where the computer graphics and text and the video pictures are displayed.

— *Input Device* : This is the user's means of communicating with the system and the program. This can be a keyboard, touch screen, mouse.

— *Interface or Overlay Cards* : A special interface or overlay device, usually in the form of an extra board or card for the computer, is needed to combine (analogue) video material with (digital) computer text and graphics.

Multimedia and other Emerging hi-tech Training Technologies

Multimedia merges a wide array of technologies to satisfy all entertainment, information and communication needs, at a single terminal the personal computer (equipped with a CD-ROM drive and an in-built sound system). An interactive disk top PC wonder which can create, juggle, receive (via on-line services) or simply run (via CD-ROMs) real-life video footage, clear audio and dazzling 3-D images all bundled together with text, and more. It integrates the work of artists, visualisers, musicians and writers with that of software programmers and project managers. "To a regular PC user, multimedia is a tool to smoothen operations, since it allow PCs to behave more like human beings than boxed pieces". It grants instant access to entertainment and information on CD-ROM. Over time, CD-ROMs are expected to become the standard format for dissemination of not just plain information, but just about anything that has visual, text and sound elements." To a communicator, multimedia provides a common base for visual, text and voice communication through a network. To the educator, it brings vividness into instruction, making things easier for the student to understand and retain. A few good teachers could reach out to millions of students. "To the corporate trainer, too, multimedia offers the benefit of conducting training sessions for large numbers without having to congregate at one place, saving time and money.

In the current multimedia market, newer digital technologies, many based on the compact disc (CD), are proliferating, but real training applications are somewhat less presently. The major developments are[6] :

— CD-DA (compact disk-digital audio). Known to most as the "compact disk", this to date has been the most successful of the CD technologies. However, it is primarily limited to home entertainment. It is only occasionally used to extend the audio capabilities of an interactive system.

— CD-V (compact disk-video). Containing a combination of analogue video and digital sound, this has little application in the training market.

— CD-I (compact disk-interactive). This provides a flexible combination of pictures, text and audio which can be self-contained, not needing an external computer.

— CD-ROM (compact disk-read only memory). This is a method of storing large volumes of digital data including text, digitized graphics and databases. It is most suitable for application where large quantities of data which do not need regular updates has to be distributed over a number of sites.

— CO-ROM XA (CD-ROM extended architecture). This adds encoding standards for audio, graphics and still pictures to the basic CD-ROM format.

— DVI (digital video interactive). Similar to CD-I, this is an all-digital medium which allows a flexible mix of multi-media information. The key to it is the methods it uses to compress video, audio and graphical information for storage and then restore it for viewing.

Evaluation of Interactive Video : The latest technology of Interactive Video offers practical advantages over earlier training aids. There are better opportunities for using different instruction and learning strategies, thus introducing greater variety into the training process. Facilities may more easily be built into the programmes to continually assess the trainee's performance and to make modification where necessary to meet his specific requirements. It is reasonable to expect him to be better motivated by his direct involvement in the determination of the content, sequencing and pacing of the project. It should nevertheless be realized that there are also problems in introducing the most advanced technology in interactive video.

A *number of benefits of I.V* have been widely stated :

* It offers increased retention due to the range of formats in which information is presented.
* It leads to a shorter training time compared to traditional classroom training I.V. can cut the required training time by up to a factor of four.
* It has a lower cost per student, because a large number of people can be trained using I.V over a limitless period of time, and because it can reduce the training time.
* It can provide effective, risk-free training, allowing trainees to explore situations without endangering themselves or their relationships with other people.

Despite these benefits, there are *problems with I.V* :

* It needs an I.V workstation on which to run. These can cost a lot.
* It is expensive, in terms of time and money, to update or revise and therefore is not suitable for use with material which may require amending. Disadvantages of CBT as compatibility, flexibility and interface problems are also relevant/apply to I.V.

Other Innovative Methods

We shall now discuss some other innovative methods:

Field Related Projects : Another training strategy is field trips/projects. Bank employees including the subordinate staff can be involved in the survey of the community around the branch (e.g. as required in the service area approach) through which customer needs can be identified and on the basis of which the performance budget of the bank can be prepared. There is need for widening the definition of training by going outside the classroom, to branches, outside a branch to customer groups and interact with the community, evolve schemes to meet the customer expectations.

Quality Circles: Quality Circles movement in banks should provide opportunities to employees for individual growth as a whole person and also let them see how they can harmonise their growth with organisation's growth. Issue of more circulars from the Head Office is not the way to initiate the movement which has to be voluntary, can be initiated best through the training system where trainers have learned to work as facilitators and can get the line executives also to work as facilitators. Canara Bank ranks first in the Banking Industry in having highest number of Quality Circle (425). The staff's problem solving skills are sharpened and involvement is redoubled. The work atmosphere is transformed and quality of work life improved. Canara Bank's striking efforts need to be emulated by the other Indian Banks and the inter bank differences in the introduction of HRD innovations like quality circle needs to be reduced.

Team Teaching: Training programmes involving simulation methods, field projects etc. should be run by a group of trainers as a team consisting of full time institutional trainers, trainers from line or staff department e.g. a personnel department officer, a participant who is expected to participate in that training programme. For example, if a programme is on performance budgeting, a branch manager who will be participating in that programme may join the team of trainers. The team teaching mode will bring in a culture of sharing information/experience, brain storming and evolving strategies appropriate to situations on the ground. It will also usher in an open participatory culture required for Quality Circle movement and for applying super market concept of banking where certain types of problems are to be solved on the shop floor and for which the employees have to show concern for the customer needs, take initiative and ensure quick decision making. It's important to promote "inquiry," a learning process which helps participants to learn on their own.

Re-engineering: Other Aspects of Training Delivery Mechanism

We shall now discuss reengineering of the following aspects: (1) Trainer effectiveness (2) Training Aids (3) Trainees Selection.

Re-Engineering Training: Trainer Effectiveness

The research and workshops on trainer effectiveness carried out by Regional Management Centre at Slough and Oxford identified a number of key areas that influence trainers effectiveness. This checklist summarizes the more important factors in each area.

Trainer Competences: Research suggested the following :

* Ability to motivate learners and to hold their interest.
* Good knowledge of the subject matter or area in which people are being trained.
* Capacity to communicate and present information, and ideas, in a meaningful way.
* Ability to relate the training to the practical world of the trainees, using appropriate examples.
* Being able to control the learning group.

Trainer Characteristics: Though the range of characteristics is clearly very diverse the research indicates the following to be important contributions to effectiveness (Bennett 1993)[7]:

* Being sensitive to the need of the learners.
* Projecting enthusiasm, motivation, interest and dedication.
* Being prepared to listen to what learners have to say.

* Being approachable, patient responsive and sensitive.
* Having confidence in and commitment to the approach adopted.
* Being seen to be 'credible'.

Trainer Role Orientation: This refers to the way in which the trainers sees their role. Two key dimensions were established from the research, and imply four basic orientations.

* An orientation to the maintenance needs of the organisation, that is, to ensuring the continuance of the existing.
* An orientation to traditional methods of training based largely on classroom-type techniques and curriculum design.
* An orientation to bringing about change within the organisation, that is, to ensure that training can respond to pressures for change.
* An orientation to methods of intervention, that is, a 'change agent' approach to training that involves greater participation in bringing about changes.

These aspects affecting the functioning of trainers have to be kept inview while re-engineering the training system of Indian Banks.

Re-engineering Training: Training Aids

Effective use of training aids isessential for re-engineering the training systems of Indian Banks. The range of aids available to help the trainers deliver successful training can be classified into a number of broad categories:

— Printed materials all texts, handouts and the like.

— Non-projected materials a variety of visual display materials, for example models, posters, flipcharts and marker-boards.

— Video materials video tape, video disc, broadcast television and film.

— Still projected material overhead projector transparencies slides and microfilm.

— Audio materials audiotape, compact disc and broadcast radio.

— Computer-based materials these may involve the application of a computer alone or a computer used in conjunction with other materials enabling multi-media based training.

Why use Training Aids? Proper training aids, or instructional materials, can enhance the effectiveness of the training/ learning process. They can:

— and variety to the learning process, maintain interaction involvement and motivation.

— provide certain stimuli not available without their use.

— benefit those learners whose learning style responds better to one type of approach than another.

— facilitate planning and preparation before the training session/lesson.

According to Bell the aids will be effective if they are chosen and used paying due regard to:

— the training objectives.

— the learners characteristics.

— the characteristics of the various aids available; and

— how the aids will be integrated with other training facets.

Appropriate Training Aids Selection: There are important considerations to contemplate when selecting the most appropriate aids for any given training need. Research indicates that most aids can perform most instructional functions, but that some are better than others for achieving certain objectives.

The starting point for planning any training must be to establish what objectives are to be achieved and whether these are best achieved by mass instruction, group or individual learning. Training aids must be relevant to the purpose for which they were created and to the learner's level of understanding. Different aids lend themselves to different types of training/ learning systems (mass, group or individual instruction).

Re-engineering Training — Trainees Selection

The effectiveness of the training programme depends on the participants proper selection. In order that the training programme should be successful, "the participant :

— should be motivated to learn.

— should have the basic education/ability to understand and assimilate the training programme offering.

— should be able/allowed to use the newly acquired skill in the near future which otherwise, he forgets if he fails to practise for a long time.[8] "

This depends to a large extent, on the management since he should be working in the area in which training has been imparted and the responsibility of providing the infrastructure and facilities rests with the management. The organisation cannot get any real benefit unless the participants use these skills in the near future for improved productivity, though the trainees may have acquired new skills to a very high degree/ specialisation.

Andragogy — Trainees as Adult Leaners: Andragogy, the art and science of helping adults to learn, is premised on at least four crucial assumptions about the characteristics of adult learners on which traditional pedagogy is promised. These assumptions are that, as a person matures:

1. his self concept moves from one of being a dependent personality toward one of being self-directing human being;
2. he accumulates a growing reservoir of experience that becomes an increasing resource for learning;

3. his readiness to learn becomes oriented increasingly to the developmental tasks of his social role; and
4. his time perspective changes from one of postponed application of knowledge to immediacy of application and accordingly his orientation toward learning shifts from one of subject centredness to one of problem-centredness.

Notes

1. Varshneya, J.S., Assessment of Training Needs, Strategies for meeting these and Preparation of Calendar of Programmes. In *Indian Journal of Training and Development*, Vol. XX, No. 5 & 6, Sept.-Dec., 90.

2. Ravi Shankar, T.S., Towards Structural Changes in Banking,-Prajanan (*Journal of NIBM,* Pune) Vol. XXI, No. 4, Jan-March, 1993, pp. 451.

3. Suneja, *Innovation in Banking Services*. Bombay: Himalayan Publishing House, 1994.

4. Rao, P.P. Deposit mobilization in Banks—Beliefs and Values and Strategies of Branch Managers—*Prajanan* Vol., XXII, No. 4, Jan-March, 1994.

5. Stewart, Jim and Winter, Rosemary, Open and Distance Learning in Steve Truelove (Ed), *Handbook of Training and Development* Blackwell Publishers, U.K. 1992.

6. Chatterton, P. and Wright, T., Emerging Technologies. In S. Hoflos (Ed), *Interactive Video Yearbook 1990*, London: NIVC.

7. Bennett, Roger, The effective Trainer checklist. In Prior, John (Ed): *Handbook of Training and Development*. Hants: Gower Publishing Company, 1993.

8. Krishna, C. Murali, Trivikrama B., Murthy, P.S.S. Are we getting the 'Right' Participants for our training programmes? New Delhi: I.S.T.D.: *Indian Journal of Training and Development*, Vol. XXIII, No. 4, October-December 1993.

7

Reengineering Training for Globalisation: Critical Training Areas

Overview: The strategy for reengineering the HRD and Training Systems of the Indian Banking Sector in order to bridge the existing gap, has so far covered aspects relating to proactive HRD interventions for improving organizational culture (Chapter 5) and parameters of effective training delivery (Chapter 6). In addition, the reengineering endeavour has to emphasize the coverage of critical training areas so that the Indian banks are able to meet the demands of globalisation/financial sector reforms/liberalization even while meeting their social obligations as required in a developing nation.

Some of these critical area which we shall be discussing are :

1) Training for preparing Indian Banks for International Operations.
2) Training for information technologies/computerisation (for keeping up with the global trends and handling the complex voluminous work load efficiently).
3) Training for improving productivity/customer service in banks (including a marketing orientation and behavioural science training for inculcating the requisite attitudes in the training personnel.)

4) Management Development Programmes, Management Self Development for enhancing the leadership/coping/problem solving capabilities of bank personnel.

The critical areas of training for effective Rural Development Banking and Women in Development/Gender Issues, we shall cover in the following chapters.

Training for Preparing Indian Banks for International Operations/Globalisation

The difficult environment in which Indian banks abroad will have to operate, the competition they will face, the needs of customers at the foreign centres demands that we prepare the banks to face the challenges of International Banking of this sort. In their operations at the international financial centres, Indian banks would have to satisfy certain minimum conditions. A major one will be the financial strength of the Indian banks and their ability to command good international ratings. Mechanisation, computerisation and electronic banking systems would be an essential pre-requisite for a bank to function at international finance centres.

The staffing pattern is another area to be looked into. Many Indian banks rely substantially on expatriate staff to satisfy the operational and managerial needs of foreign office. "While the skills of Indian staff are of high standards, the other features such as lack of familiarity with the local environment and short-term tenures abroad result in a situation where the expatriate staff are unable to give their best"[1]. This situation also discourages a large number of foreign companies from actively dealing with the Indian banks. The preparation of Indian banking personnel to cope with the extensive and intensive domain of international banking is a fundamental issue : the right man for the right job at the right time, represents the crux of managing commercial banks' international operations. With a meagre branch spread foreign banks in India have not ched a considerable share in the total profits of the banking industry in the country. This indicates how these banks have, amongst others, groomed their personnel to manage their business so well. They have trained the eyes, ears and minds of their personnel to remain at the top of the business. It is clear that if Indian commercial banks are to succeed in their international operations, they must not only pick up the correct people, both local and expatriate but also equip them with the knowledge, skills and capabilities to tap the business and service it in a scenario of intense international competition. While exposing the personnel to well-chalked-out learning programmes centred on new activities and innovations in international banking, care has to be taken to see that they do also stand adequately exposed to exploit the opportunities and handle threats in the existing and emerging market environments.

All the human and material resources, strategic plans, and training and other systems can yield results only if banks are provided with a measure of operational freedom that the international environment demands.

A Suggested Curriculum for International Banking/Global Transactions would comprise of the following:

1. Skills to manage progressive liberalization and greater competitiveness in the economy and other related challenges on the banking and financial systems of the country.

2. Understanding of the changing nature of the international capital markets.

3. Need for expanding the country's foreign trade, setting up of joint ventures abroad, attracting savings of non-resident Indians, Investment Banking.

4. Understanding the process of technology transfer.

5. Handling of a wide range of innovative financial instruments such as commercial paper, floating fixed rate bonds, currency swaps, euronotes etc.

6. Skills to deal with fluid markets and complicated international transactions particularly in view of the possible need for depending on commercial

borrowings in future because of deteriorating economic environment for official and concessional capital flows, both bilateral and multilateral.

7. Skills for evaluation of new sophisticated industries in terms of their technical, marketing and other inputs.

Indian Banks, in their international operations, in order to compete successfully with foreign banks, have to provide top quality banking services. For this, their HRD and Training systems have to be given the suggested inputs.

Re-engineering Training in the Context of Information Technology/Computerisation and Mechanisation in Indian Banks:

Background : There is a growing awareness of the need for computerisation to cope with the explosive growth in volume and variety of Indian Banking services. Computer services are also being used increasingly. The first industry level settlement relating to mechanisation and computerisation took place during 1983, a fresh settlement was arrived at during March, 1987 and subsequently Computers are already being used extensively in industry—for process control and managerial decision making. A network of information centres is also being set up at the district level for monitoring the performance of the economy beginning from metropolitan centres— Indian banks should do likewise.

Indian Banks should devote attention to bringing about gradual reduction of their non-performing assets, better cost effectiveness and higher profits, improving operational efficiency and aggressive marketing. Demands for sophisticated services will also compel banks to examine the technology alternative seriously, having regard to the cost-benefit aspects. Banks have already taken several initiatives for progressive mechanisation and computerisation; however, their range and depth must increase further. For better management control over operations, improving productivity and responding more efficiently to emerging areas, banks will have to strengthen the training sub-system — not only for improving the skill level in their employees but also the attitudinal aspects of their inter-relationship with customers. Collaborative efforts need to be fostered and specialisation encouraged as recommended by the National Banking Plan document.

Training needs in Information Technology: Training needs in information technology can be looked at from the angles of the individual level, the occupational level and the organisation level (Dell).

— *Individual level training needs* : The executives who run the banking system today and who grew up in an era when computers were not part of the society, need to be trained most through different strategies. Banks could provide all executives upto the level of, say Regional managers with a PC connected to the central computer/mini computers so that they can retrieve what they need and generate any desired output. To encourage the executives to use the computers provided to them it would be a good idea to also given them 'resource persons' — officials/employees with requisite skills in computers and software who will develop application packages, needed by the executives.

— *Training needs at other levels*: This depends on the role of the employees concerned e.g. these working in data processing centres—their needs can be met by technology-based training programmes; some working say at the foreign exchange desk their needs could be met by role-based training. 'Education has gone through distinct phases; beginning with mass education, it came down to individual education and is now moving towards group education. Computer technology too is moving from PCs to work stations, from the former's individual productivity to the latter groups productivity. Group learning should hence be the key element of technology training in banks'. For this banks can follow the *Coverdale method* whose focus is not on more knowledge acquisition and retention, but on 'applying in practice what's already known to the participants'. In the training situation, participants from different backgrounds are brought together to form stranger groups-the members in each such group work together and carryout small blocks of work, called 'tasks'.

Decentralised Computer Based Training : Computer based training divisions should be set up by all banks, headed by senior bankers, well versed in banking, educational technology and computer technology. For this `banks could set up Computer learning rooms in all their training colleges/centres and large branches. Subsequently the Computer Based Training divisions could prepare the course material on banking business and provide them to the centres, where computer learning-rooms have been set up. The responsibility for training should be entrusted to a faculty at the training set-up or a supervisory member of the branch staff. The Computer Based Training Divisions could also prepared embedded training software — i.e., teaching material relevant to each desk where computers might have been already installed.'[2]

The purpose of using technology in training is to :

— decrease the learning time.

— increase the quality of learning.

— increase the trainers efficiency without sacrificing learning quality.

— reduce costs, without affecting quality.

The items deal with the intangible aspects of educational technology called the underware as opposed to hardware and software. The emphasis is on the teaching techniques and learning rather than the aids used. The Banks should impart technology training and also use technology in doing so. The former prepares the trainees for the emerging era; the latter enables the trainees to do so faster—without sacrificing quality.

I.T. Important Training Areas : Areas[3] which would require attention in respect of computer based information technology in the immediate future would be Computer Security, Auditing, Faculty training and Attitudinal Reorientation.

— *Security*: The important threat posed by breach of security of a computer based information system in the banking context is that concerning the privacy of information pertaining to individuals and institutions due to risk of confidential information falling into wrong hands. The systems which hold and process vital data have to be protected against e.g. virus attack or failure through such measures e.g. validation checks on input data, installation of fire resistant safes to protect media as security threats may be either accidental or deliberate. Courses designed in this area could cover aspects like security of data within the computer and at the man-machine interface to overcome the wide gap between the protection under experimental conditions and that actually implemented in the banking systems.

— *Computer Auditing*: Computer auditing has to catch up with the increasing tempo of use of computers in the banking industry. EDP auditing is required by Indian Banks to determine whether a computer system safeguards assets, maintains data integrity, achieves organisational goals effectively and consumes resources at an optimum rate.

— *Faculty Training*: Computer and Communication provides the thrust towards modernisation in banking. While Colleges of banks have provided adequate faculty in respect of operational aspects relating to banking, the same cannot be said about computer/communications. There is need for augmenting and strengthening of the faculty in this area. Efforts would have to be directed to selection and training of faculty from amongst the existing ranks or even from the computer industry. Banks would follow the State Bank of India in establishing a separate Institute of Technology for imparting training on this rapidly developing discipline.

— *Reorientation of Attitudes* : Systems and procedures, check points etc. in banks are those to which the staff in the banks are accustomed. Decision support system based computer data is something which will perhaps deny many executive of the feeling of indispensability and innovativeness. The Staff Unions are also well organised and resistant. Training will have to persuade managerial cadres and Unions to respond positively and adopt to technological changes, to move from paper and file based scrutiny to interactive screen mode. People have to think/react on the keyboard rather than with a pencil/pen in hand and following printed material on paper.

Online Education and Development

As yet little-used technology in the educational and training world—*Computer mediated communications systems (CMCS)* offers enormous possibilities for enhancing educational provision by the potential they give to offer online education Computer-mediated communications systems connotes any form of communication that occurs over a network of computers — using of computers to send and receive textual communications. The text is often held in mainframe computer where it can be retrieved any time. Electronic mail demonstrated this store and retrieve principle; E-mail is most suitable for person-to-person communications. Where interactive group communication is important, *computer conferencing* allows groups of people to communicate. Electronic meeting differ from face-to-face meetings (McConnell, 1990) and requires new ways of thinking about the meaning of group work when it is mediated via computers.

The basic set up requires a host computer where the CMCS software is held, and computer terminals or personal computers capable of connecting with the host to allow users to interact with the CMCS software. If there are large numbers of users and if access is needed by several users at the same time, then the host computer will usually be a mainframe computer. Users can access the CMCS software by a variety of methods, using a variety of equipment.

Training Implications for Requisite Computing Skills: There are three levels of computing operations ideally required for computer conferencing: work processing skill, telecommunication skill; conferencing skill. This has important implications for training.

— *Word Processing Skill*: For effective use of CMCS, one should prepare the text of time, personal messages and responses before going into a conference.

— *Telecommunication Skill*: For linking the personal computer to the host computer by use of communications software. The user joins the conferences of interest to them and networks (i.e. receives on their own PC) conference text and personal messages etc.

— *Conferencing Skill*: For reading new items and responses, adding new responses, sending personal messages etc.

Online Education and Training Characteristics: Online education and training is different from face to face meetings as follows[4]:

1. People from geographically distant sites 'meet' without physically travelling to one location so there are time and travel savings (and therefore financial savings, although there will be initial capital set-up costs, and recurring costs).
2. Meetings are continuous - a meeting on line can take place over a defined time span (e.g. a week or a month) or can continue indefinitely (for months or years).
3. There is a permanent record of the meeting and of the participants contribution to it (this can be manipulated like a database).

4. Social presence, process and product of online meetings often differ from face-to-face meetings.
5. It enables people to work collaboratively in group. It can support co-operative learning and group process in ways that may be difficult to achieve in face-to-face meetings.
6. CMCS offers democratisation of educational exchanges in not having to interrupt others or talk over people in order to say what you want to say within a conference. All users have the same access to the dialogue-visual cues denoting status and power are eliminated.

Uses of CMCS: The possible uses of computer conferencing within education and training are a complete replacement for face-to-face meetings; as an adjunct to them; as a multimedia approach to teaching and learning.

— *Complete Replacement*: Computer conferencing may be used to replace conventional face-to-face meetings, either by offering these meetings electronically at a distance for geographically isolated learners, or by offering them as a viable alternative to in-house courses. It can provide continuing education courses for industry and commerce, and for teachers in service education work.

— *Adjunct Method*: Electronic communication is also suitable as an adjunct to face-to-face meetings. Electronic seminars and tutorials can add a useful and interesting focus to on-campus and in-house courses. Material covered in lectures can be added to and complemented in a computer conference. Students can question the trainer about the course, request additional information or add their own information.

— *Multi-media approach*: It is exemplified by resource — based learning which emphasizes a variety of different media and approaches to teaching and learning -- for example, in an Open University course in information technology alongwith all the usual packaged learning materials provided as part of the course (course text units: audio-cassettes; broad-cast television; a course reader, supplementary readings, course guides, and so on), students are also given access to computer conferences. The latter is one of several alternative ways of learning on the course-variety of media available to meet the varying learning needs of the students (Mason and Kaye, 1989[5]).

Applicability or CMCS to Indian Banking: A wider use of CMCS within education and training for banking industry appears feasible because of the following :

* personal computer prices are continuing to fall, and PCs are increasingly being used at home and work.

* text processing and communications software is becoming more sophisticated and user friendly.

* networks for online education and training are gradually becoming widely available—users can access CMC systems via ordinary telephone lines, via data lines or through private local area networks.

Manpower Planning and Training Strategy for Banks' Computerisation: The success of computerisation depends on the participation of people involved in the project. In networking the various parties involved include the party developing the network software and planning and the hardware configuration- usually an outside vendor. Alongwith the vendor developing the package, the banks should also appoint computer literate managers from the banks to interact with outside specialists at various stages of the project. This will help the bank to specify its requirements to the vendor, and maintain the system, once it becomes operational. It is very necessary for the banking professionals to clearly explain their application requirements to the vendor and also to develop the capability to add banks own set of messages.

Networking is a specialized area where investments in hardware and software are heavy and the bank's top management and customers will have high expectations about the service they are going to get. The success of any network depends mainly on how well the system is maintained and how widely the system is used. Hence, training the top management of the bank through awareness programme will be essential, since unless they appreciate and actively use the network, the networking of computers will be futile exercise.[6]

Specialists from junior management level who know about the hardware and software should be trained by the leading academic institutions like—National Centre for Software Technology (NCST), National Institute of Bank Management (NIBM) etc. to manage and develop applications. The strategy should be that the banking industry create a separate subsidiary to deal with networking on the lines of the National Informatic Centres and CITYCORP which is a software subsidiary of CITYBANK. There are problems particularly of manpower in the computer industry, since the number of specialists in this field are few compared to the requirement. Hence, people change the company very fast. In order to retain the professionals, the banking industry needs to evolve novel personnel policies and methods.

Computerised cheque clearing systems, on-line transactions, automatic teller machines etc. are becoming common features in banking and financial institutions even in developing countries like ours. 'Computer crime is advancing just as fast as the technology, and banks managements may not be fully aware of the potential problems. All banking and financial institutions should develop specialists skill to address every aspect of security and safety of information technology[7].'

Re-engineering HRD/Training for Improvement in Productivity/Customer Service in Indian Banks

Background and Concepts: In the last two decades of post-nationalisation period all-round expansion in banking business has brought with it problems like declining standards of customer service, poor maintenance, depleted profits and profitability of banking. This is due to increasing quantum of non-performing financial assets, increasing administration costs and decling manpower productivity.

Banks, which are service oriented organisations, in the face of increasing competition, in future shall have to develop themselves as financial super markets. "Banks the world over are becoming financial super markets providing a wide variety of services and facilities, many of which are far removed from the traditional banking activities.... In our country too, customer requirements are getting more and more sophisticated.... Be it rural banking or metropolitan banking, there is a need to enlarge the package of schemes and services offered, based on customers convenience and preferences. In a situation like ours, where banks have limited freedom in terms of offering attractive returns, the major thrust of marketing strategy should be to widen the range of products offered and improve the quality of services rendered" (Chairman, IBA 1987).

Productivity is a measure of how well the resources are brought together in an organisation and accomplishing a set of objectives — output per unit of input. It connotes reaching the highest level of performance with the least of expenditure of resources. The concept of productivity is understood in different ways/different functions—for a personnel functionary, it is a ratio between the output and the manpower, whereas for an engineer it is output per machine, improved earnings/profits/profitability can be the productivity concept for a finance executive. We shall consider productivity improvement through training in Indian Banks so as to improve customer service/other important areas. We shall view productivity as a function of both effectiveness and efficiency—effectiveness refers to performance and efficiency to resources utilisation.

Issues in productivity improvemen: With declining profitability and recruitment bar, productivity improvement is the only workable solution on manpower front. We shall consider the characteristics of the Indian Banking Industry and measurement issues in relation to productivity.

Characteristics of the Banking Service Industry

— Banking being a service industry is labour intensive where the human factor has pivotal rŏle in running the business. Men unlike machines have different attitudes, cultures and aspirations. The management of human resources attains special significance in case of banking industry.

— Measurement of quantity and quality of both input and output, is difficult in service industry. Quality control poses problems since the service is not a commodity. The demand for service is not foreseeable since service is provided on-the-spot.

— The outlets provided for rendering service to the customers are the thousands of widely dispersed branches which pose a challenge. Also banks have to offer very diverse services.

— The reliance of evaluation on a subjective judgement like service is prompt or otherwise.

— Control mechanisms such as inspection/withdrawal of the product is also not possible as the manifest behaviour on-the-spot is a service, sound or defective, that already is released.

Productivity Related Measurement Issues

— Most of the banks have a four-tier organisational structure—comprising corporate, zonal/circle, divisional/regional and branch levels. Top management confines itself to policy function, senior management to policy analysis and formulation of strategies, middle management takes up administrative coordinating functions, while the grassroots level performs routine operational activities. Productivity measurement must encompass all these decision making and implementing levels, rather than focusing on operational management.

— For productivity management indicators, certain criteria which need to be fulfilled are:

* Qualitative aspects of banking business shall have to be given due consideration alongwith the quantitative.
* The productivity norms shall relate to the performance appraisal to facilitate discrimination amongst better and poor performers.
* The indices should be simple and comprehended by staff at all levels so that their acceptability for improvement is increased.
* Work technology—present and future shall have to be given due attention due to its impact on work processes and methods of supervision.
* Intelligent segmentation of customers on the basis of their psychographic nature has to be done (e.g. business vs. service based customer, urban vs. rural and their subcategories) and banking services beamed to them specifically.[8]

Customer Service Tasks: A banker shall have to perform the following tasks in the context of customer service[9] :

(a) Identify the needs of the customer. The customer may be an illiterate or even when educated, may not be able to verbalise his needs by questioning him and other measures.

(b) Retrieve relevant information from various sources for example, other departments in the banks, government agencies.

(c) Transform the need of the customer into a banking operation e.g. when a customer likes to send money to somebody in some other town and the banking official finds out whether DD, or TT is the most appropriate operation.

(d) Take decision after weighing the different factors, the strengths and weakness of the customer/scheme and implement the decision and get other agencies to implement.

(e) Follow-up the decision-keep in touch with the customer, supervise the end use of the services offered, counsel the customer wherever necessary.

Changing Organisational Culture: At different levels and at different desks many other specific skills will be required of a banker to perform the job. These skills are required not only by executives or by officers but even by clerks and to a certain extent even by the subordinate staff all of whom have to be used for customer service. Here sermons on customers service will not produce results unless certain systems and procedures in the bank are changed e.g. mechanisation introducing computer system. Lectures alone by higher authorities are not going to be effective, monetary incentive is not positively co-related with motivation resulting in high productivity or job satisfaction. The employees in the banking organisation have crossed the stage of physiological or security needs as well as to a great extent the social needs (Maslows' need hierarchy). The banking industry is recruiting graduates from diverse disciplines who are above average in terms of their intelligence and will not automatically accept the values/practices of an organisation. This means that alongwith the change in systems and procedures, industry shall have to re-examine the organisation, structure and the psychological environment i.e. work culture in the organisation e.g. through delegation and participation. An employee gets affected if a customer is not satisfied and should synchronise his personal achievement goals with the organisational goals. The Indian Banking industry is a service industry — an important instrument of national development. To get the bank employees see this relationship between the banks roles as an instrument of national development and his role as an employee of that bank, the training strategy shall have to be suitably geared.

Training Intervention for Productivity Improvement: Training System, being the means to attain an organisational goal like productivity improvement has to undertake a significant role. HRD divisions shall have to initiate and coordinate productivity improvement programmes but the message of productivity down-the-line has to reach through the training system of each bank. The enormous applied research requirements for the task can be carried out by training systems' multi-disciplinary faculty. Relaxed environment available in a training situation enables faculty and participants to be frank with a down-to-earth approach. Productivity improvement task would require creating productivity awareness at all the levels, identifying reliable tools for carrying branch level productivity studies, creating database about the total bank in relation to productivity indicators, discussions with employees. Organisation's training system would mobilise the resources to undertake studies, provide research support and create awareness for productivity and quality through training programmes.

We shall now discuss two other important HRD/Training aspects related to improvement in customer service/ productivity in banks (1) Inculcating marketing orientation to satisfy customer needs and to target banking services for greater profitability, (2) Behavioural Science Training for such objectives as inculcating customer friendly attitudes.

HRD/Training Implications of Marketing Orientation/Mix of Indian Banking Services

Concept/need for the marketing orientation: The role of the banking sector continues to grow in a developing economy like India. It can serve the needs of the society only when it can adopt to the changing needs and preferences of its customers. In this context, marketing approach is required for banking services. Earlier banks were selling their services. But now very careful and planned marketing strategy[10] has to be evolved. Both private and public sector companies are collecting deposits directly from the public by passing even the banks and a number of funds, National Savings Certificates etc. have succeeded in collecting huge amounts of money for the exchequer directly.[11] Also other compulsions are: areas of profitability of banking business, need for innovative product development, emergence of new range of banking services, ensuring optimum use of vast banking services, ensuring optimum use of vast banking infrastructure, resources crunch and poor recovery factors. So development of marketing approach to Indian Banking becomes imperative and must be emphasised in the training/HRD programmes of the banking sector. So banks have to think of marketing their services not only in terms of their deposit mobilisation and related activities but also streamlining techniques for a healthy credit portfolio.

Marketing mix meaning 'combination of the elements which make up the marketing programmes', comprises of 4 Ps. of marketing; Product, Pricing, Place and Promotion. In case of service organisation marketing mix includes two other elements such as People and Procedures, popularly known as 6 Ps which have to cleverly adapted to the changing external environment.

HRD/Training implications of the marketing orientation: Training/HRD programmes for inculcating the marketing approach among Indian Banking personnel will have to highlight the various issues involved in marketing mix variables, which will now be discussed:

1. *Price*: Price refers to the amount of money a customer is willing to pay for the service. Though the price is one of powerful marketing tools, pricing strategy has limited scope in the banking sector because of the controls exercised by the Reserve Bank- banks should have more control over pricing strategy.

2. *Place*: Place mix refers to location of the service that the bankers have to offer to the clients—branch location and distribution are important areas of marketing of banking services, in urban, semi-urban and rural areas. While marketing banking services, the distribution strategy is mainly used to expand the branch network to those areas where potential for

deposit mobilisation and credit requirements exist. Distribution of branches along with location, work load working hours etc. has to be studied by the bankers for catering to the needs of the customers. The present working hours are not convenient for the majority of the bank's customers - in urban areas banks could be opened during the early morning and late evening hours, to facilitate customers to attend to banking transactions without any disturbance to their normal activities.

3. *Product*: Trading business first decides the products to be produced, by knowing the needs of the customers and take a number of decisions as to product additions, modifications, on the basis of marketing information. "Unless the banks quickly respond to the emerging needs of the clients, other institutions will grab the opportunity. Therefore, it is in their own interest that they anticipate, identify and provide all kinds of new services that are needed by the public." The banks products can be considered as under three categories: Credit, deposit schemes and ancillary services:

    — *Credit Schemes*: Banks have designed several credit schemes such as term loans, banks overdrafts, advances, consumer loans, Loan Linked deposit schemes, loan to pensioners, loan against Government securities, housing finance etc.

    — *Deposit Schemes* : A wide range of deposit schemes or different sections of society have been offered by the commercial banks in India—saving bank account, current accounts, recurring deposit accounts, fixed deposit accounts, cash certificates, etc. and new/innovative financial services like mutual funds, loan syndication, housing finance merchant banking, Stock invest schemes[13]:

— *Ancillary Services*: Banks also offer various ancillary services to the customers like bank drafts, telegraphic transfers, Safe deposit lockers, Credit cards and consultancy, etc.

Some of the *product related issues* which the Indian Banks have to consider are :

— *Improper market assessment:* Since the banks launched some of the deposit and credit schemes without properly assessing their market potential, the schemes had to be withdrawn. There is need to plan new products in a proper way.

— Since the schemes and features are almost uniform in every bank, the only way to create product differentiation is by providing high quality services along with the offering of the product—the qualities of services offered and courtesy with customer is deteriorating in most of the nationalised banks.

— As banks are not able to fully mobilize rural savings they should develop new schemes to suit the needs of rural customers.

— *Credit card system popularisation:* When more people take to credit cards it will reduce the cash payment and cash withdrawals at the bank counters, leading to less customers, banks will earn extra income by way of service charges, the customers will get a convenient mode of payment.

4. *Promotion*: The promotional aspects in marketing of banking services related to activities like advertising, publicity, public relations, personal selling which aim at customer information and customer communication.

— *Personal Selling*: Personal selling marketing of banking services implies a direct or face-to-face contact with the customer. Personal selling is prominent in the areas of deposit mobilisation where the employees use their personal selling skills to meet the targets set. Retaining or renewing, deposits, loan arrangements instead of premature encashment of deposits are few of the other areas where personal selling is required.

— *Public Relations*: The main goal of public relations is building a favourable opinion among the public that are neutral and attempting to change the attitude and opinions, of those who are unriendly to the organisation. In the marketing of banking services, adopting public relations and community services concept is more important to build and maintain beneficial relationships with the target groups and the community. The bank as a whole has to be more sensitive and responsive to the needs and expectations of the customer. Banks in association with social organisations should undertake various community welfare services such as organising medical and health care camps, tree plantation programmes etc., for improvement of the people's economic situation and further improving the bank's image.

5. *People*: In a service industry like banking, the quality of human resources is of vital importance as Banking is essential person-to-person business. Bank customers would prefer to do business with a bank whose staff are well informed and well disposed. Though banks have limited discretion in pricing they can acquire competitive edge in offering better customer service through their staff. For this the best personnel will be selected, motivated and trained to conduct marketing functions in a much better way via human efficiency and personalised services.

6. *Procedures*: Procedures are an integral part of the marketing of banking activities. The management should communicate the procedures involved in the banking transactions in a better manner e.g. the procedures for giving loans are cumbersome and illiterate, rural customer finds it difficult to complete these procedures. So the banks can simplify the procedures as the need of the hour is consumer orientation rather than procedure orientation.

Thus, if the Indian banks are to make big strides in the 21st century against the threats and challenges from various corners, they will have to become market-oriented. The acceptance of the marketing concept of bank management would also necessitate creation of marketing organisation in the banks. When everybody offers the same range of service with similar technology and expertise, the level of customer service will matter the most in bringing more business. Here the approach and attitude towards customers will make as much difference as the efficiency of service rendered. Serious thought will have, therefore, to be given to motivate/inspire the banking staff to deliver 'satisfaction' to the customers.

Behavioural Science Training in Banks

Relevance and Focus: Training generally imparts knowledge, improves skills and reorients attitudes: behavioural science (BS) work is used in the area of attitudinal changes which is of immense importance in a service industry like Banking. BS training in Banks is mainly done through institutional training which provide BS as one part of a large programme that they conduct in omnibus programmes like the Induction and Orientation Programmes for Clerks and Officers, General Management Programmes for Branch Managers/Accountants.

These BS sessions touch such areas as Communication, Motivation, Perception, Interpersonal Relations, Leadership, etc. The BS Training could lead to better customer service and solve some of the banks' problems (e.g. cover the seven. Is listed in the World Bank Study in Chapter 4).

BS Technology: Mostly comes through the structures, comprises of concept sessions (communication, perception etc.), exercise or "games" (tower building, prisoners dilemma etc.), Transactional Analysis to cover ego states and the nature of transactions. Sometimes films are also used on some BS subjects.

BS Trainers and Trainees: Many Banks continue to depend on guest speakers who come from diverse fields, are assigned "tops" in the BS area and they are selected on the basis of their reputation. The problem with guests is that they cannot link their inputs either with other inputs of the programme or the day-to-day situation in the Banks if they are non-bankers. Participants responses to the BS input in a general training programme range from attraction to reservation to hostility. The novelty of the subject and novelty of the technology used create an attraction. When discussion leaves participants in many doubts which cannot be further discussed for want of time, they decide to take the whole thing with reservation. Hostility would arise out of the use of the technology of exercises and instruments. Interpretation of the participant's data in an exercise may not be acceptable to the participant. For the participant, it becomes a question of his image. He takes a defensive stand. Many participants raise doubts about the trainer's ability to train. These varied responses create problems; Bank managements do not carry on these sessions with certain commitment because the responses are not uniformly positive, they do not change the content of these sessions because the resources are limited and they do not fully stop these sessions because they are not totally useless.

BS Programmes : Some banks where BS is valued sometimes conduct an entire programme with BS input mainly for the managerial class. It may be in areas like achievement motivation training, leadership, development of change agents, team building. Most Banks do such programmes with outside help either fully or jointly with inhouse faculty. Internal resources for exclusively doing such programmes are available with a very few Banks. Some programmes are in the form of

O.D. intervention-diagnosis of working groups is made and interventions using behavioural science are designed and made.

BS Training in Banks: Issues and Strategies : This indicates that the investment of Banks in this area is inadequate and wavering. Some symptoms are that (i) their Faculty are inadequately equipped for doing this work, (ii) the amount of BS Sessions is already limited and it is further reduced when required in favour of the Non-BS input and (iii) the non-institutional use of BS is very limited. Thus, although the Banking Industry is to be set with the problem of reorienting attitudes of its people, the only available process is used hesitantly. Hence, it is necessary to frame certain issues and work out strategies related to behavioural science training in banks and hope the banks will take necessary remedial measures.

— *Developing B.S Training Resources*: B.S in a bank would be as effective as the B.S Trainers themselves. Appropriate training facilities must be made available to trainers either externally or internally. Institutes like the Indian Society for Applied Behavioural Science, National Institute of Bank Management conduct programmes for this purpose. Some Banks like the State Banks of India train their Faculty at such Institutes and then organise their Internal Programmes for Developing B.S. trainers. Such training by itself is not adequate. The trained Faculty of a bank must have adequate opportunity to use his learning in his bank at different levels within his training college/centre or at the work place when O.D. interventions are planned. Training facilities available in the country for developing B.S. trainers are inadequate. So there is need for a specialised institute for doing B.S. work in Banks.

— *Development of Banks B.S. Perception*: People in Banks especially the senior and the top management, hold a variety of views about B.S.—a remedial formula for bringing about change in people's behaviour, a means of showing a person what he is, as a threat to the existing equilibrium, as an interesting break. This arises mainly on account of inadequate understanding of B.S. and faulty understanding of it at the hands of incompetent trainers. If B.S. is seen as a process-work at the socio-psychological level in the bank, the misgivings and the wrong expectations of B.S. would reduce substantially. If behaviour is an output, it is the result of an input which is processed by an individual in his unique way. B.S. work can help him to identify the input, be aware of how he has processed it. As it calls for a huge training investment, for a bank such investment needs to be made selectively in programming some trainers who in turn, facilitate such process work for other people by showing new ways of looking at the self to the participants, process-work at the level of groups is more necessary and can show some changes even faster. Since the individual or the group works under a larger environment, when process interventions in the larger environment are also made, the former two are facilitated further.

— *Organising Research and Review* : B.S. use research in the banking sector is necessary as also, review of this important area at suitable forums and through discussion groups.

So Behaviour Science Training in the Banking Sector has to be reengineered along these parameters and suitable HRD support provided for lasting behavioural changes in the banking personnel.

Re-Engineering Training: Management Development Programmes (MDP) in Indian Banks

Need for MDP: The quality of managerial personnel largely determines the performance of the organisation because the trained and competent managers not only manage resources properly but also motivate and direct the efforts of subordinates towards organisational goals. A dynamic organisation continuously develops its managers. Management development can be *defined* as the attempt to improve managerial effectiveness through a planned and deliberate learning process. Management development is one of the tools of organisation development and is conceived as a planned change involving the whole organisation as a complex system.

New developments of far-reaching consequences are taking place in banking. Bank executives would require an increasing understanding of management process, government policy. For efficiency and productivity many more skills in organisational diagnosis and negotiation skills are required. Therefore, it is essential that increased attention be given to training and development of managers, to enable them to discharge the official responsibilities, appreciate the business development as well as to implement policies and provide guidelines in particular areas of business. Recognising the need for professionalisation of bank management, the government set up a study group under B.N. Adarkar[14] to review this area and the committee's recommendations led to establishment of National Institute of Bank Management.

Issues in MDP: According to reports, the MDP programmes is rated theoretical. Institutions should develop appropriate teaching methodology, course material and faculty experience that create a climate for learning the concepts and also make them relevant in handling the potential problems of bank management. For making management education meaningful there has to be an active partnership between the organisations and the educational institution. Though MDP can give orientation to macro issues and contemporary management, it will have limitations in creating the necessary impact unless senior management personnel have an exposure to management education and unless they develop a shared perspective about the bank's problems and utility of management science to deal with the problems. Unless MDP makes a difference ultimately in his job assignment and responsibilities and unless the purpose of the programme is reinforced by the practice and ideals of the organisation, the effect of education and training fades. Management education alone is not management development. The focus of management development is on integrating the individual learning to organisational learning by giving exposure to such jobs which require innovative approaches, inter-functional exposures, job rotations.

"There must be an effective system of 'tracking' down the high performing and high potential managers, use of well thoughout performance appraisal and potential appraisal system, a reward system which encourages excellence in work.[15]" For acquiring quality management talent the banks need to take HRD measures such as developing career planning strategies, systematically developing the talent through variety of exposures including the formal management education and training, integrating specialists in the banking system and developing respect for their knowledge.

Programme Design for MDP's: Some aspects of the design of management development programme will now be considered :[16]

— Management development programmes for top executives have to be viewed basically (though not wholly) as an educational pursuit, and not as departmental or administrative activity—the primary objective has to be to educate, to contribute towards knowledge and understanding, and not the immediate and direct solution of corporate managerial problems.

— For their success as educational programmes for top level executives they demand search and identification of sharply focused themes which can generate high degrees of interest both on grounds of immediate relevance as well as wider ultimate relevance covering wider time and human perspectives.

— Success demands that for running top level management development programmes special care should be taken to arrange for best possible infrastructural facilities including reception, board and lodge, extracurricular and perfect conference-room facilities to suit the requirements of a really top level conference.

— In terms of planning and programme design, it is also necessary to divide the central theme into a few topic to be covered separately in a few separate sessions and to prepare background papers covering different topics.

— It is important that papers and other reading materials are produced and distributed in advance. Time should also be provided and built into the programme schedule for reading of material and for discussion in small groups so that intensive thinking and examination of various ideas materialises and makes conference-room discussions more productive.

— The role of the educator must have significance. They must make appearance and occupy the centre of the stage. This is achieved only when the faculty instead of withdrawing itself to the background, comes forward with all its strengths to make powerful presentations and to monitor and steer the discussions.

Management Self-development: It is an important new area within the field of Management Development Programme. The importance of management self-development is because most managers are eager to learn and require guidence in selecting appropriate material. They generally have a natural impulse to further their knowledge, both of their jobs and their outside pursuits. They may pride themselves on being able to learn from experience and self help rather than from being taught by someone else. Pedler and Boydell observe that important lessons were more likely to be learned from non-contrived experiences such as 'being confronted by a subordinate' than from 'contrived' situations. This did not in any way rule out a more formal training or teaching approach, but merely questioned the methods themselves and any priority that they may be seen to have over self-development. Managers' jobs have marked differences from those of other employees in an organization. The lives of non-managers tend to be dominated by planned situations in which the problems encountered have standard solutions. Managers, on the other hand, are concerned largely with unplanned events posing problems for which there are no 'right' answers. A different approach is therefore necessary when training managers, one that not only deals with the realities of a job which appears to have very few ground rules, but also capitalizes on the innate inquisitiveness and thirst for knowledge of the individual by Management self-development.

In general, this involves a group. The purpose of the meeting may be to assist the self-development of one or more of the group's members seeking support and assistance from their colleagues. Alternatively, the group may be task-oriented, studying problems and searching for solutions in connection with actual work situations. In either case, the group can be self-activating, or it can enlist the help of an 'outsider' such as a trainer or management development adviser, a facilitator of learning rather than a teacher or instructor.

Management self-development is becoming increasingly populars as it has a number of potent features in its favour. The managers involved are usually self-motivated volunteers whose commitment provides a sound basis for successful decision-making and problem-solving. There is an incentive to reach positive conclusions about real and pressing problems. They are not bound by a rigid training framework, trying to accomplish too many things at once. It is an activity which economizes on staff, a factor which commends it to managements with right budgets.

Effective task-oriented groups engaged on work-based projects use an action—learning approach to the solution of their problems studied by Reginald Revans. The principle at the centre of action learning theory is, in Revans' own words, "....that learning stems from responsible experience, and is reinforced when that experience is shared with others....." Action Learning distils from that comradeship in adversity which seeks responsibility through action rather than avoids it through discussions. The members of the management team, whom he very aptly styles, `comrades in adversity', are, by virtue of the relevance, of their considerable aggregated and shared experience, the only people who can do very much to improve the activity for which they are responsible.

Industrial Relation (IA) Training: This is another area of management development programme which is gaining importance in recent years due to increased emphasis on maintaining harmonious industrial relations in service organisations like Indian Banks. To ease the process of management union negotiations to create more suitable conditions in which they could take place the prerequisite is for an objective and civilized dialogue in the negotiating room or in the establishment of working conditions in which managements and the workforce can communicate sympathetically and effectively on a day-to-day basis. If the only opportunity provided for speaking to each other is when the two sides are in dispute, they are surely starting from the wrong base.

Another important factor over which training managers can have influence, and that is with respect to the training of management negotiators. It is widely assumed that practising managers are competent to carry out the negotiating role without any formal training. Yet lack of skill in analysis, strategy and the process itself can, and often does, have serious consequences. By their impulsive actions and the injudicious use of the wrong language, for example, they may create barriers to future progress. There is a growing acceptance of the need for managers to be trained in negotiating skills.

The essential elements of an IR training programme in negotiating are:

— the provision is detailed information about the organisation's industrial relations philosophy, strategies, policies and procedures.

— the process of preparation for a negotiating interview or meeting.

— the skills involved in the negotiating encounter and follow-up.

MDP-Japanese Management Principles and Courses: The Indian Banking sector can learn for the example of the innovative and relevant management courses devised by the Japan Management Association, Japan. Some examples of these courses are:

Business Process Re-engineering: Business Process Re-Engineering, also known as BPR, involves seriously questioning the existing work process of an organisation. If required, dismantling and rebuilding them, taking advantage of developments in Information Technology. All this, while keeping the customer in mind. The course objective would be:

— To understand the essence of re-engineering, and its promotion and implementation in an organisation.

— To learn how to organize a re-engineering effort in an organisation.

— To understand the intricacies of this approach through cases and examples.

Strategic Management Course: This would bring out the way of thinking and strategy formulation of most Japanese corporations that have become world leaders. The course objectives would be:

* To understand the essence of strategic management in the context of very severe state of changes that we are experiencing now.

* To develop capabilities to cope up with the dynamic changes in the external and internal environment of an organisation.

Notes

1. Bhattacharya, B: Preparing Indian Banks for International Operations under the Emerging Trends in International Banking. In Banking in the 90's Bombay: Himalaya Publishing Co.

2. Narasimhan, R: Training Needs in the Context of Computerization and Mechanization in Banks — paper presented at RBI Seminar on 'Emerging Training Needs of the Banking Industry in the 1990's.

3. Mandhyan, B.J.: Training Needs in the context of Computerization and Mechanization in Banks — Paper presented at RBI Seminar on 'Emerging Training Needs of the Banking Industry in the 1990's.

4. Haogson, U. and Mc Connel, D.: Online Education and Development in *'Handbook of Training and Development'* edited by John Prior.

5. Mason, R. and Kaye, T. Mijdweave : *Communication, Computers and Distance Education*. Oxford: Pergamon Press, 1989.

6. Dinesha K.V.: Computers and Telecommunications in International and Indian Banking Industry: Pune : *Prajanan,* Vol. XXII, No. 4 January - March, 1994.

7. Padwal, S.M. : Security and Safety of Information Technology for Banks and Financial Institutions. Pune: *Prajanan,* Vol. XXII, : No. 4, January - March, 1994.

8. Muniraj, R.: Strategies to improve customer service in banks. *The Banker,* June 1994, p. 31.

9. Kulkarni, S.S.: Training needs for bringing about attitudinal changes to improve customer service in banks. Paper presented in Reserve Bank of India Seminar on : 'Emerging Training Needs of the Banking Industry in the year 1990's.

10. Ray Corey views marketing as consisting of all activities by which a company adapts itself to its environment—creatively and profitably. Marketing has been defined by *Kotler* (Marketing Management : Analysis, Planning, Implementation and Control) as a 'social and managerial process by which individuals and groups obtain what they need and want through creating, offering and exchanging products of value with other'. The importance of marketing has been highlighted by *Peter Drucker* as: "Marketing is

so basic that it cannot be considered a separate function. It is the whole business seen from the point of view of its final result, that is, from the customer's point of view. Business success is not determined by the producer but by the customer".

11. Anbalangan, K.: Diversification of Banking Business to meet the challenges — problems and prospects of departure from Traditional Banking. *The Banker,* February 1989.
12. Saloni Rama Krishna, P.: Strategies to meet new challenges in banking, *P.N.B. Monthly Review,* February, 1994.
13. Narsimha, Murthy G. and Raji Reddy, K.: Marketing Mix for Banking Services, *The Banker,* June 1994.
14. Report of the 1988 Working Group under the Chairmanship of B.N. Adarkar appointed by the Reserve Bank of India on Training Facilities for Higher Level Bank Personnel.
15. Khandelwal, A.K.: Management Education and Training in Banks. In Khandelwal A.K. (ed.) *HRD in Banks,* Oxford and IBH, 1988. Ch. 18.
16. Nair, R.R.: Career Development Strategies and HRD in: Rao, Verma Khandelwal, Abraham (eds.)—*Alternative Approaches and Strategies of Human Resources Development,* Jaipur: Rawat Publications, 1987.

8

Reengineering HRD and Training for Rural Development Banking

Overview: In the last three chapters we have seen how reengineering endeavours can help bridge the gap in the HRD and Training systems of the Indian Banking sector through Organisational Culture/HRD, Training machinery and Critical Training Areas related interventions. Though these approaches are adaptable to different situations/requirements of Indian Banks, however, keeping in view the unique features/demands of the important rural banking segment of Indian Banking Sector, it is necessary to consider the additional/special interventions for Rural Development Banking. This forms the subject matter of this chapter of our study.

Here we shall first consider effective HRD policies required to make Rural Development Banking a success..Then we shall discuss the characteristics of the Training Strategy required to achieve these HRD objectives by the Banking net work. Alongwith general considerations, we shall focus on the training requirements of Service Area Approach. Subsequently, the innovative Organisational Development Initiative for revamping Regional Rural Banks and the requirements for effective Co-operative Banks' Training have been elaborated.

Moreover, for sustainable rural development, Banks have to engage in the total development of the rural client. This contention has been highlighted by the discussion of the topical

'Women in Development/Gender and Development' issues in the following chapter — women being the least developed/ most deprived section of the rural banks' clientele.

Re-engineering HRD and Training for Rural Development Banking: Effective HRD Policies

Indian planning places considerable emphasis on rural uplift and enhancing productivity in rural areas. So development of human resources in banks to fulfil the needs of rural development programmes assumes tremendous significance. For being effective, the rural banker has to have not only the knowledge of banking laws and practices but also various other skills required for rural lending. He has to have the right approach, attitude and style of management which is in tune with the rural environment. He has to develop empathy to appreciate the problems of rural poor more intensively and find solutions. Effective communication skills a rural banker has to possess so that he could deal with the rural poor. There is no system of pro-active HRD and training to initiate changes in the system, to spread/communicate available technology and facilities offered by the Government of India/banks to rural borrowers as done by countries like Japan. What is required now is the will to introduce changes in HRD policies, so that, rural development becomes integral to the banking activities.

Various components/suggestions on HRD and training systems like manpower planning, recruitment, training, reward and punishment system to facilitate the process of human resource development for rural development will now be discussed in the context of Re-engineering efforts required for effective/more productive operation of Rural Development Banking.

Recruitment Policies: Banks will have to change their recruitment strategies (for personnel). There are many institutions in the county which provide higher education in rural development, and carry out experiments in the field of rural higher education, provide research and extension service for the benefit of the people of the area. Institutes like Gandhi Vidyapeeth, Vedchhi, Ahmedabad; Gandhi Institute for Rural Development, Madurai; Rural Higher Education Institute, Virauli, Bihar. are some of the leading institutes which are producing a good number of people with proper rural orientation. Besides there are about 27 agriculture universities in India and about 152 gram sevak training centres, producing agriculture graduates and multi-purpose village level workers called gram sevaks. Banking Services Recruitment Boards (BSRB) can do campus recruitment both for clerical and officer cadres in such places to acquire personnel with necessary orientation for rural development work. The BSRB also needs to modify the present test system which is highly urban-oriented because it focuses only on numerical ability, reasoning ability and fluency in English, which helps the urban graduates to make their mark. There is no emphasis in the present system on rural orientation. The BSRB should also insist on proficiency in local language in the recruitment — otherwise due to the language barrier they will be unable to develop the required rapport with the local folk.

Performance Appraisal System: The performance appraisal system for officers in the bank needs to project a specific contribution and invisible work done by an officer in the rural area. The emphasis of appraisal system in banks is generally on meeting the targets of deposits and advances. Though these are important indicators of performance, there are other important dimensions such as, involvement with the local developmental task, extension services, counselling services which must be reflected in the appraisal system. There is a necessity for a separate appraisal system for rural banking. Appraisal of the performance of even controlling heads must relate an individual's contribution to rural development under his area of control on achievement of target figures and on providing counselling services to branches and pro-active steps in the area of rural development.

Placement Policies: Instead of adhocism Banks will have to come out with a positive policy statement of placement in a rural area. Rural service must be made compulsory for every officer and considered as an important yardstick for further promotion and growth in the bank. For clerical staff also, due attention should be paid to give them necessary training and exposure as also motivation to undertake rural service viaweightage during the internal promotion exercise. (75% of promotions in the banks to officers cadre are from within the ranks). According to survey conducted by the National Institute of Bank Management[1]. 31 per cent respondents felt that rural postings will help if recognition of good work in rural area is considered essential for further career development, a majority of the bank employees (85 per cent) feel that rural postings can be undertaken on the assurance that they can have postings at their desired places after they have served in rural areas. We can appreciate this point more so in view of inadequate infrastructure in rural areas as also a lack of any placement policy in the banks. The promotions and reward systems should also be linked with the achievements and contribution in the rural areas.

Team Spirit and Collaboration: For development work in rural areas to be undertaken with enthusiasm, it is necessary that the branch functionaries work in a team spirit. Working in rural areas involves dealings on one side with the rural folk and on the other side with multiple agencies headed by bureaucrats, local politicians demands on a banker and communication problems within one's own organisation. It is necessary to have a good communication machinery within the bank, so that, there is periodical feedback about the problems faced by the staff in rural areas and a time-bound grievance machinery is available to those working in rural areas since urban areas employees have better access to management through trade unions. Visits by personnel officers to rural areas should be made to have first hand appreciation of the problem, and where behavioural problems exist necessary counselling be given on the spot.

Trade Unions Contribution: Banks Trade Unions have a major role to play in rural development. There should be restraint on their part in allowing management to transfer people to rural areas, making rural service compulsory for each employee, developing a reward system based on rural contribution, periodical job rotation, enlarged job role. They will have to change their outlook about allowance based additional performance and work in collaboration with bank management to change the pattern of rural financing.

Special Training Strategy for Rural Development Banking

For the massive task of rural financing, banks have to have trained personnel in various aspects of rural development, so that, they are able to play a role of change-agent in rural areas. In fact, one of the major factors for failure of banks to touch qualitative dimension of development in rural areas has been the absence of trained manpower. Though commercial banks have provided training opportunities in rural development in their respective training establishments, the courses offered are far from adequate in terms of both content as well as impact. A majority of the banks, including some of the major banks, mainly rely on some of the courses conducted by them in their existing training establishments. There are apex training institutes—like College of Agriculture Banking, Poona and Bankers Institute for Rural Development (BIRD), Lucknow. These institutes conduct programmes for commercial banks as well as cooperative and regional rural banks (RRBs). Other apex level institutions like the National Institute of Bank Management (NIBM) and Bank Training Centre (BTC), are not doing many.programmes in the area of rural development. Thus, largely, banks have to rely on their own internal facilities for training for rural development. With the added responsibility of training RRB personnel, it is all the more necessary that banks develop suitable infrastructure to take care of training needs from clerical staff to senior management level. It does not involve merely giving capsule courses in rural development but to design comprehensive courses so that, officers with urban background can have a throrough exposure and right attitudes in the area of rural financing.[2] The aim of these courses should be to develop confidence and motivation amongst bank personnel to undertake rural development activity with enthusiasm.

The following strategy regarding the training system may be adopted to help prepare a motivated banker to undertake rural development activity:

1. Individual banks should develop policy document on "Training strategy for Rural Development" It must contain the required projections for rural development in terms of business levels and manpower requirement and existing backlog in training in rural development, chalk out a time-bound action plan in relation to training infrastructure for rural development, necessary software, development of trainers as also potential target groups. Essential training must be linked to proper placement.

2. Due to various commonalities in financing and development activities as also a huge backlog in the field of training, the banking industry would require a very large number of training establishments. Since rural development requires understanding of local socio-economic conditions as also understanding of human process in a particular locality, there is a need for inter-bank collaboration in establishment of training institution for rural development in specific areas which would greatly save the cost and duplication of efforts. For example, in a particular state, lead banks can combine to open a few training centres for a cluster of districts. This will help orienting training to specific requirements of the regions as also to undertake field studies and using such data in the curriculum. Subsequently training of bank personnel on a continuous basis can be undertaken at a low cost and at the doorstep of the developing regions.

3. The conventional institutional training arrangements are costly to maintain and in future, because of vast number of rural bankers, they may not be able to cater to them in a cost effective manner. In the future, training may have therefore to reach out to the

maximum number of bankers quickly and within easy reach of their rural centres of posting. Though essential, it may not be practically feasible to release large number of rural staff for training as the strength of a rural branch is limited and leave/training reserves are inadequate. To obviate these constraints, training and visit type of approach with Distance Learning Systems may have to be evolved. Recently National Bank has evolved the innovative scheme of Mobile Job Trainer (M.J.T) for imparting on-the-job training to officers and staff of Regional Rural Banks, where though, large number of personnel are untrained the banks find it difficult to spare them for institutional training. Under the programme, officers selected for each RRB to work as MJT are imparted orientation training by National Bank and allocated 20 branches for periodic visits initially for a period of two years. They impart training to the Branch personnel in all the areas of house-keeping, loan appraisal procedures for recovery etc. and are supported by Back up Group at Head Office of RRB, comprising Chairman, General Manager etc.

4. Conventional training techniques currently in vogue in many training centres are lecture and case study methods and use of audio-visual aids. To improve quality, methods like 'hands-on-experience', brain-storming, role play, could be used. In management development programmes, emphasis may be laid on team building, motivation, work culture etc. by having a mix of different grades of officers as successfully tried by National Bank. Under Distance Learning System banking industry may also consider establishing an open banking university[3] or Indian Institute of Bankers could evolve various courses for bankers and devise reading material in the 'Programmed Learning' approach, computer assisted Distance Learning Systems like Linear Video Instruction (LVI), Computer Based Training (CBT),

Interactive Video Instructions (IVI) could also be devised.

5. If bank officers are to sanction most of the agricultural loans without the recommendations of the technical officers, the training needs of the officers will be correspondingly higher. Branch Managers and Agricultural Divisional Managers will then have to be trained in agricultural credit, branch management etc. and receive sufficient rural exposure. Since the Rural Development Officers have to function as technical experts and also as bank officers handling credit function, they need to be imparted training in branch work, to be of help to the Branch Managers in assessing risks of agricultural loans. The technical officers, if they are to function as field officers carrying out not merely technical/advisory duties but also non-technical banking duties, they would have to be given training in routine banking work. When they opt out for a full-fledged banking career, they will have to be given detailed training in various aspects of branch work. Bankers have to adopt the latest marketing concept that it is not enough to produce goods and services but it is equally important to the borrower in their efficient use. For this, bankers have to update their knowledge in the latest technologies available for rural development and in future they may have to conduct beneficiary training programmes in the efficient use of investment.

6. The training needs of the banking industry in its developmental role in the context of the *Service Area Approach*[4] would require all banking officers to be posted as field officers or branch managers to be given training in basics of agricultural financing and technical parameters of various types of rural activities such as crop cultivation, horticulture, pisciculture, animal husbandry schemes financing, schematic lending etc. inputs regarding their role in service area scheme:village survey method, credit

planning etc. For making a success of the Service Area Approach, it is necessary for the supervisory staff posted at the rural or semi-urban branches to be given suitable training covering (Kanvinda, 1988)[5] :

(i) data collection on development programmes and development in the Service Areas.

(ii) appraisal of the extent to which backward and forward linkages required for the success of various development programmes is available or likely to be made available.

(iii) market based appraisal of the service area—size and viability of market, amount of linkage support.

(iv) budget making for the service area on the basis of this data collection and data analysis.

The banking system has so far been guided by the target approach in rural lending-overall quantitative target being achieved, but this has not been done by each rural branch contributing maximum credit feasible in its areas of operation. In many banks the special branches are concentrated in the 'thrust areas' and 'one man' branches predominate in the non-thrust areas. Since now banks will have to come up to public expectations in the Service Areas of each of their branches, it requires strengthening of all rural branches to the requisite extent and imparting requisite training to all officers posted at these branches, that they are not found wanting in the implementation of the Services Area Approach.

So, training inputs for the Service Area Approach (SAA) would include, Data collection, Skills to Translate Data into Potentials, Action Credit Plan, implementation, Monitoring, Grassroots Team (GT) Working, People's Participation and Development Perspective. Even if a particular agency or a level of it is directly responsible for a specific task, overall exposure of the entire delivery system to the broad band of inputs is necessary to initiate the new culture of villagewise planning implementation and monitoring. Lead Bank Scheme (LBS) which stands for consortiun approach espoused lateral affinity. The onus was on the lead bank officer (LBO) who had to depend on his ingenuity and liaison. Thanks to LBS and effort of LBO, there is now regular interaction among the agencies at the district level, SAA has been launched to enforce the lateral affinity at the grassroots. The onus is on the SA Branch Managers (BMs). Orientation training should gear the inputs in this direction. The feeling that BMs will be over burdened with SAA is a misconception here. SAA only introduces a method in the working of the branch. Once the culture of viewing the operations of the branch village-wise is accepted and internalized it becomes routine and would facilitate the working. The new culture of lateral affinity can and should be enforced using the vertical corporate channel. It is here 'the crucial significance of orienting the Regional Managers (RMs) arises[6]: If SAA means purpose, the new culture should be brought into operational hierarchy of banks through the RMs. Besides deposits, advances, recovery and house-keeping, the RMs should assess BMs' performance with regard to SAA. Unfortunately, RM's role in this direction was not clearly defined, which has become necessary now. Under SAA BM is accountable with other members of GT, for the overall development of the villages in his SA. RMs may have to share with the BMs lateral concern for the villages in the SA. Through the RMs we can reach all the SA BMs. The BMs in their turn would influence laterally the members of GT. RMs should supplement the LBO in his interaction with district level functionaries and other RMs. The District Development Managers (DDMs) of NABARD who are located in the districts would facilitate the process.

It is therefore, possible to envisage a training strategy where sufficient weightage is given to orientating the RMs. From each bank, selected Senior Trainers (STs) or RMs with flair for training may have to be covered in the first instance. These STs or RMs would in turn impart training to other RMs. In the second stage, RMs with the help of LBO would orient the district level functionaries of cooperatives, government agencies and other RMs. They can take the help of professional trainees or officers equipped with skills. Training is not and cannot be one shot exercise. It has to be a continuous endeavour. Lateral training both at the district and block level by the peer group trainers, as stated above, should occur at regular intervals. There should be specific inputs to provide skills for analysis of data and their translation into potentials. Taking the case study of a SA and actually working out potentials would help the transmission of skills. In addition to lecture sessions, and case study, audio-visual aids on success stories of rural development initiated by any quarter of delivery system or based on initiative from within should further help in conveying the message.

7. The exact data about the organisations of the banks in the rural areas and classification of rural branches into 'one-man' offices or 'branches with Field Officers' and 'branches with Technical personnel' is not readily available. In its absence exact quantification of the training needs/requisite training facilities cannot be made. Detailed data obout the organisation of the rural branches of commercial banks, staffing of rural branches, policy towards Technical Officers, upgradation of one-man offices, etc. should hence be collected for the industry as a whole and also for individual banks to ensure that lack of resources on the part of the smaller banks and lack of adequate

organisational attention from large banks do not interfere with the success of the Service Area Approach.

8. 'To make rural development efforts a success apart from infusion of credit, urban oriented bankers and government officials posted in rural areas require training to become effective in rural credit delivery system. So there should be frequent training meets of bankers and governmental grassroot level functionaries to enable them develop empathy for each other and work for a common cause... Bankers may have to plan training meets/workshops for beneficiaries in co-ordination with field level extension agencies, in the efficient use of appropriate technology and investment. This is likely to increase recovery of rural lending'.[7]

9. Training alongwith being viewed from corporate perspective has to be been from human resources perspective in which apart from imparting training on the skills critical to successful implementation of corporate plans the individual needs are also taken into consideration so as to have Management by Objective (MBO) approach to training. This would require more emphasis on inputs on behavioural science.

10. Since all the training institutions of public sector banks have a common objective of developing the skills knowledge of rural banking officers, it would be desirable to have coordination among the training institutions to explore the possibility of having uniform programmes and programme contents, exchange of faculty support, standardising the nomenclature of each programme so as to avoid duplication of training efforts and increase productivity of training centres.

Organisational Development Initiative for Revamping RRBs

Although the Regional Rural Banks (RRBs) have brought banking to the door steps of the poor, their very survival has been threatened by their performance on account of external factors like limited business avenues, poor recoveries etc. and internal factors like poor managerial capability, lack of work culture. As on March 31, 1993, 172 out of 196 RRBs were deeply in red and their accumulated losses of Rs. 298 crores. Realising the seriousness of their ailments, the Government of India, RBI and NABARD have taken various measures to strengthen the RRBs — the latest being revamping of selected RRBs to make them financially and organisationally strong and vibrant by the instrument of Development Action Plans (DAPs).

Insight has been gained on the problems of RRBs, many of which have developed internally due to change averse mindset of their staff. Conventional training has sought to equip RRB staff with knowledge and skills of doing their jobs better. But changing the averse mindset, the essence of the problem, has not been tackled in these programmes. The mindset is due to the work culture of these Banks's collective attitude of negativism, apathy towards clientele, false sense of job security.

Restructuring of human resources which is the crux to meaningful implementation of development plans for business and financial restructuring, involves making the RRB personnel appreciate the new realities in the context of reforms in the banking sector, developing among them a sense of belonging to their organisation, developing their abilities to find solutions themselves, inculcating group/team spirit. To find an appropriate intervention strategy whereby RRB human resources could stop organisational decay and create organisational renewal led to the evolution of a new strategy named 'Organisational Development Initiative' (ODI), rooted in organisation development theory and the application of organisational behaviour concepts to organisation rebuilding (ODI theory and methodology have been discussed under HRD and Organisational Culture in Chapter 5).

As the ODI programme in the RRB's a went on, the resistance gave way gradually to curiosity, interest and active involvement in the group process. The discussions led to many innovative ideas and schemes, which are included in the action plans. The participants also identified new systems and procedures required to implement the action plans. By the programme's end, there was involvement of the participants. The ability of the participants for innovative solutions and willingness to take greater responsibilities was encouraging. 'The ODI process is a striking working example of making people believe in their own abilities to diagnose their difficulties, design solutions thereafter, and implement the same'.

The success with the ODI approach indicates that this methodology could be adopted to solve problems related to other sectors/segments of the Indian Banking scenario. Furthermore, for making the positive changes that have taken place in the RRBs sustain over time, other supporting HRD/operational policy changes are also required to be made.

Effective Training Strategy for Cooperative Banks

(Recommendations of the ILO/NORAD/CPD Regional Symposium at Thailand on effective Cooperative Training: Excerpts) : The symposium after having considered the country reports made by the participants and the technical papers presented by the resource persons, bearing in mind the objectives of the Symposium, and accepting the role of the cooperative movement in training and education and its linkage to a self-reliant cooperative movement, arrived at the following conclusions and recommendations :

(1) One of the important recommendations of the symposium of Setting Effective Cooperative Training Policies and Standards' held in Chiang Mau 1979 was that the cooperative movement should be responsible for training its staff and educating its members. These responsibilities consist of planning and implementing

the training of the managers and other staff, management committees and the education of the members. It was felt that the cooperative movement will have to take necessary actions in raising general consciousness in the community about cooperative principles and values in addition to educating its own members. In order to discharge the above responsibilities, the movement must have at its disposal adequate human, financial and material resources. A suitable organisational structure is necessary for an effective communication between the Apex organisation and the movement as a whole. It is necessary to stress that management training and member education should lead to an economically viable cooperative movement, better services to the members and a greater participation by the members in the affairs of their cooperatives.

(2) The symposium identified a number of constraints, inter-alia the following :

— Vested interests;

— lack of political will;

— restrictive legal and administrative structures, and prevailing weaknesses in the movement such as lack of dynamic leadership limited resources, lack of adequately trained staff, lack of awareness about cooperative values among the members as well as the general public.

(3) The symposium further recommended that appropriate institutions be built up at all levels to enable the movement to effectively carry out the training, education and information functions. It was felt that the Apex organisations should execute the following functions :

— establishing of an appropriate cooperative personnel policy.

— training of staff.

- training of management committee.
- member education;
- publicity and public relation;
- research and consultancy, and
- monitoring and evaluation.

(4) The symposium was of the opinion that such a personnel policy should cover the following areas :

- detailed job descriptions and job specifications for staff at all levels;
- objective and professional recruitment procedures;
- development of suitable service conditions including satisfying scales of salary;
- provision for systematic staff training and appropriate career development systems;
- provision of performance based incentive and rewarding scheme, monetary as well as non-monetary;
- provision of periodic manpower surveys and of manpower planning;
- creation of a congenial working environment between the Management Committees and the staff by clearly defining the respective areas of responsibilities and functioning;
- maintaining an updated information on trained personnel;
- provision of opportunities of cooperative staff to be promoted to higher positions within the movement.

(5) *The Role of International Organisation* : The symposium was of the view that international agencies such as ICA, ILO, FAO, UNDP, SIDA, SOC, NORAD and the

like have an important role to play in such areas as follows :

— to act as a catalytic agent, facilitator and promoter among various cooperative movements to enable them to share experience of each other for mutual benefit;

— to provide technical, financial, consultancy and other support for development of skills and capabilities of the movements;

— to assist cooperative movements to develop inter-cooperative and international cooperative trade;

— to assist in identifying projects and donors for the various cooperative movements;

— to provide necessary forum for exchange experiences and for strengthening international cooperative relations;

— The symposium strongly recommended that the support provided by ILO/NORAD through its project on Setting Effective Cooperative Training Policies and Standards to the cooperative movements in Asia be further continued to enable the movement to reach the stage of self-reliance in the shortest possible time.

These suggestions have to be adapted to the Indian Cooperative Banking Sector in order to make it a more effective instrument of Rural Development Banking by further radical reforms in their organisational/operational/HRD policies and programmes.

Notes

1. NIBM, *Personnel Policies in Banks — An Employees Opinion Survey*, Bombay: NIBM, 1983.
2. *Report of the Committee on Training in Rural Development through Credit (TRUDEC)*, Bombay 1983.
3. Recommendations of Conference of Principals/Directors of training institutes of commercial banks imparting training in rural development banking , College of Agricultural Banking, RBI, Pune, 1989.

4. *Service Area Approach—Formulation of Credit Plan*, Rural Planning and Credit Department (RPCD), Reserve Bank of India (RBI) Bombay, 1988.

5. Kanvinde, D.J.: *Training Strategy for Meeting the Requirement of deeper involvement of Banks in Rural Development* — Paper presented at RBI seminar on 'Emerging Training Needs of the Banking Industry in the 1990's'.

6. Rao, K.D., Some aspects of Service Area Approach for Trainers — *Indian Journal of Training and Development*, March-April, 1990.

7. Saxena, V.N., *Training strategies for meeting the requirement of deeper involvement of Banks in Rural Development*. Paper presented at Reserve Bank of India Seminar on 'Emerging Training Needs of the Banking Industry in the 1990's.

9

Reengineering HRD: Gender Resource Development

Overview: In this study we have examined the HRD re-engineering endeavours required by the Indian Banking Sector for being better equipped to face the challenges of the millennium generally, and with particular reference to Rural Development Banking (through optimum Rural Human Resource Development). Apart from the rural-urban dichotomy, there is another differentiation — the vital gender dimension of the banking sector's clientele which has to be properly addressed if this sector aims to achieve a balanced growth. Gender Resource Development ('gender' being concerned with the balance of power situation between women and men) for the empowerment of disadvantaged women, hence becomes an area requiring urgent attention from the Indian Banking Sector.

In this chapter we initially explain the emergence and parameters of the Women in Development (WID.) issue in the world and within India. Through an examination of WID initiatives for the client population (by International Development Agencies like CIDA, DFID, USAID) and Equal Opportunity Measures for the sensitisation/empowerment of organisation's own personnel (vide case study of Bank of Montreal, Canada) we get acquainted with the international dimensions and cross cultural applicability of these measures.

Subsequently we look at the WID reengineering approaches (through Gender training etc.) of international developmental financial institutions like the Asian Development Bank, World Bank etc. as also the lessons they hold for the Indian Development Banking endeavours.

Gender Resource Development: The Women and Development Issue

Emergence of 'Women in Development' Issue

The twentieth century has seen the movement for women's emancipation lead to greater International conciousness about the historical suppression of rights, denial of equal opportunities/empowerment of women, gender bias, as also organisational barriers for working women (who now constitute about 30% of the global workforce). The 1979 United Nations (U.N.) Convention on the Elimination of all forms of Discrimination against women (CEDAW) enunciated the fundamental/human rights of women in the workforce, as also the development rights of rural women: The 1995 Beijing Fourth World Conference on Women asked governments to integrate a gender perspective into all economic restructuring. UNDP's 1995 `Human Development Report' proposed a Gender related Development Index (GDI) and Gender Empowerment Measure (GEM) to focus on gender equality. Aware national governments, concerned developmental/financial/other institutions and groups/individual are constantly working on women in Development (WID) issues through legislative/socio-economic/human resource development and training interventions. Though this has led to some positive outcomes, yet the feminization of poverty/gender gaps in critical parameters continue. Unequal workplace opportunities for women/paucity of women — friendly job amenities and of sensitization mechanisms like gender training remain.

Indian Working Women and Development[2]:

An important objective of development planning in India is larger and efficient use of available human resources (including the disadvantaged sections as women) to achieve poverty eradication, reduction in inequalities. Most Indian women, especially rural women, work not only to contribute to the family income but also work in the house, though this contribution is not recognised. In rural India, women work in the unorganised informal sector and their labour normally involves collection of fuel / fodder / water, household chores and the rearing of children. Agriculture and allied fields provide the largest sector for women's employment — 83% of women are involved in it. Despite forming such a large workforce, their conditions of work are poor and discriminatory. Women get very low wages, are discriminated via-a-vis men, and their work is often considered to be subsidiary to men's work. Women, however, continue to suffer because of lack of supportive mechanisms—rural women and others are provided with no creche facilities, no maternity benefits and no provision is made for their occupational health hazards. They have no control over the land and other assets in the family and therefore, cannot make decisions. There are hardly any laws for the vast majority of unorganised women labour in rural India and where the laws exist, the same are not honored.

Indian Policy Towards Women's Development :

The evolution of Indian policies towards integration of women in development has been slow. The first programme for rural development in India after the inception of planning was the community-development and rural-extension programme in which women were integrated as an after-thought. The approach toward's women's development was of a home-extension-welfare nature. In this programme women were taught some practical skills aimed at making them better housewives and using their time more fruitfully.

After the community-development programmes receded into the background, the focus of policy regarding women throughout the period of the Second to Fifth Plan (1955-80) was on welfare measures. In health and family planning, concerns about women have found explicit expression. However, only in the Sixth (1980-5) Plan document an awareness of the need for integrating women in development was shown. The Seventh Plan (1985-90) displayed a greater concern and understanding of women's issues and proposed a multi-pronged approach to women's integration in development. In rural development programmes, and particularly in the poverty alleviation programmes, the plan proposed that women should have at least a 30% share. But even in the Seventh and Eighth Plans we do not find any radical measures directed at changing women's socio-economic status.

Indian Banking Sector is involved in a big way in implementing the government's developmental policies. For sustainable rural development, Banks have to engage in the total development of the rural client-women being the least developed/most deprived of the rural banks' clientele. By incorporating Women's development/gender issues and gender training modules in the banking policies, the Indian Banking sector can fulfil its developmental responsibilities, better.

International Trends/Cross-Cultural Applicability of WID Endeavours

The process of consultation with several International/bilateral organisations (e.g. Canadian International Development Agency, CIDA vide Case Study 1/Annexure 1 to this chapter), foreign Commercial Banks (e.g. Bank of Montreal, Canada detailed vide Case Study 2/Annexure 2 to this chapter) and research/academic institutions, led to the following conclusions regarding WID policy issues which have universal applicability :

(a) This study of the Equal Opportunity/Gender Training Programmes of some International Development Financial Institutions has led to the formulation of **'BEST PRACTICES' CHECKLIST** which may, with suitable cross cultural/other adaptations, be used as a reference point by the Indian developmental financial and other public/private organisations keen on implementing such measures for not only providing women workers equality with men, but also creating conditions that are conducive to their special problems (e.g. disproportionate share of domestic/child rearing responsibilities, workplace harassment etc.). The inventory of policies, processes may be adopted for use by specific organisations as per their mission/prevalent culture/existing management philosophy and practices.

1. Management information system to gather employment equity information (e.g. through employee surveys) and special surveys to identify systemic barriers, key issues, attitudes in workforce.
2. In corporation of employment equity into annual operational plans and the linkage of Human Resource Plans to overall business plans.
3. Establishing senior management involvement/ accountability for employment equity and incorporating it into annual performance contracts/ evaluation.
4. Providing useful benefits (e.g. enhanced maternity benefits) and facilitative information on elder care/ child care arrangements etc.
5. Gender-fair recruitment and promotion e.g. by removal of systematic barriers (as the 'glass ceiling') and attaining a 'critical mass' of women in higher management/decision making.
6. Training and Development initiatives :
   — Training for new job skills;
   — Training for improving employee effectiveness on the job.
   — Educational upgrading programmes.
   — Retraining for returners.
   — Training for enhancing the Gender sensitiveness of the workforce.
7. Creating and maintaining a facilitative Organisational Culture through comprehensive Anti-Harassment Policies having explicit procedures for addressing complaints and having a support system for the complainants.

8. Addressing regional issues in organisations having widespread geographical operations, by ensuring that all employees have fair access to information on job openings and promotional opportunities. Such organisations have to also develop common corporate culture across a diverse range of worksites.

9. Targeted Recruitment, specially for non traditional occupations and provision of bridging programmes/ scholarships and internships.

10. Providing compensatory workplace training and management development support.

(b) The perusal of various WID policies of International/ bilateral organisations has provided a **CHECKLIST FOR MAINSTREAMING WOMEN IN DEVELOPMENT,** which can be implemented both at the level of the developmental institutions and in the wider national effort (through state intervention). The relevant parameters are :

1. Communicate a clear "Women & Development and gender equality" policy.

2. Promote a "gender equality enabling corporate culture" by building such organisational structures and norms that promote Gender equality.

3. Mainstream Gender equality at all organisational levels-policy formulation, program design, operation, and evaluation.

4. Procure adequate budgetary and manpower resource allocations for operational/training/advisory/other services.

5. Coordinate the institutions' women and development initiatives with other donor/NGO partners/ Government machinery.

6. Construct measurable quantitative and qualitative indices for measuring progress on mainstreaming women and development.

7. The big burden of working women for the management of their household responsibilities points to the need for policy initiatives for the improvement of the social infrastructure around women (e.g. neighbourhood child care provision).

8. The large number of women workers in the unorganised informal sector need to be reached and supported through marketing/other entrepreneurial support.

This CHECKLIST can be adapted for implementation by a developing country like India, whose Developmental and Financial Institutions play a vital role in implementing the Government's Women Development Programmes. These findings can lead to these institutions having a more gender fair organization culture/effective GT programmes.

Extent of International Corroboration/Validation of Reengineering Models Conclusions for GRD issue:

1. Organisations, including developmental financial institutions worldwide are undergoing radical redesigning/restructuring, with changes in working patterns in response to the demands of Information Technology/Globalisation etc., downsizing, flexibility in employment conditions/reduction in 'one job for a life time'. These are the conditions which affect the Indian Banking Sector as well. So the HRD related Re-engineering Interventions/Model of this study were found to be applicable to a large extent in the global context. In fact many of the new 'proactive' HRD measures proposed in this book (e.g. a 'learning' organisation culture, Strategic Human Resource Management for managing workplace diversity and implementing 'equal Opportunity'/Gender sensitive initiatives, use of Mentors etc.) are already being successfully implemented by International Agencies (as the World Bank, Canadian International Development Agency etc.)—giving strong

justification for the utilization of these measures by the Indian Organisations.

2. Progressive organisations in the west are providing continuous support throughout the career span of their employees by a suitable mix of institutional, on the job and online training modules.

3. Organisations abroad like Banking Institutions, place a lot of stress on enhancing productivity, and in improving their customer orientation as a strategy for corporate survival/meeting the challenges of globalisation induced competitiveness. This holds good for the Indian Banking Sector as well.

4. International Development Organisations are continuously working to improve the content and delivery of their 'Women and Development' programmes in their third world operations. Their approach offers many good practices for the Indian Developmental Financial Institutions like SIDBI, NABARD and other Rural Development Organisations in relation to their WID and other developmental policies/programes.

5. Considering the results of this research in terms of Human Resource Management Theories and principles as applied in both prescription and practice for the employment of Women in Organisations (considering such key features as strategic integration with business strategy, flexibility in employment contracts, high commitment work culture, emphasis on quality and performance) it is observed that HRM is not adequately sensitive to the gender aspects of employment. For both the 'soft' human — relations focus of the Harvard model and the 'hard' business —led HRM of the Michigan model a more gender sensitive HRM is required to give optimum expression to the potential of nearly half the human (woman) resources in employment.

6. The research discovered the following characteristics of organisations having effective equal opportunity/ HRD measures and plans for women employees:
   — accountability for results/involvement of both line and senior management in plan formulation.
   — setting of realistic goals and specific timetables.
   — inclusion of a comprehensive range of EO activities for remedying the short fall in women's representation.
7. Attempt at corroboration of the Reengineering Model also leads to the conclusion that despite these similarities in situation across many countries/ prevailing global trends, caution is required in adapting prescriptions to the unique requirements of the local cultures/sub-cultures of individual nations as per their national priorities/government strategies etc.

Women in Development/Gender Training

Reengineering for Human Resource and Social Development in Rural Banking

Introduction: The development oriented framework for a banker would mean basically playing two roles—functional, and promotional. The functional role would mean: quick delivery, ensuring end use of funds, anrecycling of funds. The promotional role would mainly include using credit as a lever of development, going beyond the functional role and focusing on the overall development of the customers in terms of creating awareness in them to increase their capability and confidence to handle a variety of problems faced in dealing with the environment. Bankers through education and development strategies can help in making the customer see his own inner potential to work for higher goals.

Banks can be a major resource for rural development—only with their large manpower and money power, they have to go beyond their traditional banking functions. While urban clients, with their education and socio-cultural awareness, can, with the help of bank's borrowing, lookafter their interests, the rural client is not capable of looking after his interests in the best manner. This makes the banker's role more demanding in dealing with the rural poor. Therefore, banks have a very important role in rural development, to look beyond traditional banking activities in rural areas, and have to actively engage themselves in the total development of the rural client.

This contention has been highlighted by the case study of the topical 'Women in Development'/Gender and Development' issue to be now considered—woman being the least developed and most deprived section of the rural banks' clientele. As this is a new area for the Rural Development Banking Sector of India, we shall discuss the approaches of the World Bank and Asian Development Bank in incorporating women's development/gender issues and gender training modules in their banking policies. This will serve as a model for similar initiatives by the Indian Banking Sector and its HRD/Training Systems. It will also provide insights into the enhanced developmental responsibilities of the Rural Banking sector in India which needs to be better expressed in its HRD and other operational policies.

Women in Development: Approach of Asian Development Bank

The Bank recognizes that improvements in the status of women are integral to achieving its other strategic development objectives, such as: poverty reduction, economic growth, development of a healthier and better-educated society, and overall sustainable development. Investments in women are now widely acknowledged as crucial in achieving sustainable development, in that poor health, low education and training levels, and limited access to resources not only limit women's quality of life but also their contribution to economic efficiency and growth. Public policies and investments that improve the status of women have such benefits as improved public health, low infant and maternal mortality, lower fertility rates, increased life expectancy, and reduced health and welfare costs.

The policy aims to increase the awareness of gender issues among Bank staff (taking into account the role and needs of women in all relevant facets of the development process), prepare country profiles and briefing papers to identify special circumstances and the socio-cultural context of individual developing member countries, formulate sector-specific guidelines, and create a gender-disaggregated database of selected socioeconomic indicators to facilitate monitoring of women's welfare. The Bank provides loans to support WID. It has also established a network of WID liaison coordinators in various operational departments. Coordinators, in cooperation with the WID project specialist, ensure that the role and needs of women are taken into account at all major stages of the project cycle.

Gender Issues in Lending: World Bank Study[3]

Background : Emergence of WID/Gender Issues

Since the early 1970s, numerous case-studies, social and economic research, and evaluation reports have measured the deleterious effects of World Bank projects that ignored differences in gender roles in a given setting. A series of international conferences sponsored by the United Nations served to highlight the relevance of gender issues for borrowing countries and development agencies.

Gender has become the preferred term for the inclusion of women in development planning. "Gender is preferred because it focuses on the roles of both women and men, not just women alone. In all gender training, gender refers to the social construction of men's and women's roles as distinguished from sex which refers to biological definition of men and women. There is some variation in how the word 'gender' is used". In the Harvard/World Bank frame- work the emphasis is on the depiction of men's and women's roles (activities, access to and control of resources and benefits) as they are, how these roles fit with project design and the likely impact of the project on men and women. In the Moser/

Development Planning Unit (London)/Institute for Development Studies (Sussex) model and many others, more emphasis is put on the relational aspect of gender, the relations between men and women, with women usually subordinate. Using this definition, planning more explicitly addresses the possibility of improving that subordinate position.

Early efforts to bring out the 'invisible' women in Bank-funded projects established some basic principles still found relevant in the current policy, which are as follows:

— Poverty alleviation, to address women's roles specifically within the larger policy framework of poverty alleviation.

— Mainstreaming to deal with women within the context of regular projects instead of special WID projects.

— Focusing on selected sectors, in particular, in rural and urban development, education and population, health and nutrition.

But progress in moving from rhetoric to action remained slow until the mid-1980s, when increased management support and resources made it possible to implement a more comprehensive program.

This study examined the evolution of World Bank strategy to integrate gender issues in Bank lending across sectors since 1967, and the outcomes achieved so far.

Study Findings: The study led to these conclusions:

Evolution of concepts and institutional setting: Throughout the 1970s and early 1980s, the efforts of some staff members and participation in international United Nations conferences during the International Decade for Women led the Bank to recognize the relevance of gender issues for poverty alleviation and economic growth; discuss the roles of women in Bank statements, reports and guidelines; and begin to provide staff with operational support and information.

Some principles recognized early on included the relevance of attention to women for poverty alleviation and economic growth, on grounds of improved efficiency and equity; the autonomy of member countries on culturally sensitive issues; and the desirability of focusing on sectors with the greatest pay-offs through mainstream projects, rather than projects with only women as beneficiaries.

In the second half of the 1980s, conceptual, institutional and operational changes accelerated as management took a proactive stance towards gender issues :

— Senior management and the Board provided steady, highly visible support as well as resources for gender-related action.

— A long-term, comprehensive program of operational support and research was agreed upon by women in Development staff and operations management.

— Resources earmarked for gender issues in Bank budget and trust funds greatly increased.

— A core of specialized staff was established, first in a central unit, then in the regions.

— A program of countrywide assessments of gender issues was undertaken as a basis for policy discussions with member countries regarding future projects.

Portfolio outcomes: In most cases, gender-related activities formed a relatively small part of the project, yet they were subject to the same implementation difficulties as any other component. Furthermore, the high number of area development projects among projects with gender-related action decened from FY 67 to FY 84, lowering overall performance of all projects with gender-related actions.

The following *conditions* were found associated with satisfactory achievement of gender-related actions:

— Country involvement and commitment to gender-related actions and the project as a whole.

— The clear integration of gender-related objectives with overall project objectives.

— Presence of staff with gender-experience.

— Supervision/attention to gender action.

— In some countries, there is preliminary evidence that the preparation of country-wide gender assessments helped strengthen borrowers' commitment to address gender issues, and led to more systematic integration of these issues in project identification and design.

Study Recommendations

1. To maintain the current momentum, evidence of strong support by every level of management and the Board will be essential. Sufficient resources and regular progress monitoring will also be necessary.
2. Gender-related actions are more likely to be implemented if borrower staff fully supports them and are committed to making them successful. The process of discussing gender issues at the country and sector level may help inform and convince project staff of the gender actions' relevance for successful implementation. Other steps could include the involvement of gender specialists during implementation, and participation in seminars.
3. Project design and implementation : Gender-related actions are 'more likely to be implemented if they are part of a broader social and economic analysis, and if they are well integrated into project objectives'. Social Assessment Guidelines provide guidance for early integration of social issues in project design. Managers should ensure that staff use these guidelines, and that the terms of reference for sector and operations work include explicit questions on gender issues whenever these issues are likely to be relevant.
4. To provide project managers, country planners, and the Bank with the information needed for successful implementation, progress indicators should measure outcomes on men and women separately whenever

appropriate; midterm reviews should assess progress on gender-related actions; and implementation completion reports should include gender-differentiated results in the lessons learned.

5. Gender Training: in several cases task managers modified their behaviour after having worked in the field with persons experienced in gender issues. This on-the-job training should be encouraged. The program now being initiated by the Gender Analysis and Policy team is expected to provide task managers with practical guidance through training sessions defined jointly with individual regions, and through the preparation of brief summaries of issues and operational examples. Gender issues should also continue to be integrated in sector training as appropriate.

6. Expost evaluations: The Operations Evaluation Department should look for lessons on gender issues when selecting projects for audits, impact evaluations, and country studies. Questions on differential gender effects and impact should be included in their terms of reference.

7. The history of gender in Bank lending shows how an institution organised by sectors and geography integrated an issue affecting its work in many sectors. `Networking and grassroots interest by staff were not sufficient to bring about structural and policy changes. Outside pressure, too, was useful but did not play a determining role. Strong management support, retreated often and accompanied by financial support, was needed to establish a new program.'

Gender Training at the World Bank : Lessons for Indian Rural Development Banking[4]

Introduction: Interest in gender issues-on the inclusion of women in development, on making development projects gender fair by offering equal opportunities to women and removing obstacles/discriminatory practices and empowering women — has led to several initiatives in this direction. An important endeavour is of 'Gender Training' — training on the inclusion of women in development planning/ programmes. This being a study on HRD and training systems, we shall now examine in some detail the Gender Training module of World Bank.

Gender Training at the World Bank: Training activities organised by the World Bank in the early 1980s developed a new approach to gender training that combined the case method and gender analysis. As gender issues became more visible during the 1970s, some agencies began to offer training on women in development. The World Bank sought the assistance from the Harvard Business School which had developed the case method as a pedagogical device for putting their graduate students in a situation requiring them to analyze and make judgements about business opportunities, problems, and decisions. For development cases, material includes information about the location of a project together with project objectives and resources and any other information that might be relevant in project analysis.

The Bank projects where attention to women's roles had or should have had an effect on project design and implementation were identified. Case Studies were written up from project files specifically for the workshops. Study questions and the planning assignment exercises at the end of the workshop were written from a World Bank perspective. To provide Bank project staff with a frame-work they could use to analyze the roles of women and man in a project area, the trainers reviewed Bank documents to identify the variables relevant to project outcomes on women starting from a first list of over 200 variables. The trainers and the WID advisor then elaborated an analytic framework comprising of:

— *Activity analysis*. Information on the roles of women and men with respect of socioeconomic activities namely: the reproduction and maintenance of human capital, and social functions (these are activities performed in the community that are part of traditional or political processes). These activities were to be examined according to four parameters: gender and age denomination, activity locus, remuneration form, and technology mode.

— *Access and control analysis*. The socioeconomic factors that underlie each activity, determining who does what, where and why, with particular reference to the access to and control of resources and the benefits associated with those activities.

— *Project cycle*. Understanding the women's dimension in information requirements and design opportunities at each stage of the project cycle.

Between 1984 and 1988, no Bank training on women in development or gender for World Bank staff could be identified. From 1988 to 1993, gender training was provided through courses specifically on gender, through the inclusion of gender analysis in other courses, and in some cases through courses on gender at the regional level.

Beginning in 1990, sectoral courses included an explicit gender component. The environmental assessment courses included a social analysis component focused on poverty, resettlement, gender, institution building and community participation. These are covered by lecture and some exercises in one half day of a two day course. The Bank Training Department coordinates the preparation of courses for Bank staff and provides administrative and logistic support. The content and delivery of the courses is determined principally by staff from the regions or central vice presidencies.

The Gender Analysis and Policy team of the World Bank supports mainstreaming of gender issues in operations; several innovative features devised by the GAP team are :

— Training for Bank staff tailored to operational needs at the regional level.

— `Best practices too lkits' providing task managers with a range of tools (key research findings, examples of strategies and Bank interventions, and lessons learned) on selected topics.

— Support to the regions to demonstrate, in selected countries, how gender concerns can be mainstreamed throughout preparation of country assistance strategies and operations.

Lessons for Indian Rural Banking

We shall no consider the relevant lessons from World Bank's Gender Training programme of interest to the Indian Rural Development Banking sector.

1. The conceptual framework and workshop program of the earlier World Bank WID training included awareness and skill training. The early World Bank and other institutional gender training assumed that information, a framework, and the application of reason were sufficient to persuade planners of the necessity and utility of including a gender perspective in their work. Current thinking is that 'more attention needs to be paid to the organisational context, and that incentives to use these new skills should be built into an organisation's incentive structure'.
2. Specifies on introducing and performing gender training require an extensive institutional analysis by staff experienced in gender training and in Bank thinking and procedures.
3. The recent increase in attention to participation and to anthropological and sociological perspectives in project development and decision-making provides a hospitable environment for greater inclusion of gender considerations. The Portfolio Management Task Force report emphasizes the need for better analysis during project preparation. This increases the importance of understanding the roles of women and men in the project area, and the likely impacts in terms of project success and effects on intended beneficiaries
4. A successful gender training program requires a firm commitment from management.

5. Considerable research is available from World Bank research and projects for constructing training materials. 'What is needed is a conceptual framework or an agreed upon mode of analyzing and using a gender perspective that suits or broadens the institution's objectives and information requirements'. This may need to be modified by sector or region.
6. An effective, though more gradual, approach would be to integrate a gender perspective into the most popular regular, usually sectoral, training courses.

Annexure: Case Study 1

Organisational Profile of the Canadian International Development Agency[5]

CIDA, is the Canadian government agency responsible for the Official Development Assistance program (ODA) for promoting sustainable development in developing countries through assistance in meeting basic human needs, safe-guarding human rights, women's participating in development, infrastructure services, promoting democracy and good governance, economic growth through private sector activity, and environmental protection. CIDA implements many international, national and regional initiatives in cooperation with various partners as recipient governments, the Canadian government, non-governmental organisations, private sector organisations and various international organisations and institutions. CIDA activities cover the following seven sectors: Geographic Programs, Multilateral Program, Canadian Partnership, Transition Countries, Communications, Policies and General Services.

As of March 31,1997, CIDAs workforce comprised of 1,286 people, of which 1,210 were permanent staff and 76 temporary employees. Most of these employees (82%) worked at head office in Hull, and a small proportion worked abroad (8%). The administration and foreign service category represented 60% of the Agency's employees. The administrative support category was the second largest at 24% followed by the scientific and professional category (8%), the management category (7%) and the technical and operational categories (1%). Ninety per cent (90%) of CIDA employees are unionized. As of March 31,1998 CIDA had 1,321 employees, of these 1,073 were located in headquarters, 109 in field postings.

Women were well represented at CIDA (734 women employees). The targets for women are exceeded in the Executive Group, Scientific and Professional, Administrative Foreign Service and in the Administrative Support categories, except in the Technical category where there remains a gap of 7.5% to reach the target. Compared to the Public Service's (PS) March 1996 statistics (48.2%) the Agency has a significantly higher rate (55.6%) of representation for woman. The Agency exceeded all of its recruitment targets for women resulting in an overall rate of recruitment of 66.0%. Women received lower shares than their representation in CIDA development leave opportunities, with the exception of education leave where all participants were women. The overall participation rate of women in training activities exceeded their rate of representation in the workforce by 13.3%, with the exception of women in the Executive Group where the rate of participation fell short of their representation by 11.7%. Employment equity for CIDA is, as part of honouring excellence in the Public Service, to achieve equality of representation of all designated groups in the Agency's human resources and thereby become a model federal department/ agency that has implemented the best employment equity and human resources management policies and programs.

CIDA's Employment Equity Action Plan 1998-2003 comprises of the following:

— Identify all barriers found in the employment systems review (ESR) that are within CIDA's control. Identify potential employment barriers for women.

— Support the implementation of the action plan with a pro-active communication strategy including participation of senior management.

— Review and amend present employment policies and practices so that new employment systems are barrier free. This could include actions such as:

  * develop screening grids to assess new policies and systems;

  * institute special measures to improve recruitment, training, promotion and retention opportunities for members of designated groups.

— Flexible working arrangements in the workplace available to employees, such as Tele-Work, part-time etc.

— Hire designated groups e.g. Executive Group employees according to the targets set by occupational categories.

— Establish a roster of members of under-represented groups who are interested in working with CIDA.

— Encourage the hiring of designated group students, and implement the new PSC Bridging Mechanisms for Student.

— Promote designated group employees according to the targets.

— Ensure that hiring and promotion reflects the available population of under represented groups within CIDA.

— Offer employees information/training sessions to help them prepare a resume and interview skills.

— Enhanced consultation mechanism on employment equity advisory committee including management representatives from several branches, representatives of the Human Resources Division, representatives of employees who are members of designated groups and unions members. Accurate employment equity database maintained.

In India, CIDA aims at strengthening the capacity of women's organisations to negotiate and deal with officials of the Government of India for raising women's status and facilitate policy dialogue on those economic and social policy issues which promote the status of women; support capacity building program among women's organisation which mitigate the negative impact of structural adjustment on women. CIDA endeavours to strengthen the capacity of women's groups to address environmental issues, build a knowledge base of women's participation in the private sector. Gender equality is more apt to be achieved in CIDA's WID and GE policy if alongwith other factors, certain HRD factors are considered.

* senior management commitment to gender equality.
* sufficient resources and knowledgeable personnel, along with an enabling corporate environment to promote gender equality.
* employment qualified gender equality specialists (especially locally-based ones)
* accountability frameworks.

CIDAs Women in Development Policy

CIDA adopted its first Women in Development policy guidelines 20 years ago, ahead of most of its bilateral counterparts. The Agency has long been committed to promoting women in development and gender/equity issues. The policy itself has been revised periodically since 1984, when it was first approved to reflect the changing circumstances in Canada and developing countries has been based on the principle of accountability and has emphasised measuring results. In 1995, the policy was revised and renamed the "Women in Development and Gender Equity Policy" (WID & GE) and became part of a broader trend in the Canadian government. In 1994, the government announced that Canada's Official Development Assistance (ODA) was to focus on six programming priorities including WID & GE. This recognized the fundamental importance of the role that women play in improving economic and social conditions in developing countries. Canada's international and domestic equal opportunity initiatives/gender-equity objectives complement each other. They have provided impetus for CIDA's gender-equity programs. Between 1992 and 1995, CIDA launched a major corporate renewal process for making the Agency more results oriented.

Though WID & GE practices are slowly penetrating CIDA the integration of WID & GE into agency practices continues to challenge and steady, highly visible management support is essential. Other findings include:

— the development of accountability frameworks require further effort;

— practical training in a wide variety of gender-related skills is required;

— participatory approaches to development, monitoring and evaluation are essential in raising gender issues and getting impact;

— Many agencies continue to rely on personal, individual commitment and efforts.

— professional gender specialists should be included on all project teams.

Gender Training at CIDA

Courses on WID/gender have been offered since 1985 at CIDA starting with the Harvard training model and then Social/Gender Analysis training (between 1990 and 1994). Based on a review of the SGA course that revealed the need for more experimental-type and practical learning a pilot course was delivered and evaluated over 1994-95, which established the need to base WID & Gender Equity learning programs on a multi-disciplinary team that equally comprises adult education and content expertise. This led to the developing and delivering of four modules in 1996 in the new WID & Gender Equity in Practice learning program skills based Continuous Learning intervention designed to support CIDA employees in developing WID/GE competencies in a results-based context.

The New Program comprised the following:

* Module 1
* Practising Gender Equity
* Concepts Methods and Tools
* Module 2
* Gender Sensitive Planning for Results
* Module 3
* Gender Equity
* A matter of Good Management
* Module 4
* Institutionalizing Change
* Building Successes.

The new program was assessed against effectiveness and efficiency. *Course effectiveness* measuring the value of the training experience in relation to individual learning objectives and general module outcomes revealed a gap between realization of individual learning objectives. These findings resulted in a set of recommendations. *Course efficiency* involved the examination of the factors such as which contribute to the realization of course objectives. The factors included :

* the content of modules
* the training methodology
* the time frame
* the training materials and environment.

Annexure : Case Study 2

Organisational Profile of the Bank of Montreal[6]

The Bank of Montreal is the third largest chartered bank in Canada measured by assets. It operates about 1200 branches and 1220 Automated Teller Machines in Canada, the US and

17 other countries. The Bank of Montreal has about 26,500 permanent employees. The share of permanent parttime employees in the Bank's total workforce has been rising. The largest occupational groups in the Bank's permanent full-time workforce are junior and middle managers (40%), clerical (35%) and professional (16%), Clerical workers account for 91% of permanent part-time positions. Women accounted for almost 70% of the Bank of Montreal's permanent full time workforce and over 91% of the permanent part time workforce. Women accounted for 90% of both full time and part-time clerical positions, 61% of professional jobs and 55% of middle management positions and 91% of supervisory jobs. Only 9% of executives are women.

The Bank of Montreal, like all banks in Canada, is governed by the federal Employment Equity Act. Compliance with the provisions of the Act initially shaped the Bank's approach to employment equity. However, as a result of its new Corporate Strategic Plan, the Bank of Montreal put women at the core of its human resource strategy for the nineties. The Bank believed that, in the 1990s, the driving force of gains in customer service will be the ability of employees to form a partnership with each customer. Employees development is seen as being the linchpin to providing customers with a distinctive level of service. Given that women account for about 75% of the Bank's workforce, the advancement of women was an essential element of the Bank's human resource strategy. Given the realities of organisational downsizing and flattening, advancement opportunities would embrace not only promotional opportunities but also opportunities for development and growth that will enable women to realize their full potential. The Bank of Montreal's commitment to building a fair and equitable workplace was motivated by these factors.

There was a need to remedy the imbalance between men and women at the Bank, especially the inadequate representation of women in the Bank's senior management and executive levels. In recognition of society's changing values, the Bank needed to take steps to enable its employees, both men and women to balance their multiple commitments to work and family. It made good business sense since the Bank would benefit from a better and more productive workforce —equality in the workplace was seen as part of a deeper transformation that the Bank felt it must make if it is to stay competitive from a hierarchical, top-down organisation to a flexible, quality driven and creative organisation.

The Bank of Montreal established a "Task Force on the Advancement of Women in the Bank" in 1990 to address why women were under represented at senior levels in the Bank and what should be done to remedy the problem. In response to the recommendations of the Task Force, the Bank's President committed the Bank to dramatic and systemic change to achieve equality in the workplace by initiating measures as:

(a) In order to ensure that the proportion of women and men in a given job category ultimately reflects the available labour supply for the job, the Bank is working to ensure that there is proportional representation in key recruitment programs.

(b) The merit system for advance/promotion continues to be improved. The Bank's new initiatives are designed to ensure that all employees can participate fairly and equitably in the system.

(c) A number of the Bank's benefits/policies have been designed to contribute to a fair and equitable workplace including the introduction of a child care referral service, advice on eldercare arrangements, and flexible working arrangements.

(d) The Bank of Montreal training and development policies include :

— increasing both the quantity and quality of training received by all Bank employees;

— introducing the new programs specifically designed to enhance workplace equality (such as the "Women and Men as Colleagues" program);

— placing increased emphasis on managerial training;

— integrating issues related to workplace equality into more training courses.

(e) Flexible Working Arrangements providing the employee with flexibility on when, where and how the work gets done have been initiated by the Bank e.g.

— Flexitime enables employees to arrange the start and finish time of the standard work day;

— while flexplace enable employees to arrange to perform some or virtually all of their work outside their traditional office, perhaps in another Bank location, or at home.

(f) under its sexual harassment policy the Bank is committed to providing employees an environment free of sexual and other forms of harassment. Employees are provided guidance on how they should respond in the event of an incident.

(g) A detailed strategy has been developed to ensure that employees are kept informed of every step in the Bank's march toward equality in the workplace through its regular publication for its employees, 'First Bank news', and "875 Live" which is a regularly released Bank Video.

(h) With the exception of a limited number of initiatives, the Bank of Montreal has no recruitment, training or development programs that are targeted specifically at women as the Bank feels that special targeted programs tend to alienate the workforce rather than foster its integration. The Bank's training programs have been developed to be equally accessible to both its male and female employees.

Notes

1. UNDP: *Human Development Report*, 1995.
2. Govt. of India: *Fourth World Conference on Women, Beijing 1995—Country Report*. New Delhi : GOI, 1995.
3. Murphy, Josette L.: *Gender Issues in World Bank Lending*, 1995.
4. *Ibid*.
5. Canadian International Development Agency: *CIDA's Policy on Gender Equality*. CIDA Publication, 1999.
6. Bank of Montreal, Canada: *Various Reports and Publications*.

10

Summing Up—Reengineering HRD/ Training Model for the Indian Banking Sector: Long -Term Prospects

Overview : This study began with an attempt at understanding the Indian Banking Sector including Rural Development Banking and the restructuring it is undergoing under the influence of financial sector reforms /globalisation. We then analyzed the existing HRD and Training Systems in the Indian Banking Sector, the gap in these systems and concluded that a radical reengineering effort was required for bridging this gap to make this sector effective in coping with both current and future challenges.

Subsequently, we covered various facets that should be covered by this Reengineering: HRD interventions at the organisational level, improving the training delivery mechanism, coverage of critical training areas and reengineering HRD/ Training for Rural Development Banking and for crucial concerns such as Women and Development. As would be apparent from this analysis, the reengineering envisaged is a complex multifaceted task which requires concerted action at many levels.

In this chapter, we shall attempt to draw the various strands running through this study together and propose an integrated reengineering model which will summarize the various findings of the HRD/Training interventions proposed in this study. The requisite components of the model can be utilized as per demand of the situation. We shall also elaborate on the limitations, pragmatic considerations associated with the model, and illustrate its applicability in certain situations. Lastly we shall examine this Study's limitations, and the Indian Banking Sector's long-term prospects, in the context of proposed reengineering.

Reengineering HRD/Training Model for the Indian Banking Sector

Introduction : The world economy is passing through a turbulent phase. While there is a state of depression and unheard of unemployment in the developed world, the developing countries including India while continuing to struggle with their traditional poverty related problems have also to cope with the modern problems of adjusting with the pressures of globalization, liberalization of financial sector. And the banking sector, being the chief carrier of the country's economy, has to bear the brunt of the traditional and modern problems, modernization/ diversification of the economy.

Rapid changes in the economic scene and the trend towards globalisation of the country's trade will naturally call for an enlarged and more aggressive role to be played by the Indian banking system. The traditional methods of working of these banks, still largely on manual systems and techniques require to be modernized. The advances in science and technology necessitate development of new skills and new attitudes in the large workforce of banks in all levels of management and operations. As the process of change accelerates, less emphasis can be paid on experience and increasingly more attention will need to be paid to the HRD/ Training of these people in the new techniques and new ways of working with new concepts and knowledge. Improving the planning capabilities of the top level executives to attune the banks to the changing needs and expectations had never been so vital as now. The large network of each bank spread over widely in all parts of the country calls for more meaningful and defacto decentralization and widening of delegation and autonomy and developing multi-functional capabilities in a large number of managers at different levels.

But for doing so effectively, the Indian Banking Sector has to be equipped with the requisite capabilities through legislative, organizational and HRD channels . It is in this context that the present study has made a compact analysis of current HRD and the training scenario in the Indian Banking Sector— its infrastructure, operational problems, training gap and the organizational restructuring, training reengineering efforts required for bridging the gap. The study lays special emphasis on Rural Development Banking and on addressing Women and Development/gender issues in Development Banking.

The above analysis enables us to propose a Reengineering Training Model as a component of HRD superstructure for the Indian Banking Sector which incorporates the various parameters required to provide effective HRD/training to the sector. We shall elaborate the various features/facets of this model in some detail. We shall be discussing the following:

(A) The major components of the Model.

(B) Phases/ Steps in the operation of the Model.

(C) Pragmatic Considerations to be kept in view for the successful practical operation of the Model.

(D) Practical Applicability of the Model illustrated through two hypothetical examples related to the functioning of the Indian Banking Sector.

(E) Limitations that may be present in implementing this Model.

A. Components of the Model

We shall discuss the major components of this Model under the following headings (in accordance with the plan of the study) (1) Reengineering: HRD Interventions, (2) Reengineering: Training Delivery Mechanism, (3) Reengineering: Critical Training Areas, (4) Reengineering HRD and Training for Rural Development Banking, (5)

Reengineering HRD : Gender Resource Development, (6) A Framework for choosing appropriate Training Strategy.

1. Reengineering: HRD Interventions[1]

1.1 The far-reaching changes in the Banking scenario, has thrown up a number of challenges in the operational areas as well as in HRM/HRD functions forcing the Banks to have a review of their various policy frameworks, functions and practices so as to appropriately redesign them to effectively respond to the metamorphosis that is now taking place in the business profile of the Banks.

1.2 The development of appropriate HRD/Training Inputs calls for a 'proactive approach' in conceptualizing, designing, planning and implementing appropriate HRD/Training Plans.

HRD interventions would call for (a) a philosophy of top management and the mechanism to transmit this philosophy, (b) management processes at top and other levels demonstrating use of such a philosophy in taking decisions, (c) an adequate organizational structure with clarity of roles/staff competencies to undertake the planned change,(d) internal mechanisms requiring adequate feed back to the top management, (e) the institutionalization of HRD by seeking involvement of all strategic groups and opinion makers including trade unions and associations.

1.3 The strategic categories are identified who should constitute strong partnership for revitalizing the HRM function to be able to respond to new challenges and opportunities in the Millennium. These strategic groups are: (i) Governments, (ii) Indian Banks' Association, (iii) individual banks, (iv) Trade Unions and Officers' Associations and (v) various customer groups/ associations.

1.4 Change in Banking and other laws by the government of India to give greater operational autonomy to banks to enable them to make this workforce more disciplined and accountable and hence more 'trainable'.

1.5 One of the prime issues for HRD to focus at, would be to improve the general climate of discipline, productivity of staff, eradication of restrictive practices at all the levels: Branches, which are the action point for interface with customers require allround improvement in these aspects as they experience widely prevalent practice relating to restriction of output. Low productivity, apathy to customer service and problems on account of attendance and punctuality.

1.6 Changes in personnel/HRD policies and on providing a separate route of promotion to high fliers, management of talent and rewards based on performance. Consequent to Internationalization/ launching of several allied/ancillary financial/fee-based services, a need is felt for induction of more specialists/professionals especially in the area of information technology/communication/financial analysis/ management at various levels and scouting for such top talents from within. It would be necessary to provide them a faster route for career growth.

1.7 The organizational culture of the banking sector has to become more professionalized, oriented towards becoming 'learning organization' so that self development (or auto training) is carried out informally during the entire service period of employees.

1.8 A new work culture facilitating higher productivity. job enrichment/enlargement, an environment free from restrictive/wasteful practices. Encouraging the emergence of Coaching/Mentoring phenomena should be encouraged by the Indian Banks.

1.9 Planned change in the culture, technology and management of Indian Banks can be attempted through the use of Organisation Development Initiative (ODI) to improve problem solving capabilities. Different OD interventions, both structured and unstructured may be attempted to tackle various problems in this context of banks.

1.10 The industrial relations climate in banks has to be turned from one of 'fire fighting approach' to one based on mutual faith, trust and collaborative relationship through appropriate HRD measures.

1.11 The HRD policies of the banking sector have to become proactive-'strategic' (SHRM) geared differentially to their internal differences/diversities in the work force and continuous retraining imparted to prevent obsolescence.

1.12 In the last two decades, the induction of two strategic groups, viz., SC/ST and women and on going induction of OBC's in Banking has posed new challenges in the area of training and development as well as their specialization process. Special effort is required to prepare SC/ ST employees to develop in them a sense of confidence and systematically provide them opportunities to bring the best out of them. Similarly women who now constitute about 15 per cent of the work force in some banks require special attention in view of unique problem that they face.

2. Reengineering: Training Delivery Mechanism[2]

2.1 The training efforts of individual, commercial, rural and Cooperative Banks and of their apex level controlling/Central Banks like Reserve Bank, NABARD have to be pooled together, joint strategies devised to maximize productivity while giving adequate stress to the diversities of structures and geographical spread of the industry.

2.2 The training machinery of each bank should be given more operational autonomy, decentralized functioning and greater say in the HRD policies of recruitment, manpower planning etc., corporate philosophy of the institution.

2.3 Training Needs Identification has to be done on a continuous basis at three levels : Corporate, operational and individual for all categories of staff: senior/ middle/ junior management for clerical staff for urban as well as rural banking.

2.4 The training methodology should use a mix of the classroom lecture/teaching aids and innovative/ open techniques like interactive video, computer based training, mobile job trainers for remote branches, broader development initiatives like Organisation Development Initiative the selection from the menu being decided by the specific training requirements.

2.5 The training techniques have to become more learner centred than trainer–centred and adapted to such ground realities as wide dispersal of the target learner population, limited capacity of training institutions, absence of correlation between training and current/ future placement.

2.6 The training machinery should supply training on demand, to cater to imminent specific problems of each individual employee trainee, since in this dynamic era of liberalization pressures the banking sector has to respond urgently to the emergent service requirements of all sections of a rapidly changing economy, without the loss of time involved in the formal constitutional approach.

2.7 Innovative Training Methodology has to be used to provide continuous training support throughout the career span of employees by suitable mix of institutional, on the job and on line training modules;

assignment/projects/study reports can be utilized to retain involvement and obtain feedback from the trainees.

2.8 The training software should be of high quality, topical interactive, learner-centred, adaptive to suit the requirements of different training tools and trainees' level/ background. The software should be constructed by pooling of resources of all the training institutions/HRD departments of apex and individual banks by allocation of work and supervision, by a joint consultative committee of these organizations. These training packages could then by the used by the individual banks (after suitable adaptation) to reflect the characteristics/concerns/ practical procedures unique to each institution.

2.9 Post-training situation placement should be studied carefully and impact and effectiveness of training programmes should be evaluated periodically.

3. Reengineering: Critical Training Areas[3]

3.1 The training support has to be provided to enable the bank personnel perform the traditional banking functions in a better way by minimizing the existing deficiencies related to absence of marketing/ customer orientation, poor housekeeping and proneness to frauds. The training should also enable the bankers to become equal to the emerging challenges of globalization and financial sector reforms, Information Technology and innovative rural development banking.

3.2 The future managers in banks should not only confine themselves to technical achievements but also gear themselves to discharging the functions of a marketing specialist, a public relations officer, a person capable of catching new technologies such as computerised banking and administering new financial products and services. They should also develop skills in product development, product selling, planning and administering. The Training System should be capable of imparting such skills as mentioned above to the managerial staff.

3.3 The Indian economy is progressively opening. The imperative need for expanding the country's foreign trade, setting up of joint ventures abroad, attracting savings of non-resident Indians, investment banking, raising of resources from the international capital markets etc., underline the need for effective role of Indian banks in the international banking scene.

3.4 Training should be imparted on the rapid advances in telecommunications, of Information Technology (I.T.): training should be given using I.T methods as on-line networks, multimedia, interactive video, embedded CBT etc. The contents and emphasis of training should be designed keeping in view the future banking scenario and after taking into consideration factors like technology, communication and information. Training in computers should be given, as computerization of banking operations i.e. to handle and maintain massive volume of bank accounting and book-keeping is gathering momentum.

3.5 Training should aim to improving interpersonal skills, appropriate attitudes among employees. For this, Transactional Analysis and Behavioural Sciences programmes can be made use of.

3.6 In the present context, productivity and quality consciousness and customer orientation are being identified as the pre-requisities for corporate survival and competitiveness and hence should be among the major thrust areas of training.

3.7 The Indian Banking System's phenomenal growth calls for massive efforts on developing the managerial skills in banks -it requires management development and education, but also development of skills in new operational areas.

4. ReengineeringHRDand Training for Rural Development Banking[4]

4.1 In order that rural development, in its proper perspective is achieved through economic help from the banks, it is necessary that the banks pay increasing attention to human resource development for rural banking. HRD is not a one shot affair. It would mean a planned change on a continuous basis, changing the perspective of bank personnel and motivating them to undertake rural banking jobs with a sense of dedication and commitment. The basic skill involved in the development of people through rural development programmes would require a new orientation altogether. Development of all these traits requires effective HRD/ Training interventions such as :

— Sound placement policies giving rural orientation to one and all who join banking industry;

— Suitable recruitment strategies to acquire such personnel who can identify themselves with rural processes and develop empathy for the rural mass by their very background;

— Developing reward and punishment system consistent with performance in rural areas;

— Developing systems for better communication and prompt grievance resolution of the rural employees;

— Performance linkages of creative involvement with rural development rather than merely traditional banking in rural areas; and

4.2 Rural Banking Training has to cover the areas of: Deposit, mobilization from rural customers, techniques of tapping the saving of rural masses, rescheduling the payment of dues in times of loss of earnings of specified class of customers due to sickness/ natural calamity, shift into granting loans towards a purpose oriented approach as against the traditional security-oriented approach examining the economic, technical and commercial viability of the projects.

4.3 Training for Rural Banking should aim for skill development for handling the change in the practices and procedures of rural lending due to service area concept, credit planning at the village level-assessment of credit needs-infrastructural support for command area of operations-credit dispensation. The training needs of the banking industry in its developmental role in the context of the *Service Area Approach* would require training on basis of agricultural financing, financial and technical parameters of various types of rural activities such as crop cultivation, horticulture pisciculture, animal husbandry schemes financing, schematic lending etc., inputs regarding their role in service area scheme: village survey method, credit planning etc.

4.4 Rural Bankers have to be trained for educating customers for prompt repayment of borrowed funds, long-term benefits of sound ethics and conduct in banker borrower relationship.

4.5 To make rural development efforts a success apart from infusion of credit. urban oriented bankers and government officials posted in rural areas require training to become effective in rural credit delivery system. So there should be frequent training meets of bankers and governmental grassroot level functionaries to enable them develop empathy for each other and work for a common cause.

4.6 The training for Rural Banking (alongwith institutional facilities) has also to be supplied at the doorstep wherever it is needed —the trainers reaching the remote rural bank branches (characteristic of the Indian Banking system) and impart training in consonance with the rural ethos and rural development imperatives by the use of mobile job trainers or distance learning modules, wherein the training needs of all the personnel of one branch or several neighbouring branches can be covered.

4.7 For Regional Rural Banks, conventional training has to be provided to equip RRB staff with knowledge and skills of doing their jobs better.However for changing their averse mindset, (caused by the RRB work culture) reengineering through the innovative Organization Development Initiative (ODI) is required ODI involves making the RRB personal appreciate the new realities in the context of reforms in the banking sector, developing among them a sense of belonging to their organization, making them internalize and own up to their problems, developing their abilities to find solutions themselves inculcating group/ team spirit. ODI has been successful in inculcating change in RRB staff's attitudes, beliefs organizational climate and systems and procedures.

4.8 For better effectivenessof the Cooperative Movement/Banks, necessary action has to be taken in raising general consciousness in the community about cooperative principles and values in addition to educating the members: management training and member education should lead to an economically viable cooperative movement. Appropriate institutioned/HRD mechanisms have to built up at all levels to enable the movement to effectively carry out the following training, education and information functions.

— establishing of an appropriate cooperative personnel policy.

— training staff.

— training of management committee.

— member education.

— publicity and public relation.

— research and consultancy, and monitoring and evqluation.

4.9 Since the entry of commercial banks into rural credit structure and their role as a pace setter of rural economic development, personnel of commercial banks have to learn much from cooperative banks regarding techniques of lending in rural areas, recovery problems, land records, linking credit with marketing etc.

5. **Reengineering HRD: Gender Resource Development**[5]

5.1 For sustainable rural development, the credit inputs by the banking sector by themselves being insufficient, banks have to engage in the total development of the rural client, specially of least developed/most deprived sections such as the rural poor and women. For this banks have to incorporate requisite policies e.g. for women's development/ gender issues and gender training modules in their operational banking and HRD/Training policies. The following conditions have to be fulfilled through suitable interventions for satisfactory achievement of gender-lated actions:

— Country involvement and commitment to gender related actions and the project as a whole.

— The clear integration of gender-related objectives with overall development project objectives.

— Presence of bank staff with gender-experience (for which e.g. appropriate gender training would have to be imparted).

5.2 The following aspects were observed regarding international corroboration / validation of this study's findings in the Women and Development arena:

1. Organisations worldwide are undergoing radical restructuring. Many Strategic Human Resource initiatives (including equal opportunity / Gender sensitive, initiatives, use of Mentors etc.) are already being successfully implemented by International Agencies (as the World Bank, Canadian International Development Agency etc.)–giving strong justification for the utilization of these measures by the Indian Organisations.
2. Progressive organisations in the west are providing continuous support throughout the career span of their employees by a suitable mix of institutional, on-the-job and on line training modules.
3. Organisations abroad like Banking Institutions, place a lot of stress on enhancing productivity, and in improving their customer orientation as a strategy for corporate survival, meeting the challenges of globalisation induced competitiveness. This holds good for the Indian Banking Sector as well.
4. International Development organisations are continuously working to improve the content and delivery of their 'Women and Development' programmes in their third world operations. Their approach offers many good practices for the Indian Developmental Financial Institutions like SIDBI, NABARD and other Rural Development Organisations in relation to their WID and other developmental policies/ programmes.
5. Considering the results of this research in terms of Human Resource Management Theories and

Principles as applied in both prescription and practice for the employment of women in organisations considering such key features as flexibility in employment contracts high commitment work culture. emphasis on quality and performance) it is observed that HRM is not adequately sensitive to the gender aspects of employment. For both the 'soft' human-relations focus of the Harvard model and the 'hard' business- led HRM of the Michigan model a more gender sensitive HRM is required to give optimum expression to the potential of nearly half the human (woman) resource in employment.

6. The research discovered the following characteristics of organisations having effective equal opportunity/HRD measures and plans for women employees.

   — accountability for result involvement of both line and senior management in plan formulation.

   — setting of realistic goals and specific timetables.

   — inclusion of a comprehensive range of EO activities for remedying the short fall in women's representation.

7. Attempt at the corroboration of the Reengineering Model also leads to the conclusion that despite these similarities in situations across many countries/prevailing global trends, caution is required in adapting prescriptions to the unique requirements of the local cultures,/sub-cultures of individual nations as per their national priorities, government strategies etc.

6. A Framework For Choosing Appropriate Training Strategy

Having looked at the various reengineering interventions/components of this Model we shall now workout

CRITERIA	POSSIBLE TRAINING STRATEGIES			
	On the job Training	Institutional Training	Organisation Development Initiative	Distance Learning
Organisational culture				
Training/ Learning Objectives				
Organization Training Resources				
Training Curriculum				
Trainee related factors				

an approach for deciding upon an appropriate Training Strategy in a specific Training Situation.

For determining an optimum training intervention strategy one approach could be through the application of a simple matrix which juxtaposes requirements and potential solutions. The two dimensions of the matrix would be: the key criteria which must be satisfied if the proposed strategy is to be successful and the range of possible training strategies. A possible Matrix for the Indian Banks would be as above.

The use of this matrix helps to determine which strategy will best accommodate both the opportunities and the problems inherent in a particular situation, the reasons for and against the potential choices are evaluated and the optimum or 'best fit' solution emerges. The use of the matrix however does not provide automatic solutions. Its series of questions enable careful consideration of a range of possible options. Which particular elements to include on each axis will vary according to circumstances. In making this choice, account will be taken of such factors as the banking organizations' HRD/ Training /other corporate policies, trainer and trainee related factors etc., over, all approach to training, level of sophistication of relevant staff etc.

The need to achieve training/ learning objectives is a key factor in the choice of training strategy. It is important to think carefully about possible suitable strategies, and, if necessary modify the training targets accordingly. For example, is the proposed training consistent with the banks policies.' Is the strategy adequate in the sense that it can achieve the learning objectives within the required time horizon? By asking these questions in relation to each of the possible training strategies listed on the other axis of the matrix, the degree of compatibility with the objectives can be considered and a short list compiled of the probable choice or choices.

Consideration must also be given to the support that the training may receive in the given organizational culture. Resources for training criterion has to be examined e.g. variety of learning opportunities, the time available, money, equipment and technical expertise and an evaluation made of their suitability in relation to the preferred strategies. Suitability here implies the capacity to contribute to the success of the training and that the contribution be cost effective. Trainee- related factors to take into account include the learners needs and personal agenda for training the experience and current expertise of the trainees, their preferred styles ges.

The strategies listed in the matrix above do not include all possible options -there would be other possibilities which need to be worked out as the situational requirements e.g. On-the-job Training emphasizes the potential for learning in the present job environment. This form of training is typically extremely cost effective and includes coaching, mentoring and deputizing for the boss. In other situations this may be preceded/ followed /re - placed by Institutional Training, ODI, Distance Learning or even other training strategies (like Computer Based Training, Interactive Video, Field Trips etc.)

For each case, the specific package needs to be designed by matching the training criteria, training strategy, and overall corporate HRD philosophy/perspective plan.

B. Phases/Steps in the Model's Operation

This reengineering Model for organizational HRD and Training redesign of the Indian Banking Sector has to proceed along a systematic line of action to be effective. It may be divided into four phases (which would consist of several steps): 1. Preparing for change 2. Planning for change 3. Designing Change. 4. Evaluating change, which we shall now elaborate.

First Phase : The first phase, *preparing for change* sets the foundation for future activity. This phase takes a two-pronged approach to change. The first prong involves building understanding and support in management and increasing management awareness of the need for change. The top management of Indian Banks may not be always aware of the ground realities and has to be accordingly motivated. These activities provide direction for the reengineering effort and build an internal review and approval process. The second prong prepares for a cultural shift and buy in by the organization's employees by informing the employees of their role in the upcoming change process. This may involve overcoming their resistance to change, and seeking the in-corporation of critical groups, like employee trade unions and HR diversities (e.g. women employees) in the change process.

Second Phase : The second phase, *planning for change*, operates under the assumption that organizations need to plan their future because of the constantly changing marketplace- the forces of globalization and financial sector reforms affecting the Indian Banking Organisation. Any organisation that assumes economic conditions, consumer needs and expectations, and competition in the marketplace will be the same two, three, or five years from now is being unrealistic. The planning phase provides a process by which management can envision the future (a global competitive, customer oriented market-place which needs to simultaneously cater to the modernistic demands of say export financing, merchant banking, computerised branches on one hand and of say rural financing in far flung rural branches, development of the poor/women clientele, innovations like Self Help Credit Groups on the other hand) and develop actions needed to operate effectively in that future by building on the organization's core competencies. Planning for change also provides direction and guidelines for the next phase-designing change.

Third Phase : The third phase, *designing change*, provides a method to identify, assess, map, and ultimately, redesign business processes. It offers the necessary framework for translating insights about the process being explored into quantum leaps of change. From an operational viewpoint, a process is a bound set of interrelated work activities, each having prescribed inputs and outputs; a method for doing things. Exploring the cultural aspects of the process is important because people make the process work. The organisation culture of the Indian Banking Sector has to be made supportive of the reegineering process through Strategic Human Resources Management endeavours, by turning it into productive, effective, customer friendly learning arena through appropriate HRD/Training (e.g. Organisation Development Initiative) and other necessary operational/policy interventions. Old processes may include several/cultural aspects that are highly desirable and that should be maintained in the new process.

The reegineering of business process must be driven by the organisation's core competencies and customer requirements. Some of the core competencies of the Indian Banking Sector are it's highly educated manpower, large branch network, established banking culture in the country–which, however require reengineering interventions outlined in the study in order to make this sector serve the current needs of the dynamic Indian economy in a highly effective manner. If a process is reegineered without these considerations, a lot of time and energy can be spent changing a process that does not need changing in the first place. In turn, this wasted energy tends to shift to frustration, which can significantly hinder any future reegineering effort.

Fourth Phase : The final phase, *evaluating change*, provides a means to evaluate the improvement during a predetermined time frame, usually a year, and to develop priorities for the coming years. The need to measure and thereby improve productivity of an organization is paramount. For an organization to improve and increase effectiveness-productivity and, profitability, it needs varied and complete measurements applied to a broad range of activities and processes. Several obstacles hinder the application of meaningful measurements, including management's reluctance to provide the required measurement resources. The Reengineering Model proposed in this study is a complex one, has various facets, and has to pass through several phases. It is necessary that there is an inbuilt mechanism to constantly evaluate the effectiveness and direction of the change process resulting from the application of the Model. This will ensure that the reegineering will proceed in the desired direction with minimum of undesirable side effects (e.g. employee alienation).

C. Pragmatic Considerations

We shall now discuss the pragmatic considerations which have to be kept inview in order to ensure the successful practical operation of our Reengineering Model:

1. *Anticipating Changes*: Retraining is an important aspect of preparation for reengineering related restructuring. Therefore, there is need for proaction. This is possible when we anticipate changes and plan what kind of restructuring is most appropriate to cope with technological and other changes. Restructuring may take several forms such as changes in technology, process, products, etc. Growth, modernisation, expansion, diversification, mergers, acquisition, disinvestment etc., also entail restructuring. Its effects

on jobs and skills vary with the nature of pressures/ forces of change/restructuring and the situation in which an enterprise is located.

2. *Changing Pattern of Demand/Supply for skills*: In services sectors like Indian Banks there is a gradual trend towards shift away from blue-collar to white-collar and professional, knowledge workers. This is the result of progressive shift away from muscle to machine to mind and the rapid changes in technologies, products and processes, wherever they are occurring. The shortages and mismatches between supply and demand for relevant new/emerging skills should be foreseen well ahead and appropriate actions taken to meet the requirements.

3. *Team Working*: It is an important requirement of new technologies and modern organisations, but is also a major area of weakness in Indian Banks. Therefore, organisations need to focus on training for team working and restructuring work planning and performance review systems around team performance.

4. *Training of Older Workers* : Training of older workers is a problem area. Managements may be unwilling to invest because of cost-benefit considerations. Workers' too may be reluctant or unable to learn and fear about the consequences of possible failure with new skills/tasks/work situations. This problem needs redressal.

5. *Labour-Management Co-operation*: The role of labour/ trade unions in training and retraining depends on their role in reegineering. Good communication between employers and workers' representatives will facilitate restructuring. Training is considered as a less conflictual labour-management issue. Since unions generally have come to understand that participation in training helps them obtain a large influence in the general 'restructuring' of the enterprise, bank

managements are required to solicit their cooperation for the success of the HRD/Training intervention proposed in this Model.

6. Since the staff of the banking sector continues to be largely urban educated/oriented, for applying the essence of this model to rural banking it is imperative to involve experts with a sound grasp of rural banking, who are in touch with the ground realities of extreme poverty, mental backwardness, feudal set up and oppressive government machinery functioning in the rural areas, instead of taking an idealistic view of things.

7. To cope with the existing and varied requirements of training for the Indian Banking Sector, the faculty team has to be multidisciplinary, highly qualified and innovative.

8. To resolve operational problems encountered in the day to day functioning of the banking sector, practical rather than theoretical approaches have to be devised by the training machinery.

9. Though the training is imparted necessarily on a piece-meal basis, the sight of the whole should be kept in mind and long-term prospects of the banking sector given due consideration.

10. As the implementation of the financial sector reforms is an ongoing process, the training packages have to be constantly updated to keep abreast of these changes.

D. Applicability of the Model

The practical applicability of this Re-engineering Model can be illustrated by considering possible training intervention designs for two hypothetical situations covering the extremes which the Indian Banking Sector has to provide for : a metropolitan commercial bank branch and a distant rural bank branch.

Training Design for Metropolitan Branch: In a metro branch, the training needs of staff can be determined. The training areas would be traditional banking as well as new business areas as factoring, leasing, merchant banking, foreign exchange, use of ATM's and Information Technology. While for areas like foreign exchange a combination of institutional classroom and on-the job counter training would be required, alongwith regular distant mode updates on changing government regulations on the subject, for I.T., availability of P.C.'s with embedded software (ECBT) will facilitate the staff's acquisition of this relatively new technology in the context of their work environment.

Training Design for a Rural Branch: The application of the Model to hypothetical case of taking care of the training requirements of the staff of remote rural branches of Rural Bank would be along following lines. There is usually staff constraints in such branches so that it is usually difficult to spare officials for institutional training in core areas of rural banking including thrust areas like project based financing, service area approach, non farm sector lending, self help group based lending, government sponsored latest rural development schemes.

Where the staff can be so spared, where replacements are available, they can be deputed to training centres of the RRB's sponsoring commercial banks or to apex training centres like Banker's Institute of Rural Development (BIRD). Where this is not possible, a team of mobile job trainers (MJT's) can visit the bank's branch and train the entire staff as a team. The MJT visit can be preceded by distance learning modules so that the trainees will be in a more receptive frame and ready with queries. The feedback following the training for the branch trainees could be obtained through assignments, projects etc.

And apart from the knowledge base, it is imperative for the training intervention to give rural orientation/empathy, positive attitude, gender sensitiveness to the staff so that they are more responsive in fulfilling the genuine needs of their clientele, (which include the poorest sections of society and disadvantaged groups like women) rather than merely meeting annual performance targets. In addition training could focus on borrowers' education also, as to how the branch staff can motivate them to repay the loans to improve the quality and viability of rural lending. It could try to build the capabilities of the rural poor, develop the potential of rural women, so that rural credit leads to sustainable rural development.

E. Limitations of the Model

Though this Model is oriented to practical application and if executed appropriately would lead to satisfactory outcomes, however, it has certain limitations, which we shall now examine:

1. Training is one parameter of HRD and HRD itself is only one of the parameters of productivity and effective functioning of the banking industry. Other factors such as global/national economic trends, prevailing industrial relations, work culture of the Indian public sector, the country's legal framework, political ideology/compulsions, aspects of government-banking sector interaction, infra-structural support the socio-economic characteristics such as education levels, entrepreneurial qualities etc. limit the effectiveness of the Training effort and hence of the proposed Training Model.

2. While training is undoubtedly an essential factor in developing the most important and critical resource of banks viz. the personnel, it is an integral part of the overall Human Resource Development (HRD). The HRD encompasses host of other factors like policies relating to selection, recruitment, placement, transfers, promotion, service conditions etc. The overall objective of HRD, including training, is to improve both the individual and the organisational effectiveness. It is not enough that adequate number of bank personnel is given necessary training say in the use of electronic systems, computerisation, etc.

but these should become operational through appropriate organisational interventions. Training by itself is not the panacea of all organisational problems.

3. The effectiveness of HRD/Training, interventions and so of this model is limited by the organisational climate and the prevalent attitudes towards it by the management staff and unions of the banks. The widely held attitude in Indian Banks regarding HRD as a soft cosmetic function, training as a 'paid holiday', as generally dispensable, lower considerably the benefits which could have been derived from training inputs. This is because to implement this model a massive effort is required from the banking sector which would be summoned only if the prevalent attitude to HRD/Training itself was a very favourable one. And since attitude change at the organizational level is a long drawn, tedious and difficult proposition (unless the same is achieved through very strenuous efforts) this remains a limiting factor.

4. Since job performance is a composite function of motivation, ability and opportunity, while training enhances the abilities, and through HRD measures (like creating a learning organisation) as proposed in our Model, other HRD/operational policy measures related to motivation (e.g. rational recruitment, effective reward system, accountability and expectations from the trained manpower, better correlation between training and placement etc.) have to be addressed for this training model to have optimum effect. For example, in Rural Banking, if the recruited Staff remains highly urban biased, as it is today, and if rural postings continue to be viewed as punishment postings, without additional compensation/recognition for the hardships endured, training efforts in Rural Banking will continue to have limited impact.

Limitations of this Study

Having examined the limitations of the Reengineering Model proposed by this study, we shall now discuss some of the general limitations of this study as well. These can be enumerated as below :

1. This is a theoretical project whose conclusions are based on the findings arrived at by other evaluation studies/viewpoints. Hence, this thesis would be affected by the limitations of it's data sources.
2. This study has considered Training subsystem within the context of organisational HRD system. But the HRD system is a complex/composite area, formed of several subsystems, which interact with each other and with other organisational policies and procedures. Due to constraints of space and because of the focus required by this investigation, the latter interactions (e.g. between the training subsystem and recruitment subsystem or between training and say operational policies for overdues reduction) could not be fully explored.
3. Indian Banking Sector is a complex area, formed of many tiers and components. HRD and Training practices/policies differ across this arena, between banks and even within the same bank (across regions). Though this study has tried to take a broad view point and incorporate these diversities, to the extent possible, yet this could not be done fully.
4. The Reengineering Model proposed by this study has several components and offers a general framework for making the HRD and Training systems of the Indian Banking Sector more effective and responsive to the current challenges. But, the Model has to be carefully adapted to meet the demands of specific banking institutions, keeping in view their individual requirements, situational leads and unique organizational culture.

These limitations have to be kept in mind while applying the Model for Reengineering the HRD and Training systems of the Indian Banking Scenario so that more effectiveness is attained.

Conclusion: Reengineering for better Long-Term Prospects of the Indian Banking Scenario

The future of the Indian Banking Scenario looks promising with the on going implementation of financial sector reforms, 'opening up' of the Indian economy and its integration with the World economy. The long-term prospect for the Indian Banking Sector in the years to come appear to be as follows :

1. Decentralisation and delegation of control functions from the controlling authorities to the banking system sò as to speed up the pace of transactions.

2. Gradual reduction in regulation and disintermediation. Staff will require training to adapt themselves to a change from non-price competition to price competition. Liabilities management, deployment of funds, assets quality, profit planning may acquire quite different dimensions. Financing patterns will change and techniques of credit appraisal will need fine tuning.

3. With the liberalised policy, avenues for the new types of activities such as counselling services, leasing, factoring, custodial services, etc. are coming up. These activities can be taken up by the banks.

4. With industrial growth there will be scope for improved turnover and volume of business handled by the banks. The scope will be available especially in the ancillary business like remittances, collections, bill business, etc.

5. With determined efforts to boost the exports of the country, there will be tremendous scope to increase foreign exchange business.

6. Increased agricultural and industrial outputs will increase trading activity. This will offer potential for lending to trade. There will be, thus, no dearth of demand for credit limits from this sector.
7. Infrastructure facilities development like transportation, construction, service sector etc.–this also offers scope for banks to improve their business.
8. With the increased prosperity of the middle class, there is more demand for financing consumer durables, vehicles, housing etc.
9. Changes in branch licensing policy of the Reserve Bank of India is enabling the banks to relook into the individual branch functioning profitability. By judicious decision regarding perennially less-making branches, the banks can curtail their overall losses.
10. Increasingly higher level of awareness even at district and village levels of the role of the banking system as not merely purveyors of credit but as promotors and participants in the socio-economic development. This would mean a phenomenal increase in credit demand as well as higher level of expectations from the public.
11. Rapid growth in Information Technology/telecommunications and innovations will make for speed, accuracy and compactness. Although, in the next decade, this would be confined to the urban and semi-urban areas, even this, viewed in the context of a nation of our size, will be substantial.

Reengineering for Realization of Better Long-Term Prospects

We have in this study argued that the growing trend in recent years in India towards innovative banking business and diversification of banks' activities is part of the major international trend in that direction; it represents a break from tradition, a dominance of forces of change over forces of continuity. How far and how quick new banking or the new segment of the market would grow in this country would depend largely on how quickly and to what degree the relevant national policies would be changed, infrastructural support would develop and individual banks will be left free to choose their own structures, systems, strategies and staffing patterns and finally how far and how promptly the banks will act and act in new directions. We envisage the overall reaction to be cautious and, therefore, somewhat slow and moderate success in which some banks will progress more rapidly than others.

Development of new profile manpower for new banking will prove to be the crucial factor in determining success. 'New banking demands much degree of knowledge and skills, and much higher degree of specialisation and sophistication. The emphasis is on the development of the new banker, in fact a new person'. We have to stress higher intensity and pace in training, more powerful training material and methods. The present HRD/training systems in Indian Banking industry aims at maximisation of numbers of programmes and the trainees–it has become target-oriented routinized, bureaucratized.

HRD and Training Systems of the new profile banker (for innovative and diversified banking if it has to serve the functional and not mere ritual purpose) will have to be itself innovative. And, that demands sufficient funds and resources, autonomy and freedom. 'HRD and Training are creative activities, and creativity depends on freedom to try new ideas and prove their worth'.

As has been stressed in the Reengineering Model proposed in our Study these developments must get reflected in the HRD/Training Systems of the Indian Banking Sector in order to ensure that it's long-term prospects are favourable. This sector plays a very crucial role in the country's economic growth, implementation of developmental policies and in ensuring a respectable place for the nation in the global market place. Today when the global economy is passing through a lean phase and the forces of market reform, compulsions of financial sector reforms are exerting their pressures on the

Indian economy, the Banking Sector has to make a supreme effort to meet the present and forthcoming challenges. This is possible only if this sector is able to over come its operational problems and develops its manpower to the extent that it succeeds in overcoming the adverse environmental challenges. For this a radical Reengineering of the HRD and Training Systems of the Indian Banking Sector along the lines proposed by our Reengineering Model, and as per the thinking reflected in this and other informed studies, is imperative.

Notes

1. Refer to Chapter 5 of this Book.
2. Refer to Chapter 6 of this Book.
3. Refer to Chapter 7 of this Book.
4. Refer to Chapter 8 of this Book.
5. Refer to Chapter 9 of this Book.
6. Lowenthal, J.N.: Reengineering the Organisation.

Bibliography

Agarwal, R.K.: *Evaluation of the Working of Regional Rural Bank,* New Delhi: Mittal.

Asian Development Bank: *Annual Reports.*

Athreya, M.B.: "Integrating the Human Resource Profession with Business: The challenges Ahead–HRM 2000." *Indian Perspective* ed. by K.B. Akhilesh and D.R. Nagaraj, New Delhi: Wiley Eastern Ltd., 1990.

Barthakur, Management of Training in Banks: *Indian Journal of Training and Development*, 20(2), March-April 1990.

Bentley, Trevor : *The Business of Training—Achieving success in changing world markets.* London: McGraw Hill, 1991.

Bhatt, V.V. : *Financial Systems—Innovations and Development,* New Delhi: Sage, 1995.

Canadian International Development Agency: *CIDA Policy on Gender Equality.* Ottawa: CIDA, 1999.

Daftuar, C.N. : "Integrating HRD with Line-whose responsibility is this?" *Indian Journal of Training and Development,* 27(3), July-September, 97.

Govt. of India: *Fourth World conterence on Women, Beijing 1995-Country Report.* New Delhi : GOI, 1995.

International Labour Organisation (Geneva): *An Introductory Course in Teaching and Training Methods for Management Development.* New Delhi: Sterling, 1987.

Khan, F.H.: Human Resource Development in Banks. *State Banks of India Monthly Review,* December 1993, pp. 655-660.

Khandelwal, Anil K. (Ed.), *Human Resources Development in Banks*, New Delhi: Oxford and IBH Publishing Co., 1988.

Kotler, Philip: *Marketing Management—Analysis, Planning Implementation and Control*. New Delhi: Prentice Hall of India, 1994.

Kumar, Ramesh: *Personnel Management in Banks*. New Delhi: Indian Publishers Distributors.

Lynton and Pareek: *Training for Development*, New Delhi, Sage 1990.

Mankidy, J.: Human Resource Management and Industrial Relations in Banks—Coping with, changes *Prajnan*, Vol. XXI, No. 4, January-March, 1993.

Melkote, Srinivas N. *Communication for Development in the Third World*, New Delhi: Sage, 1991.

Lowenthal, Jeffrey N.: *Reengineering the Organisation*, New Delhi: Tata McGraw Hill, 1995.

National Bank for Agriculture and Rural Development, Annual Reports.

Nadler, Leonard; "Human Resources Development" In Leonard Nadler (ed.)—*The Handbook of Human Resource Development*, New York: John Wiley & Sons, 1994, p. 1.16 to 1.22.

Pareek, Udai : *Education and Rural Development in Asia*, New Delhi: Oxford & IBH Publishing Co. Pvt. Ltd., 1982.

Pareek, Udai and Rao, T.V. : *Designing and Managing Human Resources Systems*. New Delhi: Oxford & IBH Publishing Company, 1981.

Patel K.V., and Khankhoje, D.P.: Rural Banking—Basic Issues and Scope for Restructuring—*Prajnan*, Vol. XXI, No. 4, 1993.

Podder, C.K.: Making Training effective, *Indian Journal of Training and Development*. 23(3): 69-71, July-September 1993.

Prior, John (ed.), *Handbook for Training and Development*. London Gower Publishing Co. 1993.

Rao, K.D.: Some aspects of Service Area Approach for Trainees, New Delhi: ISTD: *Indian Journal of Training and Development*, March-April, 1990.

Rao, T.V.: *Human Resources Development*, New Delhi: Oxford and IBH Publishing Co. Pvt. Ltd., 1986 p. 11.

Ravisankar, T.S., Towards Structural Changes in Banking. Pune: *Prajanan*, Vol. XXI, No. 4, January-March, 1993.

Robinson, Kenneth R.: *A Handbook for Training Management*. London: Kogan Page, 1988.

Rossett, Allison, *Training Needs Assessment*. Educational Technology Publication, 1987.

Shaw, B.G., Saiyad Udduri, M.S. and Seth, M.R. *Human Resources Management and Banking Industry—Text and Cases*. New Delhi: South Asia Publishers, 1989.

Silveria, D.N.: *Human Resources Development—The Indian Experiences*, New Delhi: New India Publication, 1988.

Singh, Kartar: *Rural Development—Principles, Policies and Management*, New Delhi: Sage, 1986.

Singh: *National Bank for Agriculture and Rural Development*, Delhi: Deep & Deep 1992.

Singh, P.N.: *Developing and Managing Human Resources*, Bombay: Suchandra Publication, 1992.

Sinha, Ajit Kumar: *New Economic Policy of India—Restructuring and Liberalising the Economy for 21st Century*, New Delhi: Indian Publishers Distributors, 1990.

Tadaro, Michael P.: *Economic Development in the Third World*. New Delhi: Orient Longman, 1993.

Truclove Steve (ed.) *Handbook of Training & Development*, London: Blackwell, 1992.

United Nations Development Programme (UNDP): Human Development Report, 1995.

Varshneya, J.S., Assessment of Training Needs, Strategies for meeting those and preparation of Calender of Programme. In ISTD, New Delhi, *Indian Journal of Training and Development*, Vol. XX, No. 5 & 6, September-December, 1990.

Vinayakam, N. (ed.), *Indian Banking by 2000 A.D.* Delhi: Kanishka Publishers Distributors, 1995.

Woodall, Jean: Human Resource Management and Women. The Vision of the Gender-blind. In Brian Towers (Ed.): The Handbook of Human Resousce Management. Oxford: Blackwell Publishers, 1996.

World Bank: *World Development Report 1994*—Infrastructure Development.

World Bank: *Gender Issues in World Bank Lending*. Washington: World Bank, 1995.

World Bank: *The World Bank and Gender in India*.NewDelhi :The World Bank, 1995.

Index

158